Mo

"Spra
acteri
critica
agrees

"Thor
ancier
ing of
that ct
eral th
ulate t
vide a
and ac
Beiner

"The v
humar
good s
cratic
want to
produc
nant lit
—Char

"*Civic*
ing nev
ideals. S
canon a
provoki
democr
. . . Thi
—Rona

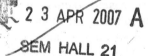

This book may be recalled b

D1609951

CIVIC LIBERALISM

Reflections on Our Democratic Ideals

Thomas A. Spragens, Jr.

ROWMAN & LITTLEFIELD PUBLISHERS, INC.
Lanham • Boulder • New York • Oxford

ROWMAN & LITTLEFIELD PUBLISHERS, INC.

Published in the United States of America
by Rowman & Littlefield Publishers, Inc.
4720 Boston Way, Lanham, Maryland 20706
http://www.rowmanlittlefield.com

12 Hid's Copse Road
Cumnor Hill, Oxford OX2 9JJ, England

British Library Cataloging in Publication Information Available

Library of Congress Cataloging-in-Publication Data

Spragens, Thomas A.
    Civic liberalism : reflections on our democratic ideals / Thomas
A. Spragens, Jr.
        p.   cm.
    Includes bibliographical references and index.
    ISBN 0-8476-9610-3 (cloth : alk. paper)   ISBN 0-8476-9611-1 (pbk. : alk. paper)
    1. Liberalism.   2. Democracy.   I. Title.
JC574.S6   1999
320'.01'1—dc21   1002215099   99-15040
                                                        CIP

Printed in the United States of America

For my students

Contents

Preface

For several years, I have taught courses at Duke University in which the students are expected to understand and are invited to assess some of the leading accounts of democratic ideals that currently contend for our allegiance. Because I want my students to appreciate the power of these competing theories and because I don't want their assessments to be biased or short-circuited by attempts to please or placate the professor, my pedagogical strategy has been to defend each of the theories in turn and largely to suppress my own judgments about them. Perhaps I have succeeded too well in my effort to referee rather than to participate in the classroom contestations, for one of my classes presented me at semester's end with a "where does he stand?" citation. Apparently, they felt curious but clueless about my own views and they had diverged in their speculations about them.

This book is intended, then, to answer their plaintive query, and I have accordingly dedicated it to them. I focus here upon those recent accounts of democratic ideals that seem most directly pertinent to our practices and policies. I try to acknowledge their strengths but also to identify the ways in which they arguably lead us in the wrong direction. And I offer my own constructive interpretations of the democratic ideals of liberty, equality, fraternity, and civic virtue—interpretations that shape and inform my own political judgments and allegiances.

Besides my puzzled students, I seek here to address two audiences. The first of these are my fellow political theorists. I want to share with them my own worries about some of the normative theories we discuss and debate in order to spur and sharpen their own critical assessments of these theories. And I also want to offer them another target to shoot at with my conception of civic liberalism. The other audience are my fellow democratic citizens—or at least the informed and concerned public among them, those who think about what our democratic ideals should be. I particularly want to address those who believe democracy is a moral enterprise rather than a mere pact of convenience, but who have serious doubts about the interpretations of that moral enterprise provided by the stylized and polarized ideological right and left in today's public discourse. To them I offer a morally robust and practically challenging democratic idealism of the middle way—a conception of the good society as composed of self-governing civic equals, sustained by an enabling state—that I hope will resonate with their own moral intuitions and political hopes.

Speaking to a dual audience unavoidably creates certain expository problems. Political theorists will find some inclusions and explanations jejune and my wider audience may find some sections too academic. I can only plead for tolerance

Preface

from both groups, asking that they realize that what they find obvious or technical may be important to other readers.

I want to express my appreciation to two groups of colleagues who have contributed greatly to my edification regarding the issues covered in this book. First, I thank the exceptional group of political theorists at Duke University: Michael Gillespie, Ruth Grant, Rom Coles, David Price, Alasdair MacIntyre, Elizabeth Kiss, Kim Curtis, Stanley Hauerwas, and Noah Pickus. Second, I thank the contingent of political theorists who have over the past couple of decades conducted what in effect has been an extended series of seminar discussions regarding the purposes and moral foundations of democratic liberalism. There are more of them than I can mention here, but important among them have been Bill Galston, Richard Dagger, Charles Anderson, Jim Fishkin, Ron Terchek, Al Damico, Pat Neal, Steve Macedo, Jean Elshtain, Amy Gutmann, Bill Connolly, Jane Mansbridge, Michael Sandel, Amitai Etzioni, Ben Barber, Carey McWilliams, Ian Shapiro, Rogers Smith, David Johnston, William Sullivan, Alan Wolfe, Terry Ball, Don Herzog, Nancy Rosenblum, Bob Thigpen, Lyle Downing, Emily Gill, Richard Flathman, Bonnie Honig, Steve Elkin, Ronald Beiner, and Donald Moon. I have learned much from each of them, even when—perhaps mostly when—we have not been in full agreement about the proper aspirations of democratic regimes.

I also thank Lillian Fennell, Susan Emery, Dana Ellington, Kim Sprunck, Marisa Law, Alicia Griffin, and Rita Dowling for their help in manuscript preparation. Steve Wrinn of Rowman & Littlefield deserves warm thanks not only for his counsel and encouragement regarding this book project but also for his significant editorial contributions to the field of political theory.

Introduction

When the Berlin Wall fell and political regimes in Eastern Europe tumbled like so many dominoes, the ideological landscape in the advanced industrial countries changed perceptibly. Among the textbooks on my shelves sits a volume entitled *The Main Debate: Communism versus Capitalism*. It was published in the late 1980s, but the controversies it canvasses are clearly no longer the main debate. Whatever analytical and critical insights Marxist philosophy may have to offer, Marxism is no longer defensible as a historical vision and no longer credible as a political blueprint. The main debate now lies elsewhere—about the nature and the aspirations of the apparently triumphant liberal democracies.

I say "apparently triumphant" advisedly. For the failure of an adversary is not the same as success. It is quite conceivable that the successor regimes in Eastern Europe, however liberal and democratic, may prove incapable of dealing with the problems communism produced and the divisions it suppressed. It is also conceivable that Western democracies, rather than advance and prosper, will undergo a process of secular decline. In the United States, for example, increased inequalities, economic setbacks, and ethnic hostilities in an increasingly diverse population could erode the quality of life and put great pressure on democratic institutions. Although the most pessimistic scenarios of democratic decline are not likely to prove right, they suggest that this is not a time for complacent self-congratulation by democratic liberals. Instead, the liberal democracies need to use the resources and attention freed up by the end of the Cold War to address their own problems and pursue their own highest aspirations.

To say that, however, only raises another question: namely, what *are* the aspirations of liberal democracy? Just as countries newly emancipated from colonialism suddenly encounter internal conflicts that had been submerged in the common effort to escape colonial rule, so the newly triumphant adherents of liberal democracy are now beginning to recognize with greater clarity and urgency than before that divergent democratic ideals pull them in several directions. As we turn, then, to address our own problems and strive for our own goals, we encounter a lack of unanimity about what these problems and goals are. There are important agreements, but significant differences as well. To cite only some of the many recent contributors to the debate about the principles animating liberal democratic politics, it is clear that John Rawls, Robert Nozick, Michael Walzer, Milton Friedman, Judith Shklar, Ronald Dworkin, Richard Rorty, William Connolly, William Galston, Robert Dahl, Charles Anderson, James Fishkin, Amy Gutmann, and Charles Taylor inter alia are all both liberals and democrats. It is equally clear, however, that their visions of what an ideal liberal democracy would look like differ significantly.

The main debate of the current decade will, therefore, be rather different from that of the previous several decades. In the countries of Eastern Europe, the main debate is likely to be over the question "how can we overcome the destructive consequences that authoritarian Marxism had upon our society and create free, democratic, and economically productive institutions?" An alternative debate, as the difficulties and dislocations of such a profound transition are felt, may be "is liberal democracy the right goal or should we retreat to the security of some new (or old) form of authoritarian nationalism?" It is to be hoped, of course, that the former of these two questions will provide the focus of public concern; but that outcome is no certainty.

In the advanced industrial societies of the West, the basic legitimacy and practical superiority of liberal democracy is not likely to be subject to serious challenge—except on the political fringes. That essential unassailability of liberal democracy is what permitted Francis Fukuyama recently to dust off Alexandre Kojève's neo-Hegelian theory about the "end of history."[1] Kojève's argument was a more metaphysical version of the "end of ideology" thesis championed by Daniel Bell and others in the early 1960s: fundamental ideological dispute is now a thing of the past, we are all liberal democrats, and the remaining issues are essentially technical and managerial. President John F. Kennedy sounded a similar theme in his commencement address at Yale University. And Kojève himself gave biographical incarnation to his claim by leaving academic philosophy to work for the European Community.

Even if these accounts capture an important aspect of the contemporary political situation, however, it would be delusionary to suppose that important normative disagreements will become a thing of the past in liberal democracies. Instead, with the decline of challenges to their ideological hegemony, some quite significant and practically important disagreements will reach new salience within the historically triumphant democracies. Evidence for this expectation can already be adduced from some of the academic controversies alluded to earlier. And quick reflection should make it clear why this development should not be surprising. For while the adherents of liberal democracy all subscribe to a common core of beliefs and central institutions, the animating purposes of liberal democratic regimes and the proper balance among their multiple values remain matters of dispute. All adherents of liberal democracy, for example, accept the fundamental moral and political equality of all citizens; they believe in the importance of individual freedoms; and they believe that legitimate government is grounded in the consent of the people. Hence they take representative government, civil liberties, and some element of economic choice as defining features of a rightly ordered politics. This basic consensus, however, can and does encompass a wide range of divergent viewpoints about the actual institutional requisites of representation, about the necessary conditions of political equality, and about the appropriate range and extent of individual civic and economic liberties. Those who concur on the rudiments of liberal democratic practices, moreover, differ among themselves about whether these practices should include among their goals the promotion of a specific conception of the human good and, if so, how such a goal can be conceived and justified in a manner consistent with other liberal values.

In an earlier study, *Reason and Democracy*, I took what might be called a quasi-foundational approach to arriving at liberal democratic norms.[2] I argued there that a conception of collective prudence or rational practice could generate a set of procedural standards—a "constitution of rational enterprises"—to provide us a more felicitous rendering of sound democratic conduct than reliance upon principles of utility, or upon rights *simpliciter*, or upon historically entrenched conventions. In this book, I want to focus more directly on the social ideals and political purposes that inform and energize the life of liberal democracies. I want to look critically and reflectively at some of the moral intuitions, empirical beliefs, and philosophical assumptions that inform these ideals. And I want to see whether and how these ideals—after critical refinement—can be incorporated into a vision of liberal democratic purposes more complex, more nuanced, and more compelling than those viewpoints that commonly contend for our allegiance.

Since the ultimate appeal is more to the moral intuitions that inform the liberal democratic enterprise than to some foundational moral axiom or axioms that allegedly ground that enterprise, the form of argument will be more rhetorical than deductive. That is, I shall, in effect, be asking myself what sense and what force the liberal democratic norms of liberty, equality, community ("fraternity"), and civic virtue have in the context of my own intuitions about the good society. Any attempts to persuade the reader must likewise invoke an appeal to his or her parallel intuitions. It should be obvious, then, that no one can reasonably pretend to have any knock-down arguments in this particular universe of discourse. The situation in this respect is like that depicted by Thomas Hobbes in his introduction to *Leviathan*. His basic approach, he says there, must be to "read himself," to look at his own desires, fears, and hopes. And then, he concludes, "when I shall have set down my own reading orderly, and perspicuously, the pains left another, will be only to consider, if he also find not the same in himself. For this kind of doctrine admitteth no other form of demonstration."[3]

Because my argument is not a foundational one and because I can hardly pretend to be writing on a clean slate, I begin by engaging critically some of the more thoughtful and influential alternative approaches to the central question of what our liberal democratic goals should be. Only then can I try to improve upon them in a dialectical and synthetic fashion. At this stage in the historical career of liberal democracy, we do not need to, cannot, and should not try to spin out a conception of democratic ideals de novo. Many of the strands for our tapestry unsurprisingly lie available in the leading extant perspectives on the problem. We can learn much both from the important insights and from what I have come to perceive as the sometimes serious weaknesses of these more conventional schools of thought about liberal purposes. To ignore alternative accounts that had a serious impact on democratic theory and practice would deprive my account of the theoretical clarity that depends on dialectic and of the political relevance that depends on at least contrast if not outright conflict. If I proceeded directly to my constructive argument without providing any critical reactions to other theories that have shaped it, the reader would apprehend much less clearly both what it is I am arguing for and why I regard it as important. Readers who want to head for the bottom line more directly, however, may wish first to read the constructive account of democratic ideals in Part Two and then to return later to Part One. This would be a perfectly acceptable strategy, since Part One does not set out essential premises that must be mastered before my construction of democratic ideals can be intelligible. What Part One provides, instead, is a comparative and critical context that brings into relief what is distinctive about civic liberalism and helps to explain its practical and political significance.

I propose, then, to take my bearings in my exploration of democratic ideals in relation to four broad schools of thought that pertain to this subject. Each of these orientations has illustrious adherents. Each has had considerable influence on the self-understanding and on the policy directions of democratic polities. Each has genuine insights to offer and compelling arguments in its repertoire. None of them, however, is sufficient, taken alone, to serve as an inclusive normative guide for democratic practice—or, at least, so I shall argue. The four schools are what I shall call liberal realism, libertarianism, liberal egalitarianism, and the liberalism of difference.

Liberal realists see democracy as the best means of bringing about a viable social order among individuals who naturally are inclined to seek their own advantage, even at another's expense. Democracy for them is, in effect, a mechanism for conflict regulation and resolution, and its constitutive goals are social peace and stability. Sometimes those who interpret liberal purposes in this manner are characterized as "modus vivendi" theorists in that the central political challenge for them is to create institutions that allow people to "get along together." For these thinkers, the major achievement of liberal democracy—and no small achievement at that—is establishing an island of relative tranquillity and safety in a dangerous and often brutal world.

The libertarian school is familiar to most of us. Its partisans see the crowning purpose of liberal democracy to be maximizing individual freedom. When it comes to democratic values, libertarians adhere to a priority rule with a vengeance: other democratic norms such as equality and community may be defensible secondary goods, but whenever they come into conflict with political, civil, or economic freedom, they must give way. Individual liberty is championed in part for its instrumental value—in producing material prosperity and social stability, for example. But freedom should in the libertarian view also be venerated as the most important intrinsic good that politics can safeguard.

Liberal egalitarians emphasize the democratic side of liberal democracy, and they construe democracy as a substantive social and economic ideal rather than as a set of narrowly political and procedural norms. The most representative and influential contemporary theorists in this context are those who—like John Rawls—conceive a morally legitimate liberal democracy as an institutional scheme for attaining distributive justice. The chapter on egalitarian liberalism, accordingly, focuses on the moral intuitions and the anthropological and sociological claims informing this account of democratic ideals.

Finally, I propose to consider the "difference liberalism" championed by Iris Young, William Connolly, and others who receive inspiration from postmodernist critiques of socially constructed political hierarchies. These difference liberals see democratic politics as the contestation of various identity groups and an imbalanced and oppressive one at that. Their own democratic ideals, therefore, center around their aspirations to end the hegemony of some groups over others; to subvert the beliefs that sustain group oppression; and to create a society in which all groups are recognized, affirmed, and empowered.

My own account of democratic ideals, which is taken up in Part Two of the book, builds on the critical analysis of these competing orientations. My intent is to see if some more nuanced and comprehensive normative conception of liberal democracy can be stitched together that incorporates as many of the strengths and avoids as many of the weaknesses of the several traditions as is possible. I suffer from no illusion that some comprehensive, all-inclusive democratic ideal can be produced that reconciles every conflict of values and satisfies everyone. Indeed, I argue that the recalcitrance of the moral world we inhabit necessarily frustrates any such aspirations. Framed in its infancy as a historical comedy, liberalism in its maturity must incorporate a recognition of the inescapable moral tragedies found in even the most intelligent and beneficent attempts to create a good and just society.

That said, I nonetheless intend to argue that we can construct and should subscribe to a normative conception of liberal democracy that is more subtle, more comprehensive, and more appealing than the usual contenders for our allegiance. Liberal democratic practice, I contend, should be guided by a complex idealism— differentiated from liberal realism by its higher reach and from the other liberalisms by its greater breadth of aspirations. I call this normative conception "civic liberalism." Mickey Kaus uses this term to describe what he affirms in his *The End of Equality*.[4] And William Connolly uses the same term to describe an outlook he critiques in his *Identity\Difference: Democratic Negotiations of Political Paradox*.[5] There is some danger in appropriating this term, therefore, because I do not endorse all of Kaus's contentions, nor do I affirm all of the beliefs that Connolly clusters under the designation. Nonetheless, I acknowledge at least a strong family resemblance between these conceptions and my own. The common theme among them all is an affirmation of liberalism's dedication to individual rights and civil liberties together with an insistence upon the parallel importance of a strong public sphere inhabited by social equals and directed toward perpetually evolving and dialogically contested common purposes. I also like the connotations carried by the word "civic": namely, the rhetorical nod toward norms of citizenship (i.e., civic-mindedness and civility) and toward the importance of mediating social institutions (i.e., civic associations) in creating and sustaining a healthy liberal polity. My adoption of this term also implies my agreement with Connolly that the pairing of "civic" and "liberalism" does not embody a category mistake. The key question here is whether the liberal commitment to individual freedoms and the civic republican pursuit of community and civic virtue are merely in tension or are genuinely irreconcilable. Any civic liberal must on this issue deny the irreconcilability thesis—and I do. Neither logic nor experience provides a persuasive case that we cannot combine protection of individual rights with the creation of a vital public sphere. [6]

Civic liberalism shares many of the concerns and emphases of the communitarian critics of deontologial liberalism. Like these communitarian critics, civic liberals insist upon the importance of responsible citizenship and upon the norms of civic virtue that sustain it. In concert with Mary Ann Glendon, therefore, a civic liberal expects that a public discourse and a political order focused almost exclusively on individual rights will tend to create a skewed social ethic and distorted public policies. [7] A civic liberal will also agree with Alan Wolfe's contention that a dominant ideological debate centering entirely on the relative merits of the market and the state neglects the vital significance of the distinctive domain of civil society—the domain that institutionalizes our natural sociability, with its nurturant and educative functions, rather than economic bargaining or political command.[8]

My use of the adjective "civic" thus conveys sympathy with much of the thrust of the communitarian agenda. My retention of the liberal label, on the other hand, represents my commitment to core liberal norms such as political equality, representative democracy, civil liberties, and the rule of law. And it suggests distance from at least some strands of the communitarian persuasion. A civic liberal cannot completely endorse the bleak assessment of liberal culture associated with Alasdair MacIntyre and Ronald Beiner, for example.[9] The civic liberal may blanch at Stephen Macedo's proclamation that "liberalism holds out the promise, or the threat, of making all the world like California." But he or she will remain within the liberal encampment precisely because of an agreement with Macedo's insistence that "liberalism properly understood stands for ideals of character far nobler than MacIntyre's unhappy and purportedly liberal trio, 'the Rich Aesthete . . . the Manager . . . and the Therapist'" and that "liberal pluralism, tolerance, change, and freedom do not stand for a moral void of arbitrary values and the will to power."[10] Although sympathetic to some civic republican ideals and concerns, moreover, a civic liberal will not allow this sympathy to push him or her toward Spartan forms of collectivism. A proper appreciation of social pluralism and individual autonomy should prevent such enthusiasms.

The democratic theory I delineate and endorse here is neither radically novel nor particularly idiosyncratic. It may involve creative reinterpretation of liberal ideals, but it remains quite consonant with the central themes and goals of mainstream liberal theorists such as Locke, Mill, Condorcet, Jefferson, and Adam Smith. The way to revitalize the liberal project, I would argue, is to recover the moral complexity found within it and then to adapt and apply this complex form of social idealism to the demands and constraints of contemporary politics. For the fact is that in its inception liberalism pursued multiple social goods. Liberty was perhaps the central theme, and it therefore gave the project its name. But it was not the only goal, and it was central at least in part because it was deemed instrumental toward the attainment of the other social goods. These other ends included greater political and social equality, which most of the liberal reformers believed would result from the diminution of economic restrictions and political distinctions mandated by the state.[11] They also included an enhancement of civic friendship, which the early liberal theorists assumed would result from breaking down invidious distinctions of rank and class. Finally, these goals included what John Stuart Mill termed "mental and moral progress" or what Condorcet optimistically foresaw as "the true perfection of mankind."

For a variety of reasons and from a variety of causes, both philosophical and sociological, the nineteenth century saw the complexity and ambition of the liberal tradition become increasingly eroded. One consequence of the industrial and the democratic revolutions, for example, was to undermine the alleged coherence of cherished liberal goals and to challenge the logic of standard liberal strategies. To be specific, the dynamics of corporate capitalism seemed to give the lie to Condorcet's sanguine assumptions about the natural tendency of wealth to equalize under the aegis of market forces. And the devolution of political power made it questionable whether state power was necessarily to be viewed as a threat to liberal goals. An ideological fissure thus began to open between those who prioritized liberty over equality (and therefore continued to view the state, however democratic, with suspicion) and those who valued equality more highly (and therefore saw a democratic state as instrumental rather than inimical to their goals).

The rise of philosophical movements such as naturalism, positivism, and historicism in the late nineteenth and early twentieth centuries, moreover, eroded the moral cognitivism and traditionalism of earlier liberal reformers. Contemporary liberals, as a result, remember the Adam Smith who explained the beneficent effects of the market but forget the Adam Smith who justified these markets within the context of a Protestant account of the moral sentiments; they remember the Mill who defended individual liberties but forget the Mill who promoted mental and moral progress; and they remember the David Hume who drove a wedge between is and ought but forget the Hume who sought to create an experimental science of morality. Contemporary liberalism has therefore largely become not a doctrine of moral perfectionism tempered by fallibilism and respect for autonomy but a doctrine of moral decisionism. This shift has altered the meaning and the justification of central liberal norms, including the norms of toleration, equality, and liberty itself.

What, then, is the proper rhetorical twist to be given to this story? What programmatic lesson is to be learned from it? Not, surely, that we can or ought to seek an escape from the current vicissitudes of liberal theory and practice by returning to some allegedly idyllic status quo ante. The fact is that this particular Humpty Dumpty cannot be put together again. We cannot and should not want to undo the economic and political changes that have challenged the coherence of liberalism's original goals. Nor can we persuasively attempt to repair to the moral Newtonianism that informed early liberal moral certitudes because we now recognize the philosophical incoherencies it incorporated.[12] Without counseling a return to the utopianism or to the philosophical blind alleys of early liberalism, however, the civic liberal nonetheless aspires to the recovery of the broader aspirations that characterized liberalism at its outset and that have become lost or attenuated during liberalism's historical trajectory.

So let us begin. It is beyond my intent to present here a fully articulated and philosophically complete theory of liberalism. Instead, I propose merely to give a name and a face to the perspective I call civic liberalism by offering some reflections on democratic ideals that lead us in that direction—and by issuing an invitation to my readers to test their own judgments by comparing them with the ones set out here.

Notes

1. Francis Fukuyama, *The End of History and the Last Man* (New York: Free Press, 1992).
2. Thomas A. Spragens, Jr., *Reason and Democracy* (Durham: Duke University Press, 1990). I call this a foundational argument in the sense that a single core normative model is delineated, and then more particular practical precepts are inferred from it. It is only quasi-foundational, however, in the sense that the core model itself can be defended on multiple philosophical grounds. In this respect, the function and logical standing of the core model of communal rational practice parallels that of the model of a "constrained conversation" in Bruce Ackerman's *Social Justice in the Liberal State* (New Haven: Yale University Press, 1980).
3. Thomas Hobbes, *Leviathan* (New York: Dutton, 1950), 5.
4. Mickey Kaus, *The End of Equality* (New York: Basic Books, 1992).
5. William Connolly, *Identity/Difference: Democratic Negotiations of Political Paradox* (Ithaca: Cornell University Press, 1991), esp. 87ff.
6. For a very thoughtful recent argument to the same effect, see Richard Dagger, *Civic Virtues: Rights, Citizenship, and Republican Liberalism* (New York: Oxford University Press, 1997).
7. Mary Ann Glendon, *Rights Talk: The Impoverishment of Political Discourse* (New York: Free Press, 1991).
8. Alan Wolfe, *Whose Keeper? Social Science and Moral Obligation* (Berkeley: University of California Press, 1989).
9. Alasdair MacIntyre, *After Virtue* (Notre Dame: University of Notre Dame Press, 1981). Ronald Beiner, *What's the Matter with Liberalism?* (Berkeley: University of California Press, 1992).
10. Stephen Macedo, *Liberal Virtues: Citizenship, Virtue, and Community in Liberal Constitutionalism* (Oxford: Clarendon Press, 1990), 278, 285, and 283.
11. Condorcet, for example, wrote that "it is easy to prove that wealth has a natural tendency to equality, and that any excessive disproportion could not exist or at least would rapidly disappear if civil laws did not [interfere in various ways]." *Sketch for a Historical Picture of the Progress of the Human Mind*, translated by June Barraclough (London: Weidenfeld and Nicolson, 1955), 180.
12. See MacIntyre, *After Virtue*, esp. chapter 5, and my *The Irony of Liberal Reason* (Chicago: University of Chicago Press, 1981).

Part One

Other Liberalisms

1

Democratic Realism:
The Liberalism of Fear

One venerable and influential account of the goals of liberal democracy embodies a relatively modest set of aspirations. Winston Churchill set the tone for this perspective when he said that democracy was the worst form of government except for all the others. We can call this perspective "democratic realism" because its hallmark is a sober realism about the intrinsic difficulties surrounding the creation of a viable political regime that is both liberal and democratic. Alternatively, one could term this outlook "democratic minimalism" because the normative consequence of this sober empirical assessment of the problematics of democracy is the belief that a liberal democracy is doing very well, thank you, if it proves capable of attaining the fairly minimal goals of social peace, rule of law, and governmental stability.

Classical political theorists who fall under the umbrella of democratic realism include Hobbes, Hume, Montaigne, Montesquieu, and Madison. Obviously, these thinkers in some ways represent different traditions and different philosophical persuasions. But they have in common a clear tendency to view the possibilities of liberal politics with a sober and skeptical eye. They are impressed by the difficulties of creating stable polities on democratic (or any other) premises. They are generally skeptical about the likelihood that people will be either capable of discerning a general good or willing to subordinate their own particular interests to it. They are suspicious about idealist enthusiasm, seeing it as frequently if not invariably a cover for personal power-seeking and as generally destabilizing in its consequences. And they consider the attainment of what is often referred to these days as a democratic modus vivendi, i.e., a way of living together peaceably, to be a considerable achievement.

Contemporary democratic realists exhibit many of these same hallmarks, and they often acknowledge their intellectual kinship with these earlier theorists. American group theorists such as Arthur Bentley and David Truman, panegyrists of democratic compromise such as T. V. Smith, and pluralists such as Robert Dahl (in his 1950s and 1960s writings) are all Madisonian in inspiration, even if they move away from Madison's eighteenth-century belief in "natural rights." Judith Shklar cites Montaigne as "the hero of every page of this book" as she defends her "liberalism of fear."[1] Patrick Neal acknowledges his debt to Hobbes as he argues for his modus vivendi theory of liberalism.[2] And Richard Rorty's postmodernist rendering of a democratic politics of peaceful accommodation, despite its neo-Nietzschean reference to the private realm as space for "strong poets," could be taken without grave distortion to be a philosophically radicalized version of Humean conventionalism. Considered together, as a loose family of minimalist liberals, these theorists provide powerful and influential arguments in support of the claim that democratic polities should be appreciated for their ability to afford security and reconcile social conflict—and that expecting much more than that may be asking for too much. Realists insist that these conflicts of interest, competing moral and religious convictions, and the psychological predisposition toward domination constitute a formidable barrier to the creation of a stable political order—particularly a liberal and democratic order that must valorize individual freedoms and empower popular will. Against the backdrop of this analysis of political problematics, democratic realists understandably depict democratic regimes as confronted by powerful forces of social entropy. The natural tendency of any political order is perceived to be toward anarchy or civil war, on the one hand, or tyranny on the other. The central task of democratic government, therefore, becomes to deal successfully with these forces and tendencies that constantly threaten to undermine it. No democratic regime can expect to survive, realists would argue, unless its leaders avoid what Alexander Hamilton called "those reveries which would seduce us into an expectation of peace and cordiality" or "deceitful dreams of a golden age" and instead focus constructively on the kinds of problems that "continually agitated" the "petty republics of Greece and Italy" and kept them "in a state of perpetual vibration between the extremes of tyranny and anarchy."[3]

Given this forbidding landscape of social entropy, it is little wonder that the political goals of democratic realism are largely depicted in negative terms. They are goals of avoidance more than goals of achievement. Like Hobbes and Madison, who sought to avoid anarchy and tyranny, contemporary democratic realists orient the liberal polity around the imperative of avoiding the most threatening evils that imperil it. Judith Shklar's powerful meditation upon the "ordinary vices" and their implications for democratic practices is a leading case in point. As she tells us in her introduction to that volume: "Thinking about the vices has, indeed, the effect of showing precisely to what extent ours is a culture of many subcultures, of layer upon layer of ancient religious and class rituals, ethnic inheritances of sensibility and manners, and ideological residues whose original purpose has by now been utterly forgotten. *With this view, liberal democracy becomes more a recipe for survival than a project for the perfectibility of mankind.*"[4]

The view of liberal democracy as a "recipe for survival" is the perspective born from what Shklar aptly calls "the liberalism of fear." This is a liberalism, Shklar notes, "that was born out of the cruelties of the religious civil wars."[5] Gestated within the sobering experiences of civil war and fratricidal violence, the liberalism of fear places cruelty at the head of its ranking of vices. "The first right," Shklar says, "is to be protected against this fear of cruelty."[6] Shklar does not explain very fully what this moral prioritizing of avoiding cruelty entails in terms of political institutions and policies. It seems, however, that she would endorse the strategic emphasis of Montesquieu and Madison upon the institutionalization of counter- vailing power. In policy terms, therefore, there is significant overlap between the liberalism of rights and the liberalism of fear; but it is important in her view to re- member that the latter is primary, in part perhaps to avoid flights of romantic in- dividualism. The core rationale of both Madison's designation of justice as the "end of government" and his and Montesquieu's concern with the dispersion of power, she insists, grows from the aversion to and defense against cruelty. "Justice itself is only a web of legal arrangements required to keep cruelty in check, espe- cially by those who have most of the instruments of intimidation closest at hand. That is why the liberalism of fear concentrates so single-mindedly on limited and predictable government.... This is not the liberalism of natural rights, but it un- derwrites rights as the politically indispensable dispersion of power, which alone can check the reign of fear and cruelty."[7]

In his recent defense of what he calls "vulgar liberalism," Patrick Neal also draws upon the perceptions and judgments characteristic of democratic realism. Neal argues that both "neutrality liberals," by whom he means theorists such as Rawls and Charles Larmore, and "perfectionist liberals," such as William Galston and Joseph Raz, are wrong to denigrate the modus vivendi model of liberalism. It is not necessary to insist upon grounding liberalism in moral principles rather than in compelling prudential considerations, Neal argues, although Rawls seems to think that his account of an overlapping consensus is importantly differenti- ated from modus vivendi models in precisely this way. Likewise, liberal perfec- tionists such as Galston should not be so anxious to identify a conception of the human good with its attendant virtues as a necessary part of a cogent defense of liberalism against its adversaries. Instead, the prudential considerations associ- ated with maintaining civil peace in a pluralistic society composed of fractious human beings should be deemed sufficiently compelling in their own right—a solid and defensible basis for justifying liberal politics and measuring liberal regimes against their competitors. Neal deplores "the tendency of ideal-based lib- eralisms to generate scorn for the mundane good of stability." And he defends his own realism and modest expectations by invoking the logic as well as the name of Hobbes.

> Hobbesians (among whom Neal includes himself) take the measure of civil polity by the yardstick of the *summum malum*, and on that instrument the mark labeled "civil peace" is not preceded by the adjective "mere." When lib- eralism is conceived according to the image of some conception of the *sum- mum bonum*, there is a tendency to forget that the mark is not a given in human affairs but an (always incomplete) achievement of human artifice.... There are, to be sure, goods greater than civil peace and personal security; but here, a Hobbesian liberal will join neutrality theorists in doubting, if not fear- ing, that these should be made the stuff of politics.[8]

Because democratic realism incorporates relatively bleak assumptions about human psychology and about the structural dynamics of political life and because it consequently sees the central task of a liberal regime as avoiding the worst possibilities intrinsic in these predisposing forces, it espouses a relatively modest set of positive goals for democracy. First on the list is the maintenance of the basic social order. George Kennan, himself often identified as a leading representative of realism in international affairs, once said that there were two sorts of social thinkers in the world, those who sought order first and those who focused on social justice. Influenced no doubt by a lifetime in diplomacy, he counted himself among the former group. Judging from their rhetoric, most democratic realists would clearly agree. Stability and civil peace are central concerns for realists, and the first virtue of liberal democracy is its degree of success in achieving these goals.

Several important subsidiary goals are related to that preoccupation with civil peace and social stability. Moderation, mutual accommodation, and effective government are all important criteria of democratic success in the realist scheme of things because each of them conduces to a peaceful and orderly society. Freedom is also an important goal, but as one might expect the first freedom is deemed to be the freedom from fear. Equality does not receive much mention. For one thing, the realist's hard-headed empiricism inclines him or her toward the view of sociological analysts like Robert Michels that all social organization inevitably produces elites. To the extent that equality receives mention, it appears in negative and defensive form—as a concern to eliminate or control those forms and degrees of inequality which allow some groups to oppress others and thereby inflame social tensions. In this respect, democratic realism follows the lead of Montaigne and Montesquieu, who were, as Judith Shklar writes, "not at all disposed to treat social equality as a positive good. Inequality mattered inasmuch as it encouraged and created opportunities for cruelty. Theirs was a purely negative egalitarianism . . . [which] is really a fear of the consequences of inequality, and especially of the dazzling effect of power, which frees its holders from all restraints."[9]

The sociological realism of the democratic pluralists in the 1950s and 1960s, together with their rhetorical privileging of moderation, accommodation, and "equilibrium," suggest that they might properly be included among our family of democratic realists. This is not particularly surprising in terms of their historical context, for the perceptions and political priorities of realism gain sustenance and urgency when oppressive, nondemocratic regimes seem threatening. When faced with the menacing visage of totalitarianism, who could deny the reasonableness of Robert Dahl's concluding evaluation of the American regime in his *Preface to Democratic Theory*? The American political system, he wrote, "appears to be a relatively efficient system for reinforcing agreement, encouraging moderation, and maintaining social peace in a restless and immoderate people operating a gigantic, powerful, diversified, and incredibly complex society. This is no negligible contribution, then, that Americans have made to the arts of government—and to that branch, which of all the arts of politics is the most difficult, the art of democratic government."[10]

There are interesting parallels here between Dahl's realistic pluralism and Richard Rorty's more recent defense of "post-modernist bourgeois liberalism." For like the pluralists, Rorty is inclined to justify our current liberal democratic practices on the (neo-?) pragmatic ground that they have been successful in maintaining a moderate and stable public order within which individuals are free to pursue their private conceptions of the good life. In his argument for a playful prioritizing of democracy over the philosophical quest for valid principles, Rorty deploys some of the rhetorical guideposts characteristic of democratic realism. He writes, in his postmodern liberal regime, people

> will get accustomed to the thought that social policy needs no more authority than successful accommodation between individuals, individuals who find themselves heir to the same historical traditions and faced with the same problems. It will be a society which encourages the "end of ideology," which takes reflective equilibrium as the only method needed in discussing social policy.[11]

On the basis of this and other similar passages, then, it is understandable why Richard Bernstein could conclude that Rorty's "celebration of a new tolerant *jouissance* of multiple language games and vocabularies is little more than an ideological *apologia* for an old-fashioned version of cold war liberalism dressed up in fashionable 'post-modern' discourse."[12]

Both Dahl and Rorty, in their different decades, expressed dismay over being characterized and criticized as ideological conservatives, since each of them considers himself a social democrat. But what triggered these characterizations and critiques was the same thing in both instances: a clearly expressed pragmatic appreciation of American liberalism for managing to maintain a reasonably stable and moderate regime wherein contending groups could reach some "equilibrating" accommodation with each other, wherein the government was somewhat responsive to public opinion, and wherein individuals were sufficiently free and secure to pursue their private happiness. In addition, because they both were committed to morally skeptical epistemologies—a positivistic empiricism for Dahl and a postmodernist conventionalism for Rorty—their accounts of liberalism lacked any critical bite. In short, their mode of characterizing the central tasks of political life and their prioritizing of contending democratic goals seemed to reflect the perspective of democratic realism. And for a variety of reasons that should be reasonably apparent, democratic realists are generally perceived as being on the conservative end of the (democratic) ideological spectrum.[13]

Preoccupied as they are with what they see as the persistently demanding task of maintaining a moderate, peaceful, and nontyrannical social order, democratic realists tend to look with suspicion upon "higher" democratic goals. They recognize that the goals of moderation, stability, and social peace seem rather pedestrian to many of more hopeful or idealistic disposition. But they are dubious about the capacity of any political regime—and certainly about the capacity of liberal regimes that by definition allow space for very imperfect human beings to pursue their own purposes—to do much in the way of improving character, creating community, or answering to some other high moral ideal. To make these ambitious demands on our politics smacks of utopianism in their view. And utopianism is always beset by the dangers that attend unreasonable expectations: frustration, anger, disillusionment, cynicism, and divisiveness. Again, Judith Shklar voices some of these concerns:

> Liberal government for bad characters did not promise us that freedom would make us good; it merely argued that it would remove the most horrible obstacles to any ethical undertaking that we might conceivably try. To demand more would not reduce vice. It would only shackle us again, and revive those pious pretenses and pious cruelties which a religious establishment had perfected and which Kant, no less than Montesquieu, regarded as one of the principal sources of public oppression.[14]

If it can generate oppression, utopianism may also bring chronic instability into democratic politics. When goals are set that are simply beyond attainment, democratic regimes are foredoomed to seem failures. They become subject to perpetual illegitimacy crises engendered more by popular delusion than by official malfeasance. In Irving Kristol's view, this destabilizing dynamic has in fact become endemic to American politics. "The consequence of this public insistence on a utopian vision of man, history, and society is that our public life is shot through with a permanent streak of hysteria" he writes. When this occurs, and a tendency "toward insistent self-dissatisfaction becomes overwhelming, then such a society is in grave trouble. . . . A more perfect recipe for permanent political instability . . . cannot be imagined."[15]

The idealistic expectations of participatory democracy are a particular and recurrent source of utopian discontent, in the view of many realists. Many people are simply not oriented toward political activity and trying to make them so can be both condescending and counterproductive. If people want to absorb themselves in the cares and exertions of private life—remaining *homo civicus* rather than *homo politicus*—that should not be cause for dismay. Moreover, the imperatives of social organization are such that a relatively small subset of the citizenry are going to run things anyway. If this inevitability is construed as illegitimate, useless and avoidable discontent is the result. Besides, as many of the realists have argued, excessive political mobilization is not desirable. No doubt with the spectres of McCarthyism and totalitarian enthusiasms in mind, realists have viewed mass politics with a jaundiced eye. As Thomas Dye wrote a few years back, "participatory democracy is a romantic fiction. The masses are incompetent in the tasks of government. . . . Mass politics is extremist, unstable, and unpredictable. The masses are not committed to democratic rules of the game; when they are politically activated, they frequently go outside these rules to engage in violence." These failings, moreover, are largely ineradicable:

> Efforts to re-educate or resocialize the masses are futile. Two hundred years ago Jefferson proposed universal free public education as a prescription [to

ameliorate] mass ignorance, incompetence, and alienation. Today the masses in America average twelve years of free public education, but, if anything, they appear less capable of governing in a wise and humane fashion than the masses of Jefferson's time. [16]

The best prescription, accordingly, is to eschew participatory imperatives and let sleeping dogs lie. A certain amount of mass political apathy is functional for the overriding goals of moderation and stability.

Given their empirical conclusions about the conflict endemic to human social interaction and the resultant difficulty of producing stable regimes which do not tyrannize their citizens, it is not surprising that democratic realists subscribe to what might be termed "a politics of containment." That tactic, made famous in the context of international politics during the Cold War, in fact aptly characterizes the strategic orientation of democratic realism *tout court*. In domestic politics as well as in the international arena, the basic imperative is to devise ways to keep the conflicting interests and passions of the people from tearing apart the social fabric and incapacitating the government.

The actual containment schemes recommended by the realists diverge. One strategy, represented by Hobbes's counsel, is to consolidate power in the hands of an authority who thereby is capable of "overawing" the potentially anarchic citizenry and keeping them in check. Hobbes complained about divided authority in the same way that Julius Nyerere once complained about Western-style two-party systems: they institutionalize incipient civil war. The best strategy of containment, therefore, is to repose in a single center of authority a power sufficient to contain those forces that would if unchecked lead to political disintegration. Hobbes's own version of this containment strategy concentrates so much power in the hands of the sovereign, in fact, that we would be inclined to say that it goes beyond the bounds of genuine democracy. But it is important to remember that his Leviathan is—putatively, at least—democratically grounded in the consent of the governed who accede to the constraint of their passions in the name of prudence.

The more common realist strategy takes the opposite tack and seeks to constrain those who would oppress others by a scheme of countervailing power. Once again, the analogy to foreign policy realism is suggestive here. Madisonian democracy in a real sense is a domestic version of Metternich's diplomacy. Contending political actors are accorded control of different levels or branches of government that must contend with and accommodate each other. Ambition, thus, in Madison's justly famous phrase, counters ambition. The same basic approach was, of course, prescribed by that other great democratic realist, Montesquieu. And it seems to be the favored recourse of Judith Shklar in her quest to organize and consolidate liberal societies dedicated most of all to the prevention of cruelty.

Another institutional mechanism for avoiding ruinous social conflict that recommends itself to democratic realists—and not only to them—is the tactic of segmentation of spheres. The idea here is to separate different social enterprises and concerns from each other so that conflicts over the criteria and conduct of one of them do not disrupt the others. To the extent that social life is considered to be and is organized as a seamless web of relationships, disagreements that break out over one aspect of the social order will ineluctably spread throughout all other aspects. Every axis of political conflict threatens to become generalized. One may seek to extol the virtues of a polity whose various constituent practices interlock and cohere in a unified fashion. But this social ideal is feasible only where a profound moral unanimity prevails—or, alternatively and not so attractively, where some subset of the populace can enforce its moral hegemony over potential dissenters. Once moral pluralism becomes endemic, as it is in most large-scale contemporary societies, this ideal of a fully reticulated social order is no longer viable. Indeed, it becomes dangerous as a guide to practice. For trying to impose extensive social coherence in the context of moral pluralism would be analogous to building a city of inflammable structures with no firebreaks. Conversely, to the extent that different spheres of the social enterprise can be dissociated from each other, conflicts arising in one domain may be contained there.

In the history of liberal practice, one central mechanism for containing social conflict via institutional segmentation has been to distinguish and disentangle the "public" and "private" realms, with the concomitant attempt to construct religious practices in such a manner that they can be mostly sequestered in the realm of private life. It is not surprising, then, that democratic realists and modus vivendi liberals depict the Act of Toleration and Locke's *Letter Concerning Toleration* as such axial moments in the development of democratic institutions. For in the century-and-a-half preceding these achievements, post-Reformation Europe had decimated itself in religious warfare; since that time, religious disputes and differences have only sporadically and less catastrophically disrupted the political order of the major liberal democracies. The diminution of the socially acceptable space for the expression of religious sentiments and imperatives is quite understandably experienced as unduly constraining by many of the religiously committed citizens of today's secularized liberal democracies. But the strategy of maintaining even a somewhat rough, porous, and contestable constitutional line between church and state has undeniably enhanced the political stability of liberal societies in exactly the way that Locke predicted it would.

In his *Spheres of Justice*, Michael Walzer has ably depicted and endorsed a similar strategy of segmentation in the area of distributive justice.[17] The things that people value, he notes, are not homogeneous but plural: wealth, friendship, honor, power, respect, health, and so on. What makes for social justice and for a free society of social equals, he argues, is not the discovery and application of some single algorithm for all goods but instead the distribution of different goods in different realms according to different relevant criteria. This "art of separation" is understood to be one of the fundamental organizational mechanisms in the creation of a free society.[18] Walzer's argument, it should be noted, is not itself couched in the terms of democratic realism or justified in terms of the realist goals of order, stability, and social peace. Instead, Walzer's concern is with the social good of what he calls "complex equality." Nonetheless, the strategy he advocates clearly is reminiscent of Robert Frost's famous admonition that "good fences make good neighbors"; and in this sense it comports exceedingly well with the realist tactic of using a pluralism of institutional domains as a means of buffering the potentially divisive consequences of moral and religious pluralism.

Most democratic realists, demurring from Kant's optimism about the efficacy of astutely crafted constitutions to deal with even the most refractory human material, recognize that institutional mechanisms alone cannot reliably produce civil peace. Social accommodation is an art rather than a science, and as such it requires sustenance not simply from technical expertise but also from behavioral norms and moral habits. The liberalism of fear, therefore, generates its own distinctive account of the civic virtues. These are the moral attributes and dispositions arguably conducive to the preservation of a stable, orderly, peaceful, and reasonably free democratic polity.

What the democratic realists most fear is what in the seventeenth century was often called "enthusiasm." Today we would probably use the term "zealotry." The enthusiast or zealot is one who is passionately and unreservedly dedicated to the furtherance of some partisan cause and/or some particular creed. The intellectual vice that generally attends zealotry is dogmatism. Zealous partisanship is inherently divisive, hence potentially threatening to social peace. And dogmatism thwarts efforts to bridge the resultant social fissures by discussion or compromise. Accordingly, democratic realists have always condemned and sought to discourage such enthusiasms. The conceptions of zealotry and hence the targets of the realists' animus have varied over the course of liberalism's historical career. But it is the common fear of and distaste for dogmatic and dictatorial enthusiasms that inform Hobbes's and Hume's aspersions against religious sectarians, Burke's attack on the philosophes, and the American pluralists' concerns about the dangers of mass politics, McCarthyism, and Marxism. In the eyes of these particular beholders, at least, each of these were a form of zealotry; each represented a standing danger to civil peace, political stability, and personal security.

The civic virtues according to democratic realism, conversely, are those passions and dispositions that pacify and stabilize. The first of these could be said to be fear itself. As Hobbes argued and Judith Shklar has recently echoed, fear is a civilizing passion. It may not be in and of itself much of a virtue, but it conduces to politically salutary behavior. Whether because they lack the intellectual awareness to perceive the predictably catastrophic consequences of certain behaviors or because of a lack of impulse control, the absolutely fearless among us are always dangerous. Teenage drivers are cases in point, as insurance statistics readily attest. With the rational fear of violent death, however, come prudence and a willingness to forbear. And these in turn conduce to social peace and stability. To value fear, it should be added, is not the same thing as to praise timorousness. It is merely to value the rational recognition of the very real and serious dangers politics presents to us, together with the emotional correlate of that recognition. Instead, the desired outcome is fortitude in the face of these dangers, a refusal to be cowed or frozen by them. As Judith Shklar writes, "courage is to be prized, since it both prevents us from being cruel, as cowards so often are, and fortifies us against fear from threats, both physical and moral. This is, to be sure, not the courage of the armed, but that of their likely victims."[19]

Perhaps the central liberal virtues for democratic realists are tolerance and self-restraint. Shklar, indeed, conjoins the two in her eloquent paean to what she regards as the ideal liberal character type.

> The alternative then set, and still before us, is not one between classical virtue and liberal self-indulgence, but between cruel military and moral repression and violence, and a self-restraining tolerance that fences in the powerful to protect the freedom and safety of every citizen, old or young, male or female, black or white. Far from being an amoral free-for-all, liberalism is, in fact, extremely difficult and constraining.[20]

A similar logic informs Richard Rorty's more recent articulation of a modus vivendi liberalism grounded in postmodernist premises. The adoption of a playful or "ironic" stance toward moral commitments should, he argues, follow from a belief in the radical contingency of all social constructions. But this stance of ironic detachment, perhaps paradoxically, is by no means devoid of moral significance. Instead, it should function beneficently in the service of "the spirit of accommodation and tolerance which is essential to democracy."[21] There is, he writes,

> a moral purpose behind . . . the air of light-minded aestheticism I am adopting toward traditional philosophical questions. . . . Such philosophical superficiality and light-mindedness helps along the disenchantment of the world. It helps make the world's inhabitants more pragmatic, more tolerant, more liberal, more receptive to the appeal of instrumental rationality. If one's moral identity consists in being a citizen of a liberal polity, then to encourage light-mindedness will serve one's moral purposes. Moral commitment, after all, does not require taking seriously all the matters which are, for moral reasons, taken seriously by one's fellow-citizens. It may require just the opposite. It may require trying to josh them out of the habit of taking those topics so seriously.[22]

Two other attributes of good democratic citizenship that attain some saliency in the realist pantheon of liberal virtues are humility and pragmatism. The moral imperative behind humility for the realists is not moral and theological, but practical and political. The concern is not with hubris that rightly offends a God who well knows our sinful hearts but rather with a grasping vanity that incurs the wrath of our neighbors, thereby disrupting the social peace of a well-ordered democracy. Pragmatism in this context means focusing on immediate problems that are inflicting real costs on real people—rather than, say, being preoccupied with long-range and more abstract goals or values. A sane and effective politics for realists is fundamentally a matter of repairs and adjustments. Good policy is, to borrow Karl Popper's phrase, "piecemeal social engineering" with a strong emphasis on the adjective. "Incrementalism" in policy-planning, stoutly defended by the pluralists, is another theme that fits into this pragmatic mode. Good policies, on this account, are cobbled together from a complex of particular judgments, each of which responds to very specific concerns and problems instead of being deduced from a predetermined coherent model. Realists accordingly assume a Burkean and Oakeshottean perspective on the proper uses of reason in politics. "Theoretical" reason— i.e., a Cartesian or Platonist-style devotion to overarching philosophical blueprints for politics—is deemed untrustworthy and potentially dangerous. The preferred alternative is not necessarily a politics of expedience or blind inertia, but a form of rationality that is heavily practical, profoundly rooted in an experiential acquaintance with the concrete particularities of specific situations.

In short, democratic realism rests upon a resolutely consequentialist ethic. Whatever can be said about the moral significance of good intentions, the fact is that the best of intentions do not guarantee good policy; and an insistence upon unwavering adherence to what one regards as principle can lead to political disasters. When the realist assesses the relevant consequences, it should be added, it is the costs and benefits of social peace and political stability that figure most prominently. For that reason, the political ethics of democratic realism approximate rather closely Hobbes's interpretation of the laws of nature as "precepts" promoting self-preservation, such as "seek peace and follow it," keep covenants, strive to accommodate yourself to the rest, "pardon the offenses past of them that repenting, desire it," do not "declare hatred or contempt of another," and be willing to submit controversies to arbitration.[23]

The realists' political heroes thus are the brokers, the peacemakers, the compromisers, the deal-makers, and the head-knockers who make the governing process work while maintaining some semblance of social comity. To moral purists, none of these types seems particular elevated, except possibly the peacemakers. And even the peacemakers may be subject to opprobrium for dealing with the devil. For the democratic realist, however, these are the people who deserve our gratitude and admiration. Apart from their talents and their willingness to undertake the often tedious and generally thankless tasks necessary to bring collective action out of a motley of contending groups, democratic politics would grind to a halt and we would be pretty much out of luck. The spectacle of a Lyndon Johnson bullying and wheedling reluctant lawmakers or of a Dan Rostenkowski handing out preferential tax breaks for particular projects in order to pass a tax bill may not seem terribly inspiring. But without such cajolery and dealing, we would not have the Civil Rights Acts of 1964 or the widely praised Tax Reform Act of 1986. The alternative to this kind of somewhat unseemly bargaining process is not some majestic march of a mythic general will but deadlock, entropy, or warfare. We should, therefore, lift our glasses in thanks to these politicos even if the squeamish among us may sometimes need to avert their gaze from these brokers' doings. For it is their mundane form of heroism that permits democracies to survive and (fitfully) to govern themselves.

This, then, is the core of what I have chosen to call "democratic realism" or, borrowing from Judith Shklar, the "liberalism of fear." It is not a sharply etched paradigm that exacts the unswerving allegiance of an identifiable party claque, but rather a relatively coherent perspective uniting an extended family of thoughtful analysts of democratic governance. It is not very idealistic in the conventional sense of that term, but it is nonetheless a normative conception of liberal democracy that prioritizes certain political goals and renders critical judgments accordingly. It may not figure prominently in the standard accounts of the ideological spectrum, but it represents an important and influential frame of reference that informs and animates both theorists and practitioners of the democratic faith.

How should we respond to the normative account of the purposes of liberal democracy presented to us by the democratic realists? Is the liberalism of fear our best guide in conceiving our goals, shaping our institutions, socializing our citizens, and measuring our achievements? Or is it beset by flaws, blind spots, or inadequacies that render it a suspect touchstone? Obviously, there is no single "right" answer to these questions. Each of us who shares the democratic faith must assess contending conceptions of liberal purposes from the vantage point provided by our moral intuitions and by our beliefs regarding the proper and feasible aspirations of a democratic society. Here I offer my own assessments—judgments grounded in the complex set of intuitions and aspirations that inform my allegiance to what I call civic liberalism.

In my view, the analytical arguments and normative claims found in democratic realism are in many respects extremely forceful and compelling. Any serious assessment of the problems and prospects of democratic governance should begin with the sober insights to be found within this theoretical tradition. If it be conceived as a comprehensive account of democratic aspirations, however, it seems ultimately inadequate. Its reach is too limited, its aspirations too low, its hopes too modest. It is a necessary but not a sufficient guide to democratic practice. It provides a solid floor but not the best ceiling for the habitation of contemporary liberalism. As William Galston has aptly said: "The fact that liberalism was born in fear does not mean that it must necessarily remain there."[24]

The greatest strength of the liberalism of fear is its hardheadedness about what Irving Kristol has called the "problematics" of democracy.[25] By problematics, Kristol refers to those difficulties and dilemmas confronting democracies that are not external and adventitious but organic and internal to the dynamics of democracy itself. For instance, to the extent that government "of the people, by the people, for the people" represents a constitutive democratic standard and to the extent that political institutions are subject to the sociological forces expressed in the "iron law of oligarchy," here lies a problem internal to the task of democratic governance. Similarly, to the extent that democracies are normatively obligated to accord legitimacy to and be responsive to popular will and to the extent that people's wills tend to be contrary to other people's rights and to the general interest (to borrow from Madison's definition of factions), here again is a difficulty that inheres in democracy as a form of government. Because of hard experience (Montaigne with the Wars of Religion, Judith Shklar with European totalitarianism, Hobbes with the English Civil War), because of their historical learning (Madison and Hobbes as students of the classical Greek republics), and/or because of their social scientific investigation of real-world politics (the pluralists' studies of urban politics and voting behavior, James Q. Wilson's study of criminal behavior), the democratic realists generally bring to the table a recognition of the constraints within which liberal democracies must function.

The liberalism of fear is also salutary in its reminders that the creation of a democratic social order which can both protect individual freedoms and produce effective governing majorities is a difficult and complex undertaking. More idealistic democratic theories seem to take the endurance of democratic regimes almost for granted and to focus principally on their distance from perfection. The realists' insistence that the attainment of stability and effectiveness by democratic regimes is always somewhat fragile is a useful corrective to this excessively sanguine assumption. Those who do not understand the great value or the requisites of the blessings of liberty are apt to lose them. In particular, the realist analysis of the perils inexorably associated with social pluralism should alert us to the folly of exacerbating social divisions either through carelessness or through romanticizing ethnic chauvinism under the rubric of identity politics.

Equally valuable is the realist illumination of the importance of buffering and restraining institutional devices in maintaining social comity in a restless and diverse liberal order. In free and pluralist societies, good fences are in fact crucial to keeping people from constantly intruding upon or dominating one another. These institutional restraints don't really turn people into good neighbors. For that, something more is required. But at least they can mitigate the collisions that generate social enmity. The realist account of civic virtues, with its emphasis on tolerance, humility, restraint, and moderation, also provides a useful counterweight to liberalism's characteristic indulgence of individual desires and ambitions.

As for the central political goals that animate democratic realism—civil peace, stability, and personal security—no one can reasonably gainsay their importance. The world is filled, it seems, with continual examples to validate Hobbes's claim that the greatest incommodity that can possibly happen to the people under any form of government "is scarce sensible in respect of the miseries and horrible calamities that accompany a civil war or that dissolute condition of masterless men without subjection to laws."[26] As I write these words, Hutu and Tutsi combatants in the nation of Rwanda are slaughtering each other and civilians on a mass scale, and Serbian troops are shelling civilian populations in Bosnia. By the time these words are read, no doubt new instances of civil warfare will be inflicting disaster upon still other populations in other spots on the globe. A possibly apocryphal tale had Judith Shklar reporting of herself that each night before going to bed she turned on the radio to assure herself that the Nazis were not coming. That sounds extreme, especially to those of us who never have shared Professor Shklar's Central European background. But the fears of the liberalism of fear are not paranoid fantasies. They are given credence by almost any daily newspaper.

Despite these many virtues, democratic realism does not provide adequate normative guidance for today's liberal democracies. The realists are far better at seeing the pitfalls and dangers democracies need to avoid than they are at conceiving the possibilities of improvement. We need to attend carefully to their sober counsel to keep from sailing the ship of state onto the rocks, but we find thin fare in this quarter to help us in charting our final destination. Like George Bush admitted of himself at one point, the liberals of fear are not that good at "the vision thing."

One way to see the thinness of the realist vision is to note the difficulty it would have responding to the rhetorical question that sets the stage for John Stuart Mill's *Considerations on Representative Government*: why would a benevolent despotism not be the best possible form of government? A benevolent despot, after all, could provide the social goods most salient for democratic realists: civil peace, security, stability, continuity, freedom from fear. With a reasonable amount of competence and a reasonably propitious political setting, such a ruler could also allow some space for individuals to be relatively free in their daily affairs. Hobbes, the first adherent of the liberalism of fear, found this logic compelling, after all. And it is not always clear why a contemporary exponent of the realist persuasion would not find countries like Brazil or Singapore compelling exemplars of good political practice.

In fact, of course, most democratic realists tacitly assume and occasionally invoke the norms of liberty, equality, and community; but these ideals would seem to require more in the way of a positive defense than they usually give them. And the realists also seem to have relatively little to say about how the pursuit of these goals should shape democratic policies and institutions.

A second problem with the liberalism of fear is that it can slide fairly easily into a liberalism of complacency. Superficially, this result may seem paradoxical, since fear breeds anxiety and anxiety seems incompatible with complacency. In political rather than psychological terms, however, the linkage is less puzzling. Those who are fearful of instability and look for little from politics will find it easier to accept a tolerably safe and stable status quo than to champion social change. Thus it is not surprising that the pluralist Robert Dahl of a few decades ago and the liberal ironist Richard Rorty should find themselves chided for their political conservatism even if they both considered themselves social democrats. The slope of their rhetoric, with its privileging of moderation, stability, and social peace—together with the relative absence or marginalization of norms possessing critical bite—leaves them sounding very much like contented apologists for things as they are. We can call this the Humean syndrome: those who, like Hume, consider peace and security to be the overriding social goods will tend toward a conservative utilitarianism of "good sense." And this tendency, in turn, will in the context of a reasonably stable and moderate society bear heavily in favor of acceptance of prevailing patterns of law and policy.[27]

A third difficulty with democratic realism, I would argue, is that it fails to distinguish properly between utopianism and romanticism. This failure, in turn, compounds the aforementioned tendency to slide into an inertial conservatism because it undermines the ambitious ideals that give democratic theory critical purchase. When theorists such as Shklar and Kristol belabor what they characterize as the dangers of utopian thinking in politics, their indictment is too broad. What is pernicious is not utopian aspirations per se but rather the flattering self-delusions about human nature which sometimes attend utopian thought but which are nonetheless clearly distinguishable from it. To borrow an example from Kristol, he is no doubt correct to say that the strident criticism of New York City public schools that surfaces every year when test scores reveal that their students are below average in reading level is, in part at least, based upon sentimentalist illusions. Those critics who profess themselves to be shocked by these results seem to assume, quite inaccurately as it happens, that all students arrive at the school door equal in their academic aptitude and interest and that students can be given an education in the same way that customers can be given Big Macs. Hence they have unreasonable expectations, which lead to unwarranted denunciations of the institutions in question, which lead to imprudent "reforms." When all that is granted, it remains true that the academic results in question are undeniably inadequate in absolute terms and that a democratic society owes its next generation of citizens better educational opportunities than they currently receive. The hysteria generated by the test scores may be inappropriate, but the quest for improvement is not misguided per se, and a blanket condemnation of utopianism in this context may undermine necessary reformist aspirations in the guise of quelling irrational overreaction.

The trick, of course, is to be hard-headed and clear-eyed about the sociological, psychological, and economic realities that inevitably constrain the horizon of possibility while at the same time to be hopeful and determined in striving for the best that can be achieved. To do that, we need indeed to avoid the romantic misconceptions that have poisoned much of modern ideology. But we also need to nourish rather than to discourage those hopes for and visions of a better world that are so essential to human improvement and social progress. However contestable his own views of social perfection may be, Allan Bloom's remarks *apropos* the necessity for visionary thinking in politics deserve endorsement. "Utopianism," he writes, "is, as Plato taught us at the outset, the fire with which we must play because it is the only way to find out what we are. We need to criticize false understandings of Utopia, but the easy way out provided by realism is deadly."[28]

Democratic realism, the liberalism of fear, provides us with the sober and solid floor for a persuasive theory of liberal democracy. But if it gives us a solid floor for our democratic practices and pursuits, the ceiling of democratic realism is too low. Its spirit is too anxious. Its adherents are too easily satisfied. Its hopes are too modest, its aspirations too limited. If it is taken to be a comprehensive account of what liberal democracy is all about, it risks becoming, in the words of Bernard Crick, "a gelded view, something so over-civilized and logically dogmatic as to deprive many of any feeling that anything, let alone free institutions, is worthwhile."[29] To give us a sense of what we should strive for, a sense of the larger and higher possibilities of democracy, we need to look elsewhere.

Notes

1. Judith Shklar, *Ordinary Vices* (Cambridge: Harvard University Press, 1984), 284.
2. Patrick Neal, "Vulgar Liberalism," *Political Theory* 21, no. 4 (November 1993): 623–42.

3. Alexander Hamilton, *Federalist* 6, 9.

4. Shklar, *Ordinary Vices*, 4 (emphasis added).

5. Shklar, *Ordinary Vices*, 5.

6. Shklar, *Ordinary Vices*, 237.

7. Shklar, *Ordinary Vices*, 237–38.

8. Neal, "Vulgar Liberalism," 638.

9. Shklar, *Ordinary Vices*, 28–29.

10. Robert Dahl, *A Preface to Democratic Theory* (Chicago: University of Chicago Press, 1956), 151.

11. Richard Rorty, "The Priority of Democracy to Philosophy," in *The Virginia Statute of Religious Freedom: Two Hundred Years After*, ed. Robert Vaughan (Madison: University of Wisconsin Press, 1988).

12. Richard Bernstein, "One Step Forward, Two Steps Backward: Richard Rorty on Liberal Democracy and Philosophy," *Political Theory* 14, no. 4 (November 1986): 556.

13. To get a sense of this parallel, compare Richard Rorty, "Thugs and Theorists: A Reply to Bernstein," *Political Theory* 15, no. 4 (November 1987): 564-80; and Robert Dahl, "Further Reflections on 'The Elitist Theory of Democracy,'" *American Political Science Review* 60, no. 2 (June 1966): 296–305.

14. Shklar, *Ordinary Vices*, 236.

15. Irving Kristol, *On the Democratic Idea in America* (New York: Harper and Row, 1972), 148–49, 137.

16. Thomas Dye and L. Harmon Zeigler, *The Irony of Democracy*, 2d ed. (Belmont, Calif.: Duxbury Press, 1972), 365–66.

17. Michael Walzer, *Spheres of Justice: A Defense of Pluralism and Equality* (New York: Basic Books, 1983).

18. Michael Walzer, "Liberalism and the Art of Separation," *Political Theory* 12, no. 3 (August 1984): 315–30.

19. Shklar, *Ordinary Vices*, 5.

20. Shklar, *Ordinary Vices*, 5.

21. Rorty, "The Priority of Democracy," 32 (ms version).

22. Rorty, "The Priority of Democracy," 39 (ms version).

23. Thomas Hobbes, *Leviathan*, part one, chapters 14 and 15.

24. William Galston, *Liberal Purposes* (Cambridge: Cambridge University Press, 1991), 12.

25. Kristol, *On the Democratic Idea*, 51ff.

26. Hobbes, *Leviathan*, part two, chapter 18.

27. See Sheldon Wolin, "Hume and Conservatism," *American Political Science Review* 48, no. 4 (December 1954): 999–1016.

28. Allan Bloom, *The Closing of the American Mind* (New York: Simon and Schuster, 1987), 67.

29. Bernard Crick, *In Defense of Politics*, 2d ed. (Harmondsworth, England: Penguin Books, 1982), 154.

2

The Appeal and Limits of Libertarianism

One enduring strand of the liberal tradition is what today goes under the label of "libertarianism." Libertarians sometimes accept that designation only with a degree of reluctance and asperity, actually, for in their view the proper name for their political orientation is liberalism. As Milton Friedman wrote in the introduction to *Capitalism and Freedom*, "the rightful and proper label . . . for the political and economic viewpoint elaborated in this book . . . is liberalism." "Unfortunately," however, he continued, in this century and in this country "the enemies of the system of private enterprise have found it expedient to appropriate that name for themselves, so that liberalism has, in the United States, come to have a very different meaning than it did in the nineteenth century or does today over much of the continent of Europe."[1] Adherents of this viewpoint, therefore, sometimes cling stubbornly to the designation of "classical liberal;" but more recent champions of that position have seemed content to accept and endorse the name of libertarianism.[2]

Whatever their label, adherents of the libertarian persuasion "emphasize freedom as the ultimate goal and the individual as the ultimate entity" in society.[3] The essence and genius of a liberal society, in their view, is that it is a contract society. That is, it is a society in which to the fullest extent possible all relationships and obligations among the citizens are the result of voluntary mutual agreement rather than the product of socially ascriptive roles or governmentally imposed mandates. As William Graham Sumner succinctly put it in 1883:

> A society based on contract is a society of free and independent men, who
> form ties without favor or obligation, and cooperate without cringing or in-
> trigue. A society based on contract, therefore, gives the utmost room and
> chance for individual development, and for all the self-reliance and dignity of
> a free man. That a society of free men, co-operating under contract, is by far
> the strongest society which has ever yet existed; that no such society has ever

yet developed the full measure of strength of which it is capable; and that the only social improvements which are now conceivable lie in the direction of more complete realization of a society of free men united by contract are points which cannot be controverted.[4]

If a contract society is so understood as the ideal society, several corollaries follow regarding the basic practices and institutions proper for liberal democracies. They are: representative government, civil liberties, the minimal state, and laissez-faire. Of these, the first two are common to all versions of liberal democracy, while the latter two are the distinctive features of the libertarian persuasion. Libertarians agree with other liberals that legitimate government comes only from the consent of the governed and that citizens should have extensive civil liberties—both because these freedoms are good in themselves and because without them government by consent is illusory. What is crucial to libertarians, though, is that the scope of government, limited by all liberals to a specified domain and functions, should be absolutely minimized and that society should not interfere in the private transactions of individuals as they contract with each other in the marketplace. Their core strategy is, to put it most simply: minimize government, maximize the market.

Although no liberal society has ever come close to removing government entirely from the economy, the nineteenth century was a time in which the "classical liberal" formula of free markets and limited government was clearly ascendant.[5] In this country, Jacksonian individualism was the dominant social philosophy, and, however socially and politically egalitarian that philosophy might have been, it left economic advancement to individual effort and to the upward mobility such effort would presumably create. Lincoln's pronouncements in this area embraced this Jacksonian philosophy; Horatio Alger famously turned it into an animating mythology; Herbert Spencer received a hero's welcome when he visited this country; and Spencer's laissez-faire gospel was proclaimed by disciples such as Sumner and Andrew Carnegie. There were some notable critics, of course, such as Henry George, but they were clearly the dissenters and not the mainstream.

The fortunes of "classical liberalism" and its laissez-faire prescriptions began to change for the worse at the turn of the twentieth century. It was not logic so much as experience that caused the classical liberals problems. Rather than delivering universal freedom and prosperity, their regime had produced the robber barons, the growth of powerful trusts and monopolies, company towns, and vast inequalities. In light of these troubling developments, the formulaic insistence that these patterns of private dominance and inequality were inevitable and ultimately benign became increasingly less convincing. Progressives such as John Dewey and Herbert Croly began to win converts to their claims that the traditional goals of liberal democracy required new means for their achievement, and central among these new means was the exertion of governmental power and agency to regulate and control the economy. As Dewey wrote in *Liberalism and Social Action*:

> The only form of enduring social organization that is now possible is one in
> which the new forces of productivity are cooperatively controlled and used in

the interest of the effective liberty and the cultural development of the individuals that constitute society. Such a social order cannot be established by an unplanned and external convergence of the actions of separate individuals each of whom is bent on personal private advantage. This idea is the Achilles heel of early liberalism.[6]

With the onset of the Great Depression and the publication of John Maynard Keynes's *General Theory*, classical liberalism seemed a faith whose day had come and gone. Classical economists could criticize Keynes and aver that it was governmental incompetence (especially in regulating the money supply) rather than some defect in the market system that caused the Depression; but they now were reduced to being the dissenters. To most social theorists and political leaders, it seemed clear that the libertarian utopia was a fantasy and that the state needed to play an active role in running the economy—not only to countervail private concentrations of power but also to maintain the viability of the economy as a successful productive apparatus.

The pump-priming, regulating, redistributing welfare state became well established and institutionalized during Franklin Delano Roosevelt's New Deal; it was essentially accepted as part of normal policy even by Republicans during the Eisenhower years, and it expanded its purchase and its ambitions under the aegis of Lyndon Johnson's Great Society in the 1960s. All of these escalating departures from the classical liberal creed elicited strenuous objections and Cassandra-like forecasts of impending disaster from that creed's remaining defenders. But for the most part, these warnings and objections were ignored.

Paradigmatic in this regard was Friedrich von Hayek's famous polemic *The Road to Serfdom*, published in 1944.[7] Von Hayek's argument, reflected in his title, was that the choice between a free market system and a socialist command economy was essentially an either/or proposition. There was no such thing as a logically coherent or empirically stable third way or middle way between these opposing alternatives. In this respect, von Hayek echoed the insistence of his mentor, Ludwig von Mises, who wrote: "There is simply no other choice than this: either to abstain from interference in the free play of the market, or to delegate the entire management of production and distribution to the government. Either capitalism or socialism: there exists no middle way."[8] Command economies, this argument continued, by their very nature necessarily wind up concentrating control of all the society's resources in the hands of their political rulers — effectively undermining civil liberties and abandoning democracy for dictatorship. Hence, by letting the state fox into the market chicken coop, those developed societies entering into the project of creating a regulatory planned economy and a redistributive welfare state were putting themselves on a slippery slope that inevitably ended in Nazi- or Soviet-style despotisms.

When I was in college in the 1960s, we were given *The Road to Serfdom* to read; but it was clearly under the heading of "for a different view, see the following." The argument set out there was considered by faculty and students alike to be the last theoretical gasp of an obsolete and reactionary ideology. But in the 1980s and

1990s, this allegedly dying gasp seemed to gain a whole new second wind. Today, influential members of Congress, mostly Republicans, such as Phil Gramm, Richard Armey, and William Archer, take their bearings from the Chicago School of neoclassical economics. Vigorous and assertive think tanks such as the Cato Institute and the Heritage Foundation develop and promote highly libertarian policy proposals. And a number of new books have recently appeared which seek to articulate and defend libertarian ideals within a contemporary setting.[9]

What accounts for this phenomenon of precipitous decline and strong renascence of the libertarian perspective over these past few decades? The precipitous decline, I believe, came because central elements of the von Hayek–von Mises argument were simply unconvincing. Not only did these die-hard defenders of laissez-faire seem basically oblivious to some of the pressing social problems and dislocations created by omnivorous and volatile market forces in industrialized economies—to patterns of class dominance, pervasive and destructive inequalities, and damagingly large hiccups in the supposedly self-equilibrating market economy—but their "no middle way" and "slippery slope to totalitarianism" claims were neither logically nor empirically persuasive. Von Mises's argument to this effect, for example, centered on the assumption that any interventionist regime would have to abandon market pricing and that a system of politically administered prices was unworkable. But there seemed to be no compelling reason to suppose that other "postprice" redistributive interventions would have to be self-defeating or unsustainable: for example, progressive taxation, unemployment insurance, social insurance, and social service provisions. And the experience of the Scandinavian mixed economies over time, which seemed reasonably workable and did not exhibit any tendencies to evolve by necessity into despotic polities, seemed to confirm these logical doubts. As a result of these evidentiary considerations, therefore, Milton Friedman had to insert a couple of noteworthy qualifying adjectives into his thesis when he sought in 1962 to reinvigorate the von Hayek–von Mises case that free societies depended on free markets: "I know of no example in time or place of a society that has been marked by a large measure of political freedom, and that has not also used *something comparable to* a free market to organize *the bulk of* economic activity."[10] The addition of the phrases "comparable to" and "the bulk of" to the von Hayek–von Mises argument represented a tacit recognition of the failure of that argument's strong form. Equally noteworthy as a sign of Friedman's de facto abandonment of the "no middle way" line was his inclusion of the Scandinavian countries under the heading of "Western capitalist societies" as he sought to make the case that "the development of capitalism has greatly lessened the extent of inequality."[11]

What made the *Road to Serfdom* argument unconvincing—and what eventually proved it false empirically—was the weakness of von Hayek's and von Mises's political and sociological analysis. As eminent economists, they well understood the functional irrationalities and incapacities of full-blown command economies —irrationalities and incapacities that at best would render such economics wasteful and stagnant and at worst could metastasize into the political system and destroy it. But they failed to see that shifting some resource allocations from the market into the hands of political authorities would not ipso facto or necessarily produce dictatorial or totalitarian regimes. This outcome occurred in Germany and in Russia not because of some inevitable slippery slope a polity starts down as soon as it places constraints on markets or adjusts market distributions; instead the descent of these countries into despotism was occasioned by their specific political institutions and culture—exacerbated by some of the contingencies of their historical situations.

In other systems and other cultures, this process would not be likely to—much less necessarily—follow a similar course. Countries with liberal cultures would instead decisively rebel against some of the restraints on their freedoms that any full-scale attempt to create a command economy would entail. And if these countries had well-established democratic institutions, these institutions would quickly make that rebellion fully effective. A paradigmatic example of this kind of process was the intense resistance to and the resultant quick repeal of the British Labour government's post–World War II attempt to enact a "control of engagements" policy that would have involved forcing some individuals into occupations determined by the government. Objections to the policy were vociferous. It was quickly repealed, and the associated policies which had seemed to necessitate it were themselves revised or abandoned. That case, and the systemic forces that shaped it, may prove the libertarian point that full-scale command economies require serious infringements upon civil liberties that democratic societies cherish. But at the same time it destroys the von Hayek–von Mises libertarian argument that free societies cannot limit and control these infringements even as they constrain and adjust the market allocation of resources.

The market constraints and resource reallocations of a welfare state need not and will not ineluctably lead to the concentration of political power in the hands of some dictatorial elite or totalitarian regime, then. Instead, those constraints and reallocations will be determined by the same forces, through the same institutions, and by the same power relations that govern the other political outcomes in the polity in question. At the present time in this country, this means that any political allocations of economic resources will be governed by the dynamics of interest-group liberalism in the context of a constitutional separation of powers, decentralized parties, and a plebiscitary presidency. Policies become enacted in these United States by legislative majorities that have to be put together anew for each occasion. Particularly when it comes to tax policy and the federal budget, legislative majorities are cobbled together from a coalition of particular interests, each of which receives its piece of the pie in return for its support of the omnibus legislation. In these crucial cases, the legislative process resembles an auction in which the proponents of competing measures make their bids—via incorporating appropriations or tax expenditures of special interest to the various legislators whose votes are up for grabs. Anyone seeking a graphic account of how this legislative auction works can consult David Stockman's chronicle, complete with his expressions of dismay, of how the Reagan budget was dramatically transformed in the process leading to its passage.[12] A parallel chronicle could no doubt be written of the various promises and concessions needed to squeak out the single-vote victory for the Clinton budget in 1993.

The upshot is that the political economy of the American welfare state does not threaten us with the specter of serfdom, as von Hayek had predicted and insisted. Far from it. Power over the formation of the budget—access to federal tax dollars—is so far from being concentrated into despotic hands that it is instead so widely disseminated that any coherent budget plan is almost impossible to effectuate. Despotic concentration of power in the society is not the problem. But very real problems and dangers of an entirely different order are nonetheless generated by the prevalent mechanisms for allocating the sizable portion of the GNP that is funded through government hands.

These problems and dangers are those best laid out for us in Theodore Lowi's *The End of Liberalism* and in Mancur Olson's *The Logic of Collective Action* and *The Rise and Decline of Nations*.[13] What Lowi explained was how and why it is that a democratic polity governed by the dynamics of interest-group liberalism "cannot plan" and "cannot achieve justice." What Olson explained in his first book was how and why it is that in such a system small intense interest groups can triumph over much larger and more diffuse general interests. And what he explained in his second book was how and why such systems tend to become increasingly stagnant economically and calcified politically.

If our interest-group liberal regime does not reduce us to serfdom or even threaten anything like it, it does generate problems of "corruption" in the form of extensive pork barrel pillaging of the treasury, problems of perverse incentives, and problems of economic stagnation and inefficiency. And, as the era of the Great Society expanded the federal share of the GNP, these problems arguably became more extensive, pervasive, and entrenched. As a result, government effectiveness and legitimacy have both suffered a pattern of secular decline, a pattern reflected in the steadily lower percentages of the electorate who express confidence and trust in their government. At the very same time, moreover, an economic marketplace in the era of the Internet seems increasingly nimble, sophisticated, and productive. At least for those who are able to cope with its demands, the new information driven economy also can be experienced as liberating and empowering with its flexibility, adaptability, and creative possibilities. And those concentrations of private power, so troubling in the days of the trusts and the robber barons, seem not as much of a threat. Indeed, the very oligopolistic firms that only a few decades ago seemed most worrisome as a potential source of private domination—IBM, General Motors, AT&T—now have to scramble and compete very hard not to be rendered obsolete in a flexible and dynamic global economy. Government enterprises, inherently coercive, slow to adapt, creaky and inefficient, and under no great incentives to be customer friendly, suffer more and more in the public estimation by contrast. We can now do our banking, make our plane reservations, and research our term papers on our computers, and we still have to wait in lines for the privilege of buying our license plates from possibly truculent civil service employees.

It is these problematic government dynamics of interest-group liberalism and these invidious contrasts that are no doubt principally responsible for the recent resurgence of interest in the diagnoses and prescriptions of libertarianism. Embracing the libertarian strategy of dramatically cutting the reach of the state and returning almost all allocative determinations to the free market is by no means the only possible way to deal with the deformations and corruptions of interest-group liberalism. Lowi counsels us, for example, to enforce the letter and spirit of the classical rule of law restrictions on government action much more stringently. If we were to reestablish in our constitutional norms the Lockean stipulation against the delegation of the legislative power, for example, and at the same time to enforce under the equal protection requirement Rousseau's stipulation that valid laws must take a general object rather than being grants of special favor to particular beneficiaries, many of the worst corruptions of our interest group liberal welfarism would be greatly diminished. If we could at the same time strengthen our national parties and allow them to assert more control and countervailing power over the various interest groups, that would help greatly as well. But if the libertarian strategy is not the only way to attack the corruptions and inefficiencies of our interest-group liberal regime, it would certainly be an effective one: if you cut off the state from having any goodies to allocate, the incentives and mechanisms that produce what Jonathan Rauch has termed "demosclerosis" would virtually disappear.[14] There is no point in lobbying the government for pecuniary favors if there are no more favors to give.

In the modern American polity, as Robert Dahl astutely observed several decades ago, we don't really have majority rule. And we don't face, therefore, any real threat of majority tyranny—at least in the ordinary course of events.

> For to an extent that would have pleased Madison enormously, the numerical majority is incapable of undertaking any co-ordinated action. It is the various components of the numerical majority that have the means for action. . . . Thus the making of government decisions is not a majestic march of great majorities united upon certain matters of basic policy. It is the steady appeasement of relatively small groups.[15]

For Dahl, this pattern of "minorities rule" was a sign and a conduit of democratic legitimacy. It meant that everybody—i.e., all groups—had access to government and had their say over government outcomes. What he did not note (perhaps because he wrote these words in 1956, prior to the Great Society expansion of the federal share of the GNP) was that this "steady appeasement of relatively small groups" might lead to the majority's subjection to a whole panoply of petty tyrannies by these organized minorities. In our democratic system, "the people" do not face much danger of being devoured by a sovereign lion (to borrow the imagery of Locke's complaint about Hobbes); but they do face the steady prospect of being nibbled to death by a host of voracious smaller pests—most of them housed on K Street in the nation's capital.

Cutting off the tap of federal largesse, as libertarians counsel us to do, would deliver us from the accumulated petty tyrannies and plunders of all those interest groups who are able to use the government's police power to carve out a protected domain or privileged status for themselves—by having the government shield them from market discipline and give them direct access to taxpayer dollars they could not win in the marketplace. We would in a libertarian regime no longer be subject to the depredations or the impositions of Archer Daniels Midland or of teachers' unions insistent upon preserving their monopolistic control over secondary education, or of the American Medical Association's artificial restraints on the delivery of health care, or of officially empowered cartels like taxi commissions, or of well-organized and well-placed ethnic or gender lobbies who get quotas and set-asides to shoulder aside nonfavored applicants with better credentials or lower bids. To many long-suffering members of the diffuse and ill-organized majority, this is a prospect to brighten their eyes and attract them to libertarian proposals.

Moreover, because these interest groups who triumph in the expansive state's bazaar and thus gain special advantage come from all sides of the political spectrum, the libertarian solution to the depredations, corruptions, and piecemeal tyrannies of the welfare state/interest-group liberal regime receives a sympathetic reception from a variety of quarters. Not only those on the right but some of those conventionally seen as in the center or toward the left have been attracted to libertarian policies. Support for voucher systems giving students and parents the ability to choose among schools does not come just from Milton Friedman, for example, but also from inner-city African Americans in Milwaukee. Not just the Cato Institute but Pat Moynihan proposes adding some privatized component to our social security system. And the "New Democrat" Progressive Policy Institute can join hands with Cato Institute libertarians in calling for an end to "corporate welfare."

Is, then, the "classical liberal" model of an individualistic contract society centered around the free market and protected by a night watchman state an idea whose time has come, then gone, and now come again? Have changes over the past few decades in the global marketplace (increasingly flexible and competitive) and in the welfare state (increasingly large and calcified) made the wave of the past the wave of the future? Should the twenty-first century seek to emulate the course of the nineteenth century rather than that of the twentieth? The libertarians answer in the affirmative, but how compelling is their case?

Before trying to answer that question, it is important to observe and acknowledge that there is greater variance among different versions of libertarianism than one might suppose. The argument for laissez-faire seems straightforward enough and the basic strategy simple enough that divergence and disagreement within the camp of libertarianism may seem anomalous. The fact is, however, that different self-styled libertarians offer significantly different rationales for the minimal state; they at times offer markedly different concrete policy prescriptions; and they embed their conceptions of libertarian utopia within quite distinctive and not entirely compatible moral and sociological visions. Let us briefly canvass these variances of, in order, policy, ethos, and rationale.

In policy terms, all libertarians seek a diminished role for the state and more extensive reliance on market transactions and allocations. They all counsel us to privatize, voluntarize, and deregulate. The variance in their specific policy mandates, however, occurs because of the slippage between the way that markets work on the economist's blackboard and the way they actually function in the real world. The invisible hand works its magic to perfection only when markets are themselves perfect. And a perfect market is one in which there are an infinite number of fully rational and independent buyers and sellers, one where all market actors are perfectly informed about all relevant variables such as prices and alternatives, one where all factors of production are entirely mobile, and one where all costs and benefits produced by market transactions are confined to the contracting parties. In the real world, of course, none of these requirements is ever completely met. Sometimes real-world conditions may approximate the market requirements sufficiently for the model to work pretty much as advertised. But at other times, the gap between the real world and the requirements of a properly functioning market may raise legitimate questions as to whether the market can work at all or whether at least some interventions may be needed to fill or lessen the gap between ideal and real circumstances. For example, in cases of technical monopoly—where market forces together with the specific circumstances of production and exchange result in a single buyer or seller—the invisible hand will not be able to exert its optimizing powers, and the ministrations of more visible hands may seem prima facie legitimate to take its place.

The phenomenon of economic externalities or neighborhood effects may be particularly vexing in the context of generating defensible libertarian strategies in particular cases. Neighborhood effects are the costs or benefits that transactions between two parties visit upon a third who is not party to the contract. In a profoundly interdependent world where individuals do not live within hermetically sealed enclosures, such effects are ubiquitous. The difficulty for libertarians, then, is that these externalities call for remedy; but the criteria for identifying them are contestable, the means of measuring them are highly imperfect, and the ways of trying to correct or compensate for them various and problematic.

The difficulties involved in identifying and properly compensating for these market externalities, then, can and do result in considerable variance among the policy prescriptions endorsed by different libertarians. At one end of the spectrum, libertarians such as Murray Rothbard wind up advocating the privatization of even police services and courts of law.[16] On the other hand, the Canadian academic libertarian theorist Jan Narveson argues that the Canadian single-payer hospital insurance program, or at least a very similar scheme, could pass muster on libertarian principles. His basic idea here is that an overwhelming majority of the populace support and would voluntarily contract with such a system, that they pretty much get the health insurance that they want and pay for, and that the redistributive aspects of the system—i.e., the provision of services to the destitute—are essentially covered by savings from the relative administrative efficiency of the single-payer system.[17] Milton Friedman, in contrast to both of these theorists, advocates a deregulated and privatized health care delivery system but supports public financial subsidies for secondary education and a negative income tax which would effectively appropriate tax dollars from the middle and upper classes to be redistributed to those below the poverty line.[18] A political convention populated entirely by libertarians, it seems, would still find itself embroiled in very spirited fights over its political platform whenever specific policies and tactics were addressed.

Equally noteworthy and insufficiently remarked are the widely divergent ways that libertarian strategies are contextualized morally. Different libertarian theorists situate, explain, and justify their policy prescriptions by invoking very different ethics, normative psychologies, and moral cosmologies. Some are as a result satisfied with certain predictive consequences of their model that would horrify others who make similar concrete proposals. A rough typology of these different stripes of libertarian would include the hard moralists, the hypercapitalists, the existentialist decisionists, and the warm and fuzzy anarchists.

The hard moralists themselves come in different versions. One school are the quasi-Nietzschean tough guys epitomized by Ayn Rand and her followers. For these libertarians, the contract society represents a system which allows the *ubermenschen* among us to exercise their superior faculties and to escape from the destructive and parasitic clutches of the statistically dominant "last men." John Galt's peroration that culminates Rand's *Atlas Shrugged* is essentially a manifesto of the supermen, a declaration of their independence from the incompetent little people who get in their way, leech off of them, and try to make them feel guilty because of their superior competencies. Rand, speaking through Galt, echoes the Nietzschean accusation that conventional morality, which seeks to encumber us with obligations to God and our neighbors, is really just an expropriative scam on the strong and able, cobbled up from a witch's brew of malice and envy. But now, he says, that game is up, we are on strike, you won't have us to kick around anymore. We owe you nothing. Henceforth we shall refuse our martyrdom at your hands and our expropriation by your minions. We are the *Queen Mary*; you are little dinghies; and from now on it's going to be every tub on its own bottom. The social world as marketplace, then, unrepentant, unadorned, unmodified, is the vehicle of liberation and justice for the strong and able. It will accord them their just deserts and leave the incompetent and parasitic to their own devices.

Other "hard" libertarian moral hermeneutics are Darwinian and Calvinist. In the nineteenth century, these often informed and reinforced each other—although they are separable logically and are ultimately not very compatible cosmologically. Herbert Spencer, for example, justified market allocative mechanisms as the vehicle of what he called the "law of conduct and consequence" and depicted the acceptance of this law as essential to the beneficence of the evolutionary process as it operated on humankind. The law of conduct and consequence meant simply that all individuals should receive the full benefits and suffer the full costs of each of their actions. Only in that way would actions that were socially advantageous be identified and encouraged. And only then would the Darwinian process of selection and survival of the fittest bring about the improvement of humankind and the social order. The same imperative expressed in Spencer's law of conduct and consequence can also be contextualized and justified in terms of the judgment of a Calvinist deity who creates a moral order that separates the sheep from the goats. The marketplace enforces the mandate of the Protestant ethic. In a contract society, the virtuous—the diligent, sober, honest, abstemious, and productive—are rewarded for the consequences of their good character, and the sinful—the slothful, covetous, and self-indulgent—suffer the consequences of their flawed souls. It is not only foolish, then, but fundamentally impious to interfere with the morally attuned just dictates of the market. This is to rob from virtuous Peter to indulge vicious Paul. Living instead within the parameters of a contract society is to inhabit a Protestant moral gymnasium with teeth. As ye sow, so shall ye reap.

Libertarian "hypercapitalists" are those who see human beings as Benthamite calculators and find a system that facilitates their preference-maximizing an inspiring spectacle. These libertarians could be said to consider narrow rational choice explanations offered by economizing sociologists (or sociologizing economists) like Gary Becker to be not only empirically convincing but normatively proper. Marx disparaged Bentham as a romanticizer of a "petty shopkeeper" mentality, and John Stuart Mill wrote that Bentham saw in human beings only what the most vulgar eye could see. But the hypercapitalist libertarian rejects these derogations of a life of the calculating pursuit of appetitive self-seeking. Instead, this glorifier of petty-bourgeois individualism endorses and extols such a life and justifies an expansive market society as the best means of organizing and making successful the lives together of basically self-interested and appetitive people.

Those we could call "existentialist" libertarians seem to depict the world in Weberian terms—that is, as devoid of any objective moral meaning. The essence of morality, then, is that it be the product of free choice. Human choice—the unconstrained determination of one's own destiny and the meaning of one's own life—is both the ultimate expression of and the ultimate source of human morality. Hence, "a major aim of the liberal is to leave the ethical problem for the individual to reckon with."[19] The virtue of the market society in moral terms is that it leaves the concrete specification of the human good in the hands of individuals to decide for themselves. It is hard to glean from the writings of libertarian theorists such as Friedman and Nozick, then, any real sense of what they would want, or suppose, or anticipate the actual content of most people's choices to be—and hence to get any real sense of what they think that life in a libertarian society would actually come to look like (except that Nozick expects that lives in his utopian society would be highly diverse). But that indeterminacy is not just an omission from their social vision; it is in a sense the essence of their vision. Life should be whatever people severally choose for it to be.

The last moral contextualization and justification of libertarian policies is what I earlier called warm-and-fuzzy anarchism. Libertarians of this stripe actually stand in the lineage of Marx and Tom Paine, both of whom thought that the state either should be reduced to miniscule proportions or would wither away. And these two theorists both fondly anticipated this radical diminution of the state's role not because they championed or expected a society of concupiscent bourgeois self-seekers to be the result. Instead, they thought that people would voluntarily join together to fill the void of state agency by spontaneously cooperating on behalf of their common goals.

The version of libertarianism recently articulated and championed by Charles Murray is an example of this perspective. To many, no doubt, applying the label "warm-and-fuzzy" to Murray, who coauthored *The Bell Curve* and argues that we should "eliminate all government social-service programs and all income transfers in case or kind," sounds not only mistaken but perverse.[20] But the crucial point in this context is that Murray champions drastic cutbacks in the welfare state not so much because he wants to see "unfit" or "sinful" people suffer their harsh just deserts. Instead, informed by Adam Smith's arguments in his *Theory of the Moral Sentiments*, by Edmund Burke's account of the central role of spontaneous "little platoons" in a free society, and by Tocqueville's observations about the ubiquity of voluntary civic associations in America, Murray counsels contraction in government to enable the work of these little platoons to expand and flourish. "Deprived of the use of force," he writes, "human beings tend to cooperate.... A return to limited government should not be confused with ending communal efforts to solve social problems. In a free society a genuine need produces response. If government is not seen as a legitimate source of intervention, individuals and associations will respond."[21] Conversely, he argues, the expansion of government's role in managing social problems not only leads to interventions that are cumbersome, inefficient, and rife with perverse incentives; it also dries up the resources and motivations that sustained the formation of private social service agencies. His goal in promoting libertarian policies is not to create an atomized society of individualistic self-seekers, but to promote spontaneous communal solutions to pursuing common goods and addressing social needs. "If you want to end the atomization of modern life, get government out of it."[22] Murray advocates curtailment of welfare state social policy, then, because he is an optimistic quasi-anarchist. He believes that—absent the perverse effects and incentives produced by governmental programs—naturally sociable human beings will organize themselves spontaneously to take care of their neighbors when and where these neighbors can't take care of themselves.

If libertarian theorists differ among themselves about particular policies and also differ in the way they contextualize the minimal state morally and sociologically, they also provide different justifications for the minimal state. The basic division here is between those who offer a prudential and utilitarian argument and those who instead emphasize a rights-based moral argument. The utilitarians are represented by von Mises, who disdains foundational forms of moral justifications for his classical liberal approach. "We liberals," he writes, "do not assert that God or nature meant all men to be free, because we are not instructed in the designs of God or Nature, and we avoid drawing God and Nature into a dispute over mundane questions." A market-centered society is instead to be preferred simply on the basis of its benign secular and prudential consequences. "What we maintain is only that a system based on freedom for all workers warrants the greatest productivity of human labor and is therefore in the interest of all the inhabitants of the earth."[23] Liberals defend the institution of private property, he continues, "not because the abolition of that institution would violate property rights.... If they considered the abolition of the institution to be in the general interest, they would advocate that it be abolished." The reason a laissez-faire system based on private property should be established and maintained, he avows, is only because without the incentives it creates "productivity would be so greatly reduced that the portion that an equal distribution would allot to each individual would be far less than what even the poorest receives today."[24]

For those libertarians who emphasize the moral rather than the prudential warrants for a market society, in contrast, "the free market's efficiency is a pleasant bonus. It would be morally superior to socialism even if it were less efficient in producing wealth."[25] It is, on this account, both dangerous and improper to rely on utilitarian arguments for the minimal state—improper because utilitarians ignore the basic moral principles at stake and dangerous because they may as a result sell out or compromise the cause. Murray Rothbard therefore complains: "To say that a utilitarian cannot be trusted to maintain libertarian principle in every specific application may sound harsh, but it puts the case fairly."[26]

The moral argument for a libertarian polity is based in this view on claims about fundamental rights possessed by all individuals. The central insistence is captured in the opening lines of Robert Nozick's *Anarchy, State and Utopia*: "Individuals have rights, and there are things no person or group may do to them [without violating their rights]. So strong and far-reaching are these rights that they raise the question of what, if anything, the state and its officials may do."[27] In explaining these rights, libertarian theorists for the most part offer very cryptic, truncated, and philosophically disembodied remnants or fragments of Aristotle, Kant, or Locke. Murray, for example, seems to echo Aristotle in his insistence that "mindful human beings require freedom and personal responsibility to live satisfying lives," i.e., that only those who are self-governing can really attain *eudaemonia*.[28] The problem with this line of argument, however, is not that it is not true, but that it seems insufficient to its libertarian intent: it is hard to make a persuasive argument that a laissez-faire regime or absolute property rights are necessary to allow people the amount of freedom sufficient for these purposes. The more common and fitting arguments in the context of trying to sustain the "far-reaching" individual rights stipulated by Nozick, therefore, invoke quasi-Kantian claims about the inviolability of individual human beings as separate loci of rational being and quasi-Lockean assertions about self-ownership. Hence Nozick argues that rights "reflect the underlying Kantian principle that individuals are ends and not merely means. . . . Individuals are inviolable."[29] This claim may also be taken to entail the corollary that, in Murray's words, "each person owns himself. Self-ownership is inalienable."[30] Accordingly, insists Rothbard, libertarianism must adopt as its "primary axiom the universal right of self-ownership, a right held by everyone by virtue of being a human being."[31] And this means both that individuals have what Murray calls "an abstract right to be left alone" and that these self-possessing human beings also have a moral entitlement to receive, and to dispose of at their discretion, the full value of their own labor.[32,33]

Libertarian theories differ among themselves, then, in many significant respects. Libertarian theorists disagree over particular policies, over exactly how minimal the minimal state should be, over what counts as a legitimate neighborhood effect warranting remedy or compensation, over the principal justifications for hewing to laissez-faire prescriptions, and over the way that a market society should interface with other and broader human and moral purposes. That variation makes it difficult to develop a critical assessment of libertarianism which is both comprehensive and specific. Criticisms pertinent to Ayn Rand might well not be pertinent to Charles Murray, and criticisms of Murray Rothbard might not be applicable to Milton Friedman or David Boaz. It is, however, quite possible to consolidate the central justifications of libertarianism into a single argument whose different parts—albeit not grounded in the same philosophical principles—are compatible with each other. And it is also possible to construct a basic model of the libertarian society that all libertarians would accept, even if they would fill in its ambiguities in different ways. This consolidated justificatory argument and the basic model it sustains, moreover, are distinctive enough to differentiate libertarian ideals clearly from other and competing normative conceptions of liberal democracy. And they are sufficiently specific, despite the open-endedness of this institutional model in some respects, to be amenable to critical assessment.

We arrive at what can be characterized as the "consolidated" justification of libertarianism simply by conjoining the moral argument on behalf of self-ownership with the practical argument regarding the beneficent consequences of reliance on the private property/free market system to allocate social and economic resources. Rights-based and utilitarian philosophies compete in principle. And they clash famously in many important instances. But in the libertarian case, the two lines of argument do not conflict in their application so much as they can be used to supplement each other. Different libertarian theorists may put more emphasis on one part of the justificatory argument than on another or may even be dismissive of parts of it. But the different aspects can cohabit quite nicely in the context of legitimating libertarian mandates for policies and procedures.

This consolidated argument, then, begins with the assertion of the separateness and integrity of individual lives. It insists upon the moral inviolability of these individuals and upon the corollary impropriety of subjecting any one of them to the status of instrumental means for another's benefit. These morally inviolable, rights-bearing individuals thus may be said to be sole and absolute owners of their selves, including their bodies. And their morally dictated right to self-disposition of their bodies entails the right to have, hold, and dispose at will of the fruits of their bodies' labor. These claims create a moral imperative on behalf of private property rights and an insistence that attempts to infringe upon these rights by other individuals or associations, including the state, are prima facie morally opprobrious. An individual must consent to another's appropriation of his or her property, either by trade or by gift. Any other transfers come under the heading of rights-violation and theft.

As it happens, the consolidated argument continues, this same morally mandatory set of arrangements and entitlements turns out to be wonderfully beneficent in its practical consequences, as well. These benefits are both economic and political. Economically, a free market system occasions the most efficient allocation of productive resources possible, and it thus maximizes a society's aggregate wealth. It furthermore creates incentives that promote constructive and imaginative innovations—better mousetraps—which in turn vastly enhance and accelerate the longer-run wealth-producing capabilities of the economy. Politically, reliance on a market system protected by a minimal state maximizes personal freedoms. It disperses power and thereby sustains those civil liberties necessary for democratic consent to be genuine and effectual. And it also promotes social stability, at least in the negative sense in that it allows what Milton Friedman calls "unanimity without conformity": that is, it allows people to enjoy variety in goods and outcomes and not to be subject to living with a single outcome dictated by the majority.

The politicoeconomic model dictated by these considerations, then, is essentially the one generated by Robert Nozick's utopian thought-experiment in the last section of *Anarchy, State, and Utopia*. In that thought-experiment, Nozick bids us imagine a world in which all persons have the right and the power to inhabit a world of their own choosing—indeed, of their own imagining. The only constraint is that all others have the same right and the same power. Therefore, I have no ability to have anyone else in my world unless they are willing to be there—unless, that is, their presence and their role in my world is the best situation they can imagine for themselves, subject to the same constraints that prevent them from compelling others to associate with them. The outcome of this choice process would be, Nozick argues, the best of all possible worlds. Whatever resulted from this process of universal self-determination would be the optimal outcome compatible with the basic human right, embodied in Kant's maxim, not to be used as means to another's ends.

In structural terms, this best of all possible worlds would have two layers. The first would be a universal formal structure that administered and enforced the choices and their terms. This would be what Nozick terms the "framework," a structural umbrella encompassing all the many particular associations created by voluntary agreement among the participants. This framework would be, then, essentially equivalent to the minimal state, the classic nightwatchman state that protects rights to life, liberty, and property and enforces contracts. The other structural layer is composed of all the particular associations created by the free choices of the individual participants. These associations would be cooperative endeavors of voluntary members, doing whatever they wanted and organized however they wanted.

What, in concrete terms, would such a two-layered best-of-all-possible-worlds actually come to look like? What associations would be formed? For what purposes? By whom? In accordance with what internal rules and procedures? Nozick refuses to answer or speculate: "I do not know, and you should not be interested in my guesses about what would occur under the framework in the near future. As for the long run, I would not attempt to guess."[34] His guesses here, he argues, would not be reliable. How could he reasonably pretend to be able to anticipate all the myriad desires, values, and choices of all the myriad individuals whose wishes will determine the answer to this query about what would finally occur? And predictions are not really necessary, he believes. For whatever would occur would be that outcome dictated by respect for the basic rights of self-owning rational beings. Whatever would occur would have to qualify on principle as the best of all possible worlds.

All libertarians would have to buy into this Nozickean depiction of their utopia. It is a model that follows logically and directly from their fundamental moral intuitions and core practical imperatives. They can, and do, differ on the details. And these details can be important. All libertarians would accept the basic model of the "framework," a minimal state of very limited powers and functions. But some libertarians would make the limits more extreme and the functions even more limited than would others.

Finally, all libertarians would accept the defining features of the constituent associations that exist under the framework's umbrella: namely, these are properly voluntary associations spontaneously generated by the individuals themselves and from which individuals are free to leave once they have discharged any contractual obligations. Where libertarian theorists differ here is in their assumptions or expectations about what this pattern of free association would look like. Nozick himself, for example, despite his demurral about providing any particulars, clearly believes in both the propriety and the likelihood of a highly diverse set of particular associations. He is a cultural pluralist, as it were, in his empirical reading of people and forms of life. And he would expect this pluralism to manifest itself in a wide variety of associations—some if not most of which would, for example, determine their own internal distribution of resources, honor, and status by noneconomizing norms. Other libertarians, on the other hand, seem to assume that the society encapsulated by the framework will be highly individualistic in its structure and highly self-interested and economizing in the motivations that drive it and the norms that govern it. The minimal state in their view, in short, would be expected to sustain and encompass one very large marketplace filled with Benthamite calculators.

Given this pattern of a consolidated libertarian justificatory argument, within which different libertarian theorists emphasize different components as most important, and a core normative institutional model, which different libertarian theorists fill in in different ways, the best way to assess the libertarian persuasion would seem to be to ask: how compelling are the constituent elements of the consolidated argument and how attractive are the features of the core model? The answer I give here is that the libertarian argument and core model incorporate several extremely important valid moral admonitions and technical truths that must be acknowledged and respected. At the same time, however, all of these truths turn out to be only partial truths or true only in a weaker sense than in the way they are often pressed upon us. And those partial truths of libertarianism also bring with them some additional weaknesses or dangers that tend to disappear into the silences or ambiguities of libertarian arguments.

The first strength of the libertarian persuasion is its insistence upon the technical incompetency and the political destructiveness of command economies. To a considerable extent, the argument between the proponents of collectivist command economies and their classical liberal critics has been decisively answered empirically by events of the past several decades—to the point, indeed, that the relevant theoretical issue is not so much whether command economies can succeed but why they fail. The development of the USSR's economy from 1917 until 1989, with its repeated pattern of disasters mitigated only by periodic retreats from Marxist principles, is virtually dispositive all by itself—when it is set against the contrasting developments of the so-called "first-world" economies of Western Europe and the United States. Comparing third-world socialist regimes with the capitalist regimes of the Asian rim produces the same experimental outcome, this time in the context of developing societies. Libertarians and their classical economist allies are right: command economies that seek to allocate resources and manage the economy without reliance upon market pricing mechanisms are at best going to be beset by staggering inefficiencies and profound irrationalities. They also will tend to be stagnant and inertial when it comes to economic and technological innovations.

If the libertarians win hands down on their negative case regarding the incompetencies of command economies and the contrasting productivity and efficiency of market economies, however, it is important to observe that theirs is only a partial victory when it comes to their positive case. Market allocative mechanisms are in fact an essential core component of a free society and a productive advanced economy. But it is not the case, demonstrably and emphatically not, that a society must accept and enforce market allocations in a total and unmodified way in order to enjoy these benefits. That either/or insistence of some libertarians from von Mises to the present day has been effectively disproved by decades of stable functioning of welfare states which allocate as much as half of their GNP through state channels. These welfare states have nonetheless been economically productive and have protected extensive civil liberties. The extreme version of the laissez-faire argument has therefore effectively been falsified empirically. And, as even the astute critic of command economies Michael Polanyi recognized, a good thing too. "The orthodox liberals," he wrote, "maintain that, if the market is limited by the fixation of some of its elements, then it must cease to function, the implication being that there exists a logical system of complete laissez-faire, the only rational alternative to which is collectivism." But that insistence plays into the hands of the collectivists by agreeing with them "that none of the evils of the market can be alleviated except by destroying the whole institution root and branch." This insistence "has been most effective in bringing contempt on the name of freedom; it sought to deprive it of all public conscience, and thereby supported the claim of collectivism to be the sole guardian of social interests."[35] It is, then, fortunate for lovers of freedom that the extreme case for laissez-faire does not hold up to logical scrutiny or to the test of historical experience. Productive economies and free societies must cede a central role to the market. But fairly extensive *post hoc* modifications of market outcomes can be made in accordance with public judgments about what is socially prudent and what is in keeping with fairness and solidarity without foregoing the very important advantages of a capitalist economy.

A second strength of the libertarian argument is its stout defense of the integrity and autonomy of individuals against the constant pressure of social impositions and state coerciveness. As I argue later on, personal autonomy is a constitutive good of liberal polities, and libertarians are perhaps the most consistent and forceful advocates and protectors of this fundamental good. This kind of forceful advocacy is well needed, for those who would invade the integrity and overrun the autonomy of their fellows are legion. For the starkest examples, one can peruse the yearly report of Amnesty International. And less dramatically, democratic majorities and organized interests constantly invoke utilitarian calculi and vague general references to "progress" or "social good" to justify extensive and sometimes discriminatory abridgments of individual rights. The libertarian moral postulate of self-ownership, therefore, is worthy of endorsement when what it means is that no one else may claim to own us. That insistence is not reactionary or merely an artifact of bourgeois consciousness. Marx himself used it as the basis of his account of how and why it is that the proletariat is exploited.

If the negative version of the libertarian claim of self-ownership—"no one else owns me, and that includes my whole self, thick with particular traits"—is an important and morally proper admonition worthy of our respect, however, the positive and absolute version of that claim is not so persuasive. Indeed, it turns out upon examination to be highly contestable, not even fully coherent, and morally and socially perverse in some of its applications. Its weaknesses are compounded, moreover, when the postulate of self-ownership is deployed to try to establish absolute individual rights to possession of external goods.

The postulate of self-ownership is expressed by Nozick in terms of his theory of "entitlement." We are "entitled" in his view to anything that we have acquired without violating anyone else's rights. Hence it follows that we are entitled to our "natural assets," our various talents and attributes, and to whatever of value our deployment of these talents and attributes can manufacture. But Nozick has to acknowledge here that we cannot in any coherent sense be said to *deserve* our natural assets. He simply insists that "it needn't be that foundations underlying desert are themselves deserved, all the way down."[36] The grounds for this insistence, however, are left entirely opaque. Surely it does matter that what Nozick pleases to call individual "entitlements" cannot be said to be deserved "all the way down." Rawls may not be justified in assuming that this lack of all-the-way-down deservingness—the ultimate "moral arbitrariness" of the distribution of our natural talents—properly devolves them into a collective asset. But Nozick is equally unjustified in concluding that we are "entitled" in any strong sense to "ownership" of these assets. (It is not accidental that he uses the term "entitlement" here, a term that connotes "desert" even as it acknowledges that such a desert claim cannot be validated. Call this tactic the making of a claim by trading upon the penumbra of a word's use that one admits cannot be logically sustained; Nozick is not really entitled, we might say, to use the word "entitlement" as he does.)

What Nozick's difficulties manifest at this juncture in his argument is precisely the ultimate groundlessness and incoherence of any absolute moral claim to own oneself. Such a claim is in fact incompatible with another core presupposition of the libertarian argument: namely, that ownership rights arise as a corollary of creating-by mixing one's labor with unappropriated raw materials—the good in question. As Nozick significantly insists in another context: "things come into being already held."[37] To the extent this is so, however, it becomes impossible to argue that we "own" ourselves in any positive and absolute sense—for we certainly did not create ourselves. One of the most patently absurd claims around is the claim to be a "self-made" person. For the one thing in the world someone obviously did not create is his or her own self. Our brute existence is the gratuitous gift of God or nature. And our most basic particular traits are generated in us through our interactions with parents, friends, and others—such as teachers—who are assigned and funded by society precisely to develop our talents for us. By the same logic libertarians use to make their claims about the sanctity of private property, we are disqualified from claiming to own ourselves. Instead, we would by that logic seem to have to recognize that we are (as in Locke's own account) God's property, nature's property, our parents' property, our society's property, or some mixture thereof.[38]

The point here is not to make this latter claim. The point instead is to insist that —based upon the normal logic of what creates constructive ownership rights— moral claims to an absolute right of self-ownership cannot be coherently justified. The libertarian postulate of self-ownership, then, is not sustainable. It could be made sustainable only by delusions of truly cosmic proportions about one's own making. We can insist, partly for the same reasons and partly on the basis of what it means and requires to be a person or rational agent, that no one can properly claim to own us or our natural assets. But we cannot claim to be our own self-creation, and we cannot therefore compellingly claim to be our own absolute and uncompromised owners. If the libertarian postulate of self-ownership properly captures the inviolable integrity of the human self against appropriative demands and hegemonic actions of others, it blinds us to our deep and pervasive moral indebtedness to all manner of others who have given of themselves to make us who and what we are.

The difficulties presented by the postulate of absolute self-ownership compound themselves when they are deployed as the basis for the justification of absolute private property rights in material goods. The main problems here center about the (Lockean) account of "mixing one's labor with" raw materials originally given to or held by humankind in common, the (Lockean) proviso that in this process of legitimate appropriation "enough and as good" must be left for others, and the standard libertarian insistence upon an absolute right to determine the conveyance of our material possessions upon our death. Even were we to grant that we should be considered absolute owners of our natural assets, hence of our bodies and our labors, rather than as stewards granted titles encumbered with obligations, these accounts have real limits and infirmities in concrete application.

Locke sustains his argument that we secure legitimate title to goods by mixing our labor with raw materials taken from the commons by contending that "ninety-nine hundredths" of their value "are wholly to be put on the account of labor."[39] But in many important instances, that simply is false. If oil bubbles up in my back yard, I may come into considerable wealth without having created any value to speak of through my labor. And the assertion of this empirically often false claim then forestalls any inquiry into the general rules or considerations that should govern cases where labor is responsible for only 1 percent or 20 percent or 50 percent of the value whose legitimate control is at issue. If I am the first to stumble upon Lake Michigan, for example, can I become its sole and absolute legitimate proprietor by pouring a package of Kool-Aid into it? Isn't instead some partial and proportionate return on our contribution more appropriate in moral terms? And why—to cite a less than self-evident contention of Locke that provides the pathway through which Marx converted the labor theory of value into a powerful tool of critique—should it be that I am entitled to possess value created by others? To value created by wage labor or to the value, as Locke wrote, of "the turfs my servant has cut?"[40] Are there no moral shadows on such forms of appropriation? Locke never really addresses these issues, and his libertarian heirs rarely do so either.

Libertarian theorists similarly tend to slide blithely over the "Lockean Proviso," Locke's recognition that it is morally unproblematic for one individual to appropriate common property (i.e., the raw materials of the earth God gave to us in common) for his or her own use *only* if that conversion to private use leaves "enough and as good" for others to have the same opportunity. Locke himself, for example, having recognized this qualification on the legitimacy of private appropriation, clearly conveys his sense that his proviso rarely presents a significant problem in the real world. He simply observes that someone who takes a "good draft" of water from a river injures no one else because a "whole river of the same water is left." He then says that "the case of land and water, where there is enough of both, is perfectly the same."[41] And he then drops the matter entirely. Nozick's account is similarly dismissive of the practical relevancy of Locke's proviso. He acknowledges its validity as a matter of principle. But he says that it should be interpreted weakly and opines that "the free operation of a market system will not actually run afoul of the Lockean proviso."[42] But these assurances are clearly far too cavalier. Drinking from a river is more the extreme case that serves as the exception, not a paradigm case adequate to demonstrate the practical irrelevance of this shadow on private appropriation. When it comes to land, for example, the first to arrive takes the best—the best soil, the most convenient location, the best supplied with water, the most scenic—and those who come later choose from what's left. Only with an infinite frontier does Locke's casualness about his own proviso seem at all appropriate—one reason, no doubt, for the peculiar success of Lockean doctrines in the New World. Contrary to Nozick, my own sense is that the Lockean proviso casts a shadow on virtually all acts of private appropriation from what God gave us in common.

All of the qualifications that these foregoing considerations would seem to impose upon moral entitlements to private property are redoubled when property holders are given full leave to designate who shall hold their property upon their demise. But libertarians characteristically insist that the absolute moral title to private property, derived from the absolute title to one's self, extends to the absolute right to bequeath one's accumulated goods at pleasure. Nozick's core distributive principle, "to each as they are chosen," carries this implication, and he complains that it is one of the defects of patterned principles of justice that they "focus on the recipient role and its supposed rights" and thus "focus on whether people should have a right to inherit, rather than or whether people have a right to bequeath."[43] Rothbard argues that "the libertarian answer is to concentrate not on the recipient . . . but to concentrate on the giver, the man who bestows the inheritance" and concludes that decedents "have the right to give their property to whomever they wish,"[44] apparently without qualification. And Milton Friedman argues that it is logically and morally untenable to distinguish between "the high returns to the individual who inherits from his parents a peculiar voice for which there is a great demand" and "the high returns to the individual who inherits property." Likewise, he argues that "it seems illogical . . . to say that a man may use his income for riotous living but may not give it to his heirs. Surely, the latter is one way to use what he produced."[45]

Pursuant to my previous objections to unqualified claims of self-ownership and rights to private appropriation, two responses can be made to these defenses of an unqualified right to bequeath according to one's pleasure. First, it does, contra Friedman's insistence to the contrary, make some sense to distinguish between one's relationship to one's own voice and one's relationship to shares of General Motors, both of which have been received by inheritance. My voice is, regardless of its receipt by (genetic) inheritance, a part of me, and I can profit from it only by taking pains to develop it and use it for the benefit of others. The shares of General Motors are not part of what I am but properties external to my person, and I can profit from them entirely passively. Second, if it be true, as I have argued, that all rights of private material possession are clouded, first, by others' role in making me who I am; second by the role that raw materials to which all are entitled without distinction have played in the creation of these goods; and, last, by the Lockean proviso, then the attempt to assert an unqualified right of the dead to determine the rights and privileges of the living from beyond the grave is doubly unacceptable. It is one thing to have received and to enjoy a right to use fruits of the earth that I have improved by my labor in recognition of my efforts, but something else altogether to convert that into a right to determine and control the material conditions of the next generation when I am no longer even here to profit from the use of those goods created in part by my labor. At this point, some focus on the recipients rather than on the putative rights of the dead donor is clearly appropriate.

So what is the moral of this mixed assessment of the libertarian doctrine of self-ownership and its deployment on behalf of a generally unqualified right to whatever property one receives by way of the market or bequest? The moral is this: the postulate of self-ownership is an important and valid moral truth that captures and defends the essential integrity and autonomy of human persons. It properly insists upon the deep prima facie wrongness of infringing upon this integrity and autonomy to bend and use people as means to your ends. It expresses the valid moral intuition that adult persons of sound mind should be credited with being the "owners" or authors of their actions and that they are, again prima facie, properly subject to reward or penalty for these actions and their foreseeable consequences. It properly sustains the insistence that persons should be seen as rights-bearers and that society should allow them to have and enjoy at least a qualified control over and use of things of value they create by their labor. But the important limitations and qualifications we have canvassed pertinent to the postulate of self-ownership justifies—and can be said to demand—parallel legitimate qualifications and limitations on private property rights. In a decent society, citizens may be expected to recognize their deep indebtedness to others who have helped to make them who they are, who have sustained and protected them, and who have supported and assisted them in the development of their talents and abilities. The citizens of a liberal polity, therefore, may legitimately establish—by their consent through the normal channels of democratic decision-making—certain obligations consequent upon this indebtedness. These obligations are a form of "giving back" to the common weal for benefits conferred, and they may include obligations to other citizens to whom less has been given and who are in need of assistance. The society is justified, moreover, in universalizing these obligations by law—as a matter of fairness in sharing the burdens of these obligations and in the prudentially justified need to prevent free-riders from undermining the success of the enterprise. Although libertarians are right to argue that a good society should for reasons of both justice and prudence grant and respect rights of private property, those rights need not be absolute and uncompromised. And although both justice (to the donor) and prudence (in the form of creating incentives to produce and conserve wealth) dictate including under private property rights some power to bequeath it at death, justice (to the recipients) and prudence (in the form of preventing social inequalities that are both excessive and undeserved) permit qualifying that right—especially in light of the common resources and the efforts of others that contributed to the individual's success in the first place.

Several other arguments and admonitions in the libertarian arsenal merit our attention and respect: their unmaking of and stout resistance against special pleading and paternalism, the insistence that the institutions of the marketplace and civil society provide salutary countervailing power against governmental monopoly of force, and the recognition that leaving allocative decisions to the market rather than to majority determination can soften social conflict and permit valuable forms of diversity. Each of these valid insights of libertarianism, however, remains a partial truth that can become counterproductive if interpreted too woodenly or applied without qualification. The admonition against special pleading, for example, becomes damaging rather than liberating if it leads—as it does for many libertarians—to the failure to acknowledge important common goods and genuine neighborhood effects warranting a collective financial response. Those libertarians, such as Murray Rothbard, who criticize Milton Friedman as a sell-out because he recognizes the (positive) neighborhood effects of education for citizenship and the (negative) neighborhood effects of poverty—and because he therefore advocates public finance of secondary education and a negative income tax—are clearly cases in point. (Friedman is also willing, incidentally, to countenance a program of government "equity investment in human beings" by financing "the training of any individual who could meet minimum quality standards." This suggestion revisits a visionary proposal put forward two centuries ago by Condorcet that a system of collective finance should "provide all children with the capital necessary for the full use of their labor, available at the age when they start work and found a family." Not even so-called progressive political leaders in this country have done much, other than provide some loan funds for college expenses, to implement this wise suggestion.)[46] But even Friedman is guilty under this heading of advocating the selling off of public parks, for example, apparently oblivious to the important role such public treasures play in sustaining national pride and identity and in symbolizing and embodying our civic equality.

Counsels against governmental paternalism, similarly, are useful enough. But they sometimes seem to distract libertarian theorists from candidly contemplating our collective responsibilities as a society to children. They acknowledge children to be legitimate objects of paternalist policy, but in the concrete they seem to assume that few serious collective issues are presented by the dependency and vulnerability of the young—and to assume as a possible justification for this neglect that children are effectively the personal property and solely the responsibility of their parents. It is all well and good, of course, to expect—and to demand through force of law—that people care for their children. But a decent society is morally obligated to set real limits on how much children are made to suffer from the incompetence or negligence of their parents. Children need protection against abuse and neglect, they need a safety net against crippling economic deprivation, and they need sufficient communal provision for their cognitive and emotional development to give them a fair chance at a satisfying life. How to meet these obligations to the next generation and how to do so without creating destructive incentives that foster parental abdication or family breakdown is one of the critical problems contemporary liberal democracies face. In recent decades, our policies have not been very successful. But libertarian prescriptions simply to leave things to individual responsibility and to the logic of the marketplace are neither realistic nor helpful in this context.

Libertarian claims regarding the market's contributions to political countervailing power and to channeling away zero-sum group conflicts are valid and important points, often insufficiently appreciated. If the concentration of all power in the same hands is not, as Jefferson wrote and Madison agreed, "precisely the definition of despotic government," it certainly provides the institutional means and the permanent temptation to the imposition of hegemonic control over society.[47] Keeping some centers of economic power beyond the direct purview of political elites or governing majorities, therefore, has real benefits. But this libertarian insistence would be more compelling if libertarians did not seem oblivious to or unconcerned by concentrations of economic power in private hands. Market enthusiasts generally depict trade union activity as merely illegitimate cartelization of the labor market and government regulation as imperialistic, when in fact these forms of collective action are often a necessary and proper exercise of countervailing power against corporate quasi-governments with despotic powers or aspirations of their own. It is instructive in this respect to consider the phenomenon of "company towns" in the late 1800s and early 1900s, such as Southern mill towns or the town that railroad car magnate George Pullman founded and ruled in Illinois. Great economic power can convert wealth into sovereignty, and when it does citizens are reduced to dependent subjects. When Richard Ely visited the town of Pullman, he wrote that "one feels that one is mingling with a dependent, servile people."[48] Those who center their political vision around the paramount goals of liberty and personal autonomy should surely be the first to be alert to such dangers and to the power dynamics behind them. Possibly in thrall to their own abstract vision of the market as the unproblematic paradigm case of purely voluntary activity, however, libertarians instead seem either innocent of or unconcerned by the way that—in the real world rather than on the economist's blackboard—economic power can itself convert into political tyranny.

Some of the most debilitating blind spots in the libertarian vision, I believe, are a product of a very important weakness of libertarian sociological analysis. Libertarian sociology is characteristically binocular: there is the state and there is "civil society," which is everything else, including and perhaps even best epitomized by self-interested market contractual behavior. Libertarians are explicit and insistent, then, about the propriety of this analytical, conceptual, and terminological dichotomizing. Thus, David Boaz writes:

> Civil society may be broadly defined as all the natural and voluntary associations in society. Some analysts distinguish between commercial and non-profit organizations, arguing that businesses are part of the market, not of civil society; but I follow the tradition that the real distinction is between associations that are coercive (the state) and those that are natural and voluntary (everything else).[49]

Now the distinction between voluntary and legally mandatory activities is obviously a fundamental and important one. But by lumping economic market institutions and all the other institutions of civil society into one undifferentiated conceptual category, extremely important distinctions and contrasts are either obscured or denied. Economic activities and market transactions are driven by the strongest and most basic of human needs and desires — the need for biological survival ("root, hog, or die!") and the desire for material gain. Economic cooperation is produced by mutual self-interest, as is the competitive battle enforced upon all producers by the discipline of the invisible hand. These features are what make market institutions so strong, effective, and reliable. As Adam Smith famously observed, they are why one need not depend upon the altruism or goodwill of the grocer for food: the grocer needs to eat, too, and provides services for us to achieve his own sustenance and profit. The other institutions of civil society, however, are generated and sustained by other motives, motives that are "softer," more complex, less urgent, and arguably more "elevated" than those that drive the market. Self-interest may be involved, of course, but the interests—in status or convivial enjoyment—are different ones. And non-self-interested motivations are also often very important: a sense of justice, charity, public spirit; felt moral obligation to God, country, future generations, or the less fortunate; love of place or community; enjoyment of noble human works; the sense of personal worth arising from achievement and creativity even when oneself is not the direct beneficiary; a commitment to standards of good professional craftsmanship; and so on. Without these complex dimensions of the human spirit, the gift of civil society humankind gives to itself does not exist.[50] Without these motives that transcend narrowly economizing modes of behavior, we don't have churches and PTA's, Kiwanis and Rotary clubs, the Salvation Army, the March of Dimes, Habitat for Humanity, Little Leagues, historical preservation societies—the panoply of civic associations that makes society so much more than an economic bazaar presided over by a police power. If our social institutions were limited to market and state, our lives might not be poor or short, but they would be solitary, brutish, and probably rather nasty.

The failure to signalize the important differences between the marketplace and the other institutions of civil society, therefore, turns out to be dangerous. If it is part of a conscious attempt to "rationalize"—i.e., marketize—all forms of social interaction, it is perverse. De facto, monopolizing enthusiasts of the market "seek the abolition of civil society."[51] They think that converting the entire social enterprise into a capitalist bazaar would make it more productive and "enlightened." But these hypercapitalists who are more Smithian than Smith and more Benthamite than Bentham would give us a materially successful world in which we knew the price of everything and the value of nothing—including ourselves and each other—a world in which the principled judgments and attendant behavioral norms incorporated into concepts like simony and prostitution would disappear. Such a triumph of what Marx lampooned as a "petty shopkeeper mentality" and what an older tradition called avarice, covetousness, and concupiscence would in fact not be a political achievement but a moral and sociological disaster.

Other libertarian theorists are not beguiled by such depressing fantasies. They recognize that most components of civil society are not the same as or reducible to the market. They value these noneconomic institutions and assume that they will and should maintain their distinctiveness and resistance to economizing norms in a libertarian society. Charles Murray's Burkean embrace of society's "little platoons" is a case in point. But their prescriptions, while not perverse, are nonetheless dangerous. They threaten civil society proper because of their sociological naivete. The central failing here is manifest most clearly in von Hayek's ubiquitous and undiscriminating reference to civil society— in which he again includes the market—as a realm of "spontaneous order," a thematic characterization that reappears as a veritable mantra in many contemporary libertarian pronouncements. The difficulty here is that "spontaneous order" is a myth. Invoking that notion in social scientific casual explanations is on a par with invocations of phlogiston in physics. It is, as Hobbes said of Scholastic explanations of gravity, to "render none at all but empty words."[52] And these empty words carry misleading prescriptive implications. If "spontaneous" here means simply "not produced by state mandate," there is no problem. But "spontaneous" clearly implies—and is intended to imply—more than that: it implies automaticity, and it correlatively implies either an outright absence of external causes or at least the absence of any need to inquire into them. But no social events, much less complicated institutions and patterns of behavior, are automatic and self-generated. The institutions of civil society do not arise spontaneously in any literal sense, then. They instead are the product of a complex panoply of cultural, psychological, sociological, and technological forces at work in a given society.

The partial truth captured by the term "spontaneous" is that among these causal forces are human needs and inclinations which are in some real sense "natural"—for example, desires for security, pleasure, companionship, and self-esteem. These needs and inclinations consequently "naturally induce" (to use Richard Hooker's phrase quoted and approved by Locke) human beings to create organizations prior to or apart from artificial governmental contrivance. But some of these organizations are more "natural" and "spontaneous" than others. The key here is the strength, the universality, and the importunity of the motivating needs and inclinations. And in this respect, the forces at work that create and sustain the marketplace give it a clear advantage over the institutions of civil society proper (or over what Boaz et al. would call the other institutions of civil society). People have to eat. They need shelter and raiment. The imperatives here are strong, and the behaviors and institutions thereby generated—i.e., economic markets—have a corresponding hardiness and resistance to forces that would weaken or destroy them. The motives and inclinations sustaining other civic associations are less importunate, less self-regarding. And these institutions whose health is so important to good liberal democratic societies are accordingly "softer," more fragile, more vulnerable. They can be eroded by cultural decay, destroyed or weakened by governmental policies that encumber them or usurp their functions, and crowded out by their tougher sibling, the market. The prescriptive implications of these differences are quite important, and they are quite obscured by blithe blanket invocations of "spontaneous order." Simply put, laissez-faire policies and a libertarian regime are indeed highly likely to produce a robust market economy—so long, at least, as certain essential cultural requisites are present. But these policies and arrangements provide no guarantee whatever that the other institutions of civil society will somehow spring up like Pallas Athena. Instead, these institutions are the fruit of deep and complex cultural forces, beliefs, and traditions that neither the state nor the market can create—and that will not appear as a simple by-product of government forbearance. This difficulty, indeed, is a principal source of the serious problems Russia is encountering in its attempts to transform itself from an authoritarian state into a free society.

Whether by perverse intent or by delusionary neglect, moreover, libertarian sociology positively promotes or passively encourages three trends dangerous to the health and prosperity (in the broad and not narrowly economic sense) of liberal democratic regimes. These corrosive tendencies are the progressive commodification of liberal society and its constituent enterprises, what Tocqueville called "individualism" but what might better be called "privatism," and what Daniel Bell has called "the cultural contradictions of capitalism."

The commodification of life and its varied pursuits is not so much a political problem as a moral one. A society whose members and their activities are exhaustively determined by pecuniary profit-maximizing choices could be reasonably stable and it would not violate anyone's rights—at least insofar as these rights are construed in the libertarian way as consisting of boundaries against other's encroachment. The costs involved bear instead upon the integrity of what MacIntyre calls "practices" and upon the character of the citizenry. Libertarians insist that the market can give an accurate rendering of the "value" of a good or service to the consumer. And so it can. But that accuracy nonetheless permits the goods and services in question to lose their integrity as part of a human practice. Or, to put it another way, things and activities change their nature when they are commodified into "goods and services," from intrinsic into instrumental goods. Sports, sex, music, and learning all become at least suspect and possibly corrupted when these intrinsically estimable goods-in-themselves become economic products for trade or hire in hard cash. When Robert Redford's character offered a cool million for the "services" of Demi Moore's character, the price may have been right and the bargain voluntary, but it was still an Indecent Proposal. And it conversely was wonderfully refreshing when, during the week I wrote these words, Jenny Chausiriporn, a collegiate golfer from my own university, passed up the rights to a rich purse and competed as an amateur all the way through four rounds, a play-off round, and sudden death overtime in the U.S. Women's Golf Open. Her amateurism (i.e., her competing for love not money) was appreciated by all fans of golf, and of sport generally, because it was testimony to the integrity and goodness-in-itself of the game. In a relentlessly commodified society, these testimonies are rare but treasured. And to the extent that libertarian norms and policies promote and encourage this relentless commodification whose rejection we so appreciate, they have their drawbacks. A society of profiteering mammonites may not be either malicious or oppressive. But it would nonetheless violate the spirit behind the Kantian maxim by turning everything and everybody into means rather than ends. Most of us would not find such a world an ideal place to live.

The second degenerative dynamic promoted or sanguinely condoned by libertarian sociology and policy is Tocquevillian "individualism." The threat to a good democratic society he warned against under this rubric is not Emersonian individualism or the individuality prized by John Stuart Mill. Instead, it is what Mill feared and condemned as the absence of public spirit. Tocqueville's "individualist" is one who has, in Mill's words,

> no unselfish sentiment of identification with the public. Every thought and feeling, either of interest or of duty, is absorbed in the individual and in the family. The man never thinks of any collective interest, of any objects to be pursued jointly with others, but only in competition with them, and in some measure at their expense. A neighbor, not being an ally or an associate is only a rival. Thus even private morality suffers, while public is actually extinct.[53]

What Mill depicts here is pretty much the essence of what the civic republican tradition styled as "corruption." And that reminder suggests that—wholly apart from the moral questions involved—there are political dangers presented to democratic societies by such privatism. As is their wont, libertarians are oblivious to these dangers because of their focus on the economic marketplace and because of their mistaken insistence that its dynamics are paradigmatic of civil society as a whole. In a purely economizing calculus, it may be that the invisible hand's regulatory power justifies the classic libertarian maxim concerning the transmutation of individual concupiscence into social economic benefit: "private vice, public virtue." But that formula does not generalize well into the rest of our social interaction with our fellow citizens. When we move beyond the marketplace into social spheres and enterprises demanding more empathy and cooperation for their success, the more apt maxim is "private vice, public disintegration."

The last, and associated, dynamic unleashed by libertarianism's hyper-Benthamism and/or its romantic anarchism concerns what Daniel Bell calls the "cultural contradictions of capitalism."[54] At issue here are the cultural requisites necessary to sustain free societies. Bell's argument, much simplified, is that Western—particularly American—society has moved over the past 200 years "from the Protestant ethic to the psychedelic bazaar." Capitalist (and liberal) societies and institutions were built, legitimated, and motivated in large measure by a culture that enshrined productivity, self-restraint, and careful stewardship. The very success of the economic system and its associated civil liberties, however, has had the somewhat paradoxical effect of undermining the ethos that sustained it and substituting for it an ethos of consumerism, self-indulgence, and hedonism. This shift from a "goodness morality" to a "fun morality," Bell writes, "leaves capitalism with no moral or transcendental ethic."[55] And it also creates a "radical disjunction between the social structure (the techno-economic order) and the culture," with the former based on "efficiency and functional rationality" and the latter centered on "prodigal, promiscuous" pleasure-seeking.[56]

Bell seems to suggest that this cultural and structural disjunction presents a challenge to the functional coherence and viability of the capitalist system. At the level of economic activity proper, however, I doubt that this is a real problem. The shifts and disjunctions he describes do produce a real change from the earlier Puritan/Protestant version of bourgeois society, where the productive virtues cohered with the regnant moral virtues and the upright labored not so much for wealth as to prove their salvation. The result of these shifts may be a more schizophrenic psyche that segments its life and adopts a "work hard, play hard" mentality—a society in which people accept the repressions and constraints necessitated by corporate efficiency norms during the day in order to have the toys to party with at night. But that pattern seems potentially perfectly stable to me, and it is a pattern that may sustain and fuel an advanced capitalist economy quite well. Indeed, those more dour and abstemious Protestant types might on principle have not generated enough aggregate demand—the expansive appetite for greater pleasures and more luxuries—to keep the productive apparatus of advanced capitalism going at full tilt. The real potential problems instead lie elsewhere: when these cultural shifts spill over into the larger polity. As commentators as diverse as Plato, Ibn Khaldun, Machiavelli, and Rousseau have pointed out, "in the hedonistic life, there is a loss of will and fortitude. More importantly, men become competitive with one another for luxuries, and lose the ability to share and sacrifice."[57]One recent result of this phenomenon has been an increasing gap—based on cultural estrangement—between America's military and civilian societies. The military life and its animating moral passions necessarily involve older ethical norms of honor, courage, and sacrifice—norms at odds with the increasingly self-indulgent civilian consumer culture. The volunteer army thus becomes a Spartan island in a Syracusean sea. This alone is a potentially dangerous disjunction. But there are broader problems here posed by the loss of a sense of solidarity and the associated lessening of any capacity of the larger society to unite and accept sacrifices in pursuit of important common purposes. College coaches have an expression, "California lazy," to capture their anxieties when they recruit in the Golden State: high school athletes who have internalized the surfer-dude ethos sometimes seem unable to accept and adapt to the rigors of high level competition. Bell's analysis reminds us that a political society can also become "California lazy." So long as the living is easy, that kind of society may happily cruise along in its sybaritic fashion. But it is not a society that will respond well to challenge and adversity.

What the foregoing considerations tell us is that Nozick's libertarian utopia—diverse voluntary associations existing within the framework of the minimal state—can be touted as an "inspiring" vision and as "the best of all possible worlds" only because of its studied ambiguities. When we interrogate the model regarding its concrete content in the real world rather than its abstract form in the imagination, its problematic features begin to appear in sharp relief. What, for example, will these associations actually look like? Whatever people want them to be, Nozick says. And his rhetorical allusions paint a scene straight out of Mill's paean to individuality in *On Liberty*: the associations will be diverse groupings of people inspired by their different forms of genius. The associations will be the fitting habitats for the variant human types represented by "Wittgenstein, Elizabeth Taylor, Bertrand Russell, Thomas Merton, Yogi Berra, Allen Ginsburg, Harry Wolfson, Thoreau, . . . Picasso, Moses, Einstein, Hugh Heffner, Socrates, Henry Ford, . . . Gandhi, . . . Buddha, . . . Freud, . . . Thomas Jefferson, . . . Ralph Ellison."[58] Just a diverse bunch of average guys and gals. The mind wanders. What about Jeffrey Dahmer, Charles Manson, David Duke, Louis Farakhan, Timothy McVeigh, Larry Flynt? Or what if the empty antinomianism and laissez-faire incentives of the framework simply generate more and more Nietzschean "last men," larger and larger hordes of self-centered, driveling consumerist idiots? The point here is simply that the real-world results of implementing Nozick's libertarian model might be considerably less inspiring than his rhetoric suggests. His refusal to speculate makes some sense both for reasons of libertarian principle and proper humility when it comes to making predictions about futures and possibilities. But it is also significantly evasive and, coupled with his rhetorical allusions, misleading.

Answers are also not given to other very important questions: for example, how would the constituent associations of the libertarian utopia relate to each other? And what would be the likely or logical consequences of the criteria for admission into the various associations that Nozick suggests would be operative? Nozick specifically and candidly asserts that entry into particular associations will be governed by the logic of the marketplace. Thus,

> associations competing for my membership are the same structurally as firms competing to employ me. In each case I receive my marginal contribution. Thus, it seems, we have the result that in every stable association, each person receives his marginal contribution. . . . No association will admit me if I take more from the association than I give to it. They will not choose to lose by admitting me . . . From no association will I be able to get something worth more to them than what I contribute is worth to them. [59]

Now these important dynamics governing admission into the various associations are fundamental to Nozick's libertarian logic. And he seems to regard their operation as not only unproblematic but proper and admirable. But even rather cursory reflection about the concrete implications of these selective processes leads to some fairly obvious and sobering difficulties with the whole scheme. The obvious equilibrium point of this process is a society composed of associations that are not only diverse in their orienting passions and values but also dramatically unequal. The internal cohesion and external diversity of the associations would in the real world very probably produce racial, religious, and ethnic enclaves. And these in turn would logically be subdivided into clearly hierarchical (in terms of wealth and talents) groups of winners and losers. No one, recall, will get from any association more than what they can give to it. Those with less to contribute will therefore either have to accept a subordinate position to join an association composed of those who have more to offer. Or else they will have to join their own more homogeneous association of inferiors. And what of those who have less to offer than what is required for their subsistence? Logically, they get into no association and simply perish between the cracks. Or perhaps associations composed of generous and philanthropic spirits will admit them. If so, these associations would then likely become swamped by their voluntarily accepted charitable burden, since the other more "rational" associations would happily be free-riders—if, that is, we presume that they take any comfort in the survival of the unfit.

Given the likely composition of and the deep differences among the various associations that would logically result from their entry rules, problems would seem endemic in their relations with each other. Presumably, these associations would have to work together cooperatively in some ways and could not live in isolation like a group version of hermits. Nozick's thought experiment leaves the impression that these groups could float around unrelated in abstract space, keep to themselves, and pursue their very disparate life plans. But in the real world, they would have common spaces to inhabit, a common environment to shape and protect, common or cooperative economic ventures and organizations to establish and sustain, a common defense to maintain, possibly—depending on circumstances—common educational institutions to construct, and so on. These associations would, however, be animated by very different values, would in a pluralist society likely have radically different ethnic and religious compositions, and would—admitting members on the basis of marginal productivity—be radically unequal in wealth and ability. This would seem to be a structural recipe for mutual incomprehension, resentment, dislike, suspicion, and hostility, not a good or even a viable basis for the cooperative endeavors necessitated by living together— even under the loose umbrella of the minimal state.

In short, Nozick's utopia can seem "inspiring" (and possibly even functionally viable) only so long as it is depicted as operating in an imaginary and disembodied world and only so long as its developmental logic remains unexplored. The more we return his model to the real world, pursue its logic, and fill in its likely consequences, the less appealing it becomes. It offers us a liberating vision, but it is something of a pipe dream—of a piece, and not accidentally so, with the economist's tendency to assume away the most vexing problems.

What, then, should we conclude about the libertarian rendering of democratic ideals? We should, I think, be appreciative but unsatisfied. Libertarian theorists are right to insist that the blessings of liberty are fundamental and irreplaceable. They are helpful in reminding us that democratic decisions can be oppressive and violate rights. They are right to insist upon the deep infirmities of command economies and the consequent necessity to accept some material inequalities as the price of economic productivity and innovation. They provide us with astute critiques of the way that the special pleading of interest groups corrupts and ossifies the public household. They make wonderful allies in the perennial fight against the paternalistic arrogance of those who claim to know what's good for us and want to use state power to discipline us accordingly. They rightly insist that programs of social insurance and collective provision bring unintended and destructive consequences if they too fully shield people from the consequences of their own foolish or dangerous actions. All this said, however, the libertarian account of democratic ideals is in important respects inadequate and misleading.

Libertarians are entirely too simplistic, ambiguous, and uncritical when it comes to their own paramount ideal of liberty. Whether because of their reflexive individualism and antiauthoritarianism or because of their prereflective absorption in the antinomianism of American culture, libertarians pay surprisingly little attention to detailing the particulars of freedom and to explaining why it is properly to be understood as the axial human good. Libertarians generally take liberty to mean what Hobbes defined it as being: "absence of impediment." But Hobbes and Sir Robert Filmer, who defined freedom as "a liberty for everyone to do what he lists, to mean he pleases," were authoritarian antagonists of those who, like Locke, argued for limited government. This was not accidental, for Hobbes and Filmer traded upon this undifferentiated construction of freedom as negative liberty to insist upon its moral unworthiness as an ideal and upon its incoherence and self-undermining tendencies as a political norm. If liberty is indistinguishable from slavish obedience to appetite, impulse, blind habit, or arbitrary whim, then it is not pellucidly clear why it should carry much moral weight. And if all are left unconstrained to behave "licentiously," the predictable social consequences are not very pretty. One might, with Alexander Hamilton, either then anticipate an authoritarian reaction—exemplified in the "state of perpetual vibration between the extremes of anarchy and tyranny" that vexed "the petty republics of Greece and Italy."[60] Or one might simply advocate a preemptive strike against the anticipated political disintegration, as did Hobbes and Filmer. That is why Locke always thematized the freedom he prized in conjunction with lawfulness and rationality. The early liberal reformers celebrated by libertarians, Locke and Adam Smith in particular, understood liberty, like Aristotle and Kant, as the independent self-determination of rational personhood. It was their enemies who depicted liberty as existentialist freedom or as random whimsy. This is not a merely academic or metaphysical point, but one quite pertinent to how demo-cratic regimes should craft their procedures and policies. For the capacity for rational self-determination is a complex social achievement and not something that automatically happens if only government will keep its hands off. For true lovers of liberty, laissez-faire is not enough.

Moreover, liberty itself is not enough—not enough to create a genuinely good and humanly satisfying society in the absence of other complementary and supplementary goods. Libertarians rip liberty out of context. They fail to understand that liberty can flourish and prevail only when it works in tandem with other enabling conditions of a good life together. Liberty functions properly and beneficently only in the context of civic equality, civic friendship, and civic virtue. The abstractions, oversimplifications, and indeterminacies of libertarianism take liberty "on a holiday", as Wittgenstein would say. Time to get back to rough ground.

Notes

1. Milton Friedman, *Capitalism and Freedom* (Chicago: University of Chicago Press, 1962), 5.

2. Thus Ludwig von Mises changed the title of his book *Liberalismus* to *The Free and Prosperous Commonwealth* when it appeared in the English translation in 1962, but his followers opted to use the title *Liberalism in the Classical Tradition* for the 1977 reprint. On the other hand, Charles Murray and David Boaz both were content to use the term libertarian to designate their viewpoint in books they published in 1997; Murray, *What It Means to Be a Libertarian* (New York: Broadway Books, 1997); Boaz, *Libertarianism: A Primer* (New York: The Free Press, 1997).

3. Friedman, *Capitalism and Freedom*, 5.

4. William Graham Sumner, "What Social Classes Owe to Each Other," in *Political Thought in America*, 2d ed., ed. Michael Levy (Chicago: Dorsey Press, 1988), 327.

5. See Karl Polanyi, *The Great Transformation* (Boston: Beacon Press, 1965).

6. John Dewey, "Liberalism and Social Action," in *Political Thought in America*, ed. Levy, 418.

7. Friedrich von Hayek, *The Road to Serfdom* (Chicago: University of Chicago Press, 1944).

8. Ludwig von Mises, *Liberalism in the Classical Tradition*, trans. Ralph Raico (San Francisco: Cobden Press, 1985), 79.

9. Besides the books by Charles Murray and David Boaz, cited earlier, that were published in 1997, see also: Murray Rothbard, *For A New Liberty: The Libertarian Manifesto*, rev. ed. (New York: Libertarian Review Foundation, 1985); Jan Narveson, *The Libertarian Idea* (Philadelphia: Temple University Press, 1988); and Robert Nozick, *Anarchy, State, and Utopia* (New York: Basic Books, 1974). Richard Epstein has written a whole series of books on specific domains of law and policy that collectively amount to a libertarian critique of the regulatory state. See, for example, his *Takings: Private Property and the Power of Eminent Domain* (Cambridge: Harvard University Press, 1985) and *Forbidden Grounds: The Case against Employment Discrimination Laws* (Cambridge: Harvard University Press, 1992). Public choice arguments, such as those of James Buchanan and Gordon Tullock, *The Calculus of Consent: Logical Foundations of Constitutional Democracy* (Ann Arbor: University of Michigan Press, 1962) are also pertinent to libertarian concerns. And a variety of supporters, including the Cato Institute and the Heritage Foundation, have joined forces to produce a new twenty-two-volume edition of von Hayek's collected works.

10. Friedman, *Capitalism and Freedom*, 9 (emphasis added).

11. Friedman, *Capitalism and Freedom*, 169.

12. David Stockman, *The Triumph of Politics* (New York: Harper and Row, 1986).

13. Theodore Lowi, *The End of Liberalism* (New York: Norton, 1969); Mancur Olson, *The Logic of Collective Action* (Cambridge: Harvard University Press, 1965) and *The Rise and Decline of Nations* (New Haven: Yale University Press, 1982).

14. Jonathan Rauch, *Demosclerosis: The Silent Killer of American Government* (New York: Random House, 1994).

15. Robert Dahl, *A Preface to Democratic Theory* (Chicago: University of Chicago Press, 1956), 146.

16. Rothbard, *For a New Liberty*, chapter 12.

17. Narveson, *The Libertarian Idea*, 251–57.

18. Friedman, *Capitalism and Freedom*, chapters 6, 9, and 12.

19. Friedman, *Capitalism and Freedom*, 12.

20. Murray, *What It Means to Be a Libertarian*, 124.

21. Murray, *What It Means to Be a Libertarian*, 81 and 59.

22. Murray, *What It Means to Be a Libertarian*, 135–36.

23. Von Mises, *Liberalism in the Classical Tradition*, 22.

24. Von Mises, *Liberalism in the Classical Tradition*, 30–31.

25. Murray, *What It Means to Be a Libertarian*, 27.

26. Rothbard, *For a New Liberty*, 27.

27. Nozick, *Anarchy, State, and Utopia*, ix.

28. Murray, *What It Means to Be a Libertarian*, 18.

29. Nozick, *Anarchy, State, and Utopia*, 30–31.

30. Murray, *What It Means to Be a Libertarian*, 6.

31. Rothbard, *For a New Liberty*, 29–30.

32. Murray, *What It Means to Be a Libertarian*, 18.

33. Rothbard thus writes: "The central core of the libertarian creed, then, is to establish the absolute right to private property of every man: first, in his own body, and second in the previously unused natural resources which he first transforms by his labor." *For a New Liberty*, 39.

34. Nozick, *Anarchy, State, and Utopia*, 332.

35. Michael Polanyi, *The Contempt of Freedom* (New York: Arno Press, 1975), 58–59.

36. Nozick, *Anarchy, State, and Utopia*, 225 (emphasis in original).

37. Nozick, *Anarchy, State, and Utopia*, 219.

38. "For men being all the workmanship of one omnipotent and infinitely wise Maker; all the servants of one sovereign Master, sent into the world by His order and about His Business; they are His property." Locke, *Second Treatise of Civil Government*, chapter 2, section 6.

39. Locke, *Second Treatise*, chapter 5, section 40.

40. Locke, *Second Treatise*, chapter 5, section 28.

41. Locke, *Second Treatise*, chapter 5, section 33.

42. Nozick, *Anarchy, State, and Utopia*, 182.

43. Nozick, *Anarchy, State, and Utopia*, 168.

44. Rothbard, *For a New Liberty*, 41.

45. Friedman, *Capitalism and Freedom*, 164.

46. Friedman, *Capitalism and Freedom*, 105; Condorcet, *Progress of the Human Mind*, 181.

47. Madison, *Federalist* #48.

48. Quoted by Walzer, *Spheres of Justice: A Defense of Pluralism and Equality* (New York: Basic Books, 1983), 297.

49. Boaz, *Libertarianism*, 127–28.

50. This phrase is Alan Wolfe's. *Whose Keeper?* 261.

51. Wolfe, *Whose Keeper?* 41.

52. Hobbes, *Leviathan*, part four, chapter 46.

53. John Stuart Mill, *Considerations on Representative Government* (Chicago: Henry Regnery, 1962), 73.

54. Daniel Bell, *The Cultural Contradictions of Capitalism* (New York: Basic Books, 1976).

55. Bell, *Cultural Contradictions*, 71.

56. Bell, *Cultural Contradictions*, 37.

57. Bell, *Cultural Contradictions*, 83.

58. Nozick, *Anarchy, State, and Utopia*, 310.

59. Nozick, *Anarchy, State, and Utopia*, 301–2.

60. Alexander Hamilton, *Federalist Papers* no. 9.

3

The Weaknesses and Dangers
of Liberal Egalitarianism

In the academic world, the most insistent and compelling arguments on behalf of conceiving democratic society as a cooperative endeavor devoted to an egalitarian ideal of social justice have recently come mainly from those informed and inspired by the moral philosopher John Rawls. Whether Rawls and his followers have influenced and shaped the goals and policies of the liberal left or whether their ideals and arguments instead have mirrored and rationalized ideological and moral reactions to specific historical events is, I think, impossible to answer. No doubt the causal arrows run both ways. What is crucial for our purposes, however, is the isomorphy between Rawls's account of the moral foundations of democratic liberalism and the animating ideals of many contemporary egalitarian liberals. For although Rawls may have been misled to suppose that this theory of justice captures the "basic intuitive ideas that are embedded in the political institutions of a constitutional democratic regime," his theory does seem to capture very well the social beliefs and moral intuitions of much of the egalitarian left.[1] Although Rawls has been the subject of voluminous commentary and criticism, therefore, it nonetheless seems important to identify what arguably are the weaknesses and dangers of Rawlsian-inspired liberal egalitarianism. Doing so is necessary both to make clear why this influential perspective is not an adequate guide for our political labors and also to make explicit some of the deficiencies that a more compelling vision of democratic ideals would have to make good.

The impetus for Rawls's highly influential account of democratic ideals stems from his conviction that the traditional moral arguments for democratic liberalism are unacceptable. These traditional arguments include utilitarian, "intuitionist," *modus vivendi*, and comprehensive liberalisms. Utilitarian theories of democracy depict democratic institutions as the logical embodiment of the "greatest good for the greatest number" and would judge policy options by that standard. What Rawls terms "intuitionist" theories would counsel some form of largely *ad hoc* balancing of multiple social goods in assessing democratic policies. *Modus vivendi* theories argue that democratic institutions are justified simply because they best advance the interests of the parties to the social contract. And comprehensive liberalisms seek to justify and evaluate democratic polities on the basis of moral beliefs that encompass the meaning of human existence and its embracing moral purposes.

Each of these traditional understandings and justifications of democratic liberalism is problematic, Rawls argues. Utilitarianism is morally flawed because it "does not take seriously the distinction between persons."[2] It "does not matter" to utilitarianism, "how [a] sum of satisfactions is distributed among individuals."[3] But clearly, Rawls suggests, our moral intuitions about justice tell us that, since individuals are distinctive entities with their own unique and separate interests and purposes, it does indeed matter very much what the pattern of distribution among individuals is—that the highest aggregate sum of satisfactions is not necessarily the best outcome irrespective of how these satisfactions are allocated. It is also morally problematical, Rawls argues, that "in utilitarianism the satisfaction of any desire has some value in itself which might be taken into account in deciding what is right."[4] Thus, if people take pleasure in others' pain or misfortune and if they enjoy discriminating against them, these morally objectionable pleasures will nonetheless be figured into—and hence contaminate—the utilitarian normative calculus.

The problem with "intuitionism" for Rawls is that it is insufficiently determinate: it cannot give us any definitive answers to what should be done or what goals pursued whenever the multiple values it accredits point in different directions. Intuitionism "denies that there exists any useful and explicit solution to the priority problem."[5] If that denial is simply recognition of the limits of our moral judgment, then we must, of course, accede to it. But Rawls wants to argue that valid priority rules are possible for us to ascertain. And he tries to make good on that claim by producing exactly that: persuasive standards for prioritizing and choosing among competing goods when it comes to making policy decisions. He would disprove the moral logical equivalent of a claim that all swans are white by producing a healthy black swan.

It is also undesirable, Rawls maintains, to try to base democratic practices and the social cooperation that sustains them solely upon the self-interest of the parties, as *modus vivendi* theories do. The basic problem here is that democratic norms are reduced to merely instrumental goods and democratic societies to mere pacts of convenience. Democracy thus loses the genuinely moral stature to which Rawls believes it is entitled. This loss in turn exacts significant costs with respect to the legitimacy and stability of democratic polities: a democratic consensus based upon moral conviction should be much stronger and more durable than a consensus based on interest alone, Rawls argues, because the latter "depends on happenstance and a balance of relative forces" which obviously can shift dramatically over time.[6]

Finally, any democratic theories or practices predicated upon a specific comprehensive moral or religious doctrine are both practically infeasible and morally improper. They are infeasible because of the simple but consequentially important reality that in today's pluralistic societies people have allegiances to different and competing comprehensive moral viewpoints. Hence any attempt to privilege one of these viewpoints over the others will arouse resistance rather than acceptance of the norms and procedures justified in this manner. And such attempts would simultaneously be violative of moral strictures against coercion and hegemony, for they could prevail only by "the sanctions of state power."[7]

It follows from these critiques of other forms of democratic theory that a morally acceptable and practically feasible framework of democratic ideals would have to, *inter alia*, be grounded in moral convictions and not in purely prudential interests, take the separateness of persons and hence distributive criteria seriously, be normatively determinate by establishing priority rules, and be capable of eliciting the uncoerced allegiance of all citizens—or at least all reasonable citizens. In a pluralist society, moreover, the last requirement entails the further stipulation that an acceptable theory must be "political" rather than comprehensive in its foundations; that is, it must not depend upon the truth of any one comprehensive moral doctrine but must instead derive from freestanding moral beliefs and empirical perceptions that can be accepted by reasonable citizens regardless of their ultimate religious or philosophical convictions.

As is familiar to all students of contemporary democratic theory, Rawls seeks to establish normative guidelines for democracy that satisfy these criteria by updating the idea of the social contract. Proceeding on the fundamental premise that legitimate power comes only from the consent of the governed, paradigmatic liberal theorists such as Locke, Hobbes, and Rousseau derived their conceptions of democracy by asking what kind of government free, equal, and rational people would agree to obey. Rawls asks the same speculative question, but with one major difference. For the traditional theorists, the authoritative contract situation—the proper way to conceive the circumstances of the contracting parties—was what they called the "state of nature." The state of nature represented the conditions of human life prior to or apart from all "artificial" institutions contrived by human beings. The intuitive idea was that the proper normative baseline from which to judge governmental legitimacy was the human condition as it came from the hand of God or nature. Rawls rejects that moral intuition on the grounds that a legitimate regime must be based upon a scheme of justice, justice being "the first virtue of social institutions."[8] If that be so, then the natural condition of humankind is not the appropriate setting to pose the question of the social contract, for that condition incorporates much that is unfair or "morally arbitrary." Some are born healthy, some sickly. Some are born bright and others slow. Some are comely, others homely. Moreover, pregovernmental social forces such as family situations advantage some and disadvantage others. Justice would seem to require not the ratification but the rectification of such undeserved inequalities. Accordingly, Rawls argues that the appropriate "original position" in which to imagine the contracting parties should not be a state of nature but rather a state of perfect fairness—or at least a state in which the contractors are precluded from knowing and hence factoring into their choices any morally arbitrary or irrelevant considerations.

Rational parties blocked from knowing any of the arbitrary or irrelevant contingencies that would bias their judgment, Rawls argues, would agree to certain specifiable terms of association to govern their cooperative endeavors. Because these terms are generated from a condition of perfect fairness, we are entitled to call them principles of justice. And because they are the product of the uncoerced consent of free and equal people, we can take these principles of justice as "the most appropriate moral basis for a democratic society."[9]

These principles of justice, Rawls avers, "are a special case of a more general conception of justice that can be expressed as follows: all social values—liberty and opportunity, income and wealth, and the bases of self-respect—are to be distributed equally unless an unequal distribution of any, or all, of these values is to everyone's advantage."[10] And, Rawls adds, "to everyone's advantage," given the integrity and separateness of persons, cannot mean an aggregate or average advantage but must instead mean "to the greatest benefit of the least advantaged."[11] The regulative principles of the well-ordered democratic society, then, Rawls concludes, must be devoted to maximizing the absolute welfare of its least well-off members. Hence Rawls's liberalism is heavily egalitarian in its substantive imperatives.[12]

The ideal democratic society, then, is for Rawls one whose first priority is social justice—that is, the fair distribution of the fruits of the cooperation among its members. And "fair" here must mean conducive to the maximum absolute advantage of the least well-off members of the society. Regulating its affairs in accord with this conception of social justice is not only morally proper, Rawls believes, it is also highly advantageous in a practical sense as well—at least within the context of today's highly pluralistic societies. For if a Hobbesian compact grounded purely in self-interest represents too weak and fragile a basis for necessary social cooperation, an Aristotelian compact centered about a commonly shared conception of the good life is unattainable. People inhabiting divergent comprehensive moral and religious belief systems will *pari passu* not be able to agree upon the human good they seek, Rawls argues. But they need not be forced to fall back upon self-interest and prudence alone, he contends, because they can—notwithstanding their allegiance to different moral world views—converge upon consensual principles of justice and fairness. At least, says Rawls, all adherents of "reasonable" comprehensive moral doctrines could reach this consensus. For this consensus is a function of "basic intuitive ideas" that are accepted and affirmed by "all the opposing philosophical and religious doctrines likely to persist and to gain adherents in a more or less just constitutional democracy."[13] The principles of justice then, not only serve to give genuine moral stature to democratic governance, they also provide the basis for bringing political unity and stability to today's pluralist democracies.

Critiquing Rawls

When Rawls's magisterial account of the moral basis of democratic society first appeared, I—like many others—found myself extremely sympathetic to his argument. I found welcome his insistence that liberal democratic regimes are not mere pacts of convenience but are instead animated by serious moral purpose. I was also attracted to his insistence that, in a good society, citizens in some real sense "share one another's fate" and are not merely a concatenation of self-seeking strangers.[14] And I concurred with his view that liberal justice could not be adequately conceived or justified in strictly utilitarian terms. Moreover, as a political theorist, I found his argument an exhilarating attempt to provide a coherent and systematic philosophical foundation for reform liberalism and the welfare state instead of leaving it to be seen as an *ad hoc* pragmatic compromise between the intellectually coherent but morally and prudentially faulty orthodoxies of laissez-faire capitalism and Marxist socialism.

The more I reflected upon some of the basic assumptions and moral intuitions driving Rawls's account of democratic social justice, however, the more serious reservations I began to have about his whole scheme. These reservations were further consolidated by many thoughtful discussions of Rawls's ideas with my students and pushed along by the voluminous secondary literature devoted to critical analysis of Rawls and deontological liberalism more generally.[15] I now would argue that, for all its many merits, Rawls's account of liberalism—and hence the democratic ideals and policies animated by such an account—is deficient in a number of significant respects. Specifically, it depends upon certain fundamental moral intuitions that turn out upon examination to be problematic. It relies upon other sociological and epistemological judgments that are dubious. And as a consequence, it underwrites political norms and strategies that are or would be deleterious to the legitimacy and well-being of democratic societies. Understanding these dangers and difficulties, moreover, provides important clues to what a more persuasive account of democratic ideals should look like. Space does not permit a full consideration of all these complex and controversial issues. But in the remainder of this chapter, I want to identify as succinctly as possible some of the more important of these weaknesses and dangers.

The first problematic moral intuition behind Rawls's democratic ideal—and behind deontological liberalism more generally—is the claim that "justice is the first virtue of social institutions, as truth is of systems of thought."[16] Toward the end of *A Theory of Justice*, Rawls offers some supporting arguments for this claim, but these arguments are themselves problematic for a variety of reasons. Rawls first says that "wanting to be fair with our friends and wanting to give justice to those we care for is as much a part of these affections as the desire to be with them and to feel sad at their loss."[17] True enough, but this explanation of the importance of justice seems to belie its primacy by deriving it from the demands of friendship and *caritas*. He says that justice is primary because "participating in the life of a well-ordered society is a great good."[18] True enough, but that supports the primacy of justice only if one supposes what is at issue here, namely that a "well-ordered society" is one in which justice takes precedence over all other social goods and moral imperatives. And he says that we can "express our nature as a free and equal rational being . . . only by acting on the principles of right and justice as having first priority. . . . What we cannot do is express our nature by following a plan that views the sense of justice as but one desire to be weighed against others."[19] Possibly so. But Rawls has since abandoned any metaphysical claims about the self; and the question is not whether justice must be given precedence over other desires but rather over other moral imperatives.[20] Therefore, the best way to proceed is probably simply to address the question head on: does it in fact square with our considered moral judgments to consider justice "the first virtue of social institutions, as truth is of systems of thought?"

The answer to this question turns out to depend upon what the meanings of the central terms are taken to be. Depending upon how "justice" and "first virtue" are understood, the claim about the primacy of justice may take a very strong form or it may take weaker forms. Rawls never distinguishes these different meanings adequately, and his claim therefore becomes an ambiguous and inadequately justified one. A weaker version of the claim does in fact, I would argue, accord with our considered moral intuitions. And even this weaker version is important because it disqualifies utilitarianism's claim to be a comprehensive moral guide for social policy. But the stronger version is not so compelling, much less as simply intuitive as Rawls suggests. And that leaves his larger case against all teleological or "intuitionist" (i.e., accounts of social goods as plural and not susceptible to clear priority rules) theories at best incomplete. His account of the moral basis of democratic society may still be preferable to these competing accounts, but if so it is not because they are disqualified by their failure to abide by a compelling intuition about the primacy of justice.

To grasp the important difference between the strong and weak versions of the primacy of justice thesis, it is necessary first to distinguish between two possible meanings of "first virtue," both of which have textual warrant in Rawls's account. One of these is that of "essential requisite," the other that of "paramount and overriding goal." The former interpretation is suggested by Rawls's insistence that "laws and institutions no matter how efficient and well-arranged must be reformed or abolished if they are unjust."[21] That is, no society can be considered well-ordered if it is unjust. This is the weaker, and intuitively persuasive, claim. It properly serves to deny legitimacy to regimes that violate the dignity, integrity, and rights of its citizens—even in order to maximize some putative collective utility. A stronger claim than this is indicated, however, by Rawls's analogy between the role of justice in social institutions and the role of truth in intellectual inquiry. (Justice is the first virtue in politics, says Rawls, "as truth is of systems of thought.") For the attainment of truth can reasonably be construed as the whole point of systems of thought—as their entire and consuming purpose. But this analogy—together with its implicit claim that attaining justice is the sole constitutive purpose of social cooperation—should be rejected. As Hume pointedly observed, justice is a "remedial" virtue; were the members of a human association more benevolent and/or their economic circumstances either exceptionally fortunate (an economy of universal abundance) or exceptionally dire (an economy of base subsistence), norms of social justice would become otiose. Taken in its strong sense, therefore, Rawls's dictum deflects us from recognizing that political societies—including liberal and pluralist ones—may and should seek other and higher goods (what Hume describes as "much nobler virtues") besides justice. Civic friendship is one of these goods; what Mill called "mental and moral development" is possibly another. Like utility, these goods do not excuse genuine social injustice. Indeed, they are probably unattainable where such injustice prevails. But if "first virtue" is taken to mean the sole and consuming purpose—as it seems to be when truth is characterized as the first virtue of systems of thought—then according justice this status diverts our attention and efforts from the other and nobler goods to which a democratic society can legitimately aspire.

The other crucial ambiguity in Rawls's claim relates to the meaning of the term "justice" itself. When Madison says something that sounds at first blush identical to Rawls's contention, namely that "justice is the end of government," he actually means something quite different and something considerably less ambitious or demanding.[22] "Justice" in his lexicon means the absence of tyranny, which in turn refers to the infringement of natural rights. Political regimes are just when they derive their powers from consent and when they respect the lives, liberties, and estates of their citizenry. Institutionally, justice so understood is achieved, or at least best approximated, by free elections, bills of rights, and countervailing power. For Rawls, in contrast, justice refers to distributive justice—i.e., fairness in the allocation of the benefits and burdens of civil association. Justice so understood would have to be embodied not only in procedural and institutional restrictions on government but also in specific allocative policies bearing upon the distribution of wealth and income, opportunities, educational resources, and the like. For justice to be understood in this more expansive way as the first virtue in either the strong or weak sense, it becomes necessary, of course to suppose or to demonstrate that societies have available to them an unequivocal and determinate standard of substantive distributive justice. Presumably, such a standard would have to be warranted by logical demonstration, near-universal acceptance, or both. Therefore, the possibility of distributive justice being the first virtue of social institutions is contingent upon the success of Rawls's attempts to produce a compelling "moral geometry" or to produce a compelling interpretation of a moral consensus transcending all the various moral disagreements that otherwise mark free and pluralistic societies. And despite Rawls's own best efforts along these lines, it seems clear that there is and can be no such thing as a true moral geometry and that there is not and is never likely to be such a consensus about what a fair and morally proper criterion for the distribution of social goods might be.[23]

Rawls's claims about the primacy of justice, then, can be accepted only with regard to the weaker understandings of both "justice" and "first virtue." It is in fact persuasive to argue, in accord with some widespread and deep moral intuitions, that an essential requisite of a well-ordered society is the protection of its citizens against both private and public tyrannizing. When it comes to a democratic society's distributive rules and arrangements, moreover, these rules and arrangements must be compatible with the postulate of moral and political equity and with the prohibition against arbitrary or partisan mandates which is embodied in the norms of rule of law, equal protection, and due process. Beyond these important but limited constraints, however, the legitimate indeterminacy of what is distributively fair and just must be respected. Room must be left for the reasonable and morally serious disagreements found in almost all societies regarding the competing claims of need, entitlement, and desert.[24] Besides according respect to the internal indeterminacy of standards of distributive justice, moreover, a well-ordered society must also recognize that attempts to eliminate all sources of unfairness—all undeserved inequalities—will unfortunately impinge destructively upon other social practices and relationships that not only have great value to society but also have strong moral standing in their own right. Paramount among these practices and relationships are affiliations of blood and affection, including family ties. Not only are these relationships the source and the natural home of some of Hume's "nobler virtues" such as love and generosity, but a society bereft of the enormous contributions to nurturance, socialization, and economic support made in the context of and as a consequence of these affiliations would surely be in deep trouble.[25]

The strong version of Rawls's stipulation that justice is the first virtue of social institutions, then, cannot be sustained. To insist upon this imperative falsifies our best moral intuitions and creates false hopes about a spontaneous moral consensus that can serve as the basis of social cooperation and comity. It also diverts our attention from other important—perhaps even "nobler"—and morally legitimate social goods that also are worthy of our respect and aspiration. It improperly discredits thoughtful, morally sensitive, and widely held dissenting views about fairness and desert. And it blinds us to some of the tragic conflicts among competing but valid moral imperatives and social goods that require hard choices and compromises rather than the simple imposition of a single preeminent norm.

Contrary to Rawls's claim that his account of democratic ideals is grounded in the "familiar intuitive ideas and principles" and in "the most firmly held considered convictions" of our democratic culture, moreover, his account of the principles of justice and their determinative role in a well-ordered society turns out instead to depend upon significant departures from these traditional and prevalent moral intuitions.[26] Rawls can and does offer arguments in support of his nontraditional (though not idiosyncratic) views in these areas. But his arguments are not likely to prevail. And the departures from more conventional views in these respects not only belie his nonfoundationalist claim to ground his theory in prevalent moral conventions but also create serious political difficulties for those who would base social programs upon them.

These difficulties become apparent in his account of human agency and his normative account of what he calls "a social division of responsibility." These accounts are central to the justification of his democratic ideals, linking as they do what he calls the "moral and political conception of personhood"—which plays an increasingly visible role in his thought—with the principles of justice. Indeed, as Rawls seems clearly to appreciate, he must insist upon his interpretation of what people are and are not to be held accountable for so as to not risk forfeiting his general conception of justice.

In *Political Liberalism*, his most recent book, Rawls argues on behalf of a social division of responsibility that takes the following form: "society . . . accepts responsibility for maintaining the equal basic liberties and fair equality of opportunity, and for providing a fair share of the primary goods for all within this framework; while citizens as individuals and associations accept responsibility for revising and adjusting their ends and aspirations in view of the all-purpose means they can expect, given their present and foreseeable situation."[27] The individual responsibility assigned here to citizens for their "ends and aspirations" is linked by Rawls to one of the two fundamental "moral powers" he attributes to democratic persons—namely, the power to formulate and pursue a plan of life. Rawls expresses this connection in the following way: "given their capacity to assume responsibility for their ends, we do not view citizens as passive carriers of desires. That capacity is part of the moral power to form, to revise, and rationally to pursue a conception of the good."[28] Thus, Rawls continues, "we arrive at the idea that citizens as free and equal are to be at liberty to take charge of their lives and each is expected by others to adapt their conception of the good to their expected fair share of primary goods."[29]

Rawls's democratic citizens are conceived as "taking charge of their lives" only in the fairly narrow and specific sense, however, that they are deemed free to choose a plan of life and to be responsible for their choice. The freedom referred to here, moreover, represents a political entitlement rather than a "metaphysical" capacity: democratic citizens are free in the sense that their society gives them leave to form their own plan of life, but they are not necessarily thereby deemed to be free agents in the usual sense. The freedom and responsibility of Rawlsian citizens, therefore, consists in the political entitlement accorded them to choose their own plan of life without interference or judgment on the part of society and by their being held responsible for that choice by society. Since all plans of life are on principle to be deemed equal by a well-ordered democratic regime, being "held responsible" for their desires/ends/plan of life means in practice not that they are held answerable for that choice by some social authority possessing some standard of what a better or worse choice might be. It means simply that the democratic society, having itself no responsibility for that choice, is under no obligation to make accommodation for differences among particular plans of life in its allocation of benefits and burdens among the different individuals.

On the other hand, Rawls has made it clear from the outset of presenting his theory of justice that democratic citizens are not to be held responsible for their effort or lack of effort, at least in the economic domain. In establishing its operative principles of justice, Rawls insists, a democratic society should disregard as morally irrelevant the level of effort put forth by individuals—including but not limited to the effort put forth in developing one's natural talents. This disregard for effort from the standpoint of justice, Rawls avers, is proper because "the willingness to make an effort, to try, and so to be deserving in the ordinary sense is itself dependent upon happy family and social circumstances."[30] Returning to the same point, he later elaborates: "The assertion that a man deserves the superior character that enables him to make the effort to cultivate his abilities is equally problematic; for his character depends in large part upon fortunate family and social circumstances for which he can claim no credit."[31] Stripped to its essentials, then, Rawls's core argument invokes a determinative causal chain: our effort level is a product of our capacity to exert ourselves, which is a facet of our character, which is in turn a product of external (family and social) circumstances. Our efforts are, then, ultimately the outcome of circumstances or contingencies beyond our control. Hence we should not be held responsible for them.

Now, the notion of effort is very intimately connected with the concept of will, and both of these are in turn deeply implicated in the logical grammar of the verb "to do." That is, to "do" something—as contrasted with merely having something happen to you—implies that the act in question was willed by you. This is a logical connection embodied, for example, in the legal standard of *mens rea*. To have committed a criminal act, the deed in question must have been willed by the perpetrator: he or she must have had "criminal intent." Otherwise, there was only a happening and not a deed; and mere happenings cannot be criminal acts because they cannot really be seen as acts at all. To say, then, that people should not be held accountable for their efforts is logically tantamount to saying that they should not be held accountable for what they "do"—because they did not in the sense relevant to the issue at hand actually "do" anything. Rawls's account of individual responsibility thus winds up holding democratic citizens responsible for their desires/ends/purposes but not for their efforts/deeds.

This view of responsibility creates serious difficulties for Rawls, however. The first of these is an inconsistency between his account of distributive justice and his (much less developed) account of retributive justice. For Rawls tells us that "a prospensity to commit [criminal] acts is a mark of bad character, and in a just society legal punishment will only fall upon those who display these faults."[32] Aware of the clear disjunction between this acceptance of the moral propriety of punishment for criminal acts and his rejection of the moral propriety of a lesser allocation of primary goods to the slothful, Rawls simply asserts that the cases of distributive and retributive justice are "entirely different" and that to think of them "as converses of one another is completely misleading." But it is not at all clear why this is so, and the only reasoning Rawls offers in support of his claim is logically circular: any inequalities in distributive shares, he says, are purely prudential in their warrants; they are justified completely and solely by their functional role in "covering the costs of training and education, attracting individuals to places and associations where they are most needed from a social point of view, and so on."[33] But that rationale for distributive justice simply reiterates his own previous insistence to that effect, an insistence that depended upon the disqualification of preinstitutional moral desert as playing any proper role in distributive justice. And that disqualification was in turn dependent upon the insistence that people are not responsible for their "characters," which are instead a function of "circumstances" beyond their control—an insistence he seems to repudiate in explaining why criminal punishment is proper. Rawls's assurances to the contrary notwithstanding, the complaints of commentators such as Sandel, Honig, and Scheffler that he landed himself in a significant inconsistency problem seem entirely justified.[34]

The core account of personal responsibility or the lack thereof in the context of distributive justice and the model of the "social division of responsibility" also commit Rawls to a very odd moral psychology, a moral psychology that—quite in tension with Rawls's claim that justice as fairness is grounded in the "fundamental intuitive ideas" and "deeper bases of agreement" and is "acceptable to the most firmly held considered convictions" of our culture—clearly clashes with our commonly held fundamental moral intuitions and beliefs about human agency.

By an odd moral psychology, I mean the following. Rawls's account attributes to his democratic citizens a capacity to control and hence a responsibility for their "plan of life" and hence for their desires and ends. It denies, however, that they have (any? much?) capacity to control and hence to be responsible for their actions—given that effort means effective will and effective will is a necessary component of voluntary action and hence for action for which one may coherently be held responsible and given that Rawls attributes the capacity for making an effort to contingent circumstances for which one cannot be held accountable. This pattern of attribution of control over (hence responsibility for) one's desires and denial of control over (hence responsibility for) one's efforts/actions, however, seems to invert the realities of human experience in a very odd way. Most of us, I think, would accord ourselves considerably less capacity to control our desires and ends than to control our efforts. I may understandably feel, for example, that I have relatively little control over my attraction to chocolate ice cream, members of the opposite sex, good foreign films, and a commodious life. Hence I would find it hard to accept responsibility for or to feel guilty about having these desires. I can however, exercise a great deal of control over whether in pursuit of these desires I eat to excess, engage in sexual harassment, attend the cinema to the neglect of my parental duties, or become an embezzler. Hence I do accept a responsibility for avoiding these sins and crimes, and I would feel genuinely guilty if I succumbed to them. But Rawls wants this pattern turned on its head. He would attribute to us a power over our desires and ends, which in our experience are more visited upon us than freely chosen; and he would not attribute to us the capacity to exercise control over the actions we take on behalf of attaining (or restraining) those desires. To the extent that his account of responsibility rests upon this odd account of human capacities and desires—and, to the extent that "ought implies can," it does rest upon it—that account becomes very precarious.

It is, moreover, important to appreciate how essential this odd moral psychology and this problematic account of responsibility are to Rawls's overall theory and core purposes—how deeply committed he must be to these accounts as a matter of logic. Even relatively knowledgeable students of Rawls at times seem unable to understand that Rawls cannot relinquish his commitment to these claims without abandoning some of his most cherished prescriptive claims and putative philosophical accomplishments. One anonymous reviewer of an earlier version of this chapter, for example, wrote: "To my knowledge it is true that Rawls never repudiates his view of moral responsibility in *A Theory of Justice*. But the implications the author draws are overblown. Surely, Rawls's claim that people are not morally responsible for their ability to work hard, as they are not responsible for the fact that their family is wealthy or well-positioned, is limited to exceptional circumstances." Against any such protestation it must be insisted that it is not accidental but imperative for the maintenance of his central argument that Rawls has never repudiated the account of responsibility he provides in *A Theory of Justice*; and the claim that people are not morally responsible for their ability to work hard, so far from being "limited to exceptional circumstances," must be the rule.

Rawls must affirm as the rule and not as an exception his account of responsibility as set out here because if he does not do so the "moral geometry" that produces his general conception of social justice collapses. His version of the "social division of responsibility" provides an essential barrier to claims which could otherwise be made on behalf of the moral propriety and perhaps even the moral obligatoriness of unequal proportional shares of resources. And if such claims have merit, the carefully constructed rational choice logic so basic to his argument simply falls apart. That Rawls himself understands this intimate connection between his specific attributions (and exculpations) of responsibility and his principles of justice is made very clear by the way that he directly follows his conclusions regarding both halves of his social division of responsibility with the pertinent implications for distributive norms. Both where Rawls attributes responsibility to individuals and where he denies it, he immediately follows these claims with prescriptive lessons. The sentence that follows Rawls's contention that "citizens have some part in forming and cultivating their final ends and preferences" is: "Hence it is not by itself an objection to the use of primary goods that an index does not accommodate those with unusual or expensive tastes."[35] Elsewhere he makes this linkage within a single sentence: "This division of responsibility relies on the capacity of persons to assume responsibility for their ends and to moderate the claims they make on their social institutions accordingly."[36] In short, individuals are assigned responsibility for choosing their ends and desires in order that they may invoke neither the unusual expensiveness of their tastes nor the unusual strength and zealousness of their feelings and aspirations to claim a proportionately greater share of social resources. In the same way, Rawls's denial of individual responsibility for one's effort level is immediately invoked to defeat claims from a different quarter (i.e., on the basis of differential merit) for a larger share of social goods. He directly follows his contention that effort depends upon "family and social circumstances" with the normative inference that "the notion of desert seems not to apply to these cases. Thus the more advantaged representative man cannot say that he deserves and therefore has a right to a scheme of cooperation in which he is permitted to acquire benefits in ways that do not contribute to the welfare of others. There is no basis for making this claim."[37]

It is not entirely clear whether Rawls's account of responsibility is driven by or predicated upon what Scheffler calls "philosophical naturalism"—i.e., a profoundly deterministic set of assumptions about the causes of human behavior— or whether it is instead directly and wholly generated by a moral passion for a more equal distribution of social resources than that enforced by most societies, including our own.[38] Either way, the results are the same. His account of responsibility, as William Galston writes, "severs the link between what we do and what we deserve" and generates a "conception of free and equal moral personality [that] diverges radically from [the broadly consensual] American understanding of freedom and equality and leads to principles of justice significantly different from those most Americans embrace."[39] Moreover, Galston continues, "there is little evidence to support—and much to refute—Rawls's hope that his conception of personality will prove acceptable to us once its implications are fully grasped. Yet his 'constructivist' metatheory leaves him no other grounds of persuasion or verification."[40]

Strictly in formal terms, then, Rawls's argument leads him to an impasse. His hermeneutic turn—his antifoundationalist appeal to dominant conventions and general consensus—seems clearly unable to sustain and provide warrants for his core substantive claims about democratic persons and social justice. Moreover, this disjunction between his theory of justice and the actual dominant moral intuitions in American and other democratic cultures causes political difficulties for those who espouse his views along with their attendant policy implications. As Galston hypothesizes, the political consequences of this disjunction "are mirrored in the national electoral disasters of contemporary liberalism."[41] And at a deeper level still, the problematic aspects of his account of personhood and social responsibility arguably threaten the moral basis of the democratic commitment to equality and undermine his own cherished social goal of a society in which citizens are disposed to share one another's fate.

These problems arise from the logical impact of his doctrine of responsibility upon the crucial norm of respect for persons—an impact that can, perhaps, best be appreciated by juxtaposing Rawls with a figure he ostensibly takes as a source of inspiration and illumination, namely Kant. As is turns out, Rawls's claims about responsibility place him at odds with Kant in one important respect, even as he adopts a Kantian perspective in other contexts. Methodologically, Rawls embraces what he calls "Kantian constructivism." Morally, he pledges his allegiance to the Kantian maxim. His anthropology, however, offers a more mixed outcome vis-à-vis Kantian doctrine. Because Rawls's self—i.e., the democratic person—is accorded responsibility for choosing his or her ends, that self is, like the Kantian practical ego, a radically self-defining agent. This is the aspect of Rawls's account that leads Sandel to implicate him in an alleged adherence to a conception of "unencumbered" selfhood—a self that exists prior to ends and purposes which it subsequently "chooses." And, regardless of whether Rawls has any metaphysical commitment to such a conception, his political conception of the democratic person/citizen/self continues to embody this pattern. Thus, Sandel's account of Rawls's anthropology as Kantian "deontology with a Humean face" remains an apt characterization of his anthropology in this respect, even if it applies only on the political plane and has no metaphysical import. [42]

In another respect, however, Rawls's anthropology is more Benthamite than Kantian. His skeptical/neutralist doctrine of the human good recalls Bentham's insistence that pushpin is as good as poetry: combing blades of grass, at least, is depicted as on a moral par with more poetic pursuits. And, what is more directly pertinent here, the depiction of democratic persons as not to be held responsible for their efforts/actions mimics Bentham's rejection of the reality or at least the significance of human freedom: call them robots if you like, Bentham said of the citizenry of his utilitarian republic, I don't care—so long as they be happy. This part of Rawls's doctrine of responsibility and the heavily deterministic account of human behavior he offers in its defense stand in stark contrast to Kant's ideas on the same subject—and to Rousseau's account of freedom and responsibility that Kant took as his inspiration.

We should recall that, in his quest to identify those attributes which distinguish human beings from (other) animals, Rousseau reached the following conclusion: "it is not so much the understanding that constitutes the specific difference between the man and the brute, as the human quality of free agency. Nature lays her commands on every animal, and the brute obeys her voice. Man receives the same impulsion, but at the same time knows himself at liberty to acquiesce or resist: and it is particularly in his consciousness of this liberty that the spirituality of his soul is displayed."[43] Kant took this claim and thematized it in his account of morality and practical reason. He argued that human beings are unique—and, uniquely, creatures subject to moral tension—because they dwell both in the world of sense (phenomena) and in the world of intelligence (noumena). And it is precisely this latter membership in the noumenal domain—i.e., the status of having a will, being free, not being entirely subject to the mechanism of nature—that gives human beings their moral dignity, their membership in the kingdom of ends, and hence their entitlement to be treated with respect—i.e., as ends-in-themselves, as proper objects for protection by the categorical imperative. Because he makes his democratic citizens responsible for choosing their ends, Rawls avoids falling into Bentham's authoritarian willingness to *make* people happy, exemplified by his infatuation with his Panopticon. But Rawls nonetheless leaves himself with a serious problem of a different order. He wants his well-ordered society to obey the Kantian maxim, and he features his own obeisance to it, but he has jettisoned what Kant presumed to be its basis: respect for the status of a free will that accepts responsibility for actions. Like Bentham and Kant, Rawls treats citizens as moral equals. Unlike Bentham, he accords them integrity as separate beings. Unlike Kant, he does not hold them responsible for their actions and—at least if the justification he offers for this stance is taken seriously—he does not consider them possessed of free agency in the Kantian sense but instead sees them as governed by what Rousseau called the mechanism of nature.

One very important question presented by Rawls's attempt to retain the Kantian maxim while abandoning its grounds is a political, not metaphysical, one. Namely, how would this doctrine play out in a society governed by it? That is, what would happen in a society governed in accordance with Rawls's principles of justice—principles that demand that citizens share one another's fate while they are answerable for what they want but not for what they do pursuant to these wants? For it would seem impossible that this premise regarding the "social division of responsibility" could be suppressed, like some noble lie, from public view. That doctrine would have to be invoked in response to any citizen who challenged the propriety of equal outcomes for unequal effort and argued instead for some form of proportional justice. In short, the claim that people should not be held responsible for their effort level—or for the character that purportedly determined it—would have to function in the public discourse of what he calls the well-ordered society in exactly the same way that it functions in Rawls's own argument.

This is clearly a speculative question, but I would nonetheless hazard a guess that the likely outcome would not be to Rawls's liking. My experience with human moral behavior leads me to conjecture that this attempt would lead to the discovery of another practical paradox embedded in a normative social scheme that insists upon being deontological, egalitarian, and political (in Rawls's sense) simultaneously. The practical paradox is that an acceptance of Rawls's doctrine of responsibility would weaken the acceptance of the very principles it was devised to sustain. Simply put, people who were convinced by the (Rawlsian) contention that their fellow citizens were beings of the sort not to be held responsible for their efforts would be for that very reason disinclined to feel themselves morally obligated to share their fate. Why am I, an autonomous moral agent in Kant's sense and therefore willing to stand responsible for what I do, under an obligation to share the fate of fellow citizens (would that appellation cogently apply, even, in this case?) who are, in contrast, a different order of creature—ones whose actions are governed by the mechanism of nature? Indeed, how *could* I do so? How could I bridge the ontological gap that separates noumenal from phenomenal existence in order to accomplish this feat? I could, of course, in accord with the difference principle less poetically construed, simply cough up the requisite share of my primary goods. But even here my willingness to do so would be compromised. I would be sharing from a sense of compassion for suffering animals, as it were (recalling both Rousseau's account of natural pity and his account of free agency as the defining difference between humans and brutes), not from a sense of respect. And the measure of pity, unlike that of respect, is not likely to be equality.[44]

This speculative thought experiment supposes, of course, that I continue to experience myself as responsible for my own efforts and actions. Theoretically, I might, however—and probably logically should—construe not only my fellow citizens but myself as not so responsible. Rawls's case is made no easier by this change, however. Indeed, it is not at all clear that anyone can coherently so conceive oneself and simultaneously ponder what he or she is morally obligated to do. As Kant recognized, any being without some element of free will—any being who does not "know himself at liberty to acquiesce or resist" natural impulses, as Rousseau put it—cannot coherently be considered subject to moral obligation at all. Hence it becomes entirely opaque what the likely consequence of such a self-conception would be vis-a-vis one's fellow citizens. In any case, it seems impossible to provide a cogent argument on these premises that the logical outcome would be a disposition, whether for moral or psychological reasons, to share one another's fate.

Additional difficulties arise from one of the important corollaries of Rawls's central argument: his claim that all the natural talents of people in a well-ordered society should be regarded as assets to be held in common by everyone. All the personal abilities, capacities, and attributes which we have as individuals and which function as productive resources are not in Rawls's view to be considered as properly belonging to us as individuals. Our energies, intelligence, artistic skills, athletic abilities, strength, beauty, and so on—all the fungible traits that make up our unique and distinctive selves—are to be seen as belonging equally and indifferently to the whole body of citizens. Or, to be more specific, the fruits of these capacities and attributes are in moral terms to be conceived as having the same status Locke accorded to things of the earth: they are "given . . . to men in common." As Rawls says, his principles of justice represent "an agreement to regard the distribution of natural talents as a common asset and to share in the benefits of this distribution whatever it turns out to be."[45]

Rawls justifies his claim that our natural talents should be regarded as common assets by invoking his basic position that morally arbitrary inequalities should be mitigated. Our natural talents are gifts. We did nothing to deserve them, but received them as free bounty from God or nature. And our gifts are not equal. In many cases, indeed, they are radically different in their value. Our possession of them therefore not only lacks moral purchase but is morally problematic: it embodies undeserved inequalities, and such inequalities are unfair. A society with a sense of justice will therefore seek to eliminate so far as possible the effects of these morally arbitrary inequalities. And it can do so by appropriating their fruits as common assets and distributing them in accordance with criteria of justice instead of in accordance with the capriciousness of nature.

This argument is the functional equivalent but substantive opposite of the standard libertarian doctrine of self-ownership. Alas, like the libertarian argument, Rawls's argument falls short. Like the argument on behalf of self-ownership, the argument for treating natural talents as common assets is logically incomplete. And, again like the libertarian argument, the common asset claim contravenes or ignores other important moral considerations.

The logical inadequacy of Rawls's argument is that the conclusion—treat natural talents as a common asset—does not follow from the largely incontestable insistence that the de facto unequal distribution of natural talents is morally arbitrary. (I say largely rather than wholly incontestable because one can certainly conceive of a theological argument that could function not so much to deny as to override Rawls's point. That is, without trying to claim that people deserve their different and unequal natural capacities, a believer could nonetheless argue that these disparities are divinely ordained—that God desires and legitimates difference and that they, however undeserved, carry moral weight. The biblical parable of the talents, for example, takes for granted and offers no moral objection to God's unequal allocation to his servants. They are not considered to have any grounds to complain about the relative level of their assets, which they received as a gift. Instead, they are deemed to be under an obligation to make the most of the unequal endowments they received.) A libertarian like Nozick, for example, freely concedes that our natural capacities are undeserved. But he denies that they therefore should be appropriated from us as individuals and relegated to a common pool of resources. After all, nobody else can claim to deserve the talents either. The question is: what is the proper default position in the case of undeserved goods? Libertarians say that rights are trump, that the arbitrary distribution violated no one's rights, and that possession should therefore be the law. Rawls opts instead for "fairness," saying that in the absence of a case for individual desert equality should be the rule. But this latter claim is by no means incontestable. It does not embody a strong positive argument for the recommended allocation, but is rather an argument for what the proper default position is in the absence of any strong positive argument for any particular allocation.

In the absence of relevant competing moral considerations, Rawls's argument for common ownership based on "fairness" might well be compelling. The difficulty is that he ignores at least one very strong competing moral consideration that works against his preferred outcome—namely, the moral imperative to respect the integrity of persons. Indeed, the case can be made that although Rawls makes good upon utilitarianism's failure to "take seriously the distinction between persons," he himself fails to take seriously the integrity of persons.[46] Integrity here means a combination of two things: wholeness and inviolability. Or, to put it more precisely, Rawls respects the inviolability of persons but not their wholeness; and he thus winds up respecting the inviolability only of philosophically abstract "persons" but not that of real-world whole persons, who are constituted by and inextricably related to the very traits and capacities Rawls would detach from their control and throw into a pool of common assets. Despite the unpersuasiveness of his own strong doctrine of individual entitlement or self-ownership, Nozick is on target here in his pointed demurral to Rawls's contention that his principles of justice conform to the Kantian injunction (expressed in the categorical imperative) never to treat anyone as a means to someone else's welfare. That is so, Nozick observes, "only if one presses *very* hard on the distinction between men and their talents, assets, abilities, and special traits. Whether any coherent conception of a person remains when the distinction is so pressed is an open question. Why we, thick with particular traits, should be cheered that (only) the thus purified men within us are not regarded as means is also unclear."[47] Libertarian claims about self-ownership fail because they are blind to the many profound obligations we all incur in the process of becoming a self in the first place. But Rawls's claims about collective assets fail because he loses sight of the necessary conditions of personal integrity. His fixation upon the remediation of everything morally arbitrary leads him astray. For the fact is that in our gratuitously created world the very existence of persons is morally arbitrary. As a consequence, we cannot delegitimate everything morally arbitrary without paradoxically eliminating a major premise underlying the very notion of morality itself.

Rawls's aspirations to build upon our sense of justice alone a democratic society whose members feel both obligated and motivated to share one another's fate are, for the several reasons canvassed above, doomed to disappointment. His account of justice as fairness is ultimately based upon his fundamental intuition that no one deserves to have more than anyone else because no one really deserves anything. But this intuition and the important implications that flow from it are highly contestable, are not likely to have widespread political appeal, would not necessarily compel all who accredit them to behave in the way Rawls would like, and carry unsettling consequences for other deeply held and widely shared moral convictions regarding human agency and personal integrity.

The problems of taking Rawls's theory of justice to be the basis for a more egalitarian democratic society, are further compounded by Rawls's attempt to deflect us from trying to shore up what would seem to be the most promising alternative foundation for such a society—namely, a robust sense of community or civic friendship. Older versions of democratic theory embraced "fraternity" as a democratic ideal and—rightly, in my view—saw the sense of solidarity they sought not only as valuable in itself but also as an important impetus to greater equality. But Rawls would cut the props from under such an enterprise and its attendant hopes in two ways. First, he unnecessarily and unconvincingly disparages as chimerical any attempts to build into a well-ordered society any sense of common purpose or common identity that would transcend a common devotion to abstract equity. Second, he consequently truncates the classic meaning of fraternity, depriving it of its capacity to animate social cooperation and mutual assistance.

"A well ordered democratic society" Rawls tells us, "is neither a community nor an association."[48] By the term "community" Rawls here designates "a special kind of association, one united by a comprehensive doctrine, for example, a church."[49] Thus "community" functions for him as a term of art, one that is situated within his account of the nature and functions of "comprehensive moral and religious doctrines." Comprehensive doctrines are all-inclusive accounts of the meaning and purpose of human life. Hence, it is essentially a truism, i.e., true by definition, that any pluralistic society—one that encompasses citizens adhering to different religious persuasions or other comparable moral beliefs—cannot be a community. A church, then, as Rawls says, would be an example of a community. But to say it is merely an example is a bit misleading, for *only* a society that functioned intellectually, morally, and sociologically as a church would be a "community" in Rawls's specific and rarified sense of that term. In any case, once it is understood what Rawls means by "community," it is not controversial that a democratic society cannot be a community.

The more problematic and important claim is that a well-ordered democratic society cannot even be an "association." In contrast with the members of a community, who are united by allegiance to a common comprehensive doctrine, Rawls tells us, "members of other associations often have shared ends but these do not make up a comprehensive doctrine and may even be purely instrumental."[50] So why can even a pluralistic democratic society not function as an association of this sort, with such limited shared ends? Rawls's answer is very cryptic, rather opaque, and seems to rely upon a failure to respect his own definition of an association. He tells us that "there are two differences between a democratic society and an association." The first difference is that "a democratic society, like any political society, is to be viewed as a complete and closed social system." It is "closed" in the sense that we join associations but are born into a society. And it is "complete in that it is self-sufficient and has a place for all the main purposes of human life." The second difference is that a democratic society "has no final ends and aims in the way that persons or association do. Here by ends and aims I mean those that have a special place in comprehensive doctrines."[51]

Neither of these distinctions seems persuasive. It is not at all clear that a democratic society is properly seen as a "complete" social system, one that "is self-sufficient and has a place for all the main purposes of human life." If the verb "has" here is taken to mean "provides," then the democratic society would seem to turn into a community. If "has" means instead "leaves a place for"—as in a protected and private domain beyond the purview of the society—then it would not seem to be "complete" in any sense that necessarily distinguishes the society from an association. Either way, Rawls loses: a democratic society is not a form of organization necessarily distinct in principle from both a community and an association. The alleged second difference is equally unavailing. A democratic society is held to be different from an association because it "has no final ends and aims in the way that . . . associations do." But this contrast seems to violate Rawls's own distinction between an association and a community: he says that these final ends and aims which characterize an association but not a democratic society are "those that have a special place in comprehensive doctrines," but this seems inconsistent with his stipulation that in an association these shared ends "do *not* make up a comprehensive doctrine and may even be purely instrumental." Unless there is some convincing and pertinent meaning to the phrase "special place" in this formulation—one that Rawls does not provide and that I cannot imagine— this argument falls apart. Associations cannot be distinguished from a democratic society by the alleged constitutive *presence* within them of "final ends" tied to comprehensive doctrines and then distinguished from communities by the alleged *absence* of such ends.[52]

So bereft of the shared ends that characterize a community or association, Rawls's democratic society is deprived of a principal basis for and impetus toward "fraternity" or civic friendship. Rawls does not want to banish fraternity completely as an element of his well-ordered society. But because he limits the society's grounds of social cohesion to self-interested prudence together with a general commitment to abstract fairness, his conception of democratic civic friendship necessarily becomes itself very diluted and abstract. He offers us as citizens of a modern democratic society only the prospect of a very impersonal form of civic friendship, one essentially devoid of affectivity and one whose vitality seems questionable.

"The ideal of fraternity," Rawls writes, "is sometimes thought to involve ties of sentiment and feeling which it is unrealistic to expect between members of the wider society. And this is surely a further reason for its relative neglect in democratic theory. Many have felt that it has no proper place in political affairs. But if it is interpreted as incorporating the requirements of the difference principle, it is not an impracticable conception."[53] (Despite the use of the passive voice it seems clear from his account of the nature of pluralism and the functions of comprehensive moral doctrines that Rawls shares the skepticism expressed in the first sentence.) Insofar as it can be made a plausible ideal for contemporary democratic societies, then, fraternity "corresponds . . . to the difference principle" and finds its expression in the "definite requirements" that principle imposes on the basic structure of society.[54]

This attempt to transform the idea of fraternity and thus to assimilate it to his theory of justice and to his account of the dynamics of a well-ordered society, however, creates some serious difficulties—not only for a robust understanding of democratic ideals but also for Rawls's own aspirations. Purging the idea of fraternity of its affective features—the "ties of sentiment and feeling"—as "unrealistic" is not to tinker with the periphery of fraternity but to strike at its heart. Affection, good will, and mutual understanding are not mere accidents of civic friendship but its essence. To say that Rawls's understanding of fraternity is truncated, then, is an understatement of the first order.

In a later chapter, I try to make the case that a more traditional conception of fraternity remains a possibility and constitutes a very important resource even for pluralistic democracies. Here, however, the pertinent point is that Rawls's revisionist and skeptical account of democratic fraternity renders it useless for his own central aspirations: unlike the traditional understanding, his account leaves nothing there to serve as a stimulus to the willingness of citizens to behave as though they shared one another's fate. The key question here is: What inclines, encourages, or motivates people to accept a redistributive precept such as the difference principle in the first place? In response to this sociological and causal question, to say that fraternity "corresponds to" the difference principle is useless and circular. As analysts of friendship from Aristotle onward have observed, friendship has as one of its most significant consequences a tendency to empathize with each other and to offer needed assistance. But when fraternity is reduced to being the abstract correlate of a rule mandating such assistance, there is nothing left to it to cause these consequences in the first place. An important empirical dynamic of cause and consequence has been reduced by Rawls to a purely theoretical and causally impotent structural parallelism.

Rawls thus weakens rather than bolsters the chances in the real world that democratic citizens will be inclined to believe and to act as though they shared each other's fate. His purely formalistic conception of fraternity damages the prospects for achieving what he would endorse as a well-ordered society. Rawls must insist that his citizens will be moved to accept the difference principle through their purely rational apprehension of their duties consequent upon a logically compelling notion of formal equity. Their abstract sense of justice will provide all the impetus they need. But this is a very fragile and somewhat wistful expectation, one he is left clinging to in the absence of the fraternal sympathies and motivations whose basis he has undermined. In falling into this difficulty, Rawls experiences one of his most genuinely Kantian moments. He replicates here in politics the same dilemma that Kant created for himself in trying to give a convincing account of moral action. For as Kant recognized, one of his greatest difficulties was to make plausible "how pure reason can be practical of itself without the aid of any impulse to action . . . that is, how it can supply an impulse of itself without any object of the will in which one could antecedently take any original interest." As he conceded, "all this is beyond the power of human reason to explain." And as he recognized, the resultant danger is that reason may "impotently raise its wings in the empty space of transcendent concepts . . . without being able to move and so lose itself amidst chimeras."[55] For Kant, the disturbing prospect of the possible failure of his principles to succeed in moving the human will was that our moral sensibility would collapse back into the "lax and even low habit of thought" exemplified by Hume's identification of the human good with the useful and agreeable. For Rawls, the disturbing prospect of the potential inability of his ideal of fairness to determine the will on its own recognizance is that our democratic society will devolve into the contractual collaboration of mutually disinterested strangers who pursue their individual interests without sharing one another's fate. And this, I would argue, is a very real threat. Just as one could say that Kant's stringent dismissal of all heteronmous emotive resources (e.g., Aristotelian happiness, Platonic *eros*, or Christian charity) that transcend mere utility may have played into the hands of latter day Humeans, so Rawls's dismissal of the fraternal sentiments and feelings that can impel people to share one another's fate may play into the hands of the libertarians. Only time will tell, I suppose. But the impact of Rawlsian ideas upon the electoral fortunes of the Democratic Party together with the conclusions my students are inclined to draw from their disaffection with Rawls's argument give me little cause for optimism.

Conclusion

Rawls's highly influential reading of democratic ideals has many important virtues. Many of his moral intuitions and his insights into the requisites of a well-ordered society warrant our appreciation and should be incorporated into any persuasive account of liberal purposes. His account of what he calls a political liberalism organized around a consensus upon principles of distributive justice, however, also exhibits serious weaknesses whose acceptance would distort and damage the democratic enterprise—even detracting from the prospects of some of Rawls's own most basic hopes.

On the positive side of the ledger, Rawls rightly insists that liberal democracies have always been and need to remain fundamentally moral enterprises. They are not and cannot happily become mere pacts of convenience and prudence narrowly defined. He properly insists that these moral foundations cannot be limited to the protection of rights conceived as the simple prohibition of boundary crossings—that in that direction comes a common life reduced to what both Aristotle and Mill analogized to animals grazing side by side, a society less capable of cooperative endeavor than it needs to be or than is good for its stability and productivity. He reminds us that democratic citizens need to have some sense of working together for their common benefit and that we should shape our institutions and policies accordingly. He properly insists that the utilitarian calculus gives us an inadequate reading of this common benefit because it fails to take our separateness as distinct persons seriously. He rightly, if by no means uniquely, cautions us that pluralist democracies cannot install as orthodoxy any single comprehensive moral doctrine. He beckons us to recognize that citizens in a well-ordered society need to exhibit political virtues of civility, fairness, and tolerance—and that they owe their fellow citizens reasoned justification for their contestable political pursuits. He reminds us that many inequalities and misfortunes result from arbitrary causes, that a decent society should therefore seek to miti-gate the resulting social and economic disparities, and that a society committed to democratic norms must above all keep these disparities from turning some of its members into subjects rather than citizens of equal standing.

These virtues conceded, Rawls's account of the purposes, ideals, and governing principles of a liberal democratic society is nonetheless inadequate and in some respects counterproductive. He narrows and distorts the full range of democratic ideals that should have purchase on us. By stipulating that justice is the "first virtue" in a strong sense, Rawls loses sight of the other and arguably more noble virtues to which a well-ordered society should aspire. His questionable exegesis of the moral intuitions informing liberal constitutionalism brings him to offer the false and misleading hope that a single and determinate conception of distributive justice can play the central and decisive role in a democratic overlapping consen-sus. In seeking to undermine all claims of proportional justice, Rawls is driven to promulgate and endorse a constricted and reductive account of moral selfhood and democratic persons. He espouses a dangerously diminished conception of human agency and accountability, one whose wider ramifications are highly problematic for the normal expectations imposed upon civilized adults—not to mention democratic citizens. In so doing, he seriously attenuates the traditional basis of our beliefs in human dignity and endangers the norm of respect entailed by these beliefs. He loosens inhibitions against the violation of personal integrity by objectifying and externalizing constituent parts of us under the rubric of "as-sets" and by depicting their alienation as morally unproblematic. He exaggerates the incommensurability and the completeness of comprehensive moral doctrines and as a consequence unpersuasively and unhelpfully denies the capacity of a democratic society to function as an association of associations.[56] The same logic leads him to denigrate and cast aside possibilities for encouraging the linea-ments of civic friendship that are extremely conducive and possibly even neces-sary to the success of democratic regimes.

For all of its contributions, its insights, and its morally sensitive awareness of the contingencies that produce unfair disparities in people's lives and threaten the best hopes of a democratic society, Rawls's version of liberalism does not provide us a fully satisfactory account of democratic ideals. Its reading of the moral intu-itions informing the democratic project is in important respects simply inaccu-rate—both as intellectual history and as an interpretation of the philosophical assumptions presupposed by the institutions of contemporary liberal democratic constitutionalism. Its aspirations to achieve a moral geometry are delusionary. Its account of the overlapping consensus of a democratic society is faulty, both in what it includes and what it excludes. It compromises the integrity and autonomy of democratic citizens. It neglects and disparages the cultivation of civic friend-ship transcending the fault lines of a pluralist society. And it thereby paradoxically undermines some of the most important beliefs and social resources that conduce to greater civic equality.

Those who, like Rawls, would encourage us to build a democratic society in which citizens genuinely share one another's fate need to do better than this. We should embrace the commitment to greater civic equality and the hopes for mutuality of concern that have animated Rawls's imaginative attempt to recast and revitalize democratic theory. But we need to situate these aspirations within a framework that affirms rather than undermines other moral intuitions and hopes needed to sustain democracy at its best. For it is difficult to imagine a society of self-governing equal citizens and vibrant communities absent widespread belief in the autonomy and responsible agency of our fellow citizens, profound respect for personal integrity, and a commitment to join together in common endeavor on behalf of common goods.

Notes

1. John Rawls, "Justice as Fairness: Political Not Metaphysical," *Philosophy and Public Affairs* 14, no. 3 (Summer 1985): 225.

2. John Rawls, *A Theory of Justice* (Cambridge: Harvard University Press, 1971), 27.

3. Rawls, *Theory of Justice*, 26.

4. Rawls, *Theory of Justice*, 30.

5. Rawls, *Theory of Justice*, 40.

6. John Rawls, *Political Liberalism* (New York: Columbia University Press, 1993), 148.

7. John Rawls, *Political Liberalism*, 37.

8. Rawls, *Theory of Justice*, 3.

9. Rawls, *Theory of Justice*, viii.

10. Rawls, *Theory of Justice*, 62.

11. Rawls, *Theory of Justice*, 83.

12. Rawls writes that "the difference principle is a strongly egalitarian conception" (*Theory of Justice*, 76). Because Rawls's ideal democracy would tolerate those inequalities that improved the absolute welfare of the least well-off and would not concern itself with anyone's relative standing, some rigorous egalitarians challenge this self-characterization. One reviewer of an article I once wrote chided me, for example, for "confusion arising from the [idea] that the difference principle is an egalitarian principle when, in reality it is compatible with the status quo of present liberal societies." I leave it to the reader's judgment whether the current distribution of wealth and opportunity in contemporary liberal societies squares with the dictates of the difference principle (the stipulation that distributions should be determined by what most benefits the absolute welfare of the least well-off), but I find that claim extremely dubious. As for the question of principle, Rawls would argue—I believe correctly—that his conception of justice mandates as much equality as a moral argument can mandate without giving moral accreditation to envy. (See, e.g., *Theory of Justice*, 530ff. and 143–44.)

13. Rawls, "Justice as Fairness," 225–26.

14. Rawls, *Theory of Justice*, 102.

15. I won't try to cite all of the relevant literature here, since it now encompasses, as one writer has aptly said, a whole cottage industry. Some of the more helpful insights, however, have come from the following sources, which represent a wide range of perspectives in terms of their own constructive democratic ideals: Michael Sandel, *Liberalism and the Limits of Justice* (Cambridge: Cambridge University Press, 1982); William Galston, *Liberal Purposes* (Cambridge: Cambridge University Press, 1991), esp. chapters 6 and 7; Nozick, *Anarchy, State, and Utopia*, esp. chapter 7; Ronald Beiner, *What's the Matter with Liberal-*

ism? (Berkeley: University of California Press, 1992), esp. part two; Bonnie Honig, *Political Theory and the Displacement of Politics* (Ithaca: Cornell University Press, 1993), esp. chapter 5; Roberto Alejandro, "What Is Political about Rawls's Political Liberalism?" *The Journal of Politics* 58, no. 1 (February 1996): 1–24; Samuel Scheffler, "Responsibility, Reactive Attitudes, and Liberalism in Philosophy and Politics," *Philosophy and Public Affairs* 21, no. 4 (Fall 1992): 300–314.

16. Rawls, *Theory of Justice*, 3.

17. Rawls, *Theory of Justice*, 570.

18. Rawls, *Theory of Justice*, 571.

19. Rawls, *Theory of Justice*, 574–75

20. Regarding the theory of justice as fairness, he writes, "no particular metaphysical doctrine about the nature of persons, distinctive and opposed to other metaphysical doctrines, appears among its premises." "Justice as Fairness," 240n.

21. Rawls, *Theory of Justice*, 3.

22. Madison, *Federalist Papers* 51.

23. The grounds for this rather preemptory judgment can be found in my article "The Antinomies of Social Justice," *The Review of Politics* 55, no. 2 (Spring 1993): 193–216 and in some of the reservations about Rawls's argument canvassed later in this chapter. The doubts about the presence or possibility of a genuine "overlapping consensus" regarding substantive criteria of distributive justice can be grounded in even rather cursory observations of real-world political disputes or in the results of any relevant survey of public opinion. Concerning the latter, see also the results—which cause her some dismay—of Jennifer Hochschild's interviews regarding *What's Fair? American Beliefs about Distributive Justice* (Cambridge: Harvard University Press, 1981).

24. For a thoughtful and persuasive argument along those lines, see Galston, *Liberal Purposes*, chapter 9.

25. For an extended essay that brings home the practical and moral dilemmas entailed by some of these facts of life and competing goods, see James Fishkin, *Justice, Equal Opportunity and the Family* (New Haven: Yale University Press, 1983).

26. Rawls, "Justice as Fairness," 229.

27. Rawls, *Political Liberalism*, 189.

28. Rawls, *Political Liberalism*, 186.

29. Rawls, *Political Liberalism*, 189–90.

30. Rawls, *Theory of Justice*, 74.

31. Rawls, *Theory of Justice*, 104.

32. Rawls, *Theory of Justice*, 315.

33. Rawls, *Theory of Justice*, 315.

34. See Sandel, *Liberalism and the Limits of Justice*, 89–91; Honig, *Political Theory and the Displacement of Politics*, 139; Scheffler, "Responsibility, Reactive Attitudes, and Liberalism," 312, n. 7.

35. Rawls, *Political Liberalism*, 186.

36. Rawls, *Political Liberalism*, 189.

37. Rawls, *Theory of Justice*, 104.

38. Scheffler argues that "the unwillingness of liberal philosophers to rely on any pre-institutional conception of desert is due in part to their internalization of a broadly naturalistic outlook, and to their skeptical understanding of how robust a notion of individual agency is compatible with such an outlook." "Responsibility, Reactive Attitudes, and Liberalism," 309.

39. Galston, *Liberal Purposes*, 160.

40. Galston, *Liberal Purposes*, 161.

41. Galston, *Liberal Purposes*, 162.

42. Sandel, *Liberalism and the Limits of Justice*, 14.

43. Rousseau, "A Discourse on the Origin of Inequality," in *The Social Contract and Discourses*, translated by G. D. N. Cole (New York: Dutton, 1950), 208.

44. Some people notoriously care more for their pets than they do for most other human beings, of course. So perhaps those conceived as being less than fully human responsible agents would be treated generously. Even pampered domestic animals are not treated as objects of equal respect, however. So I would not want to hazard wagering the welfare of the disadvantaged solely upon compassion for their suffering.

45. Rawls, *Theory of Justice*, 101.

46. Rawls, *Theory of Justice*, 27.

47. Nozick, *Anarchy, State, and Utopia*, 228.

48. Rawls, *Political Liberalism*, 40.

49. Rawls, *Political Liberalism*, 40, n. 43.

50. Rawls, *Political Liberalism*, 40, n. 43.

51. Rawls, *Political Liberalism*, 40–41.

52. Once again, perhaps, Rawls is driven into making a questionable argument because of his overriding concern with protecting the difference principle. For he follows his denial that a democratic society can be an association with the following moral: "This means that citizens do not think there are antecedent social ends that justify them in viewing some people as having more or less than others and assigning them different basic rights and privileges accordingly." (*Political Liberalism*, 41). To which three rejoinders can be made: (1) the members of all societies think some of their number are worth more than others to their enterprise—that's what honors such as the Congressional Medal of Honor or admission to the French Academy are all about; (2) that judgment need not entail assigning people different basic rights and privileges; (3) refusing to acknowledge the associational features of a democratic society may accord theoretical protection to the difference principle, but the practical effect of purging from a society any sense of shared ends would be destructive of one of the principal motivational bases for its citizens to believe and act as though they shared one another's fate.

53. Rawls, *Theory of Justice*, 106.

54. Rawls, *Theory of Justice*, 106.

55. Immanuel Kant, "Metaphysical Foundations of Morals," in *The Philosophy of Kant*, ed. Carl Friedrich (New York: Random House, 1949), 206–7. Kant ultimately pinned his hopes in this context on the ability of the "magnificent ideal of a universal realm of ends in themselves (of rational beings)" to produce in us "a lively interest in the moral law" ("Metaphysic of Morals," 207). Rawls might conceivably argue the same thing on behalf of this ideal of a well-ordered society of democratic persons. Rawls has a problem here, however, that can compromise this neo-Kantian hopefulness—namely that many morally sensitive readers/citizens have not found his construction of democratic personhood, with its contestable boundaries of the self, its decisionism vis-a-vis-the good, and its drastically limited moral accountability, so unproblematically magnificent. There are, moreover, significant contrasts between his democratic persons and Kant's rational beings.

56. I here translate into Rawls's terms Amitai Etzioni's characterization of a good democracy as a "community of communities."

4

Identity Politics and the Liberalism of Difference

In recent years, another variant of egalitarian theory/praxis has emerged. The adherents of this version of democratic liberalism do not necessarily disagree with the distributive prescriptions offered by Rawls and his followers; but the axis of their concerns is a different one. In the view of these "difference liberals," material inequalities in democratic societies are important and need attending to; but they are not as fundamental a threat to justice and human flourishing as the more radical and deeply entrenched inequalities that pervade—even constitute—the politics of identity. Material inequalities may indeed be debilitating and injurious to the capacity of the disadvantaged successfully to pursue their plan of life. But human societies—including contemporary liberal democracies inclined to tout their tolerance and devotion to human equality—are also in some senses predicated upon normative constructions of what it means to be fully and acceptably human that, so the difference liberals argue, exclude and assault the self-understanding and the aspirations of some of their citizens/subjects.

The central message of difference liberalism runs roughly as follows. The animating values of democracy are equality, freedom, and human dignity. A commitment to equality and dignity requires an even-handed respect for all forms of human life—for all identities—as being worthy and morally on a par. Attempts to make and to enforce evaluative hierarchies among the diverse forms of human existence constitute a political "privileging" that is both philosophically indefensible and morally illicit. These hierarchical and discriminatory distinctions are embedded in our language/discourse and then embodied in laws, institutions, and distributions of power. They use the cover of a perverse moralism to enshrine a particular version of identity/aspirations and to impose it on others, derogating and oppressing them in the process. Despite our democratic rhetoric of toleration and equality, this pattern of oppression is fundamental to our own society, and it is displayed paradigmatically in Eurocentrism, patriarchy, and heterosexism. The central mission of genuine democratic governance in our time, therefore, is the elimination of these discriminatory hierarchies with a view toward giving equal status and empowerment to the historically marginalized and oppressed groups.

This democratic hermeneutic produces an ambivalent response to the more traditional form of egalitarianism found in Rawls. On the one hand, difference liberals generally accept the traditional egalitarian contention that contemporary democratic regimes are characterized by distributive injustices and they want to see these remedied. On the other hand, they believe that the focus of traditional egalitarianism on these distributive issues is too narrow and that its norms and strategies may serve to perpetuate those forms of oppression/inequality that turn around issues of cultural identity. William Connolly expresses this ambivalence in the following terms:

> The most general (and idealistic) idea is to subdue the politics of generalized resentment by moving on two fronts—first, by removing social injustices that exclude a large variety of constituencies from the material and cultural life of the whole and, second, by criticizing modes of existential resentment that intensify social dogmatism with respect to identity, responsibility, and otherness. These two "fronts" are neither separable nor fully harmonious within this vision. They are interdependent in that a politics of freedom cannot make much progress on either without making some on both. They enter into strife in that each can easily become a staging area for infringements on the other.[1]

Viewed through the prism of the sociology of knowledge, the contrasts between the interest-oriented egalitarian norms paradigmatically displayed in Rawlsian theory and the identity-oriented egalitarian norms endorsed by difference theorists are no doubt in part the product of different generational experiences. The perceptions and concerns that animate Rawlsian egalitarianism grew out of the civil rights revolution and the War on Poverty. They are sociologically situated prior to 1968. The perceptions and concerns animating difference liberals are situated in the politics of the late 1960s and 1970s. They gestate out of the emergence of feminism, black power, and gay pride. Both Rawlsian liberals and difference liberals are devoted to easing the plight of those caught on the downside of prevailing social hierarchies. But "otherness" to traditional egalitarians tends to conjure Michael Harrington's "other America": people shut out by structural poverty from full inclusion in the good life promised by democracy. In contrast, "the other" for difference liberals refers to those whose cultural identities—whether ethnic, gender related, racial, or psychosexual—rendered them relative outcasts in post-World War II America. The seminal event for the Rawlsian imagination, one is inclined to say, was John Kennedy's discovery of Appalachia; for the newer cultural egalitarians, it was the Stonewall rebellion. Rawls offers us a neo-Kantian pluralism within the bounds of reason, conceived in the sense of justice, and dedicated to the proposition that the disadvantaged citizens of a liberal democracy should receive the highest practically feasible share of that society's "primary goods." Difference liberalism offers the vision of a more broadly inclusive and nondiscriminating pluralism, a society that champions social diversity as a positive good rather than giving priority to the watery redistributive "fraternity" of the difference principle, a place where everyone has the equal ability and freedom to be who they are without suffering the slings and arrows of social condescension or political manipulation.

The cultural and philosophical resources of the newer egalitarianism are both indigenous and imported. In a way, indeed, it is somewhat surprising that difference liberals have invoked their indigenous ancestry so sparingly. For political reasons alone, such invocations would seem to be more promising rhetorically and strategically than the invocations of semi-intelligible foreigners. For the moral passions and intuitions resident within their widely tolerant democratic pluralism were given a powerful poetic expression in the democratic vistas limned by the poet laureate of democracy, Walt Whitman. His lyrical vision of the democratic future seems sympathetically attuned to their own hopes. He wrote, for example, that all human beings are "on a common level, utterly regardless of the distinctions of intellect, virtue, station, or any height or lowliness whatever." He asserted that the ultimate object of all government is "not merely to rule, to repress disorder, but to develop, to open up to cultivation . . . that aspiration for independence and the pride and self-respect latent in all characters." He looked forward with conviction to the time that "the women of America" would "become the robust equals, workers, and, it may be, even practical and political deciders with the men." He celebrated the multiple and polyglot "shows and forms presented by Nature, the sensuous luxuriance, the beautiful in living men and women, the actual play of passions, in history and life." And he offered the broadly inclusive vision of America as the land "of copious races, cheerful, healthy, tolerant, free . . . —the modern composite nation, formed from all immigrants . . . not the man's nation only, but the woman's nation."[2]

This democratic embrace of a positive and polyglot pluralism also received expression, as George Kateb has reminded us, in the thought of Whitman's transcendentalist contemporaries, Emerson and Thoreau.[3] And for those willing to stretch the notion of indigenous tradition to include classical British liberalism, John Stuart Mill's celebration of diversity as socially valuable "experiments in living" also serves as available inspiration.

Contemporary exponents of multicultural democracy have for the most part, however, not been inclined to situate themselves within this tradition or to draw upon its resources. This disinclination likely occurs for several reasons. In the first place, few contemporary theorists find themselves very attracted to the philosophical paradigms that animated these traditional indigenous pluralists. Whitman's syncretic neo-Hegelian pantheism, Emerson's neo-Platonic transcendentalist idealism, and Mill's revisionist version of utilitarianism all seem to them rather dated and obsolescent. Second, these indigenous pluralists tend to conceive the clientele they champion in individualistic terms. Difference to them means what is distinctive to individual persons. Contemporary multiculturalists, in contrast, for good or for ill, conceive "identity" largely in terms of group attributes. And last, contemporary multicultural democrats find the empirical sociology that arguably informs these earlier versions of positive pluralism to be outdated and misleading if applied to today's politics. As Connolly says vis-a-vis Kateb's exposition of Emerson and Whitman: "Notice the assumptions of early nineteenth-century America that form the silent background" of this viewpoint. "But the past ain't what it used to be. What's more, it probably never was. We do not reside today in a world where individuality can flourish if state, corporate, and associational institutions of normalization are left to their own devices."[4]

For all these reasons, difference liberals are most likely to draw their principal philosophical sustenance from continental postmodernist thinkers. The ideas they find in Nietzsche, Heidegger, Derrida, and Foucault mesh very well with their basic moral intuitions and their political aspirations. Additionally, this intellectual tradition offers them with a vocabulary and analytical tools congenial to their sensibility and useful for their purposes.

Philosophically, the central goal of these postmodernists is to escape the confines and putative distortions of "metaphysics," which they see as endemic to Western philosophy. In anthropological and moral terms, which are most directly pertinent to social theory and hence to our concerns here, the corollary of the desired escape from the clutches of "metaphysics" is the abandonment of "essentialism": the idea that there is some fundamental ontological and normative structure to being human. From the postmodernist perspective, essentialist presuppositions (encapsulated in what Heidegger calls the "ontotheological" tradition of the West) are not only false; they also serve as the backdrop and justification for authoritatively enforced language games or "discourses" that serve to legitimate regimes of discipline and control over all those who do not conform, for whatever reason, to the relevant essentialist norm.

In opposition to all forms of essentialism, the fundamental anthropological claim of postmodernism is that everything human is, through-and-through, a social construct. Escape from the alleged delusions of metaphysics brings the putatively liberating and equalizing recognition that everything human is thoroughly contingent in origin and content. Based on this fundamental assumption, postmodernist social theory encapsulates within its analytical terminology a thoroughgoing historicism and conventionalism. Any sociological or normative theories incorporating claims that fail to adhere to this assumption are deemed to disqualify themselves from the outset as a consequence of their erroneous—and probably politically malign—attempts to "naturalize" or "normalize" some aspect of human life or some social goal. In this context, genealogy—as practiced paradigmatically in various works of Foucault—and deconstruction—as practiced by Derrida—serve as powerful tools for the unmasking and undermining of these widespread and allegedly oppressive ideological discourses. Genealogical investigation tracks down the sociohistorical origins of and the political interests behind these justificatory rationales for regimes of surveillance, discipline, and punishment. And deconstructive analyses upset and implode the linguistic embodiments of these naturalizing and normalizing conceits by challenging the various tropes and binaries—e.g., masculine/feminine and rational/irrational—that encapsulate and propagate them.

Genealogy and deconstruction are powerful tools of critique and delegitimation. Indeed, they are so powerful that when they are deployed in a dogmatic and undiscriminating fashion, they may be too powerful even for the purposes of those who deploy them. One is reminded of the apt characterization Terence Ball once invoked in a different but parallel context: using a stringent form of the verificationist principle to attack opposing social theories, he noted, was tantamount to "going duck hunting with anti-aircraft guns." Highly effective weaponry no doubt, but a form of overkill that carried with it concealed dangers even to those who used it. In like manner, most enthusiasts of genealogy/deconstruction gleefully unleash their critical tools upon the putative oppressors of the modern world—mostly, European white bourgeois heterosexual males—with relatively little attention to the question of what norms or social ideals are to be left standing at the end of their deconstructive orgy. The implicit assumption seems to be that what counts as legitimate democracy is to be identified as what survives at the end of the demolition derby: delegitimize and destroy all the vestiges of hierarchy together with their justificatory naturalizing and normalizing mystifications, and true democracy will be what is left at the end of the cathartic leveling process. But this sanguine conceit is patently delusionary. All social orders, all form of governance—and democratic regimes are no exception—embody and institutionalize crucial and powerful normative distinctions and evaluative hierarchies. The contrast between a classless and a class-based society, for example, may be politically antihierarchical in its rhetorical force, but it embodies a theoretical and normative "hierarchical" distinction, as does the fundamental democratic distinction between consent and manipulation. The danger of genealogy/deconstruction as social theory, therefore, is that it threatens to replicate the constructive incompetencies Marx discerned in the Young Hegelians. It may simply "exhaust itself in critique."[5]

The two most serious and interesting recent attempts by political theorists to go beyond the purely critical deployment of genealogy and deconstruction in order to offer a constructive model of a democratic society centered about the dynamics of group identity and difference have come from Iris Young and William Connolly. Their accounts are not cut entirely from the same cloth.[6] But they take their point of departure from many of the same sources, and they each provide us an account of democratic ideals worthy of our attention. What are these accounts, then, and how compelling should we find them?

In *Justice and the Politics of Difference*, Young argues that abstract and universalizing approaches to the definition of social justice are bound to be defective. Drawing upon her interpretation of critical theory, she "rejects as illusory the effort to construct a universal normative system insulated from a particular society."[7] Besides being "illusory," the effort to conceive justice by "adopting an impersonal and impartial point of view" is theoretically distortive and politically destructive. The "ideal of impartiality" is alleged to "express a logic of identity that seeks to reduce differences to unity," to generate false and destructive binaries— e.g., between private and public, reason and passion—and to perform "ideological functions . . . masking the ways in which the particular perspectives of dominant groups claim universality," thereby justifying hierarchical political structures.[8] A theoretically adequate and politically emancipatory theory of justice must, in contrast, be concrete and specific—explicitly situated within the particular and contingent realities of the social order in question. "The normative ideals used to criticize a society are rooted in experience of and reflection on that very society, and [those] norms can come from nowhere else."[9]

Young also depicts the "distributive paradigm" of social justice within which Rawls and most other moral theorists operate as faulty and misleading. By implicitly conceiving the central issue of social justice to be the proper criteria governing the distribution of things—even when the paradigm is stretched and massaged to include nonmaterial "things" such as self-esteem and opportunities—these moral theories "produce a misleading conception of the issues of justice involved." The distributive paradigm "reifies aspects of social life that are better understood as a function of rules and relations than as things. And it conceptualizes social justice primarily in terms of end-state patterns, rather than focusing on social processes."[10] To avoid these distortions, therefore, Young recommends that the concept of distribution should be limited to material goods and that justice should be conceived in broader "structural" terms. Specifically, it should be focused "on issues of decisionmaking, division of labor, and culture."[11]

Accordingly, the tacitly individualist "social ontology" informing the universal rights/distributive model needs to be jettisoned and replaced by an explicit social theory. This social theory, in turn, needs, in Young's view, to center around the presence and functions of social groups and their structural relations with each other. A social group is defined as "a collective of persons differentiated by cultural forms, practices, or way of life." These social groups "constitute individuals" rather than vice versa, as the contract model of society suggests. And this constitutive process involves the creation of "people's identities" via their inculturation into "group meanings."[12] When examined from a vantage point that makes the situations of and mutual relationships among social/cultural identity groups focal, she contends, it turns out that "American society contains deep institutional injustices."[13] These injustices are best characterized as the oppression of groups rather than as the morally arbitrary relative deprivation of individuals. And oppression, in turn, is specified as some combination of five structural features of a pluralistic society which give some groups a privileged or dominant position vis-a-vis other groups. These features, the subspecies and stigmata of oppression, are economic exploitation, social marginalization, political powerlessness, cultural imperialism, and outright violence.

Justice, therefore, becomes on this view a process of rectification. It is the very specific righting of very specific wrongs. Justice is not attained by the application of universal and impartial distributive criteria intended to "mitigate the effects of natural accident and social circumstance," as Rawls would have it.[14] Instead, it is the transformation of existing political institutions, social relationships, and cultural practices that lead to oppression. The goal is not the effectuation of a difference principle to regulate social distributions. It is, rather, to establish an "egalitarian politics of difference" that operates on behalf of what Young, borrowing from Christine Littleton, calls an "acceptance model of equality."[15] Justice entails social equality, and social equality "refers primarily to the full participation and inclusion of everyone in a society's major institutions, and the socially supported substantive opportunity for all to develop and exercise their capacities and realize their choices." And for this to occur, Young insists, the "specific experience, culture, and social contributions" of all cultural identity groups must be not simply tolerated but "publicly affirmed and recognized."[16] In a sense, the replacement of distributive egalitarianism by an egalitarian politics of difference that puts "acceptance" and "affirmation" at its center is tantamount to replacing a Kohlberg-style political ethic with one inspired by Carol Gilligan.[17] Rather than maintaining a scrupulous principled neutrality vis-a-vis the multiple and contending groups under its purview, a democratic regime should attend to the distinctive identity of each group and give them all—or at least the oppressed ones—a caring hug of affirmation and assistance directed at the group's specific needs.

Democratic and socially just institutions should not, therefore—as in the popular depiction of a blindfolded justice holding her scales aloft—be blind to group-differences. Precisely the contrary. A well-ordered democratic regime must instead be specifically and intensely group conscious. "A culturally pluralist democratic ideal," Young argues, "supports group-conscious policies not only as means to the end of equality, but also as intrinsic to the ideal of social equality itself."[18] This explicit attention to group differences and conscious promotion of the interests and identity of groups who qualify as oppressed, Young contends, should take place in all the major social venues: group-conscious rectification should shape the representative institutions of the political system, the content of social policy, the rules of economic allocation, and the norms of cultural practices.

Democratic representative institutions should, on this model, employ "institutional mechanisms and public resources" to support: (1) the organization of groups in pursuit of their "collective empowerment," (2) the generation of policy in institutionalized contexts where decision-makers should be required to show that they have taken group perspectives into account, and (3) "group veto power regarding specific policies that affect a group directly."[19] It is not all groups that should be accorded group-specific representational entitlements of this sort, however: "the principle of group representation . . . calls for specific representation only of oppressed or disadvantaged groups."[20] Electorally, one might suppose that this normative ideal should lead to an insistence on devices to effectuate proportional representation; for PR electoral arrangements, as John Stuart Mill argued long ago, provide the only guarantee that numerical minority groups have the potential to attain direct representation in the councils of government.[21] But Young does not pursue this line of argument. Instead, her representative ideal centers around a broader and less specific model of group caucuses.[22] She offers as models for emulation Jesse Jackson's Rainbow Coalition, the National Women's Studies Association, and the Sandinista regime in Nicaragua. She values the organizational principles of the Rainbow Coalition because "each of the constituent groups affirms the presence of the others as well as the specificity of their experience and perspective on social issues. . . . Ideally, a Rainbow Coalition affirms the presence and supports the claims of each of the oppressed groups or political movements constituting it, and arrives at a political program not by voicing some principles of unity that hide difference, but rather by allowing each constituency to analyze economic and social issues from the perspective of its experience."[23] The virtue of the National Women's Studies Association governance model is that it "has a complex and effective system of representation for group caucuses in its decision-making bodies."[24] Sandinista Nicaragua appeals to her because of its "experiments with institutionalized self-organization among women, indigenous peoples, workers, peasants, and students."[25]

In the realm of social policy, Young argues against what she calls "the assimilationist ideal" of "treating everyone according to the same principles, rules, and standards." Instead of this illusory and unfair standard of impartiality, she advocates "special treatment to groups." "Equality as the participation and inclusion of all groups sometimes requires different treatment for oppressed or disadvantaged groups."[26] For example, laws and practices relating to pregnancy and birth need not be folded into gender-neutral leave policies; linguistic minorities should be supported in their desire "to maintain their specific culture and speak their language and still receive the benefits of citizenship, such as voting rights, decent education, and job opportunities;" and Native American groups should retain special rights and autonomy that cannot be "altered or eliminated" by government decree, while maintaining at the same time rights "to full participation and inclusion in the polity."[27,28]

Economic allocations in a democratic society should, in Young's view, be politically determined much more than is now the case. Here, as elsewhere, it seems to be the welfare of the putatively oppressed that is key to her prescriptions. Allocations of scarce desirable jobs or places in selective institutions in accord with assessed "merit" have not resulted in the proportional success of all groups. And the determination of salary levels and job tasks by market mechanisms has likewise produced identifiable differentials among groups—as, for example, in the relative overrepresentation of women in lower paying job categories. Young therefore argues that "merit" is mostly a myth and that gender bias skews wage structures. Hence, whereas "the ideology of merit seeks to depoliticize the establishment of criteria and standards for allocating positions and awarding benefits," in fact merit evaluation is always political and therefore "decisions that establish and apply criteria of qualification should be made democratically."[29] It is not made clear exactly how these political determinations would be made. But since they would be governed by the group consciousness embedded in Young's account of democratic procedure and since the criteria are recognized as political in substance, one result is that the case for affirmative action-style group preferences would be consolidated and, presumably, such practices could be systematized. "No longer need affirmative action be seen as an exception to the otherwise operative principle of nondiscrimination. Instead, it becomes one of many group-conscious policies instrumental in undermining oppression."[30] Young also embraces "comparable worth" policies that would require setting salary scales by applying a standard of "equal pay for work of comparable worth." Presumably, such a policy would work to lessen differences between pay for culturally defined "masculine" and "feminine" jobs. However, it is not made clear how the untenability of claims to be able to assess "merit" in an objective way is compatible with the claim of comparable worth advocates that it is possible to provide an objective measure of the relative worth of different skills, abilities, and job conditions.

Finally, the "egalitarian politics of difference" is deemed to support and require the "politicization of culture" in which the line between public and private realms is attenuated or abolished and "certain everyday symbols, practices, and ways of speaking" are to become "the subject of public discussion and explicitly matters of choice and decision." Any cultural "practices, habits, attitudes, comportments, images, symbols, and so on" that "contribute to social domination and group oppression" call for "collective transformation."[31] Indeed, Young insists that "no social practices or activities should be excluded as improper subjects for public discussion, expression, or collective choice."[32] These "collective choices" should be given the force of law, moreover, to mandate the avoidance of even "unconscious and unintended actions" that "contribute to the disadvantage" of oppressed groups. Such mandates can include judicially imposed "forward-looking remedies" and the use of sexual harassment rules to discipline males who behave in ways "that women collectively judge annoying, humiliating, or coercive."[33]

A full assessment of Young's argument could fill several volumes. Her argument involves a wide-ranging set of empirical, theoretical, hermeneutic, moral, and prudential claims—almost all of which are both complex and contestable. Since many of these claims have been influential in recent years and because I have significant doubts and reservations about many of them, however, it is necessary to indicate the nature of these doubts, even if they are unavoidably stated somewhat cryptically and dogmatically.

On the positive side of the ledger, it should be happily and forthrightly acknowledged that the multifaceted cultural and social transformations that provide the background of Young's work have been important and beneficial changes consonant with the spirit of both liberalism and democracy. These transformations, distinguishable and in some respects different but also related and mutually reinforcing, have concerned the status and role of racial minorities, women, and gays and lesbians. The civil rights revolution that eliminated *de jure* racial segregation and discrimination and dismantled Jim Crow institutions removed what had always been the greatest moral anomaly within and the greatest blight upon American democratic practices. A transformation of social conventions governing gender roles, produced by a combination of moral convictions and technological advances that rendered many aspects of traditional gender roles obsolescent, has given women of this generation a whole range of new opportunities largely unavailable to their mothers and grandmothers. And although homosexuality is not accepted in all quarters as morally or socially unproblematic, the stigmatization and persecution that gays and lesbians faced a generation ago have been greatly attenuated and in some locales virtually eliminated. Future historians will, no doubt, regard these changes as one of the remarkable and defining features of the last half of twentieth century America. And any democratic vision that does not recognize these changes as important and welcome aspects of social democratization in their movement toward inclusiveness, tolerance, equality, and opportunity must be regarded as highly suspect. It is the great virtue of Young's argument—and of multicultural egalitarianism and identity politics in general—that it recognizes and embraces these social changes as highly important advances in democratic practice.

It is another thing entirely, however, to fashion and promote an ideal of democratic institutions and policies driven by the desire to consolidate these social changes and to give them juridical form. Turning democratic politics into a normative politics of group identity creates serious distortions and carries significant costs. Careful reflection on Young's recommendations and some of their implications and likely consequences, I would argue, brings some of these difficulties into relief.

Doubts about the imperatives generated by democratic multiculturalism should begin with the notion of identity itself. The politics of identity starts from the recognition that selves are neither created nor defined apart from social relations with other selves. Who and what people are, their identities, are constituted by the forms of life of the social groups they inhabit and by the roles they play within these forms of life. This recognition represents a helpful correction to mistakes arising from taking the individualistic abstractions and norms of classical liberal contract theory too literally; and it is entirely justified, I would argue, by what psychology and sociology have to tell us. So far, so good. The problem arises from the interpretation that advocates of identity politics give to these dynamics of identity formation and group membership. In the first place, the process of identity formation is conceived as a form of social imprinting, as it were, in which the self passively receives rather than dialectically interacts with his or her social environment. An identity is "how I am recognized rather than what I choose, want, or consent to."[34] Second, the defining features of an identity are conceived—consistent with this passive recipient imagery, perhaps—as a concatenation of the external accidents of one's being. My identity is the aggregate total of whether I am male or female, black/brown/yellow/red/white, hetero- or homosexual, and so on. Last, the specific accidents or "socially recognized differences" deemed crucial are those that center around race, gender, and sexual orientation.[35] Those other group memberships that are more particular, more national or universal, or more voluntary are somehow deemed subordinate or even inconsequential. An identity, then, becomes something that is passively received, externally defined, and tied specifically to one's putative "membership" in certain intermediate-level social groups that are deemed most salient and significant.

This account of identity formation is empirically quite suspect. But it may be that it is more a matter of a stipulative definition governed by a political agenda than it is an empirical theory. In any event, conceiving identity in this fashion and giving it normative force arguably carries significant social and moral costs. It is constraining to individuals, divisive for the larger society, and impoverishing to both. The analytical perspective behind Young's politics reifies group stereotypes, and the organization of democratic politics around group caucuses would entrench them institutionally. Group identification turns into a straightjacket forced upon people who would and should possess more complex, capacious, and idiosyncratic identities and more varied and flexible modes of political activity. Democratic society is conceived and organized as a collage of different and competing teams, and woe betide anyone who won't wear a uniform. Multicultural democracy on this account is a kind of "estates' rights" system, with identity groups as the constitutive estates. And it imposes the same costs on the larger society and on local minorities as "states' rights" did. The larger, more inclusive "national" community loses coherence and authority. And individuals are dominated by the local majorities who can dictate the terms of membership to them.

In Young's democracy, social solidarity and a sense of common purpose are effectively confined within social groups. The only broader social solidarity she has a place for is that of the "rainbow coalition" variety, in which various groups affirm each other and cooperate politically on the basis of their status as oppressed. She laments that the "promise" of the Jesse Jackson Rainbow Coalition campaign "has not been fulfilled."[36] But she fails to understand that the narcissistic particularism engendered by preoccupation with group identity militates against such success. She imagines that putatively similar experiences of oppression will create social bonds, without realizing that if all that matters to me and my self-realization occurs within the bounds of my particular social group, then the only thing that matters to me politically will be the relief of my own group's oppression. Indeed, to the very extent that other groups are instrumentalities of other identities/ways of life, they must be seen ultimately as by their very existence being contributory to my oppression—whether or not they themselves are oppressed by some third party. As a dedicated feminist convinced of her own subjection to oppressive forces, Young may empathize with other groups she adjudges to be somewhat similarly oppressed. But the logic of her social psychology and her politics provides little sustenance for making common cause across the lines of difference she hypostasizes.

The subjection of individuals by local majorities within the group to which the politics of difference consigns them is all too apparent. As Roberto Alejandro aptly observes: "In Young's views, as in the Anti-federalists, the principle of difference does not refer to the identity which the group makes possible. That identity, apparently, should not be challenged. . . . Within the group, the values of 'group specificity' and 'cultural pride' may require the same uniformity which is not deemed acceptable for society as a whole."[37] The result of what styles itself as a politics of difference is, paradoxically enough, an institutionalized bias toward cookie-cutter individuals who conform unproblematically to stylized group identities. Those who do not so conform are subjected to social ostracism and—as long as caucus decision-making is the rule—to political homelessness. The practical effect of the politics of identity is actually to suppress rather than to encourage human diversity.[38] Rather than the rich and varied flourishing of human potentiality in all of its multifarious forms, the yoking of identity to membership in externally defined groups creates a small and prefabricated handful of "identities." The wonderful array of human characters that Whitman depicted and delighted in as the culmination of democracy is nowhere in sight. The "fullness of life" Mill held up as the promise of liberal society is diminished rather than enhanced. Genuine human diversity is compressed into its grotesque similacrum: the reified psychological artifacts of a group nationalism that bleeds the public interest and herds individuals into politically sanctioned corrals.

The insistence of the politics of identity upon effacing or obliterating the line between public and private also is problematic. True, "the personal is political" in the sense that politically constructed institutions and practices shape personal identities and can generate personal problems and also in the sense that the expression of personal identity can be impeded by politically established norms, practices, and institutions. It is true, moreover, that the line between the public and private realms is neither immutable nor set in accordance with some transcendent or objective standard. Therefore, it is both likely and proper that the specific placement and operations of this dividing line be contestable and contested. Nevertheless, so long as a society is pluralistic in the sense that it is inhabited by people with different moral and religious beliefs, maintaining a protected "private" space in which the ways of life predicated upon these competing beliefs can be freely and safely pursued is both morally proper and prudentially necessary. A protected private space accords freedom and dignity to the adherents of different lifestyles, and it simultaneously removes from public determination issues that would be sharply divisive were they necessary to decide by majoritarian mandate.

It follows, then, that it is both improper and imprudent to seek effacement of the line, however blurry and mutable it may be, that separates public and private domains in a democratic society. The attempt to efface that line is particularly ill advised, one might add, for minority groups, since they would be the losers if all behavioral norms were set and enforced by public majorities. By investing matters of personal (group) identity with public significance and by demanding not simply toleration—which is deemed to be grudging and "demeaning"—but "affirmation and recognition" as essential to not being oppressed, Young and other advocates of identity politics wind up pushing in that direction. She states as a basic principle, for example, that "no actions or aspects of a person's life should be forced into privacy" and that "no social . . . practices should be excluded *a priori* from being a proper subject for public discussion and expression."[39]

The central difficulty here is that it may seem benign, enlightened, and morally uplifting to insist that every aspect of everyone's identity be "publicly affirmed and recognized."[40] But so long as a society is morally and religiously pluralistic, so long as it encompasses a variety of different and in some respects mutually antagonistic ways of life and moral commitments, such a demand is not merely unrealistic but morally improper. Given the political tragedy/limitations endemic to moral pluralism, in fact, such a demand is in a sense self-contradictory. To demand that you "affirm" my identity, when that identity inextricably incorporates behavior that the premises underlying your identity construes as immoral, is to demand that you effectively renounce your own identity. Like it or not, your toleration is the most I can reasonably expect and the most I can properly demand.

For example, suppose that I am one of a social group known as "the pork people." For us, the consumption of pork is a favorite activity—sufficiently central and gratifying to our desires even to have become vested with religious and moral overtones. Many of us also savor and occupy ourselves with the aesthetic trappings that surround pork consumption: we experiment with different recipes for barbecue sauce, we display photography of artfully displayed boars on a spit with apples in their mouths, and so on. Some of us make a living as restauranteurs, featuring pork delicacies. Now so long as everyone else in our polity is also a pork person or so long as everyone in our polity who is not a pork person considers our gustatory enthusiasms to be a morally indifferent matter of taste, we have no political problems consequent upon our particular identity. Suppose, however, that a preponderance of the citizenry in our country are Muslims, who consider pork consumption to be a divinely proscribed moral offense. How should the resulting tension be handled politically, legally, and institutionally?

The theocratic or political "unitarian" solution would be to allow the dominant group to dictate behavior through legal force as well as through social compulsion. Dedicated pork people would have to emigrate, go underground, or endure persecution. The liberal solution, the logic of which was well laid out by John Locke in his *Letter Concerning Toleration*, imposes, in contrast, some very serious restraints upon the passions and actions of the dominant groups. However offensive the dominant Muslim population may find the pork people's behavior, they are nonetheless obliged to tolerate it. Specifically, they must forbear and allow the pork people to consume pork, to merchandise their wares, and to publish articles extolling the virtues of their way of life. This vast improvement in the lot of the pork people is the result of the liberal regime's policy of defending universal individual rights, a conception that Young confusedly and improperly denigrates as "assimilationist."[41]

By Young's standards, however, those of us who are pork people are still entitled to consider ourselves oppressed. Rather than settling for toleration, accommodation, and the private space to do our thing, we are entitled to insist upon receiving "public affirmation and recognition." We demand that barbecue be served in school lunches and that school children be taught that eating pork is "just as good as" eating chicken or vegetables. We may demand an end to any disapproving looks from Muslims when we eat ribs in public, and we may want the introduction of mandatory consciousness-raising sessions in the workplace in which biases against pork-eaters are to be exposed and extirpated. Is this more expansive political strategy prudent? Is it normatively proper?

Whether the more ambitious strategy is prudent involves a complex calculation of costs and benefits that can't really be adjudicated in the abstract. The answer will vary with circumstances, will change with different priorities, and will depend upon whose interests are at stake. The costs to the polity as a whole stem from the increase in acrimony with its attendant political consequences. From the point of view of us pork eaters, of course, our gains in visibility, self-assertion, and the like may make this cost worth bearing. Asking whether it would be normatively proper for the polity to accede to the pork people's demands for "affirmation and recognition," on the other hand, leads to the acknowledgment of an element of moral and political tragedy in this situation that cannot be entirely reconciled or eliminated. The source of the tragedy is that some "identities" or moral beliefs are not merely different but contradictory. Practices deemed constitutive by one way of life are deemed morally opprobrious by another way of life. If there must be a public determination of the issue, one identity necessarily is derogated. For Muslims to accept the teaching that eating pork is "just as good as" any other dietary practice is for Muslims *de facto* to renounce their faith and to declare themselves benighted. Whether dietary practices are matters of mere taste or matters of significant moral moment is precisely what is at issue; the different identities hinge about contradictory answers to that question and hence any public determination of the question ineluctably derogates one identity or another. There can be here no hope of eliminating oppression, as defined by Young; it is only a question of who shall be oppressed.

The central point here is that a demand that all identities be publicly "affirmed" potentially suffers from a practical self-contradiction. Whether this potential self-contradiction becomes actualized is a function of sociological contingencies. If the various cultural identities within a society are merely different, all of them may be publicly affirmed and recognized without creating any difficulties of principle. But if there are identities that clash—as in the confrontation between Muslims and pork people—rather than merely diverge, any attempt to end oppression by public affirmation is futile. The oppression may be shifted around, but it cannot be eliminated. Moreover, the denigration of a rights-based politics of toleration and the effacement of the public/private distinction by an insistence that "the personal is political" arguably results in a net increase in oppression rather than in its abatement. Under more favorable sociological circumstances, this tragic result might not occur. But where identities/moralities involve zero-sum clashes in which the rightness of one ineluctably implies the wrongness of the other, the sum total of oppression is lessened when the public domain prescinds from any attempt to adjudicate the issue and makes it a private matter, giving the latitude to each antagonistic cultural group to live as it sees fit within this protected domain. The alternative to carving out a private domain, confining some behaviors to it, and according it protection is not equal affirmation for all, since that is a will-o-the-wisp. The alternative is a choice between cultural imperialisms, and that should be unattractive to anyone except those belligerents in the culture wars who want to take no prisoners.[42]

To forestall any potential misunderstanding, let it be clear that I am not here trying to adjudicate the issues that set the Muslim faithful and the pork eaters in my example at odds with each other—or to adjudicate by analogy the clash between, say, fundamentalists and gay/lesbian groups that is probably the current real-world clash in this country that conforms most closely to my hypothetical case. Indeed, part of the problem is precisely that it is impossible to adjudicate these issues in any objective and definitive way—however strong may be our personal convictions on these matters. The central points here are these: Young, and most advocates of identity politics, fail to acknowledge the tragic zero-sum contradictions that sometimes obtain in the real world between the constitutive moral premises/commitments that inform different identities; the presence of such contradictions renders the call for universal "affirmation and recognition" of all identities in their particularity incoherent and utopian; and under such circumstances, the more traditional liberal strategy that protects individual rights, mandates toleration, and creates a private sphere that serves as a safe haven from adverse collective judgments and controls is both more practically viable and morally defensible than a broad expansion of public determination pursuant to the insistence that "the personal is political."

The expansive interpretation of oppression provided by Young, in conjunction with its crucial distributive consequences, also creates serious difficulties for her democratic ideal. These difficulties are compounded by the political battles that unavoidably must determine what and who is to be categorized as oppressed. Achieving official designation as "oppressed," it should be recalled, represents a real political prize; for groups who achieve this designation thereby accrue an entitlement to "special treatment," ranging from economic and cultural favoritism enforced by judicial and bureaucratic mandates to the guarantee of specific political entrenchments—including the holding of veto power over decisions that "affect them directly." The problems that ensue from the broad construction of oppression, from the inescapably political nature of designating who counts as oppressed, and from the profound advantages attained by such designation include, once again, both matters of principle and of practicality.

Because democracy demands justice and because justice consists in the relief from oppression, Young's very capacious definition of that term generates some rather odd moral claims, particularly in the questionably extensive obligations it imposes on the nonoppressed. It follows from Young's argument, for example, that if I choose to move my family to Spain, if we are allowed residence there, and if we wish to retain our language and our American cultural identity, we thereby may be deemed "marginalized" victims of "cultural imperialism" and hence qualify as an oppressed group. It then would become morally incumbent upon the Spaniards to undertake strenuous efforts to make our decision to hold on to the language and culture of our origins a costless one to us. We would be entitled to demand of the regime that it "ensure the possibility of [our] full inclusion and participations . . . in all society's institutions and at the same time preserve and affirm [our] group-specific identity." Should the Spaniards not undertake to create the institutions and to provide the special resources necessary to meet this extraordinarily demanding standard, they seemingly would become guilty of imposing "an assimilationist ideal" that "amounts to genocide."[43] The old adage "when in Rome, do as the Romans do" turns out to be an ideology of oppression. The new democratic standard becomes "when in Rome, the Romans have a lot to do to make you happy."[44]

Because the distributive advantages in terms of both resources and power are so substantial for those who can gain official designation as oppressed, it becomes a serious question as to how exactly those designations are to be made. Young recognizes the problem, but gives no useful response to it, calling it "a paradox of political origins . . . which no philosophical argument can resolve." She offers only the rather lame and politically anesthetized suggestion that groups seeking the advantages conferred by being officially recognized as "oppressed" will "have to petition with arguments that may or may not be persuasive."[45] This is, to put it mildly, a rather romanticized description of the contentious battling that her scheme and its determinative criteria make almost mandatory, as various groups scramble for comparative advantage in the political spoils system she sets up. All the incentives are there for the emergence of an "oppression sweepstakes," in which the advocates for various groups jockey rhetorically and tactically for the status of most oppressed group. The model for this rather unseemly and counterproductive form of political squabbling, perhaps, appeared recently in my university's school newspaper. In respective letters to the editor, two students, one black and one Jewish, quarreled bitterly over the relative degrees of oppression and suffering endured by their group forebears. The black student practically quivered with indignation as she sought to downplay the enormity of the Holocaust, an event that paled in significance in her view by comparison with the Middle Passage endured by slaves being shipped to the New World. This polemical donnybrook between two students in an elite university who, by any reasonable standard, have to be counted among the most fortunate and privileged members of the human race was profoundly dispiriting. But it was a perfectly logical consequence of the distributive criteria enjoined upon us by Young's influential version of multicultural egalitarianism. In her ideal democracy, the last shall indeed be first, and one gains the coveted position of those who shall inherit the earth by one's success in the competition to be officially designated as the most oppressed group around. In this system, to turn another old adage on its head, "to the officially designated victims go the spoils."

Considered *in toto* as a democratic ideal, then, the identity group caucus version of the "egalitarian politics of difference" has genuine virtues but also serious flaws. The principal virtue of the model is its dedication to a politics and a culture of inclusiveness and generosity. It insists both properly in moral terms and prudently in political terms that all of the diverse cultural groups that make up a pluralist democracy should have a place within its public life and its decision-making process. Also welcome and important is Young's insistence that mechanisms be in place that allow all voices to be heard in the public deliberations that shape the formulation of a democratic society's purposes and policies.

The specific institutional incarnation that Young gives to these admirable goals, however, has a number of serious costs and dangers. First, her whole scheme hinges around a specific standard of substantive justice that—like all such standards—is both reasonably contestable and actually contested. In her case, justice is effectively defined as the absence of oppression. Hence it is dependent for its definition and validity upon the highly contestable abstract definition and equally contestable concrete applications that Young gives to that concept. I have already noted some of the problems with the capacious definition Young gives to the concept of oppression. Here it should also be noted that she tends to accept claims of oppression quite uncritically. As a veteran of feminist discussions and campaigns, for example, she seems to accept allegations about oppression from that quarter—such as the claim that the nuclear family is "patriarchical" and that "the norms of heterosexuality are oriented around male pleasure"—as though they were epistemically on a par with "water freezes at 32 degrees Fahrenheit." The point here is not whether these claims are warranted or unwarranted. The point is that the standards of justice hinge around the answers given to highly contestable questions about what counts as oppression, both in general and in particular cases. Absent widespread agreement on these issues and absent some clear and objective standards for adjudicating them, Young's democratic ideal leads *de facto* to the imposition by the winning political coalition of its version of justice upon the losers. As a true believer, like Rawls, in the moral verity of a particular notion of justice, Young would take that outcome—the electoral success of her rainbow coalition?—as virtue triumphant. Those of us more skeptical about the moral and epistemic standing of definitive claims about social justice would be more inclined to see the outcome largely as the victory of an alternative coalition of interests.

The unwarranted moral certitude displayed by Young is doubly unsetting because of the alacrity with which she envisions and endorses highly coercive and intrusive measures to enforce her own preferred perceptions and distributions. She is an enthusiastic exponent of mandatory "consciousness-raising workshops for male managers and other male employees" and other therapeutic interventions, for instance. (It is remarkable how many social reformers who like to deploy Foucault's insights about domination when interpreting liberal society become such enthusiastic therapists themselves when they get the chance.) And she wants courts to issue "forward-looking remedies of institutions" to prohibit even "unconscious and unintended actions" that could be alleged to contribute to the disadvantage of the oppressed.[46] For all the talk about democracy and persuasion, advocates of the politics of difference seem happy to lean on the most undemocratic institutions in society to promote and enforce their desired ends.

Finally, the preferred ideal of an egalitarian politics of difference institutionalized around identity caucuses creates a polity centered around specific partial associations (Rousseau's phrase) or factions (Madison's term). Centering the democratic political process around these officially recognized and empowered groups—some of which are designated as oppressed and thereby turned into vehicles of social preferment for their members—heightens the social divisions that are always a threat to pluralist societies. Young's democracy is all *pluribus* and no *unum*, an idealized Bosnia without (as yet) organized gunfire. Once the romantic gloss is rubbed off her envisioned "egalitarian politics of difference," it looks remarkably similar to many of today's college campuses: students encouraged by their culturally hypersensitive faculty and counselors and lobbied by their peers to huddle into explicitly defined and recognized identity groups fragmented by race, gender, and sexual orientation who then sally forth to complain and preen and quarrel with each other or to demand something from the administration. All in all, it is a scene more dispiriting than inspiring, and it induces the conviction that we ought to be able to find better ways than this to be inclusive and to celebrate our pluralism. When it comes to envisioning the way diversity enriches democracy, Whitman and Mill are better prophets—even if their visions need to be adapted to the constraints and possibilities of the twenty-first century—than are the exponents of an institutionalized politics of group difference.

The other account of an egalitarian politics of difference that demands consideration is William Connolly's provocative conception of "agonistic democracy." Connolly's version of difference liberalism is admirable for several reasons. First, it is based upon a well-informed, creative reconstruction of two philosophers/social theorists who have been paradigmatic for many postmodernist assessments of democracy: Nietzsche and Foucault. Second, Connolly is well aware that deconstructionist and genealogical critiques do not in themselves constitute a political theory.[47] Third, unlike many who, perhaps misled by their endorsement of Heidegger's critique of Western metaphysics, think they have somehow transcended the fiduciary contingencies of all claims to knowledge, Connolly is well aware that postmodernist philosophy has no Archimedean point on which to stand. His favored philosophical position, he recognizes, "is not above metaphysics" and is instead "a highly contestable rendering of the fundaments of being" that "we can never demonstrate . . . to be true and necessary."[48] Finally, his political aspirations are not suffused with utopianism but acknowledge the political tensions and paradoxes that are almost surely uneliminable in a politics of difference—or any other politics for that matter. And that avoidance of utopianism saves him from succumbing to the temptation to implement his favored goals by undemocratic, intrusive, and manipulative means. Even when these many and important virtues of his theoretical orientation are acknowledged, however, I would argue that significant problems remain.

The philosophical and sociological underpinnings of Connolly's democratic vision are, to use his term, "post-Nietzschean" and heavily indebted to Foucault. Because many of these premises were set out in the earlier account of the postmodernist inspiration of multicultural egalitarianism and because some of them are shared with Young, I can state them rather summarily:

(1) There is no such thing as a true, natural, normal, or essential identity. That is to say, there is no universally grounded or valid model of human actualization, perfection, or fulfillment.

(2) Instead, all identities—both the existing identities of real-world people and the ideal conceptions of human identity that shape and judge them—are fashioned totally from historically contingent components. We are all, in short, both who we are and who we strive to be, a concatenation of "accidents" generated by historically variable circumstances that could well have been different than they are.

(3) "Identity requires difference in order to be."[49] Like a picture needs a frame or a foreground needs a background, an identity becomes recognizable and crystallized only by contrast with something that it is not. We know who and what we are *via* a simultaneous recognition of alternative configurations of human features that we do not share.

(4) Strong pressures are at work to convert difference into otherness. "Other" is "different" with an evaluative negative sign added. It is difference seen as evil and as threat.

(5) In order to consolidate and justify the evaluative contrast between one's own identity and that of the other, the adherents of a particular identity—a particular conception of ideal humanity—tend to "fix the truth of identity by grounding it in the commands of a god or the dictates of nature or the requirements of reason or a free consensus."[50] As a necessary corollary to this cosmic self-elevation, the other becomes stylized as "intrinsically evil, irrational, abnormal, mad, sick, primitive, monstrous, dangerous, or anarchical."[51] These naturalizations of self and the concomitant demonizing of the other, however, are in principle an untenable mystification. (See premise 1.)

(6) These evaluative categorizations—despite their untenability or perhaps because of their consequent precariousness—will seek political incarnation, institutional embodiment, authoritative enforcement.

(7) This political entrenchment and enforcement results in cruelty and repression. Those who seek to conform to the norms of the officially established identity are forced to repress those attributes and inclinations which do not fit within the confines of the idealized self. Those who cannot or will not accept and conform to these norms are derided, stigmatized, persecuted, manipulated, and/or vilified. Touting itself as the social embodiment of the human good, a society adheres to its idealized self-image through policies that subject its adherents and its deviants alike to various forms of discipline and punishment.

One feature of Western notions of essential identity that comes in for Connolly's special scrutiny is the norm of responsibility—the idea that the normal human self is a free moral agent who can and should be held responsible for, accountable for, all of his or her actions. In a compelling interrogation of Augustinian theology and ethics, he details how Augustine in effect created a human other, loaded with sin and guilt, in order to save the (perfect) identity of his God. The requisites of theodicy generated a strong doctrine of human responsibility. Augustine's core dilemma was to account for the existence of evil in the world while holding fast to the insistence that God was both perfectly good and—contrary to Manicheanism—all powerful. The only solution to the dilemma was to say that God had created human beings as free agents and that they had abused this freedom in destructive ways. In short, it was sinful mankind who had brought evil into the world and who could properly be held entirely accountable for it.

The modern, secular, post-Christian subject, Connolly continues, may not be conceived as a miserable sinner. But the modern subject nonetheless retains intact the attribution of free agency and, with it, the liability for being held fully responsible for its actions. In a way, the imposition of full responsibility upon the human subject for the world's ills is even intensified. If the pagan gods and the Christian God are both banished in the dispensation of scientific secularism, there is no one else left to blame. Moreover, the modern self, paradigmatically displayed in the Cartesian *cogito*, is more radically free metaphysically than the finite pagan self or the created Christian soul. Hence, even if theodicy no longer exerts its imperatives, the burden of responsibility remains fully intact on the modern subject—as embodied, for example, in Kant's demanding ethics and in Sartre's condemnations of "bad faith." The problem, however, is that, as Connolly puts it: "We are not predesigned to be responsible agents. . . . Life exceeds, resists, and overflows the mold of responsibility imposed upon it."[52] The imposition of stringent norms of personal responsibility, therefore, produces some of the same kinds of cruelties, repressions, and resentments as those generated by the reification and political enforcement of a particular conception of identity. Human beings who are just doing what comes naturally find themselves maligned, punished, and scapegoated for the unfortunate or unacceptable consequences of their behavior. It is not really their fault, in the sense that they are not in fact wholly free and undetermined agents but creatures of instinct and unbidden desires who have some (limited) capacity for foresight and self-control. Holding such creatures accountable as though they were truly and wholly free and self-determining is therefore morally overdemanding, destructive, and unjustifiably punitive.

In the face of this understanding of the human (political) condition, then, what would Connolly have us do? What prescriptions would he offer as ways to attenuate the repression and cruelty he sees as endemic to the dynamics of identity\difference? to drain the existential resentments? to blunt the punitiveness? What should be our aspirations for democracy?

For his constructive democratic ideal, Connolly turns for inspiration to the same figures who shape his diagnostic analysis; to Nietzsche and Foucault. He recognizes, of course, that deriving a democratic ethic from the relentlessly and imperiously aristocratic Nietzsche requires some fairly creative reformulations. As he writes, "a democrat who draws upon Nietzsche to think about contemporary issues of identity, ethics, and politics will soon be compelled to take several steps away from him."[53] What Connolly takes from Nietzsche is a tragic sense of life together with an attitude that he variously styles as "nontheistic reverence for existence" or "affirmation of the abundance of life." The emphasis is not upon Nietzsche's political ideas, but upon his "apolitical idealism." Of particular importance in this democratic reconfiguration of the Nietzschean tragic vision is that Connolly transforms the central contrast between "last man" and "overman" from a class distinction between human types—between the vast masses of petty self-seekers consumed by resentment and the few magnanimous self-affirmers—into a "set of dispositions that may compete for presence in any self."[54] Like Foucault, moreover, Connolly shifts the focus from Nietzsche's heroes and classical tragic figures to everyday tragic misfits, thereby seeking to convey the extraordinary character of the latter and to "fold Nietzschean agonism into the fabric of ordinary life."[55]

What emerges from this democratic reconfiguration of Nietzsche under the aegis of Foucault, then, is what Connolly recommends as a democratic "ethic of cultivation." Connolly begins his account of a democratic ethic with a Rortyan move. Recognition that human life has nothing essential or natural to it but is instead a serendipitous congeries of contingencies should lead us to live our identities with an element of ironic detachment and self-effacement. The genealogically sophisticated post-Nietzschean spirit laughs at its own pretensions and at its own impulses toward moral elevation and cosmic reassurance.[56] That ironic self-awareness carries with it a leaching away of moralism, punitiveness, and manipulative designs upon those who are different.

But Connolly does not rest there. His ironism does not end in a form of Humean complacency, but in an ethos of "reciprocal generosity" and "adversarial care and respect." Irony towards oneself is combined with a sense of reverence for the multifarious and diverse panoply of life the world gives us. Nietzsche's aristocratic magnanimity is softened and democratized into a generosity that "proceeds from the abundance of being over identity" and an "obligation to difference that proceeds from acknowledgment of the indebtedness of your contingent identities to those differences that make them possible."[57]

Appreciation of the "abundance of being" and recognition of one's indebtedness to the presence of difference lead next, Connolly hopefully surmises, to an "ethic of care for life" and to adversarial respect. The tragic vision of life derived from Nietzsche and Foucault can elicit care from the bearers of this faith, Connolly avers, through a sense of sympathetic identification with those who differ from us: however different in particular identity, they, like us, are products of contingency; they, like us, struggle with mortality.[58] And respect is elicited in the same manner that one gains respect for a foe who resists and challenges you. Like gladiators who embrace after the battle, like Agassi/Sampras or Evert/Navratilova, "one sometimes selects as a friend one whom one respects most as an adversary."[59]

The political ideal that flows from this ethical stance is one of "agonistic democracy." Agonistic democracy does not, like liberal neutrality, prioritize the right to the good and try to push competing claims to identity off the agenda of the democratic polity. It does not enshrine a liberal individualism that privileges a particular kind of self, particular goals, and particular values. And it does not seek to center politics around an elusive quest for the common good, a notion Connolly sees as ineluctably hegemonic in its effects if not in its intent. The agonistic democrat champions a form of democracy "in which divergent orientations to the mysteries of existence find overt expression in public life. Spaces for difference to be are established through the play of political contestation."[60] Agonistic democracy is pluralistic all the way down. It encompasses and in some sense is built upon contention among clashing identities who respect each others' self-affirmations. It incorporates special care, perhaps, for society's misfits, who should be seen as tragic figures caught in a world not well suited to their own unique desires and propensities. And it hopefully incorporates, amid the strife of contending identities, "selective collaboration between multiple, overlapping constituencies" that can in turn produce "a politics of creative coalitions . . . to enable action in concert through the state while cultivating attunement to new drives to pluralization."[61]

In many respects, this is an appealing vision of democratic possibilities. It encompasses most of the virtues of Iris Young's model of an egalitarian politics of difference: generosity of spirit, creative acceptance of human differences, a commitment to the flourishing and dignity of all citizens. Additionally, it offers a therapeutic solvent for the resentments and punitiveness that systematically disfigure democratic—not to mention nondemocratic—politics. By comparison with Young's prescriptive remedies, moreover, Connolly seems more realistic about some of the unavoidable trade-offs, paradoxes, and ambiguities that are uneliminable in any politics. And he seems less inclined to countenance manipulative and intrusive measures to pursue his favored ends. One is left, nonetheless, with several areas of concern regarding the adequacy and the structural solidity of Connolly's vision of democratic agonism. The principal worry about agonistic democracy centers around the fragility of its ethical base. If the case for nontheistic reverence for existence and adversarial care and respect is shaky, the whole edifice becomes exceedingly precarious. The question here is not whether reverence for life, care, and respect are ethically worthy responses to the world and to other people; surely they are. The question is whether these responses are reasonably to be expected as the attitudinal corollaries of the animating vision behind them. Connolly himself acknowledges that "these post-Nietzschean sources of goodness and obligation are fragile and fugitive."[62] But they may be even more fragile than he concedes both in their psychological sources and in the sometimes tenuous connection between these sources and their alleged behavioral consequences.

Why should the tragic vision of life as a teeming chaos of diverse contingencies be expected to inspire in the beholder a sense of reverence? Why logically should it do so? The hope that this will happen seems crucial to the agonistic project, but convincing warrants for this hope are hard to come by. Confronted by the riotous abundance of a pulsing accidental cosmos, why is not the likely reaction one of despair? Why not a sense of metaphysical nausea? This is a vision of the world as a tale told by an idiot, full of sound and fury, signifying nothing. It is a world in which the correlate of abundance is meaninglessness. Why, then, are not the responses of Shakespeare's MacBeth or Sartre's Roquentin more likely and more logical than Connolly's reverence? Why, moreover, is a sense of reverence morally proper in this context? Why not moral as well as metaphysical nausea? Given that the diversity of existence encompasses not just black and white, straight and gay, male and female, but Jeffrey Dahmer and Joseph Mengele, the Jukes and the Kallikaks, isn't reverence as inappropriate as it is unlikely?

What then happens to the hopes for the fostering of care and respect in this world of contingency and difference? Connolly says that he, Nietzsche, and Foucault "strive to tap into a protean care for the diversity of life which, according to these faiths, already inhabits almost everyone to some degree or other."[63] But is the evidence in support of this "protean spirituality" that strong? Or is it, like Rousseau's "natural pity" and Condorcet's "fine and generous sensibility which nature has implanted in the hearts of all" more of an autobiographical report than a warranted empirical generalization? And if the evidence for this hope is suspect, what about the logic? Why should we expect people to be naturally or spontaneously caring or respectful to others, particularly when those others are conceived as different from them and not in some essential way the same or engaged in common enterprise? They may indeed "struggle with mortality" like us. But what if our own struggle can be eased by terminating theirs? Should we not suspect that Connolly's hopes represent a triumph of his moral habituation over his logic? *Caritas*, after all, is the axis of a Christian ethic; respect, the fulcrum of the Kantian imperative. These profoundly humane moral injunctions are deeply em

bedded in our culture—and, no doubt, in the patterns of socialization that produced the humane and ethically attuned sensibility of a William Connolly. But if
these traditions are jettisoned as products of a mythical metaphysic, will the care
and respect they sustain survive them?

What, moreover, are the practical implications—for policies and institutions—of Connolly's critique of responsibility as an onerous construct foisted
onto human material not predesigned to accommodate it? One possible prescriptive conclusion that might follow from Connolly's anthropology could be to
counsel the complete and total removal of responsibility as a reasonable norm or
proper expectation in social policies or institutions. But Connolly does not embrace this alternative.[64] Instead, he avers that responsibility is "indispensable to
life"—a construct to be sure and one that does not well fit those who bear it, but
one society cannot do without.[65] And this concession is no doubt a wise one, not
only for the practical reasons suggested by the language of "indispensability," but
for more profound political and moral reasons as well. For the practical correlate
of relieving the ordinary run of human beings of all responsibility on the (charitable? or contemptuous?) grounds that they aren't really up to it and that it is
therefore both cruel and unrealistic to demand it of them has always been some
form of benignly construed despotism—whether of the Grand Inquisitor, Bentham's wardens, Platonic philosopher-kings, or Helvetian "true doctors of morality." Total absolution from responsibility presages eligibility for total subjection.

If Connolly wisely avoids the political and moral quagmire surrounding the
abandonment of attributions of responsibility, however, it remains unclear what
practical implications do follow. Perhaps this is only consistent with his persistent
invocations of the uneliminable ambiguities in political life. But at some point
policies have to be formulated, institutions have to be fashioned. Should these differ from what we have now? Or must we live with them as they are, since we cannot dispense with them? One gathers that compassion, mercy, and a lack of
vindictiveness are the moral attitudes entailed by Connolly's tragic view of life.
But does refraining from "blaming the victim," as it were, entail that norms of responsible behavior should be waived for those who were not well socialized into
them? Do we refrain from punishing criminals? Or simply wring our hands in
sorrow as we send them off to jail? Do we refrain from rehabilitative designs on
the grounds that they implicitly enforce contestable ideals of normal identity?
Unless and until more concrete answers are given to questions such as these, Connolly's critique of the "overdetermined" or "strong" Western norm of responsibility constitutes a counsel of attitude adjustment based on a metaphysical
anthropology, but it lacks political purchase. The clear rhetorical effect of Connolly's hermeneutic is to cast doubt on the legitimacy and the *bona fides* of all
those who exercise some form of authority/control even in (or particularly in?) a
liberal society. But it is not clear what would legitimate their exertions of power or
what, in the alternative, should replace them.

Last, it can at least be argued that Connolly's hopeful aspirations for democratic cooperation among his contending identities may be both too optimistic and
too pessimistic at the same time. He hopes to see "selective collaboration" among

the "multiple constituencies" he depicts, a "politics of creative coalitions . . . to enable action in concert through the state." But one can doubt that his account of the dynamics of identity and the exigencies of an insistent pluralism will in fact lend themselves very well to such collaboration. When does the contestation and the agonism end and the cooperation begin? Why does it not simply deepen into antagonism, mutual detestation, and political fragmentation? What causes or inspires or sustains the hoped for coalitions? Common mortality and contingency seem too little to work with.

What is most valuable, perhaps, about Connolly's admonitions, particularly for those of us inclined toward invocations of some common good, however elusive, is his cautionary note about the tendency of ideals of community to be or become *de facto* hegemonic. To maintain or pretend harmony of purpose, some must be ignored or shortchanged or suppressed or cast aside. All idealizations of democratic community have to take this concern with great seriousness—both to seek to avoid hegemonic imposition as much as possible and also to admit to the elements of tension that no conception of the public interest can ever entirely overcome and to the attendant and unevenly allocated price that is paid for a politics of common good. Once this is conceded, though, it remains possible to insist that Connolly's arguably unwarranted optimism about the possibilities of democratic cooperation in his pluralistic and agonistic identity-oriented polity is conjoined with an excessive pessimism about the possibilities of democratic community centered around more extensive, robust, and concrete elements of common cause and general welfare than the very abstract metaphysical commonality of mortality and contingency that he holds out to us as our only common threads. A democratic community is always a work of political art, something that takes conscious fashioning and continual sustenance, rather than a natural or spontaneous occurrence. This form of political art is crucial to the statesmanship of all democratic societies—especially pluralistic ones—although it is not an art that has received much theoretical (or empirical) attention and sustenance in recent decades. Those who undertake to pursue this art, however, have more to work with than Connolly concedes to them: strands of common humanity that exceed the struggle with mortality and the facts of contingent fate, a common geography, some common—or at least very widely held—values, common experiences, common burdens, common interests. With all that divides the members of a pluralist democracy, both in interests and in identities, there is more to sustain the creation of a democratic community than Connolly allows us. And a good thing, too; for as the democratic realists well understand, we need all the help along these lines that we can get.

Notes

1. William E. Connolly, *Identity\Difference: Democratic Negotiations of Political Paradox* (Ithaca: Cornell University Press, 1991), 33–34. For a similar ambivalent assessment of the relationship between the ideals of traditional distributive egalitarianism and those of

identity egalitarianism, see Bonnie Honig, *Political Theory and the Displacement of Politics* (Ithaca: Cornell University Press, 1993), 159–60: "the aspiration of the difference principle is admirable . . . [but it can be embraced] only by rejecting the rational packing in which Rawls wraps his difference principle."

2. Walt Whitman, "Democratic Vistas" and "1872 Preface to As a Strong Bird on Pinions Free," in *The Complete Prose of Walt Whitman*, vol. 2, ed. Malcolm Cowley (New York: Pellegrini and Cudahy, 1948), 221–22, 229, 253, 283.

3. See, for example, George Kateb, "Democratic Individuality and the Claims of Politics," *Political Theory* 12, no. 3 (August 1984): 331–60.

4. Connolly, *Identity\Difference*, 83–84

5. It is hard, in fact, to read Marx's remarks about Feuerbach, Bauer, and Stirner in the preface to Volume One of *The German Ideology* without noting their potential applicability to contemporary poststructuralist radicalism. Marx characterizes the animating assumptions of the Young Hegelians as follows: "Hitherto men have constantly made up for themselves false conceptions about themselves, about what they are and what they ought to be. They have arranged their relationship according to their ideas of God, of normal man, etc. The phantoms of their brains have gained the mastery over them . . . Let us liberate them from the chimeras, the ideas, dogmas, imaginary beings under the yoke of which they are pining away . . . ; and existing reality will collapse." To these excessively "idealist" assumptions, Marx ripostes by parable: "Once upon a time an honest fellow had the idea that men were drowned in water only because they were possessed with the idea of gravity. If they were to knock this idea out of their heads . . . they would be sublimely proof against any danger from water. His whole life long be fought against the illusion of gravity, of whose harmful results all statistics brought him new and manifold evidence. This honest fellow was the type of the new revolutionary philosophers in Germany." *The Portable Karl Marx*, ed. Eugene Kamenka (New York: Penguin Books, 1983), 162–63.

6. See their exchange in *Political Theory* 20, no. 3 (August 1992): 511–14 and *Political Theory* 21, no. 1 (February 1993): 128–31.

7. Iris Marion Young, *Justice and the Politics of Difference* (Princeton: Princeton University Press, 1990), 5.

8. Young, *Justice and the Politics of Difference*, 97.

9. Young, *Justice and the Politics of Difference*, 5.

10. Young, *Justice and the Politics of Difference*, 25.

11. Young, *Justice and the Politics of Difference*, 33.

12. Young, *Justice and the Politics of Difference*, 43–45.

13. Young, *Justice and the Politics of Difference*, 7.

14. Rawls, *Theory of Justice*, 100.

15. Young, *Justice and the Politics of Difference*, 157 and 177.

16. Young, *Justice and the Politics of Difference*, 173–74.

17. See Lawrence Kohlberg, *The Philosophy of Moral Development: Moral Stages and the Idea of Justice* (San Francisco: Harper and Row, 1981) and Carol Gilligan, *In a Different Voice: Psychological Theory and Women's Development* (Cambridge: Harvard University Press, 1993).

18. Young, *Justice and the Politics of Difference*, 174.

19. Young, *Justice and the Politics of Difference*, 184.

20. Young, *Justice and the Politics of Difference*, 187. "Privileged groups," in contrast, do not need specific representation because they "are already represented, in the sense that their voice, experiences, values, and priorities are already heard and acted upon."

21. John Stuart Mill, *Considerations on Representative Government*, chapter 7.

22. Proportional representation *per se* is apparently deemed inadequate because (1) the electoral rosters and voting behavior might turn around interests or parties rather than around cultural identity groups and (2) because PR, in its reliance upon the one person one vote principle, "retains the assumption that it is primarily individuals who must be represented in decision making bodies." *Justice and the Politics of Difference*, 187.

23. Young, *Justice and the Politics of Difference*, 188–89.

24. Young, *Justice and the Politics of Difference*, 188.

25. Young, *Justice and the Politics of Difference*, 191.

26. Young, *Justice and the Politics of Difference*, 158.

27. Young, *Justice and the Politics of Difference*, 160.

28. Young, *Justice and the Politics of Difference*, 183.

29. Young, *Justice and the Politics of Difference*, 212.

30. Young, *Justice and the Politics of Difference*, 195.

31. Young, *Justice and the Politics of Difference*, 86.

32. Young, *Justice and the Politics of Difference*, 120.

33. Young, *Justice and the Politics of Difference*, 151 and 154.

34. Connolly, *Identity\Difference*, 64.

35. Connolly, *Identity\Difference*, 64.

36. Young, *Justice and the Politics of Difference*, 189.

37. Roberto Alejandro, *Hermeneutics, Citizenship, and the Public Sphere*, 127.

38. For an expression of similar concerns, see George Kateb, "Notes on Pluralism," *Social Research* 61, no. 3 (Fall 1994): 511–37.

39. Young, *Justice and the Politics of Difference*, 120.

40. "Groups cannot be socially equal unless their specific experience, culture, and social contributions are publicly affirmed and recognized." Young, *Justice and the Politics of Difference*, 174.

41. See Young, *Justice and the Politics of Difference*, 97 and 158 *inter alia*. For an explication of the confusion involved in this characterization, see Alejandro, *Hermeneutics, Citizenship, and the Public Sphere*, 125. Alejandro writes that "her argument about the 'assimilationist' ideal of justice . . . suggests a confusion between a universal background of rights and a universal culture identity, two categories that overlap in her analysis." In fact, he notes, the universality of the principle of rights "since the beginning . . . was meant to protect, not a universal identity of interests and even less a universal culture, but, quite to the contrary, the universality of different talents, levels of property, and religious perspectives."

42. It might be objected that this formulation implies that a liberal state cannot enforce laws against, say, racial discrimination on the grounds that such enforcement is culturally imperialistic vis-a-vis certain identity groups—e.g., racists. But that does not follow. For one thing, the distinction between traits—such as skin color—and behavior is an important one, however much it tends to be elided under the rubric of "identity." A democratic regime is not only entitled to but obligated to prohibit behavior in the public domain that invidiously discriminates against any citizen on the basis of race, color, or gender *per se*. To fail to do so eviscerates the meaning of democratic citizenship and violates the fundamental axiom of political and legal equality constitutive of democratic governance. The Slaughterhouse cases, one might say, demonstrated this proposition in a perversely backward fashion.

43. Young, *Justice and the Politics of Difference*, 181–82.

44. Young's very expansive construction of oppression is an instance of a fairly widespread phenomenon in egalitarian social theory, a phenomenon we might call the "conceptual inflation of negative normative categories." I refer to the tendency to take a pe-

jorative term pertaining to illegitimately hierarchical social relations and to interpret it so broadly, and to apply it so indiscriminately, that it implies the presence of extensive entitlements for the less fortunately situated and a corresponding obligation on those arguably better-off to undertake remedial action requiring self-sacrifice and/or the assumption of guilt. One example of this conceptual inflation that mimics Young's account of oppression is Bruce Ackerman's expansion of the term "exploitation" to cover any instance of undeserved inequality. By his definition, every time an athletic incompetent is born, Michael Jordan becomes more of an exploiter—unless he is willing to make additional sacrifices to even up the distribution of assets. See Ackerman *Social Justice in the Liberal State* (New Haven: Yale University Press, 1980), chapter 8. Another example is the expansion of the notion of "rape" by some feminists to cover any sexual encounter that a female comes to deem unsatisfactory, even *ex post facto* upon sober second thought.

45. Young, *Justice and the Politics of Difference*, 190.

46. Young, *Justice and the Politics of Difference*, 154–55 and 151.

47. "Contemporary followers of Nietzsche such as Foucault and Deleuze, who have politicized the spirit of Nietzsche's thought and thereby reconstituted some of its key dimensions, have not pursued this project far enough to sustain a political theory." Connolly, *Identity\Difference*, 185.

48. William Connolly, "Pluralism, Partisanship, and Ethics," in *Political Theory and Partisan Politics*, ed. Edward Portis, Adolf Gundersen and Ruth Shively (Suny Press), 8 . Another way to characterize this virtue of Connolly's thought is to say that he, as a good student of Karl Mannheim, does not fall into the comforting and delusory self-certitude that results from remaining frozen at the ultimately untenable level of awareness Mannheim calls the "special form" of the "total conception of ideology." Those who never move on to the less comfortable but logically unavoidable "general form" of the total conception of ideology entertain the delusion that only their adversaries' views are determined by social contingencies and not their own. See Mannheim, *Ideology and Utopia*, trans. by Louis Wirth and Edward Shils (New York: Harcourt, Brace and World, 1936), 77.

49. Connolly, *Identity\Difference*, 64.

50. Connolly, *Identity\Difference*, 65.

51. Connolly, *Identity\Difference*, 65.

52. Connolly, *Identity\Difference*, 115–16.

53. Connolly, *Identity\Difference*, 184.

54. Connolly, *Identity\Difference*, 187.

55. Connolly, *Identity\Difference*, 187.

56. Connolly, *Identity\Difference*, 180.

57. Connolly, "*Pluralism, Partisanship, and Ethics*," 23 (ms).

58. "The very contingency of identity and the universality of the struggle with mortality can sometimes solicit in the self a fugitive experience of identification with life that stretches below and above any particular identity." Connolly, *Identity\Difference*, 166.

59. Connolly, *Identity\Difference*, 197.

60. Connolly, *Identity\Difference*, 211.

61. Connolly, "Pluralism, Partisanship, and Ethics," 24–25 (ms).

62. Connolly, "Pluralism, Partisanship, and Ethics," 23 (ms).

63. Connolly, "Pluralism, Partisanship, and Ethics," 13 (ms).

64. Others have been willing to do so, following out what seems to be the logic of a thoroughgoing naturalism or determinism. See, for example, Bruce N. Waller, *Freedom Without Responsibility* (Philadelphia: Temple University Press, 1990).

65. Connolly, *Identity\Difference*, 115.

Part Two

Civic Liberal Ideals

Introduction

The foregoing review of several leading variants of contemporary liberal theories is, of course, far from complete or comprehensive. But it does cover some of the most popular and influential conceptions of democratic ideals operative in American politics today. Democratic realism, perhaps, is more of an academic orientation than a popular ideology. But it is for that reason a persuasive perspective among political elites and policy intellectuals. And the libertarian, egalitarian, and multicultural ideas we examined arguably constitute the heart of current ideological debate and partisan struggle in this country.

The burden of my argument so far has been, however, that none of these theories provides a fully adequate or compelling account of liberal democratic ideals and purposes. The realist perspective is one crucial part of a serious understanding and appreciation of liberal democracy. What is missing from realist accounts for the most part, however, is any real sense of the higher reaches and aspirations proper to liberal democracy. What is missing is a serious and sustained answer to the question Mill posed at the outset of his *Considerations on Representative Government*: why is a liberal democratic regime better than a benign and competent despotism? The latter, after all, could presumably provide what the realists offer as the central virtues of liberal democracy: security, stability, and some degree of personal liberty, including freedom from depredations by fellow subjects.

The answer given that question by the libertarians is that liberal democracy is better than any form of despotism—including majoritarian despotism—because when properly conceived and organized it maximizes individual freedom. Individual liberty is the raison d'être of democracy, the pearl beyond any price. But this answer is open to serious questions. Liberty is a good, but why is it a good? How does it connect with human flourishing? Should all other human goods be subordinated to any incremental addition to individual absence of impediment, however small? Is merely formal equality sufficient for a democratic society? How can maximizing liberty be reasonably expected by itself to result in a healthy community life? Or is that unimportant? Isn't there something inadequate, misleading, and simplistic about libertarian ideals?

The principal alternative answer given to Mill's question by contemporary theorists focuses on the goal of equality. The central aspiration of liberal democracy, from the egalitarian perspective, is to eliminate as far as is possible and prudent the disparities of power and position among its citizens. But when the theoretical justification of this conception of liberal purposes is examined, other questions arise. Is equality per se a good? Why? Given the moral tragedies inherent in life, can any society really attain "fairness"? Are there no tensions between equality of condition and individual liberty? If there are, how much sacrifice of the latter is proper to produce incremental diminutions of inequality? Can equality as a normative end-state be squared with respect for the dignity and integrity of individuals, including the correlates of personal desert and responsibility? If so, how? If not, are there not serious costs to evading these moral tensions?

If the norms and institutional strategies of libertarianism were carried through to their logical conclusion, the result would seem to be a society of estranged enclaves or anomic individuals engaged in barter and competition. It would be a world in which the privatistic individualism Tocqueville worried about would reign supreme, with any larger sense of community and public spiritedness atrophied almost completely. The legislative and other representative institutions in society would become, to borrow Burke's words, not a "deliberative assembly" but a "congress of ambassadors from different and hostile interests." Overall, the society might be prosperous, so long as the costs of containing its inner divisions did not bleed it economically; but the social order would encompass vast and profound inequalities, with some segments of the population destitute and adrift. Individuals would, so far as their means permitted, have great latitude of behavior, but taken as a whole it seems doubtful that this would be a society an outside observer would characterize as good or happy.

Taking the norms and institutional strategies of the egalitarian theories we surveyed to their logical conclusion would also, however, lead to significant distortions. In some respects, the unfavorable results would actually overlap with those in the opposing libertarian scenario. For there is little in a Rawlsian egalitarian imperative that would provide much sustenance and support for the public realm and for the intermediary institutions of civil society. Under the aegis of Rawls's difference principle, the bonds of community seem to run almost entirely through the hands of the Internal Revenue Service and the other agencies of the redistributive branch of government. Sharing each others' fate means sharing their pocketbook and little else.[1] Indeed, the possibilities of community and what Rawls terms "associations" are derogated as impossible or oppressive in the context of moral and social pluralism. Tocqueville's privatism is thus not avoided. It simply is contextualized differently. For here, it is not the market that reigns supreme, but the government, the collective power of the majority or of a caste of moral guardians, lawyers, and bureaucratic elites able to insinuate themselves into positions of power. The prospect looms that Tocqueville's other great fear about the democratic future would be realized: "Above this race of men stands an immense and tutelary power, which takes upon itself alone to secure their gratifications and to watch over their fate. . . . It would be like the authority of a parent, if, like that authority, its object was to prepare men for manhood; but it seeks, on the contrary, to keep them in perpetual childhood."[2] A democratic society organized in accord with egalitarian liberal theory, then, might be benign and compassionate, and it would avoid the perils and practical costs of the great inequalities that libertarians would countenance. But it would be rather like a school run by beneficent schoolmarms: a regime of putative fairness and noble intent, but one that was neither very free nor very adult. From the perspective of civic republicans, who also prized political equality, it would seem more like a patron–client regime with one big patron and a host of querulous clientele groups than like a healthy democratic republic.

The ideals and policy prescriptions of the liberalism of difference are similarly flawed. Difference liberals usefully remind us that the ideals of both liberty and equality need to be expanded and transposed into cultural terms in today's ethnically and morally pluralistic societies. But they offer no compelling account of how a society so fixated upon cultural differences and so subservient to demands based upon them can work cooperatively on behalf of effective democratic governance.

What seems lacking in the leading extant theories of democratic ideals is balance and complexity. They fail to account adequately for the plurality of human goods pertinent to a democratic polity and they fail to appreciate relevant nuances within the particular goods, especially as they are related of necessity to each other. My thought, then, is that we can do better than this. Surely we can conceive of our liberal democratic purposes and aspirations in a more capacious and complex way that does justice to all the various elements of a free and flourishing community of political equals.

The purpose of the remaining chapters, then, is to sketch an alternative liberal democratic ideal—an alternative way to understand the norms and goals that should guide our policy-making and our institution-building. What follows will be in effect an exercise in what C. L. Stevenson has called "persuasive definition."[3] Our central democratic ideals are somewhat vague and open ended. They have a relatively stable core of abstract meaning, but both the concrete particulars and the periphery are neither entirely clear nor agreed upon. Full definitions of the concepts may be contestable, then, and where they bear upon moral and practical issues they are almost certain to be in some dispute.[4] Our definitions are significantly constrained because their core meanings cannot be effaced or altered beyond recognition. Without entering an Orwellian world or Alice's Wonderland, we cannot simply twist an appraisive concept to our immediate idiosyncratic ends. Freedom can't be twisted to mean bondage to others or equality twisted to mean hierarchical subordination. On the periphery, however, things are more fluid. Here we can try to bend and shape our normative concepts in order to make them more serviceable to us. Here rhetoric and personal judgment must come into play. Some would argue, as a result, that here things come down to politics narrowly conceived, to self-interest, and to emotion. Persuasion essentially consists in trying to manipulate the perceptions of others to render them compatible with your own interests. But this account is too permissive. Even on the periphery there are tests and standards, criteria—somewhat porous, to be sure—for what counts as a good definition that can make legitimate claims on our acceptance. To succeed in being persuasive, a proffered definition needs to meet both empirical and practical tests. Empirically, it needs to be true to our experience of the world; it needs to be able to render that experience more fully intelligible than its competitors. Practically, it needs to be a good tool, to borrow Wittgenstein's analogy. It needs to be more useful than alternative conceptions in allowing us to meet our needs and attain our desired ends. What makes this test not merely subjective or purely partisan, moreover, is the reference to "our" needs and ends. The test here is not objective in any positivistic sense, but it is also not a matter of purely individual will or preference. What Hume says of moral terms generally is on target here: in order to be intelligible, useful, and therefore accepted, the terms must answer to a common perspective and to general interests. What I am trying to accomplish by these chapters in rhetorical terms, therefore, is to convince you, my reader, that the interpretations I set out serve more effectively than the available alternatives to accord with your moral intuitions, to make your experiences intelligible, and to make our lives as democratic citizens better.

My reflections on our democratic ideals have led me to several general conclusions concerning them. I state these summarily here to give preliminary shape to the more particularized discussions that follow:

(1) A democratic society should not be organized around a single, overarching goal or value that claims hegemony over all other goals and values. Liberal democracy is characterized by certain core values, central among them liberty and equality; but neither of these—or any other goal—can claim to be *the* ruling standard or *telos* of a good society. A healthy liberal democracy must acknowledge the essential plurality of human goods and must give each its due.

(2) Democratic ideals are profoundly shaped and informed by a number of animating values and beliefs that generally do not appear on the masthead, as it were, but nonetheless play a key role in the democratic scheme. These are the not-so-evident truths that operate just beneath the surface of the more focal norms of liberty, equality, and community. I would include under this heading of "subterranean" liberal values respect for human dignity, belief in the efficacy and legitimacy of practical rationality, and a concern with the cultivation of personal responsibility.

(3) The central democratic ideals turn out to be somewhat complex and nuanced ideas in themselves. This is true not only with respect to their content but also with respect to their status—the way they properly function within the overall liberal scheme of things. A great deal of confusion, for example, is caused by conceiving all the liberal values as teleological—as end-state conditions that should be maximized.

(4) Properly understood, the various democratic ideals do not, for the most part, collide head-on—as in liberty versus equality, for example. In many ways

they support and supplement each other. It is hard to imagine that people could ever become autonomous, for example, apart from a sustaining community. And it is equally hard to conceive of genuine community or civic friendship in the modern world that is not in some fundamental sense a relationship among moral equals.

(5) Notwithstanding the synergy that obtains among the major democratic purposes, they are not always fully or completely reconcilable. Elements of tension always will remain among them. Trade-offs will be unavoidable in applying them. The plurality of human goods creates some moral tragedies, as Sir Isaiah Berlin has properly insisted, that neither the best will nor the best technology can eliminate. It follows, moreover, that liberal democratic norms can never be fully determinate, in the sense of dictating a specific outcome or policy as the unequivocally right one.

(6) "Politics," therefore, will be both proper and constant in a good liberal democracy, as Bernard Crick has eloquently insisted. Politics is not merely a residual chaos produced by theoretical failings, institutional inadequacies, or malign will. A democratic citizenry will always have to make choices and will have to do so through making corrigible judgments, by seeking to persuade each other, and by bargaining among themselves. This would be the case even if we all were civic liberals, and it certainly will be the case in the real world where other versions of democratic ideals will always remain to contest the field.

Notes

1. In *Political Liberalism*, Rawls goes beyond his tendency in *A Theory of Justice* to identify democratic fraternity with the institutionalization of the difference principle (*Theory of Justice*, 106) to cite participation in the dialogue of public reason and adherence to its norms as part of civic friendship (*Political Liberalism*, 253). This is a welcome addition to his earlier and more attenuated construction of fraternity. But it is arguably compromised by his circumscription of what counts as reasonable (see endnote 30, chapter 8) and undermined by his dismissive account of the associational bonds needed to sustain a genuine and robust democratic conversation.

2. Alexis de Tocqueville, *Democracy in America*, ed. Richard Haffner (New York: Menton Books, 1956), 303.

3. C. L. Stevenson, "Persuasive Definitions," *Mind* 47, no. 187 (July 1938): 331–50.

4. See W. B. Gallie, "Essentially Contested Concepts," in *The Importance of Language*, ed. Max Black (Englewood Cliffs: Prentice–Hall, 1962), 121–46. See also William Connolly, *The Terms of Political Discourse* (Lexington: Heath, 1974).

5

Political Liberty and the Good of Autonomy

Although all democratic liberals privilege liberty and equality in their scheme of political values, they do not necessarily interpret them in the same way. These are very broad and abstract notions, and they admit of considerable variation when people get around to specifying in any concrete sense what exactly they entail. Moreover, since these two axial norms can exist in some tension with each other, different schools of liberalism can and do relate and prioritize them in divergent ways. However unanimous the liberal embrace of liberty and equality, therefore, these ideals are very much essentially contested concepts. As a consequence, the abstract and prima facie concurrence of liberal theorists and citizens of liberal regimes often falls apart rather quickly when it is brought to bear on real-world issues.

In this chapter and the one to follow, I want to provide a civic liberal reading of these potent but ambiguous social ideals. I want to delineate a civic liberal perspective on what these core values should mean and to make the case that this perspective is coherent and somewhat distinctive. I also want to make the case that the civic liberal view on these matters is at least as well anchored in the tradition of liberal thought and practice as are its competitors. And finally, I offer some reasons—though not a systematic or sustained argument—for why the civic liberal account should be seen as morally and practically more compelling than other versions of liberalism. There are, of course, no knock-down arguments in this particular arena. As Quentin Skinner has well said, "in moral and political debate, it will always be possible to speak *in utramque partem*, and will never be possible to couch our moral and political theories in deductive form. The appropriate model will always be that of a dialogue, the appropriate stance a willingness to negotiate over rival intuitions concerning the applicability of evaluative terms. We strive to reach understanding and resolve disputes in a conversational way."[1] My hope is to deepen and enrich this conversation/contestation about the defining norms of democratic liberalism. I do not imagine that my argument will settle the controversies about these ideals, only that the controversies can be extended in an illuminating and productive manner.

In reflecting upon the nature and appeal of liberty and equality as crucial political norms, it is important to keep them well situated in two respects: first, within the dynamics of a good human life and, second, within the history and tradition of the liberal democratic project. It is important to keep political ideals well situated because they are heavily context dependent for their meaning. It can be said of terms designating political ideals what Wittgenstein insisted regarding words generally: their meaning is their use. And their use is discernible only within the setting of the language game in which they function. When words are abstracted out of their natural and historical habitats, as it were, they may confuse rather than illuminate, leading us into thickets rather than where we want to go. The problem here, as Wittgenstein put it, is that language has lost its traction, gone "on a holiday." To alleviate the confusion and avoid misdirection, it is necessary to recall the language game whose logic had given the words their use in the first place. Terms of normative political discourse are certainly subject to the same debilities, and Wittgenstein's admonitions are thus equally appropriate with respect to them. Political ideals emerge from specific historical contexts and mean what they do in relation to the concrete problem situation that generated them. If we do not keep these generative circumstances in mind, we permit the ideals to go on a holiday and lead us afield. This is not to say that a political ideal cannot take on some life and logic of its own, evolving into a new and broader notion that may turn out to be compelling. But even then this pattern of evolution is likely to be productive rather than malign only so long as some connection is maintained with the originating function of the ideal.

This cautionary admonition is, I would argue, particularly relevant to the core liberal ideals of liberty and equality—for two principal reasons. First, these core liberal ideals were in their incipience what Giovanni Sartori has called "protest ideals."[2] They are symbols of aspiration to escape or transform specific situations that were experienced as unnecessarily or intolerably confining on the one hand or unjustly and inappropriately discriminatory on the other. It is therefore especially pertinent to the task of getting a good handle on what political liberty and equality were felt to be about to recall what these constraints and discriminations were and why they were deemed improper. If these are inaccurately supposed or fabricated, the point and intention of the ideals may be altogether transformed. One very likely consequence, for example, is what Stephen Holmes aptly refers to as "antonym substitution." As he tellingly observes, the whole thrust of liberalism is distorted if we forget that private property rights were defended not as an alternative to charity but to princely confiscation, that skepticism was juxtaposed not to moral commitment but to authoritarian dogmatism and irrational enthusiasm, and that interest-based compromises were defended not against an alternative of rational consensus but against the horrors of religious fratricide.[3]

The second reason that adequately situating the norms of liberty and equality is particularly important is that these ideals are especially prone to being lifted out of context and turned into abstract and hegemonic standards precisely because they are so fundamental to liberal aspirations and moral intuitions. Precisely because we, as modern democratic liberals, are so deeply convinced of the moral force of liberty and equality, we are susceptible to the notion that they can be hypostasized into transcendent goods to be maximized. But when they are handled in that fashion, the results are rarely either illuminating or benign. Much of the ideological disputation that goes on between the competing wings of liberalism may be taken as a bleak illustration of this phenomenon. One leading school of thought seems content to suppose that liberty in the form of an abstract and open-ended individual freedom to choose is worthy of being elevated into an uncompromisable absolute. Others seem to consider equality so sacrosanct that they want to impose verbal taboos on any reference to even the most obvious and incontrovertible instances of uneven human endowment or attainment. In both cases, the commitment to a profoundly worthy and compelling moral ideal engenders perversely rigid imperatives because the ideal has been wrested from its moorings and turned into an idol. The initiating commitment is laudable, the consequences not always very plausible or attractive. Time to get back to rough ground.

Liberty as Autonomy

In the fall of 1958, Sir Isaiah Berlin delivered his Inaugural Lecture at Oxford University. His topic was "Two Concepts of Liberty," and the published lecture has since become a *locus classicus* among scholarly reflections on political liberty and its various forms.[4] Adapting a distinction that Benjamin Constant made between the liberty of the ancients and the liberty of the moderns, Berlin argued that a major source of contention between competing twentieth-century political regimes and their animating systems of ideas was their adherence to one or another of two very different conceptions of liberty. These he succinctly dubbed the "negative" and "positive" conceptions. Negative liberty is freedom from, positive liberty a capacity to do. A person is free in the negative sense whenever he or she "can act unobstructed by others."[5] The definition given to positive liberty is somewhat less clear, but Berlin basically characterized it as possessing the ability to attain one's "true purpose" in life.[6]

Berlin coupled this analytical thesis with a normative one. The only proper use of the terms "freedom" and "liberty," he insisted, pertains to the negative version. We should recognize that freedom properly so called can only refer to the happy situation of being uncoerced by other human agents. Freedom so understood is by no means the only human good, and we should concede that it may be in tension in our imperfect world with other human goods. But it is a great good. And we should avoid the temptation to try to reconcile it with other goods by redefining it. When we do that, we risk losing the precious reality of genuine freedom while hiding that fact from ourselves (or others) by our (mis-)appropriation of the very name in which protests against political coercion—whether benign or deliberately exploitative—must be waged.

Specifically, he argued, the positive conception of liberty is disastrously prone to being abused in this fashion. If freedom is understood as self-realization, the crucial element of noncoercion is in danger of being lost. If I am "free" when I have actualized my "true self," others may claim to know better than I what my self-realization consists in, and they may use that claim as warrant for "forcing me to be free." Thus the positive conception of liberty "lends itself . . . to this splitting of personality into two: the transcendent, dominant controller, and the empirical bundle of desires and passions to be disciplined and brought to heel." The ideal of positive liberty is "at the heart of many of the nationalist, communist, authoritarian, and totalitarian creeds of our day."[7] Rousseau begets Robespierre and Jacobin terror. Hegel, via Marx, begets Bolshevik policies of "moulding communist humanity" through "proletarian coercion, in all its forms, from executions to forced labor."[8] Negative liberty, then, is not an all-encompassing political good, but it is a cherished and genuine good that should neither be forfeited in the real world nor defined away in the world of ideas. Positive liberty, in contrast, sounds very elevated, all-encompassing, and benign; but it leads all too easily and frequently to monstrous and manipulative political regimes and practices.

Berlin's notable essay has many virtues. It insightfully demonstrates the significant variations of understanding and aspiration that may be obscured by invocation of the common term of "liberty." It makes a compelling case for the importance of what Constant called "the liberty of the moderns." It casts a searching eye upon the distressing habit of self-righteous and self-assured elites employing the notion of freedom as self-realization to justify technocratic tyrannies. And it forcefully reminds us that all legitimate political projects and ideologies must forthrightly acknowledge and deal with what might be called the fact of tragedy—the unfortunate truth that "not all good things are compatible, still less all the ideals of mankind."[9]

That conceded, Berlin's argument taken as a whole is analytically inadequate and normatively misleading. The basic problem is that his conceptual typology is inappropriately dichotomous. He takes a range of various and reticulated notions of free agency and sorts them out like sheep and goats into two categorical pens of positive and negative. This relentlessly bifocal approach obscures some important distinctions, creates some very strange philosophical and political bedfellows, and leads to an unnecessarily confining political morality. Several of Berlin's hermeneutic judgments, I would argue, give us clues to where his basic argument goes awry. First, he implicitly assimilates what Constant calls the liberty of the ancients with twentieth-century totalitarian programs of contrived self-realization of the masses. But clearly this is cutting with a very dull analytical blade. Aristotle, Marx, and Hegel may all endorse the notion that human beings have essential potentialities that a well-ordered society should seek to actualize. But participating in self-governance (the classical notion of political liberty) is a long way from serving as malleable human material for the technocratic master-builders generated by left-wing neo-Hegelians. Second, when Berlin avers that "the classical English political philosophers" meant "not being interfered with by others" and no more when they used the term "liberty," he references Hobbes. But then a few pages later it turns out that Locke (along with Burke and the continental liberals Montesquieu and Kant) is consigned to the proto-Jacobin camp of positive liberty theorists for claiming that "where there is no law there is no freedom."[10] Mill is portrayed as unproblematically an exponent of negative liberty, even though the epigram for *On Liberty* references Wilhelm von Humboldt's paean to "human development" (self-realization by another name) and even though the core argument in the crucial third chapter of that work ("Of Individuality") incorporates a number of concepts and claims that seem more at home with the idea of positive liberty than of negative liberty, if we are to be forced into that dichotomous choice. And Bentham is then invoked as a paradigmatic defender of unambiguous negative liberty against the backsliding Locke. The result is that Hobbes, who gave us *Leviathan,* and Bentham, who gave us the Panopticon (arguably a paradigmatic embodiment of technocratic tyranny), are styled as exponents of the good (negative) kind of liberty, whereas Locke, who gave us one of the greatest defenses of limited government, is construed as a suspect sympathizer with the bad (positive) kind of liberty. Third, Berlin explicitly concedes that his preferred notion of liberty "is not incompatible with some kinds of autocracy," an avowal that makes one wonder why it was that the appeal to the good of liberty functioned historically in the rise of liberalism as a protest ideal in the fight against autocratic forms of governance.[11]

Berlin's analysis produces these anomalous characterizations, I would argue, because his dichotomizing conceptual razor slices apart the idea of autonomy, which should be seen as clearly distinct from and not reducible to Berlin's constructions of "positive" and "negative" liberty. Berlin mentions the idea of autonomy in his essay. But he rather abruptly and unpersuasively seeks to assimilate it to self-realization and hence to "positive" liberty, and in the process of doing so he leaves his own ideal of "negative" liberty more amorphous and less attractive than it needs to be. From the civic liberal perspective, it is precisely the notion of autonomy—which gets butchered by Berlin's bimodal typology—that should be seen as the core meaning of the defining liberal norm of liberty. The ideal of human autonomy is, I would argue, not only more humanly and morally compelling than either of Berlin's constructions, "negative" and "positive" liberty. It also is more faithful to the central concerns and aspirations of the liberal tradition, considered both as a philosophical tradition and as a political movement.

To understand the ideal of autonomy, it is perhaps best to begin by contemplating its opposites. This method of definition by contrast makes particular sense in the case of political ideals because political ideals characteristically arise in response to particular historical states of affairs felt to be problematical. That is why Stephen Holmes's insistence, cited earlier, that one must always attend closely to the originating antonyms of a political ideal is so pertinent. That is also why I have argued elsewhere that epic political theories always need to be understood in the context of the crises that prompted the theorist's inquiry in the first place.[12]

The impetus to autonomy that drove the liberal project historically was a campaign against three principal forms of illegitimate and improper political domination: subjection to absolute and/or arbitrary power, dependency, and paternalism. These are not entirely distinct categories of subjugation, of course. Anyone subject to absolute power is in a state of dependency, for example. But one can be dependent on others without their power being absolute in scope, arbitrary in form, or paternalistic in rationale. Dependency, then, is the most generic conception of the political condition that early liberals attacked. The specific subcategories of absolute, arbitrary, and paternalistic control were singled out for their particular relevance to leading extant examples of enforced dependency. The special objects of Enlightenment opprobrium, monarchs and prelates, served as almost paradigmatic examples of the abuses under attack: they claimed and sometimes exercised absolute or arbitrary authority in the name of God or Caesar or both, and they justified the forced dependency of their subjects in paternalistic terms—as fathers of the country or shepherds of the sheep.

It was John Locke who wrote most directly and eloquently about the unjustifiability of absolute and arbitrary political power, especially in his *Second Treatise of Civil Government*. Once it is conceded that no one is a slave by nature or a subject by God's divinely granted political patrimony (Locke's *First Treatise* was directed principally against the second of these claims) it can be established that arbitrary and absolute power are essentially and intrinsically illegitimate because no rational person would consent to be subject to such power. Locke summarizes the grounds for his rejection of absolute or arbitrary power in Chapter 11 of the *Second Treatise*. This form of excessive power, he tells us, cannot "consist with the ends of society and government." If people gave their rulers such absolute or arbitrary power over their persons and estates, they would "put themselves into a worse condition than the state of nature." By doing so, they would "have disarmed themselves, and armed him to make a prey of them when he pleases."[13]

Locke also took care to insist upon the distinction between paternal and political power and to draw from that distinction the conclusion that political power can never be justified on the basis of paternalistic claims. "These two powers, political and paternal," he wrote, "are so perfectly distinct and separate, and built upon so different foundations, and given to so different ends, that every subject that is a father has as much a paternal power over his children as the prince has over his." Thus, "the freedom of a man at years of discretion, and the subjection of a child to his parents, while yet short of it, are so consistent and so distinguishable that the most blinded contenders for monarchy 'by right of fatherhood' cannot miss of it."[14] Kant likewise zeroed in on the evils of paternalistic regimes for competent adults, making escape from them the centerpiece of his interpretation of the politics of enlightenment. "Paternalism," he wrote, "is the greatest despotism imaginable."[15] What enlightenment is fundamentally about, therefore, is escape from subjection—albeit possibly a willing subjection—to paternalistic authority: "Enlightenment," reads the opening line of Kant's famous essay on that topic, "is man's emergence from his self-imposed immaturity."[16] ("Immaturity" here is the translation offered for the German "Unmundigkeit," or "minority," a condition of being unable to make decisions for oneself.) "Immaturity," Kant continued, "is the inability to use one's understanding without guidance from another." This inability is often self-imposed, "because its cause lies not in lack of understanding, but in lack of resolve and courage to use it." This irresolution, however, Kant observed, is often deliberately encouraged by those in authority, who take upon themselves the role of paternalist guidance.

> The guardians who have so benevolently taken over the supervision of men have carefully seen to it that the far greatest part of them (including the entire fair sex) regard taking the step to maturity as very dangerous, not to mention difficult. Having first made their domestic livestock dumb, and having carefully made sure that these docile creatures will not take a single step without the go-cart to which they are harnessed, these guardians then show them the danger that threatens them, should they attempt to walk alone.[17]

Absolute power, arbitrary power, and paternalistic power are then the specifically relevant cases of the unfreedom which liberal reformers sought to escape. The generic evil, of which these conditions are paradigmatic and concrete instances, is dependency. The core intuition underlying the focus upon liberty as a political ideal is the perception that it is both morally improper and socially deleterious for mature, competent human beings to live in a state of abject dependency upon others. To live in this way is, first of all, less than fully human and, second, it drains the social enterprise of the aggregate energy and intelligence that could make it more productive and creative.

Rousseau perhaps comes to mind first as the theorist who identified and emphasized the role of dependency as the central political evil—one that he sees especially deeply entrenched within bourgeois society.[18] In a famous passage he tells us that "there are two sorts of dependence: dependence on things, which is from nature; dependence on men, which is from society. Dependence on things, since it has no morality, is in no way detrimental to freedom and engenders no vices. Dependence on men, since it is without order, engenders all the vices, and by it, master and slave are mutually corrupted."[19] Because Rousseau's critique of dependency eventuated in a politics of the general will and prompted him to style its triumph as a valid instance of forcing people to be free, one might seem justified in concluding prima facie that a focus upon dependency is associated with the deformities and dangers of "positive liberty" cited by Berlin. But Rousseau was somewhat distinctive in the psychological tack of his analysis of the nature and dynamics of dependency, and he was equally distinctive in his normative conclusions. Where he was not so distinctive was in his identification of dependency as the central debility a democratic politics should seek to overcome. Other leading liberal theorists concurred in this judgment, but they took a more institutional and less psychological view of the causes and content of dependency. And they therefore were not implicated in Rousseau's more radical and strained solutions to the problem.

Adam Smith, for example, could be as eloquent as Rousseau in his indictment of dependency as humanly and socially destructive. In his *Lectures on Jurisprudence,* he wrote that: "Nothing tends so much to corrupt and enervate and debase the mind as dependency, and nothing gives such noble and generous notions of probity as freedom and independency."[20] For Smith, however, it is not bourgeois society that is most culpable in creating the evil of dependency; it is, rather, the dynamics of a traditional society and economy that is more to blame. In the first place, Smith was not so quick as Rousseau to pronounce dependency on things to be, as Rousseau claimed, "in no way detrimental to freedom." Smith romanticized neither nature nor the poverty that afflicts primitive economies. Dependency on things, too, can be degrading. "No society can surely be flourishing and happy, of which the far greater part of the members are poor and miserable," he wrote.[21] And poverty and misery are what static economies tend to create.

Moreover, in the static and traditional societies that house these economies, the lower orders of people are forced into extreme dependency on their feudal superiors. Serfdom is virtually a synonym for dependency. Even if not actually in a state of villeinage, moreover, tenant farmers in these traditional agricultural economies existed in a state of dire dependency upon the landowner. "A tenant at will, who possesses land sufficient to maintain his family for little more than a quit-rent, is as dependent upon the proprietor as any servant or retainer whatever, and must obey him with as little reserve."[22] It is not the institution of the general will but rather the institution of the market, Smith argued, that liberates people from the degrading condition of dependency—both upon things and upon others. That is the moral and political point of the famous passage in which Smith said that "it is not from the benevolence of the butcher, the brewer, or the baker that we expect our dinner, but from their regard to their self-interest." The point is not that self-interest is better than benevolence. Rather the point is that those who must rely on the benevolence of others are cast into dependency upon them: "Nobody but a beggar chooses to depend chiefly upon the benevolence of his fellow citizens." If dependent in this way upon another's benevolence, people are forced to behave like puppies with their dam or spaniels with their master, Smith wrote, to "endeavor by every servile and fawning attention to obtain their good will."[23] Thus Smith's political prescriptions, considerably different from Rousseau's, were just as much shaped by a moral revulsion against the degrading consequences of living a life of dependency.

Two other classical liberals bear mention in this context: Condorcet and Jefferson. For both of them, the institutional reforms that meant most were predicated upon the perceived need to create a society in which democratic citizens were not trapped into dependency on others. For Condorcet, of course, who in classic Enlightenment fashion pinned his hopes for future progress on advances in the attainment and dissemination of knowledge, greater equality in education was of paramount concern. When he asked the question, "How equal must education be?" his answer turned about the problem of dependency. "The degree of equality in education that we can reasonably hope to attain, but that should be adequate, is that which excludes all dependence, either forced or voluntary." The central task, he argued, was to educate everyone to the point that each could "escape the deceits of charlatans who would lay snares for his fortune, his health, his freedom of thought and his conscience" and that none "will be compelled to yield . . . to the ablest of their number . . . absolute power in a spirit of blind confidence." In a word, what is most important to the advance of liberty, justice, political equality, and economic progress is that the citizen "not be in a state of blind dependence upon those to whom he must entrust his affairs or the exercise of his rights."[24]

Jefferson's political philosophy was similarly preoccupied with the need to organize a democratic republic so as to eliminate the vice of dependency. Some of his most characteristic and distinctive efforts at institutional reform were dictated by this concern. His fight against the laws of primogeniture and entail, for example, and his espousal of a ward system were driven by his quest to produce independent citizens with the competence and self-sufficiency to participate actively and effectively in the governance of their own political affairs. His famous insistence upon the virtues of an agrarian society flowed from the same preoccupation. Part of the reason he opined that "those who labor in the earth are the chosen people of God" was that he thought they possessed a firmer sense of the nature and limits of reality and possibility than did their urban counterparts. Those who encounter only artifacts, media images, and other people may be deluded into thinking that the world is merely—to borrow today's parlance—a social construction. Hence they may also be tempted to suppose that others are always to blame for any miseries they endure and that the world is infinitely malleable. Those who, in contrast, spend their days deploying their energies with and against the forces and regularities of nature—nurturing plants and animals and fighting things like drought, blue mold, and hoof-and-mouth disease—are safe from such reveries. But the crucial consideration behind Jefferson's preference for the agrarian life related not to a farmer's relationship with nature but to the freeholding landowner's status of nondependency. "Dependence," he wrote, "begets subservience and venality, suffocates the germ of virtue, and prepares fit tools for the signs of ambition." Those who rely upon "their own soil and industry, as does the husbandman, for their subsistence" are sociologically situated in a way that keeps them from falling prey to this moral and political debility. Jefferson's great fear was anything that would reduce "the bulk of the society . . . to be mere automatons of misery, and to have no sensibilities left but for sinning and suffering."[25]

Although Locke and Rousseau, Smith, Condorcet, and Jefferson championed different political institutions and strategies, then, they were all preoccupied with the same evil: the condition of being inescapably dependent upon the agency of others—whether benevolent or malign—for one's subsistence and direction. The fundamental human good of autonomy, conversely, is the transcendence of this dependency and subjection so that one has the capacity to be self-directing and has sufficient social space and resources to put this capacity to work. Linguistically expressed, to be autonomous is to be able meaningfully to use the first person pronoun in narrating one's life, to be an "I" and not simply a "me," to be an agent and not merely an object or a dependent variable.

To be autonomous, then, is to be—in Kantian language—not heteronomous, not merely a passive plaything of external causal circumstances. It also means, however, that a person is not anomic in one's patterns of behavior. The classical liberals did not contrast the desirable state of autonomy with guidance *per se* but with determination from the outside. The goal was not to lead a life of sheer impulse and whimsy, but to be self-governed. The goal was, and properly is, a political order in which all citizens are able to sail their own ships, as it were, and not to be either subservient crew members in the conduct of their own lives or adrift in boats with no rudders and luffing sails.

It is the norm of autonomy, of self-governance, that generates the powerful and—correctly understood—entirely proper insistence upon "individuality" as a core norm and aspiration of liberal governance. Democratic individuality, as one of its most eloquent contemporary expositors suitably reminds us, should not be confused with "individualism," either in the Tocquevillian sense of submersion within a circumscribed privatistic world or in the stereotypical sense of social atomism. Instead, writes George Kateb, the true and proper meaning of democratic individualism—a meaning that coheres with the liberal logic of autonomy—"resides in being, to some important degree, a person of one's own creating, making, choosing, rather than in being merely a creature or a socially manufactured, conditioned, manipulated thing."[26] As the bard of American democracy, Walt Whitman, wrote in *Democratic Vistas*: "The mission of government, henceforth, in civilized lands is . . . to train communities through all their grades, beginning with individuals and ending there again, to rule themselves."[27]

This is where and why the notion of having a "plan of life" becomes pertinent to liberal theory and governance. Not adventitiously, it was in the third chapter of *On Liberty*, entitled "Of Individuality," that John Stuart Mill elucidated the value of what he called "spontaneity," but what he more properly should have called autonomy. "It is the privilege and proper condition of a human being, arrived at the maturity of his faculties," he wrote, "to use and interpret experience in his own way. . . . He who lets the world, or his portion of it, choose his plan of life for him has no need of any other faculty than the ape-like one of imitation. He who chooses his plan for himself employs all his faculties. He must use observation to see, reasoning and judgment to foresee, activity to gather materials for decision, discrimination to decide, and when he has decided, firmness and self-control to hold to his deliberate decision."[28]

John Rawls has more recently incorporated this core aspect of autonomy into the conception of moral personhood that informs his theory of justice and his model of a well-ordered society. With an appropriate nod to Aristotle, Rawls argues that it is a "natural fact" that "other things equal, human beings enjoy the exercise of their realized capacities (their innate or trained abilities), and this enjoyment increases the more the capacity is realized, or the greater its complexity." Rawls then links this "Aristotelian Principle," as he calls it, with Mill's notion of having a plan of life: "A rational plan—constrained as always by the principles of right—allows a person to flourish, so far as circumstances permit, and to exercise his realized abilities as much as he can." The capacity to have "a conception of their good as expressed by a rational plan of life" thus becomes one of the two basic moral capacities of human beings.[29] That capacity is then attributed to the inhabitants of the original position, giving life and point to their self-interested calculations and hence entering crucially into the rationale for the principles of justice.

The normative point of this hermeneutic exercise, then, is this. Civic liberalism affirms what this sampling of seminal figures in the liberal tradition suggests: the liberty treasured by that tradition is best understood as the achievement of autonomy. Civic liberalism seeks a polity in which all citizens can be as self-governing as the limitations and constraints of social life permit. The goal is a society where all have the capability and the opportunity to pursue a plan of life of their own choosing. Liberty so understood and cherished is neither "negative" nor "positive" liberty as Isaiah Berlin limned those influential conceptions. From the vantage point of civic liberalism, "negative" liberty is all *auto* and no *nomos*, whereas "positive" liberty is all *nomos* and no *auto*.

Antonomy is not merely negative liberty because it requires more than—to borrow Hobbes's phrase—"absence of impediment." Achieving citizen autonomy is a complex and demanding task, both for the individual and for the society. An autonomous life is more than the unimpeded expression of whimsy, impulse, caprice, or inertia. As our review of prominent liberal theorists made clear, the kind of freedom sought by liberal regimes is not found in or attainable by beasts, mechanisms, or small children. Human selves that are no more than a bundle of appetites or unmediated drives are not autonomous and hence not really free in any humanly meaningful sense. They may be uncoerced by other human beings, but they are still unfree because they are fully governed by heteronomous forces. Their existence is not a human life; they behave but they do not act. For citizens to be free in the sense championed by the historic mainstream of liberal theory and by civic liberalism, they must be self-governing. They are exempted from the control of others because they can and do control themselves. Such an ideal also demands more of the society than does negative liberty. For societies cannot produce autonomous citizens by mere forbearance. People attain autonomy, if ever, not simply *via* an absence of imposition from the outside but from the presence of complex systems of nurturance and development and from being placed in situations in which they have the wherewithal to choose and to act. Even those liberal theorists who sought to limit the scope of the state most stringently, therefore, knew full well that liberal societies had to establish strong and vital institutions to nourish, educate, and sustain the autonomy of their citizens and especially their citizens-in-the-making.

If the autonomy espoused by civic liberalism is more than negative liberty, it is not—despite Berlin's worries and intimations to the contrary—subject to the deformations of "positive" liberty. It always requires Orwellian distortions of language and studious evasions of obvious issues to enlist the ideal of autonomy in the cause of domination. One thinks in this context not simply of Rousseau's dangerous language about forcing people to be free, but also of the verbal gyrations that Lenin performs in *What Is to Be Done?* when he very uncomfortably confronts the question of whether the actual will and judgment of the working class leads to socialism and whether it is entitled to the moral respect of socialist elites like himself. He answers yes to both questions to comport with the moral force of the ideal of autonomy, but then reverses the practical significance of his concession by adding a magnificently Orwellian proviso: working class autonomy ("spontaneity") is to be respected by socialist theory *provided* (his emphasis) that "this theory does not itself yield to spontaneity, *provided* it subordinates spontaneity to itself."[30] Such a claim for technocratic authority is rightly to be both derided and feared, as Berlin argues. But it is difficult to see how the idea of autonomy can be blamed for willful distortions of its core meaning. For it should be reasonably clear that for anyone to misappropriate the idea of autonomy in this way they must ignore part of its plain meaning: plainly, although self-governance may be contrasted with capriciousness, it contrasts most directly with being controlled and mastered and coerced by others, however ostensibly benevolent and knowledgeable these others may claim to be. As David Johnston has judiciously put it: "The liberal conception of autonomy provides amply for negative freedom in Berlin's sense. One of the principal conditions for the attainment of autonomy [as leading liberal theorists conceive it] is the existence of significant alternatives from which individuals may fashion their lives and identities. A strong concern for negative freedom is built into this conception of individual autonomy."[31]

Autonomy as a Constitutive and Threshold Good

In considering a political good or ideal, it is not enough to know what it means—what the content of the ideal is. It is equally important to understand its function—its role within the complex of other political goods that are also a part of the overall normative conception. The proper core meaning of liberty within the framework of a civic liberal perspective, I have argued, is that of autonomy or self-governance. But what *kind* of good is autonomy? What is its status and its role?

Three specific questions regarding the status and role of the good of autonomy within the complex of civic liberal political goods seem particularly relevant. First, should autonomy be deemed an intrinsic good or an instrumental good? Second, should it be considered a maximizing or a threshold good? Third, should it be seen as part of a comprehensive ethic or part of a political ethic more narrowly defined? I argue that (1) autonomy should be understood as a "constitutive" good rather than as an intrinsic or instrumental good *simpliciter*, (2) autonomy should be considered a threshold good rather than as a maximizing one, and (3) it makes little practical difference whether autonomy is conceived as part of a comprehensive ethic or as a more specifically political good.

First, the issue of intrinsic versus instrumental goodness. The problem here is that neither notion, by and of itself, captures exactly the role that autonomy plays in a good life. Some liberal theorists and moralists have been understandably inclined to say that autonomy is an intrinsic good. It is good in itself and not for any further instrumental uses to which it might or might not be put. Now this claim of intrinsic worth is understandable because it seeks to capture the recognition that autonomy is a necessary element in a fully human life. Those who are nonautonomous function as beasts or machines, however benignly. To function in a fully and distinctively human way, people must act autonomously at least to a certain as yet undefined extent. That is the consideration that led Rousseau, for example, and later Kant after him—in a mode shaped by their Cartesian meta-physic—to insist that genuine human status is attained only when one has the "in-ner" knowledge of his or her freedom and uses that awareness to acquiesce in or resist the "outer" heteronomous impulses that impinge on us.

But to style autonomy as an intrinsic good is misleading in a couple of respects. In the first place, it leads us to suppose that autonomy is good in itself; but that may not be so. We can easily think of a myriad of human actors and actions that were clearly autonomous but evil. Adolf Hitler, Jeffrey Dahmer, and Benedict Arnold all were arguably autonomous agents. They had reflectively conceived purposes that animated their plans of life, and they pursued these freely and, in the narrow technical sense, "rationally." But these were not good purposes and not good lives. Second, saying that autonomy is an intrinsic good also seems to imply that it is a teleological or final good—that it is something that one should pursue as a central goal or *telos* of our strivings. But that also is not really the case. As Will Kymlicka has succinctly put it, freedom of choice or autonomy "while central to a valuable life, is not the value which is centrally pursued in such a life."[32] The diffi-culty in each of these two logical but inappropriate inferences that follow from wanting to style autonomy as an intrinsic good is that the function of autonomy is adverbial rather than nominative. We live autonomous*ly* or not, pursue goods autonomous*ly* or not. But autonomy is not the *thing* pursued; it is instead a qual-ity of our pursuit.

These considerations thus may lead us toward characterizing autonomy as an instrumental good, good not in itself but only as a means to the attainment of other goods which are in and of themselves desirable. If we are autonomous be-ings, we will be more successful in achieving our ends and purposes, but auton-omy is not one of these goods and not something that is desirable in its own right apart from these other goals. Prompted by these considerations, Kymlicka draws what seems to be the appropriate conclusion and construes autonomy instru-mentally. "Freedom of choice," he says, "isn't pursued for its own sake, but as a precondition for pursuing those projects and practices that are valued for their own sake."[33] But it turns out upon examination that it is equally misleading to conceive of autonomy as a purely instrumental good. When we say that a good or property is related to another only instrumentally, we imply two things about that relationship which do not seem to hold in the case of autonomy. The implication is that the instrumental good is both fungible and external to the final good, but neither of these things is true of autonomy. (These two considerations overlap in part. Fungibility presupposes externality.) An airplane is instrumental to the good of a Florida vacation for a snowbound Chicagoan. But the airplane is fungible in the sense that a train or an automobile might be substituted for it without com-promising the attainment of the final good or destination. And the instrumental good that serves as but a means to an intrinsic good can be fungible only because it is "external" to that final good: i.e., it is not itself somehow inextricably related to or a constituent element of the final good.[34]

Autonomy is not, however, simply instrumentally related to other goods that we pursue because it is not purely external to these goods—or at least, it is not

purely external to the status of these goods, a status they need in order to be persuasively construed as intrinsic human goods. These final goods are thus themselves partly constituted by the autonomy that enables us to pursue them. This
point may be elucidated by recalling the language Kymlicka invokes in order to
deny autonomy the status of an intrinsic good. Autonomy, he says, is not pursued
"for its own sake, but as a precondition for pursuing those projects and practices
that are valued for their own sake."[35] The pertinent observation is that "precondition" here cannot properly denote a purely instrumental connection between autonomy and the that-for-the-sake-of-which one acts autonomously. The
connection is not external but internal: the projects and practices that are valued
"for their own sake" are not entitled to the status of being "projects" or "practices"
unless they are to some extent autonomously pursued. Autonomy, in other words,
is part of the defining penumbra of the notion of a project or a practice. Machines
have functions; animals have impulses; only human beings can properly be said to
have projects or practices, and that is because only they can act autonomously.
And when human beings do not act autonomously, it is misleading to speak of
them as engaged in the conduct of a project. If I, for example, am a prisoner being
forced by the state to break rocks, I am not engaged in a "project" of breaking
rocks. Rather the project is that of the state's punishing me *via* forcing me to go
through the exertions in question.

It is for these reasons that autonomy is best described as a *constitutive* good
rather than as either intrinsic or instrumental in the usual sense of those terms.
Autonomy is not a final good in itself and by itself, but it relates to the intrinsic
goods of our lives in a more than instrumental way. *It plays a necessary role in constituting these goods as genuinely human goods because human goods come under
the heading of purposes and we cannot properly be said to have purposes unless we
possess some measure of autonomy.* Without necessarily agreeing with everything
that Joseph Raz claims for autonomy as a good, I think that the phrase he deploys
to characterize its role in our lives is about right: autonomy is an "essential ingredient" of a good and fully human life.[36] Or as James Rachels and William Ruddick
put it, liberty is not "like air, causally necessary for lives. Rather, it is like motion,
a component of living. Liberty constitutes our lives through the free choices and
actions that embody it."[37]

Understanding autonomy as a "constitutive" good in this manner already begins to answer the next question as to whether it should be conceived as a maximizing good or as a threshold good. The initial answer has to be that autonomy is
better conceived as a threshold good—something for which there exists a necessary minimum level—than as a maximizing good—something you would like to
have as much as possible. The metaphor packed into Raz's phrase "essential ingredient" captures this point rather well. Baking soda is an essential ingredient in certain baked goods. But that does not mean that you would like to consume it by
itself or that you should dump as much as you can into the flour. Without it, the
culinary project is a failure; but the logic of maximization doesn't apply here.

Similarly, in the case of autonomy a strategy or standard of maximization
would be chimerical and destructive. To be wholly autonomous is not within the

power of created and contingent beings. We do not and cannot create ourselves *ex nihilo* and hence are incapable in an ontological sense of being completely autonomous in the strong sense of that term. Moreover, it makes little sense even within these ontological limits to pursue a maximizing strategy. Maximum autonomy alone does not create the good life. Instead, we properly seek a kind of optimizing equilibrium within the dialetic of autonomy and interdependency that characterizes a satisfying human life. Autonomy should not cannibalize our connectedness, our "situatedness," to borrow a term from Michael Sandel and Charles Taylor. We can achieve and practice autonomy, somewhat paradoxically, only within the context of and with some sustenance from a supporting web of social association. As Benjamin Barber expresses this point: "Self-direction brings freedom only when the self . . . is associated with intentions and purposes that by their nature can only arise within the guiding limits of a society and a culture. To be unimpeded and infinitely mobile is not freedom but deracination, unless by 'free' we mean only 'homeless.'"[38]

Maximization also makes little sense vis-a-vis those other notions that inform the concept of autonomy, the notions of "plan of life," "reflective self-direction," and "unity of self."[39] We all have encountered individuals who embody the parodic form of life that maximization would lead to in this context. These are the people who practically incapacitate themselves by treating every choice they confront in their daily lives—french fries or mashed potatoes?—into an occasion for extensive deliberation. To act in this manner, to demand that each and every choice one makes be closely tied to a rigid conception of one's "plan of life," is to put oneself in a ludicrous straitjacket. This is the kernal of truth contained within Bonnie Honig's complaint against John Rawls's privileging of deliberatively rational selves: "Is it irrational . . . to resent planning [one's] life as a career? Is nothing foregone in this unification of a life? What about promiscuity, spontaneity, experimentation, the will to live in the present?"[40]

Once again, as with regard to the core concept of autonomy, the appropriate tack is optimization and not maximization. Alasdair MacIntyre's notion of the "unity of a narrative" is a useful vehicle for understanding this contention.[41] The unity properly characteristic of a human self or agent is essentially the kind of unity that characterizes a good story. A good story, like a good life and the "plan" that shapes it, has a real unity that arises from its animating purposes and values, but this is not the unity of total closure, deductive determination, or lack of novelty and spontaneity. As MacIntyre describes it: "Unpredictability and teleology therefore coexist as part of our lives; like characters in a fictional narrative we do not know what will happen next, but nonetheless our lives have a certain form which projects itself towards our future."[42] Thus the notions of unity of self, reflective self-direction, and plan of life are not, properly understood, incapable of accommodating Honig's praise of "spontaneity" or "experimentation." Without these elements, a human life would lack growth, development, and excitement. It would in fact represent a futile attempt to escape the fundamental contingencies of historicity. On the other hand, some elements of planning, deliberation, and unity of self are necessary if our lives are to hang together in the way a genuine narrative must. And when selves do not hang together in a fundamental way, they become both painful and destructive.[43]

To return to the main point, it would seem to be clear that autonomy should be deemed a threshold good rather than a maximizing one. It is essential to a good, fully human life; but it is not an end-in-itself that should be pursued in a maximizing way. Having said that, however, it is worth noting that calling autonomy a threshold good may also be somewhat misleading. The reason is that there is some gap between the minimum threshold of autonomy that figures into important tests of liberal politics and jurisprudence, on the one hand, and an optimal level of self-governance and effective agency, on the other. The minimum level of autonomy is that which qualifies individuals as being "competent." It is embodied in such notions as reaching the "age of consent" and being "of sound mind and body." These criteria embody crucial distinctions for law and policy. But one can meet them and still fall short of a more optimal level of autonomy. To approach this latter somewhat higher standard, a person needs to feel that he or she possesses the abilities and the wherewithal to exercise some significant control over the course of his or her life. Perhaps, then, we should adopt Johnston's characterization of autonomy as a "satiable" norm, understanding that this refers to a necessary threshold and a somewhat higher optimum without implying that more is better ad infinitum.[44]

The last status and function issue surrounding the ideal of autonomy is whether it should be understood as a specifically political good or as an ethical good that is part of an all-encompassing conception of the good life. This question, and the distinction informing it, arises from Rawls's emphasis on this distinction and its significance in the context of framing and championing his conception of "political liberalism."

Rawls's central distinction is between "political" and "comprehensive" moral doctrines. One might suppose, prima facie, that the logical opposite of comprehensive is partial. But Rawls allows for what he calls "partially comprehensive" doctrines, so his distinction becomes somewhat tricky at the very outset. A "partially comprehensive" doctrine is one that falls short of covering "all recognized values and virtues" (in which case it would be "fully comprehensive"—a seeming redundancy terminologically) but that exceeds the scope of "the political virtues" and "comprises certain but not all nonpolitical values and virtues."[45] Since the basic distinction is one of scope and the crucial consideration is the absence of "full comprehensiveness," the important distinction relates to the proper scope of the political domain and its animating doctrines within the larger domain of morality more generally.

This distinction is important to Rawls for both moral and practical reasons. It is morally important because any attempt to ratify and enforce a moral doctrine not freely subscribed to by all citizens constitutes unjustified coercion. "Call this," he writes, "the fact of oppression."[46] But in any free contemporary society there will be no unanimity regarding comprehensive moral doctrines. This is "the fact of pluralism."[47] Hence any regime that is founded upon and seeks to effectuate a comprehensive moral doctrine, including a comprehensive liberal doctrine, whether partially or fully comprehensive, will necessarily be oppressive. The liberalisms of Kant and Mill, Rawls contends, are examples of comprehensive liberalisms, apparently in significant part because they are held to embrace autonomy and individuality as "ethical values ... which may apply to the whole of life."[48] Justice as fairness, in contrast, Rawls says, "affirms political autonomy for all but leaves the weight of ethical autonomy to be decided severally in light of their comprehensive doctrines."[49]

The question, then, is where civic liberalism comes down on this issue. Does it accord some more-than-political ethical value to autonomy? Does it then become oppressive? Does it diverge significantly at this point from "political" liberalism as a consequence? The summary answers to these three questions, are: (1) probably but not necessarily, (2) no, and (3) not really. In addressing each of these questions, it is useful to recall what has been said heretofore about the role and status of autonomy as a good—and what has been said about the nature of autonomy itself. Specifically, it should be kept in mind in addressing these questions that autonomy means independence and self-governance, that autonomy is deemed to be not the sum and substance of the good life but rather an "essential ingredient" of the good life, and that autonomy is not a final good to be maximized whenever possible.

It is fair to concede, then, that civic liberalism in all candor tends to understand autonomy as an ethical good with import and application that exceed the political domain strictly defined. Autonomy possesses this ethical status because it is deemed to be a constitutive element of having a life, being an agent, being genuinely and fully human. And the ethical value of having a (fully human) life would seem to extend beyond the realm of politics. To admit this, however, is not to say that one could not embrace civic liberal values as "merely" "political." That is really a question of grounds and scope rather than of content. But that stance would probably amount to a kind of principled ingenuousness. Autonomy is held to be a defining good of liberalism because it is held to be good for human beings generally.

It is hard to see, however, how a commitment to promoting and defending human autonomy, even candidly recognized as a (partially comprehensive) ethical value, renders civic liberalism "oppressive" in its implications. It is important, in the first place, to insist upon the importance of the "essential ingredient" metaphor and upon the denial that autonomy should be construed in a maximizing fashion. Some ethical doctrines may conceive autonomy as *the* self-subsistent and preeminent standard of the ethically good life, but civic liberalism clearly does not make this error. Kant, with his insistence that nothing is truly good but a good will, that a good will is one that is rational in his specific sense, and that a rational will is an autonomous will, might conceivably be said to be committed to such a view. But nothing about the civic liberal reading of the virtues, political or otherwise, forces it into embracing this kind of position. Civic liberalism, for similar logical reasons, does not endorse the claim put forward by Stephen Macedo that liberal autonomy leads to and is paradigmatically expressed in a consumerist or "California" way of life.[50] As a matter of empirical sociology there may be some

truth to the claim that a liberal culture, especially in the context of an affluent capitalist political economy, tends to make a fetish of "choice." But there is nothing in
the civic liberal insistence upon the fundamental value of human autonomy to
give normative support to this conception of the good life. Instead, it would seem
to be a semiparodic caricature of the good life—one that results from the failure
to keep in mind exactly the important specifics of the nature and status of autonomy as a human good that have been delineated here. It is a result of the misconceived notion that autonomy is a final good to be maximized rather than a
constitutive good to be optimized as well as of the correlative failure to keep autonomy properly situated within other moral and political goods. Insofar as the
consumerist or California model of the liberal self can be considered as a normative ideal, it is based on a confusion between living an autonomous life and having a protean existence, a confusion between self-authorship and self-indulgence.
In short, then, civic liberalism is not—simply because it tends to accord autonomy ethical and not merely political value—implicated in either the Kantian or
the consumerist versions of conceiving the good life *in toto* as a form of maximal
autonomy. And for both these substantive and also procedural considerations of
legitimacy, civic liberalism would never endorse forcing these or any other (fully)
comprehensive conception of the good life upon a democratic citizenry.

It is, moreover, rather hard to make much sense—without recourse to Orwellian deformations of reasoning and language—of the notion that a regime
could coherently be said to oppress its citizens by virtue of a commitment to promoting and defending their autonomy. The worry that a more-than-political liberalism would try to (or be able to) "force you to be free" might be coherent
against the background of a "positive" conception of liberty as a form of self-realization known to the ruling class or caste or group. But, as we have seen, the civic
liberal understanding of autonomy, to recall David Johnston's words, "provides
amply for negative freedom." Respect for negative freedom and hence the fore-
bearance proper to such respect "is built into this conception of individual autonomy."[51] And so long as that is true, the concern about oppression-in-
the-cause-of-autonomy seems tantamount to worrying that someone might try
to push me around with a string. A liberal society, in the civic liberal view,
should—in keeping with its animating values and purposes—seek to provide its
citizens with the capacities and the requisite space and opportunities to act autonomously. There is no coerciveness involved in this commitment to citizen autonomy or in the provision of resources or in the protection of private space. It
would not only violate this moral commitment itself to use force against those
who do not appreciate or respond to these rights and privileges, it would be oxy-
moronic to do so, a transgression against the very meaning and logic of autonomy. Rawls's worry about the potential oppressiveness of a liberalism that
embraces autonomy as an ethical value—as a more than merely political good—
seems too much a function of abstract implications deduced from the abstract
category of "comprehensive doctrine." When the specifics of the doctrine in question are supplied, it seems hard to make this worry politically or practically compelling.

As it turns out, the one real-world political venue in which this concern seems to arise is that of public education. Specifically, the specter of an oppressive commitment to the value of autonomy surfaces when it comes to the public education of the children of communities that seem to disdain or fear some of the elements of or capacities seemingly important to autonomy. The leading instances of this problem are cases in which traditionalist or fundamentalist religious communities seek to insulate their children against what they regard as contaminating influences and do so by trying to limit their exposure to a secular education or by trying to censor the content of that education. There are indeed important and complex issues of liberal morality, constitutional law, and prudent public policy presented by these cases. But it is hard to characterize the situation as one in which an aggrandizing liberal state committed to a more-than-political ethic of autonomy seeks to oppress its citizens. The problem arises because there is a triad of relevant parties here rather than a dyad. The question involves not the state vis-a-vis citizens who reject an ethical norm of autonomy for their own lives. Here there would be no problem: the state must and would properly forbear. But in these cases the question concerns proper state action where tensions exist between the rights, interests, and desires of parents and their children. The issue here is the relative authority of parents and the state over children, and the problem arises because what the state considers it owes the children—i.e., an education that provides them the knowledge and capacities necessary for the exercise of their rights and responsibilities as citizens—is feared by the parents as something that might allow/lead/seduce their children into abandoning a way of life they love and cherish. The problem arises here because the norm of promoting and defending autonomy cannot be unproblematically acted upon; the autonomy claims of the parents conflict with the autonomy rights of the children to acquire the wherewithal to lead independent lives. The state is put into a quandary because it feels both the obligation and the right to equip the children to become good democratic citizens, but it has no right and should have no desire to impose or proselytize on behalf of a particular comprehensive ethical conception of the good over the objections of citizens who reject it.

Civic liberalism has within its conceptual and normative arsenal no resources to solve unequivocally all the practical and moral dilemmas presented by these cases. But then neither does any other credible form of liberal theory. Leading liberal theorists have staked out somewhat different positions on these cases. And I say a few more words about them in a later chapter. But these positions are more the product of marginally different casuistic judgments than the consequence of deductive inferences from divergent fundamental principles.[52]

Our central concern here is the significance of the contrast Rawls makes between embracing autonomy as a purely political virtue and according it "partially comprehensive" value as an "essential ingredient" in a good, fully human life. The key question then becomes whether this contrast carries much weight in dealing with a policy issue that seems to be the leading candidate for bringing the practical implications of the contrast into view. And the answer, I suggest, is that the practical bearing of the contrast is quite negligible. Political liberalism would forbear from forcing a general autonomy ethic on its citizens because it does not sub-scribe to autonomy—or anything else—as a comprehensive doctrine. Civil liber-alism would forbear in the same way because it does subscribe in a fundamental ("partially comprehensive") way to the ethical importance of respecting citizen autonomy. Thus a civic liberal would find little to disagree with in Rawls's own ju-dicious, but not uncontroversial or cost-free, attempt to deal with these cases. "So-ciety's concern with their education" (i.e., the education of the children of parents "who wish to withdraw from the modern world in accordance with the injunc-tions of their religion"), writes Rawls, "lies in their role as future citizens, and so in such essential things as their acquiring the capacity to understand the public cul-ture and to participate in its institutions, in their being economically independent and self-supporting members of society over a complete life, and in their devel-oping the political virtues, all this from within a political point of view."[53] The only part of this formulation that a civic liberal could not conceivably endorse is the final phrase: "all this from within a political point of view." Which is to say, the actual practical difference between endorsing autonomy as a "political" virtue and subscribing to it in a more (but still partially) "comprehensive" way, as does civic liberalism, is negligible.

If one moves beyond the abstract contrast Rawls makes between "political" and "comprehensive" doctrines to look at the specific content and functions of the no-tion of autonomy in justice as fairness and in civic liberalism, this result is not re-ally surprising. Justice as fairness, even if it is a political and not a comprehensive doctrine, is profoundly committed to the importance of citizen autonomy. A ca-pacity for autonomy is one of the "two moral powers" that Rawls distills from the basic normative conception of personhood appropriate to democratic citizens, and the logic of the whole scheme behind the derivation of the principles of justice is predicated upon these moral powers. For that reason, in turn, Rawls's "political virtues" include the obligations of respect appropriate to autonomous persons.[54] Therefore, however much Rawls wishes to emphasize his neutrality vis-a-vis com-prehensive moral doctrines and the limited scope of the moral commitments he would bring to bear on political issues, de facto he privileges autonomy very deci-sively in his political morality. When push comes to shove, then, the moral priority of autonomy becomes one of those affirmations he is forced to acknowledge even if doing so is "the kind of thing we had hoped to avoid." And in doing so, Rawls concedes, he is asserting "at least certain aspects of [his] own comprehensive . . . doctrine."[55] At this point, the putative gap between affirming autonomy as a polit-ical norm, as does Rawls, and affirming it as part of a partially comprehensive eth-ical doctrine, as does civic liberalism, narrows to the vanishing point. The only difference is, to turn another of Rawls's phrases around, metaphysical not political.

Defending Autonomy

The civic liberal account of liberty as the constitutive good of autonomy, then, dif-fers from Rawls's account of autonomy as a moral power and a political good only at the margins. The differences here appear only when the question of the theoretical status of autonomy arises and not when the practical and political bearing of a liberal society's devotion to autonomy is at stake. The differences between our account and other versions of democratic ideals, however, do take on practical significance that needs remarking.

The contrast between the civic liberal embrace of autonomy and the libertarian enshrinement of individual freedom should be clear on the basis of what has been said already—in this chapter and in the earlier chapter critiquing libertarian ideals. Libertarians essentially see liberty as Isaiah Berlin's "negative liberty" and as Hobbes's "absence of impediment." By absolutizing and prioritizing liberty as the paramount democratic ideal, moreover, they construe it de facto as a maximizing good. In contrast, the civic liberal account distinguishes autonomy or self-governance from sheer whimsy or slavish subordination to impulse, it situates autonomy within other democratic goods, and it considers it a satiable good rather than a maximizing good. As a consequence, civic liberals will be less inclined to prioritize individual license when it comes into tension with other democratic purposes and ideals such as equality and fraternity. And, by contrast with libertarians, civic liberals will not see liberty as necessarily optimized by simple government forbearance. For becoming autonomous is an achievement, not simply the absence of external constraint. And it is an achievement that requires resources, social protection, and social sustenance for people to be able to develop the constitutive capabilities of self-governance. In the view of civic liberalism, then, benign neglect is not likely to be the social policy best adapted to optimizing citizen autonomy. Instead, strong institutional protection and promotion of public health, education, and employability may reasonably be seen as necessary to liberate democratic citizens from dependency.

The interpretation and defense of liberty as the constitutive good of autonomy offered here also brings with it an important caveat vis-a-vis the communitarian critique of liberalism and its associated agenda. In many respects, what I am calling civic liberalism coincides with communitarian perspectives: the denial that liberalism is predicated upon moral neutrality, the endorsement of civic friendship and norms of civic virtue, the championing of personal responsibility and the institutions of civil society. But the status given by civic liberalism to autonomy is not compatible with arguments that would push aside rights of self-governance in the name of some stipulative doctrine of the human good that is enforced by governmental authority. The civic liberal defense of autonomy is not compatible, for example, with a position that Michael Sandel has recently staked out in *Democracy's Discontent*.[56] Specifically, the understanding of autonomy as a constitutive good that should be respected and nurtured by democratic society poses a challenge to Sandel's critique of what he calls "the procedural republic" and to the constitutional jurisprudence he derives from this critique.

It is Sandel's view that the constitutional jurisprudence of the past several decades has embodied an acceptance of a normative model of democracy as a purely procedural system that enshrines and protects citizens as "freely choosing" individuals. These "freely choosing" citizens are, in his view, the legal and political incarnation of the metaphysical conception of the human self presupposed and promoted by deontological liberals such as Rawls. As a consequence of this imputation, Sandel fuses into this notion of the "freely choosing" individual two quite distinguishable notions which he nonetheless links together very tightly: the first is the metaphysical conception of an "unencumbered self" and the second is the normative conception of the independent political agent. The metaphysical conception invokes the neo-Kantian/Weberian model of a self existing prior to and apart from any constitutive purposes or commitments and who thus acquires these purposes—and his or her identity—only *via* these free and unencumbered decisions. The political conception signifies the independent agent who possesses the autonomy to determine his or her own political commitments and plan of life. The former self is metaphysically free—unencumbered or unconstrained by any objective or preexisting moral meanings or purposes embedded in what Locke called "the visible structure and argument of this world."[57] The latter self is politically free, undominated by anyone with the power or authority to force upon him or her a particular moral or religious commitment or a prefabricated plan of life.

The core difficulty with Sandel's analysis of "the procedural republic" and with the critical jurisprudence he bases upon it resides in his implicit insistence that the latter political conception is logically dependent upon or indistinguishable from the former metaphysical conception. This insistence, is, I would argue, a mistaken one, and it is a mistake that both distorts Sandel's critique of recent trends in constitutional law and raises doubts about the status and protection he would have us accord individual liberties.

Even if it be true that Rawls's "method of avoidance" leads him to claim more metaphysical indeterminacy for his own normative and political conception of democratic personhood than might be convincing or desirable, his basic claim that the metaphysical presuppositions needed to sustain it are sufficiently general that they do not depend upon a highly distinctive metaphysics of selfhood is both persuasive and pertinent here.[58] In the present context, the civic liberal commitment to the constitutive good of autonomy no doubt presupposes that human selves possess the capacity for deliberative self-determination and hence for morally meaningful choice. But that does not require, as Sandel implies, any embrace of or commitment to the metaphysical conception of a cosmologically "unencumbered" self. It is necessary only to affirm, as Mill insisted, that a genuinely human life requires some real component of self-determination and that it therefore cannot consist of mere "ape-like imitation." And it is further necessary to draw from this core supposition not Weber's lesson that the human self be treated as a "moral Atlas" (the precursor of today's "strong poets") but only Jefferson's lesson that none are "born with saddles and spurred, ready to ride them legitimately, by the grace of God.[59]

Sandel's misleading conflation of metaphysical decisionist freedom with political autonomy leads him to render some odd judgments regarding constitutional jurisprudence. He tells us, for example, that with the Supreme Court's decision in *West Virginia v. Barnette*, 319 U.S. 624 (1943), "the procedural republic had arrived."[60] This was a case in which the Court sustained the contention of several Jehovah's Witnesses that their children should not be compelled by public school authorities to salute the flag over their religious objections to such rituals and upon pain of expulsion from the schools. This decision overturned an earlier case from only three years before, *Minersville v. Gobitis,* 310 U.S. 586 (1940), in which the Court had upheld a virtually identical Pennsylvania statute requiring all public school children to salute the flag and recite the pledge of allegiance. Sandel imputes to the *Barnette* decision acceptance of the tenets of "the procedural republic" because it in his view rests upon making the right prior to the good, upon "the idea that the Constitution is neutral among ends, that government may not impose a particular conception of the good life," and upon "a conception of persons as free and independent agents, capable of choosing their ends for themselves."[61]

But this rendering of the Court's position as an embrace of deontological liberalism is not persuasive. The Court here does not and need not prioritize the right over the good *tout court.* It accords priority to one particular right—i.e., the freedom of religious conscience—above the government's right to utilize a particular means—i.e., compelling school children to salute the flag—in the service of a particular good—i.e., "the binding tie of cohesive sentiment." The Court does not say that a liberal regime does not rest upon some particular convictions about the good life, only that the *government* should not *impose* upon some recalcitrant citizens an obligation to affirm some particular conception of the good against their religious beliefs. And the Court does indeed rely upon the belief that citizens should be treated as "free and independent agents, capable of choosing their ends for themselves"; but that needs to mean only that citizens must be accorded the respect due rational beings and therefore protected from having other citizens, acting through government mandate, force upon them a profession of beliefs and commitments they do not in fact hold—not that citizens must be construed as radically unencumbered selves.

Moreover, Sandel does not make clear what he would have had the Court do and say instead. Would he have had the Court affirm *Gobitis* and allow state compulsion of profession of beliefs contrary to one's religious convictions? Would that endorsement of majoritarian compulsion be necessitated by recognizing that a liberal regime is not neutral *vis-a-vis* the constituent elements of a good life? Would he deny the assertion of the Court that "no official, high or petty, can prescribe what shall be orthodox in politics, nationalism, religion, or other matters of opinion" and that "love of country must spring from willing hearts and free minds"?[62]

Sandel never answers these questions directly. But his clear intimation that the *Barnette* decision and the cited assertions are questionable outcomes of an inadequate theory of liberalism are quite troubling. Perhaps indeed he would allow state officials to "prescribe what shall be orthodox" when it comes to substantive issues of morality. For later, reflecting upon the cases of American Nazis wanting to march in Skokie and Martin Luther King wanting to march in Selma, he argues that it is "not always possible to adjudicate rights without passing judgment on the morality of the cause they would advance".[63] And he would have had the court decide differently in the case of *Bowers v. Hardwick,* 478 U.S. 186 (1986), where the Court upheld the state of Georgia's criminalization of consenting homosexual practices, *not* on the grounds that such criminalization violates the autonomy of citizens in their private lives but rather on the basis of the substantive proposition that homosexual intimacy "may realize important human goods."[64] Instead of having the courts protect the constitutive liberal good of autonomy embedded in constitutional protections against intrusive and oppressive state action, Sandel would have judges decide cases by imposing upon the rest of us their own substantive judgments about the good life. Ultimately, Sandel's putatively "communitarian" jurisprudence seems to issue not into a rights-threatening majoritarianism, as many critics of communitarianism have contended, but rather into a form of judicial imperialism in which judges are emboldened to decide what rights are to be protected and what state actions permitted on the basis of their own substantive convictions about the human good. Sandel's jurisprudence turns out to be not simply antideontological but illiberal and not only illiberal but undemocratic.

The civic liberal posture on these issues is quite different. The civic liberal would endorse the Court's judgment in *Barnette.* Civic liberalism would, moreover, agree with the Court that citizens must be deemed capable of choosing their ends for themselves rather than having them imposed by local majorities or by state action. It would deny to state officials—including federal judges—the authority to impose their own conceptions of the human good upon the rest of society. It would consider *Bowers v. Hardwick* to have been wrongly decided, but on what Sandel calls "voluntarist" grounds rather than on the grounds that the Court's judgment about what is humanly good should take precedence over the contrary judgments of the citizens of the state of Georgia.

These civic liberal judgments are not grounded in the deontological prioritizing of the right over the good or upon the delusion that liberal regimes and practices are neutral *vis-a-vis* the good or upon a neo-Kantian or Weberian or existentialist insistence that all moral meaning comes from the "demonically" free choices of metaphysically "unencumbered" selves. Instead, these affirmations are based upon the conviction that personal autonomy (in the sense of freedom from outside determination by other selves, *not* in the sense of exemption from all moral obligations that are not constructed ex nihilo by the individual) is a necessary condition of the good life; that liberal democratic purposes, practices, and institutions embody that conviction; and that this good of autonomy is embedded in constitutional protections and prohibitions the courts are bound to honor and enforce.

The central point *vis-a-vis* liberal purposes is this. A threshold level of personal autonomy is a constitutive human good, a necessary condition and essential component of a good life. Enabling and protecting that autonomy is one of the core moral purposes of well-ordered liberal regimes. Although it is without question true, as thoughtful communitarian critics of liberalism have insisted, that the most dominant contemporary strands of liberal theory—including both deontological egalitarianism and libertarianism—have been excessively individualistic and have as a result encouraged the neglect and consequent erosion of civic friendship and civic virtue, it is neither necessary nor proper to campaign for the sacrifice of personal autonomy on the altar of community and rectitude. Such an agenda is not only wrong in principle but self-defeating in practice. For it is one of liberalism's defining insights that genuine social solidarity and human virtue cannot be produced by coercion or manipulation, however well intentioned. The ultimate goal of democratic liberalism is a free people, civic equals, who support and cooperate with each other out of common interests, compassion, mutual respect, and commitment to human flourishing. No doubt that is an ambitious goal, but it cannot be either abandoned or fragmented. And it certainly cannot be successfully pursued by allowing the community to bully recalcitrant members into professions of faith they do not hold or by authorizing jurists to impose their judgments about the humanly good life upon a community that harbors other convictions or prioritizes goods differently.

The Autonomy of Social Enterprises

One final observation needs to be made regarding the civic liberal understanding of the norm of autonomy: it applies to the conduct of social enterprises as well as to the conduct of individual lives.

By "social enterprise" I mean to designate those institutionalized collective endeavors of a society or social group that develop around some significant human need or social task. I am not here particularly concerned with the question of whether these needs and tasks should be deemed to be natural or socially constructed. They could be either. The only relevant consideration is that a society considers them sufficiently important undertakings to institutionalize them—and that their animating purposes do not contravene any basic moral constraints.

Many obvious and important examples of these enterprises come readily to mind. The social production of wealth is an enterprise, as is the preservation of public health, the conduct of learning and education, the creation of works of art, the organization of worship and religious life, and so on. The conduct of these enterprises becomes embodied in institutions such as schools and churches, corporations and stock exchanges, families and the various professions. Indeed one could reasonably argue that these enterprises comprise most of the organized efforts of human life and that the political regime, in the narrow and specific sense of the agencies of state or government, is engaged basically in supporting, coordinating, and regulating them. This is why, pursuant to some perhaps unlikely but not entirely fanciful suppositions, it might be possible to imagine that the state could conceivably wither away. But the social enterprises themselves would have to endure. They are coterminous with the life of organized society itself, and their death would entail its demise.

These social enterprises develop within themselves criteria and standards of excellence and good performance. These standards of performance are not arbitrary or adventitious; rather they are a function of the *telos* of the enterprise. Good performances are those which most effectively conduce to the successful attainment of the purposes of the enterprises. We speak meaningfully, for example, of standards of good educational practice or of good business practice and the like. Invocation of these standards may receive important recognition and application in legal contexts: medical malpractice suits, for example, turn around ascertaining what constitutes prevailing standards of acceptable practice and whether the medical actions and judgments in question did or did not conform to them.[65]

It is commonly supposed that the liberal norm of autonomy is concerned specifically and perhaps exclusively with the integrity and freedom of individuals. The overriding preoccupation of liberalism is held to be carving out for individuals a protected domain within which they are accorded the social elbow room to pursue their individual lives free from intrusive interference by other citizens or by the state. And of course that is a valid and important concern of all versions of liberalism, one captured by metaphors like the nightwatchman state and embodied in liberalism's preoccupation with individual rights. A liberalism not concerned to defend the integrity and civil liberties of individuals would not be a liberalism at all.

Nonetheless, this linkage of autonomy solely to individual lives is at best a half-truth. Taken as a full account of the logic of liberalism it is both inaccurate and inadequate. The too-exclusive focus on individual autonomy is a misconception that likely is fostered by a too-exclusive focus on liberal treatises on obligation and legitimacy. For these theoretical arguments, such as Hobbes's *Leviathan*, Locke's *Second Treatise*, and Rousseau's *Social Contract*, do in fact take the free and equal individual as their normative starting point. In the context of the question "What makes government power legitimate?" when it is denied that political authority over others is conveyed to some by God or by nature, starting with unfettered individuals in a "state of nature" makes perfect moral and logical sense. However important may be this question of how political authority can be legitimately derived from an initial state of individual freedom, though, looking at it alone results in a narrow and distorted view of the liberal understanding of autonomy, its warrants, and its imperatives for social organization.

Without gainsaying for a moment the importance of the legitimacy issue and the crucial significance of individual rights, a broader and more complete understanding of what liberalism historically has sought under the rubric of autonomy or self-governance, and why, can be achieved only if we turn away for a moment from theoretical arguments about obligation to reflect upon the concrete institutional reforms early liberals sought to achieve. For the concrete institutional goals of liberal reform clearly turned every bit as much around the aspiration to accord a proper autonomy to social enterprises as to the desire to accord protected space to individuals.

Three social enterprises in particular served as the focus of early liberal social criticism and political reform: the production of wealth, the conduct of inquiry, and the practice of religion. When liberal theorists and political leaders eulogized liberty, they had in mind not so much a concern with freeing individuals from social control generally but a concern with freeing these important social enterprises from the control of political authorities and social elites. In fact, it arguably was not until what might be styled as a second wave of liberal theory—the nineteenth-century liberalisms of Mill, Constant, Tocqueville, and Emerson—that the issue of protecting and promoting "individuality" come to the fore. That concern came, in fact, not so much from the original liberal attack on elite dominance as from a later developing recognition that the triumph of democratic reforms brought new and unanticipated problems. Mill provides a very pertinent and revealing genealogy of his concern with individuality in his introduction to *On Liberty*. As he observes there, it was only after the success of the original liberal agenda of self-governance that the question of the proper relationship between individual citizens and the democratically self-governing majority came into relief: "success discloses faults and infirmities which failure might have concealed from observation."[66]

In the seventeenth and eighteenth centuries, at least, the principal political aspiration encoded into the rhetorical appeal to liberty was arguably a determination to emancipate religious, educational, and economic enterprises from domination by outside actors and by extraneous criteria of performance. A central impetus for the limitation of state power sought by liberalism was the goal of "rationalizing" the governance of these crucial social enterprises, and this rationalization meant vesting authority in the hands of those who possessed the relevant expertise and who would exercise their authority in accordance with the norms of good performance appropriate to and generated by the nature of the enterprise.

In the case of religion, as Locke argued in his *Letter Concerning Toleration*, this meant that "the magistrate"—i.e., the civil government—had no business trying to run things. The magistrate did not possess any relevant competency to determine what was correct or heretical doctrine. He was not vested by the consent of the believers with any authority to regulate their religious lives where these did not intrude upon the proper concerns of the state. And his disciplinary recourse, the use of force, was unavailing when it came to the care of souls and the attainment of salvation.

In the case of economic pursuits, as the physiocrats, Condorcet, and Adam Smith insisted, the state was not the proper vehicle for the determination of how the productive resources of the society should be allocated. If the point of economic enterprise is to produce wealth most efficiently, then the internal discipline of the marketplace rather than the mandates of political authorities should govern. As Condorcet wrote, "men should be able to use their faculties, dispose of their wealth and provide for their needs in complete freedom." They should have that freedom, Condorcet explained, not simply or even primarily because their individual freedom should be maximized or deemed a goal above all others. They should instead be left free to pursue their best interests in the economic realm without extraneous interference because the consequence of the judgments they make and the actions they take will be to further "the interests of society" and "minister to the welfare of all."[67]

Finally, the case of scientific inquiry and its governance provided almost a paradigm case for the benefits of enterprise autonomy, as liberal theorists took pleasure in pointing out. The imposition of state power was a retardant force when it came to scientific advance. If the proper goal of the scientific enterprise, of learning and scholarship, is the attainment and dissemination of truth, society is best served by letting scientists and scholars govern their own endeavors in this sphere. Whenever the state—or clerical authorities backed by state power—sought to control the scientific enterprise, the results were always counterproductive. Scientists acting on their own recognizance made discoveries; state authorities "contributed" by suppressing telescopes and burning books. The only truly constructive role the state could play in promoting scientific progress was that of patron. State abdication in matters of scientific governance did not entail some sort of descent into organizational anarchy. Instead, the scientific estate would govern itself and distribute its positions, influence, and access to resources in accordance with its own internally generated norms of excellence. And from that "enterprise autonomy" society as a whole would benefit.

In continuity with these insights that informed the historical liberal project from its inception, civic liberalism emphasizes enterprise autonomy as an important component of the ideal of liberty. A free society is one in which the institutions of civil society are strong and vital. Individual freedom is not, of course, identical with or reducible to enterprise autonomy. In a good society, individual citizens should have the leeway to retire to Walden Pond like Thoreau or to pursue their idiosyncratic quests like Foucault. But, in a very real and concrete sense, individual liberty is meaningful and effectual only when the organized enterprises of civil society provide frameworks for their meaningful expression. Without organized communications media, the freedom of thought and speech does not amount to much, resembling Bishop Berkeley's tree that falls with no one to hear it. Without churches and denominations, freedom of religion would be a cipher. Without markets, economic freedoms would be unavailing. An embodied liberty, one that is not merely abstract and hypothetical, is to a greater extent than generally realized a function of flourishing, well institutionalized, and broadly autonomous civic enterprises. As Michael Walzer eloquently and succinctly writes: "Men and women are free when they live within autonomous institutions."[68]

One very important caveat needs to be entered regarding the norm of enterprise autonomy, however, in order to forestall a potential misunderstanding concerning its implications. To insist upon the autonomy of the various civic enterprises as a key constituent element of liberty does not entail any notion that this autonomy should be absolute or unqualified. And it does not, for some of the same reasons, entail the idea that the state either can or should wither away or confine itself to a very narrow nightwatchman role. Rather like individuals, organized enterprises tend toward hegemony. Moreover, their internal purposes and norms of performance necessarily represent only one segment of the various and extensive legitimate purposes of a society. And finally, the conduct of a social enterprise will inevitably be shaped not only by its distinctive purposes but also by the particular interests of its participants. As a consequence, however crucial the autonomy of these enterprises may be for the overall effective liberty and flourishing of the society, they nevertheless behave in some ways like Madisonian factions: when guided only from within, they may act in ways detrimental to the general interest and to the rights of others. For example, left entirely to their own devices, scientific disciplines have conducted potentially damaging experiments on unknowing subjects, clerical authorities have undertaken not simply to guide their own congregations but also to function as moral censors of the larger community, medical associations not only promote public health but function as price and income inflating cartels, and large corporations or business enterprises have undertaken to exercise a kind of omnibus control over their "company towns."

It is, therefore, entirely appropriate—indeed necessary—for the larger public to be accorded some role in defining the operative purposes and norms of the various social enterprises, and it is also necessary for the public, here acting through state agency, to regulate and manage the relationships among the various enterprises, keeping each from transgressing upon the others and from usurping the powers of the people as a whole.

Concerning the public's input into the definition of an enterprise's purposes, Charles Anderson argues persuasively that

> the stipulation of function for an enterprise is not properly the prerogative of the state. Nor do I think we believe it exclusively the affair of the contracting parties. I do not believe we are willing to say that a family is anything to which consenting adults decide to apply the term, or that it is up to the owners to determine what a corporation *is*, how it is entitled to act and how it is properly constituted.[69]

The participants in the enterprise itself, therefore, should rightly be granted the leading role in shaping the purposes and internal governance of their activities. But the public should have its say as well and not abandon control entirely to the private professionals. "The relationship of state to enterprise is not defined in a single, one-time settlement . . . [but] is a continuing process of monitoring the performance of enterprise, in which the public policymakers, the officials of enterprise, the practitioners and citizens, are commonly engaged." No simple algorithm of division of power or cooperative governance can really be stipulated in the abstract or in advance. "It is a matter in each case of striking a balance between the particular aims of enterprises and the general values and interests of the liberal commonwealth."[70] This will always be a rather messy process filled with compromises and political contestation. And the way in which we try to strike the balance Anderson hopes for will always be imperfect. Think, for example, of the role of boards of directors of corporations or boards of trustees of universities. Often they are too weak and at times positively pernicious. But they are an institutional embodiment of the regulatory principle Anderson invokes. They are created and empowered to provide some degree of public or quasi-public review over and input into the management and control over large-scale enterprises which perform functions that affect the larger public domain but are for the most part self-governing. The second major regulatory role of the state *vis-a-vis* social enterprises is what Michael Walzer has characterized as the task of "boundary maintenance."[71] That is, it falls to state agency, presumably guided by public deliberation and judgment, to stake out and enforce the jurisdictional fences that surround the various enterprises and hedge in the hegemonic tendencies of their norms and the hegemonic aspirations of their practitioners. As in the case of stipulation of purposes, there are here also no set algorithms of decision or permanent fence posts. "We never know exactly where to put the fences; they have no natural location. The goods they distinguish are artifacts; as they were made, so they can be unmade."[72] And the process will always be a site of political contestation. Consider in this context the perpetual jockeying for position that goes on among the bureaucratic agencies in a government or among the disciplines in a university. But this does not mean that there are no reasonable standards or relevant arguments in deciding where to draw the boundaries. Hume said of the rules of justice that they are artificial but not arbitrary. The same can be said of the boundaries of enterprises.

The price of liberty, it has been said, is eternal vigilance. If, as has been claimed here, an important part of liberty is the autonomy of social enterprises and the concomitant vitality of civil society, then an important part of that vigilance is assiduous attention to Walzer's "art of separation"—to the task of maintaining the fences that prevent one sphere from achieving dominion over other legitimate spheres that should be governed by their own logic, their own standards, their own authority. In the context of contemporary politics, this means that civic liberalism counsels and promotes resistance against the tendency of both state and market to weaken and distort other spheres by penetrating or absorbing them. Egalitarian liberals worry about the market; libertarians worry about the state; civic liberals worry about both. With egalitarian liberals, civic liberals recognize that a good society is not an agglomeration of self-interested individual preference maximizers; but the alternative to that should not be an intrusive and paternalistic state. It may take a village to raise a child, as a currently popular homily goes. But if "the village" translates here simply into teams of lawyers and bureaucrats, not only the child but the society is in trouble. With libertarians, then, civic liberals recognize that a good society is not a benevolent welfare apparatus; but the alternative to that should not be a modus vivendi truce among aggrandizing yuppies joined only by contracts. Alan Wolfe has recently explained why. He cautions market enthusiasts that "to the degree that Chicago school economics describes what is taking place in society, it describes a society that is in decline because its members are not willing to adhere to the rules that make it work." To welfare enthusiasts, on the other hand, he offers the sobering observation that "the Scandinavian welfare states, which express so well a sense of obligation to distant strangers, are beginning to make it more difficult to express a sense of obligation to those with whom one shares family ties. The irony of this development may be that as intimate ties weaken, so will distant ones, thus undermining the very moral strengths the welfare state has shown." Moreover, "the new welfare state, in assuming greater responsibilities, has led to a decline in a sense of individual moral responsibility that threatens the ability of Scandinavian societies to find new sources of moral energy." The core problem, especially in a time wherein both state and market are driven by strongly aggrandizing forces and legitimated by dominant ideologies, is that "When the market and the state exist without civil society, neither can work as promised."[73] There are no easy answers to this problem, but surely the first requisite is a clear awareness of the irreducible functions performed by the often fragile (because they are not driven by unalloyed self-interest or enforced by law) institutions of civil society such as families, neighborhoods, churches, civic associations, and schools. A free society cannot be concerned simply to defend and nurture the autonomy of individuals. It must also take care to defend the autonomy of its constituent social enterprises. That also is a part of the liberty we celebrate and enjoy.

Notes

1. Quentin Skinner, *Reason and Rhetoric in the Philosophy of Hobbes* (Cambridge: Cambridge University Press, 1996), 15–16.

2. Giovanni Sartori, *Democratic Theory* (New York: Praeger, 1967), 327.

3. Stephen Holmes, *The Anatomy of Antiliberalism* (Cambridge: Harvard University Press, 1993), 253–56.

4. Isaiah Berlin, "Two Concepts of Liberty," in *Four Essays on Liberty* (London: Oxford University Press, 1969), 118–72.

5. Berlin, "Two Concepts," 122.

6. Berlin, "Two Concepts," 133.

7. Berlin, "Two Concepts," 134 and 144.

8. Berlin, "Two Concepts," 137n.

9. Berlin, "Two Concepts," 167.

10. Berlin, "Two Concepts," 123 and 147.

11. Berlin, "Two Concepts," 129.

12. See my *Understanding Political Theory* (New York: St. Martin's Press, 1976).

13. John Locke, *Second Treatise of Civil Government*, XI, 137.

14. Locke, *Second Treatise*, VI, 71, 61.

15. Immanuel Kant, cited by Berlin, "Two Concepts," 137.

16. Immanuel Kant, "What Is Enlightenment?" In *Perpetual Peace and Other Essays*, trans. by Ted Humphrey (Indianapolis: Hackett, 1983), 41.

17. Kant, "What Is Enlightenment?" 41.

18. See Arthur Melzer, "Rousseau and the Problem of Bourgeois Society," *American Political Science Review* 74, no. 4 (December 1980): 1018–33.

19. Jean-Jacques Rousseau, *Emile*, trans. by Allan Bloom (New York: Basic Books, 1979), 85.

20. Adam Smith, *Lectures on Jurisprudence*, ed. R. L. Meck, D. D. Raphael, and L. G. Stein (Indianapolis: Liberty Classics, 1982), 333.

21. Adam Smith, *An Inquiry into the Nature and Causes of the Wealth of Nations* (New York: Modern Library, 1985), 80.

22. Adam Smith, *Wealth of Nations*, 186.

23. Adam Smith, *Wealth of Nations*, 15.

24. Condorcet, *Progress of the Human Mind*, 182–83.

25. Thomas Jefferson, "Letter to Samuel Kersheval" July 12, 1816; and *Notes on the State of Virginia*, in *Great American Political Thinkers*, Vol. 1, ed. Bernard Brown (New York: Avon Books, 1983), 358 and 328.

26. George Kateb, "Democratic Individuality and the Claims of Politics," *Political Theory* 12, no. 3 (August 1984): 343.

27. Whitman, "Democratic Vistas," in *The Complete Prose*, 222.

28. John Stuart Mill, *On Liberty* (Indianapolis: Bobbs–Merrill, 1956), 70–71.

29. The quotations in this paragraph are all from Rawls, *Theory of Justice*, 428, 427, 429, and 505.

30. V. I. Lenin, "What Is to Be Done?" in *Selected Works*, Vol. I (New York: International, 1967), 132.

31. David Johnston, *The Idea of a Liberal Theory* (ms version), 80.

32. Will Kymlicka, *Liberalism, Community, and Culture* (Oxford: Clarendon Press, 1989), 50.

33. Kymlicka, *Liberalism, Community*, 48.

34. Alasdair MacIntyre elaborates the distinction between internal and external goods in his account of the virtues. See *After Virtue* (Notre Dame: University of Notre Dame Press, 1981), esp. chapter 14.

35. Kymlicka, *Liberalism, Community*, 48.

36. Joseph Raz, *The Morality of Freedom* (Oxford: Clarendon Press, 1986), 415.

37. James Rachels and William Ruddick, "Lives and Liberty," in *The Inner Citadel: Essays on Individual Autonomy* (Oxford: Oxford University Press, 1989), 231.

38. Benjamin Barber, *Strong Democracy* (Berkeley: University of California Press, 1984), 100.

39. For an insightful account of this normative conception in John Locke and its bearing on the American constitutional tradition, see Rogers Smith, *Liberalism and American Constitutional Law* (Cambridge: Harvard University Press, 1985).

40. Bonnie Honig, *Political Theory and the Displacement of Politics* (Ithaca: Cornell University Press, 1993), 151.

41. MacIntyre, *After Virtue*, esp. chapter 15.

42. MacIntyre, *After Virtue*, 201.

43. For some interesting reflections on this issue, see James Glass, *Shattered Selves: Multiple Personality in a Postmodern World* (Ithaca: Cornell University Press, 1993).

44. Johnston, *Idea of a Liberal Theory*, 71. (ms version).

45. Rawls, *Political Liberalism*, 175.

46. Rawls, *Political Liberalism*, 37.

47. Rawls, *Political Liberalism*, 36.

48. Rawls, *Political Liberalism*, 78. Rawls habitually lumps Kant and Mill together whenever this issue arises, which may not be entirely justified – at least as far as the question of the "comprehensive" ethical value accorded autonomy (and its full meaning) is concerned.

49. Rawls, *Political Liberalism*, 78.

50. Macedo writes that "liberalism holds out the promise, or the threat, of making all the world like California." *Liberal Virtues* (Oxford: Clarendon Press, 1990), 278.

51. Johnston, *Idea of a Liberal Theory*, 80. (ms version).

52. For several illuminating discussions of these issues, see Amy Gutmann, "Undemocratic Education" and William Galston, "Civic Education in the Liberal State," in *Liberalism and the Moral Life*, ed. Nancy Rosenblum (Cambridge: Harvard University Press, 1989), and Bruce Ackerman, *Social Justice in the Liberal State* (New Haven: Yale University Press, 1980), chapter 5.

53. Rawls, *Political Liberalism*, 200. That this conclusion, however thoughtful and moderate, does not entirely solve the problems or overcome the conflicts and tension in

these cases should be apparent if it is recalled that the parents in question often do not want their children to acquire "the capacity to understand the public culture" and that these same parents may see some of Rawls's "political virtues" as vices—e.g., religious toleration.

54. See for example, Rawls, *Political Liberalism*, 194–95.

55. Rawls, *Political Liberalism*, 152.

56. Michael Sandel, *Democracy's Discontent: America in Search of a Public Philosophy* (Cambridge: Harvard University Press, 1996).

57. John Locke, *Essays on the Law of Nature*, ed. W. von Leyden (Oxford: Clarendon Press, 1954), 133.

58. See John Rawls, "Justice as Fairness: Political Not Metaphysical," *Philosophy and Public Affairs* 14, no. 3 (Summer 1985): 240n.

59. Thomas Jefferson, "Letter to Robert C. Weightman," June 24, 1826, in *Political Thought in America*, 2nd ed., ed. Michael Levy (Chicago: Dorsey Press, 1988), 84.

60. Sandel, *Democracy's Discontent*, 54.

61. Sandel, *Democracy's Discontent*, 53–54.

62. Justice Frankfurter, speaking for the Court in *Gobitis*, quoted by Sandel, *Democracy's Discontent*, 54.

63. Sandel, *Democracy's Discontent*, 90.

64. Sandel, *Democracy's Discontent*, 105.

65. Social enterprises are salient examples, then, of what Alasdair MacIntyre generically refers to as "practices." They are "coherent and complex forms of socially established cooperative human activity through which goods internal to that form of activity are realized in the course of trying to achieve those standards of excellence which are appropriate to, and partially definitive of, that form of activity." *After Virtue*, 175.

66. Mill, *On Liberty*, 6.

67. Condorcet, *Progress of the Human Mind*, 130–31.

68. Michael Walzer, "Liberalism and the Art of Separation," *Political Theory* 12, no. 3 (August 1984): 326.

69. Charles W. Anderson, *Pragmatic Liberalism* (Chicago: University of Chicago Press, 1990), 84.

70. Anderson, *Pragmatic Liberalism*, 70, 81.

71. "Complex equality requires the defense of boundaries." Walzer, *Spheres of Justice*, 28.

72. Walzer, *Spheres of Justice*, 319.

73. Alan Wolfe, *Whose Keeper?* 259, 142, 181, 258.

6

The Moral Imperative and Political Value of Equality

In a democratic era, the ideal of equality seems a self-evident truth, one of those givens everyone understands and no one would gainsay. Tocqueville, writing as a somewhat skeptical aristocrat, saw the desire for equality as the "ruling passion" of democratic ages. But the truth is that equality is an ambiguous and multivalent norm. It is in some respects highly counterintuitive. Taken literally, it seems problematic in some of its implications. Despite its role as a virtually unchallengeable liberal democratic ideal, it is not at all obvious what the grounds for it are, what the point of it is, and what specific imperatives it has for the institutions, policies, and procedures of those societies that enshrine it.

Like other political ideals, the ideal of equality did not float down to earth as part of an abstract utopia. Instead, it represented a moral protest against historically specific political distinctions and privileges which were experienced as improper and arbitrary. These specific distinctions and privileges were different in different times and countries, and the specific meaning and coloration of the idea of equality tended to vary correspondingly. Liberals in seventeenth-century England, for example, were especially offended by what they saw as the arbitrarily and capriciously divergent treatment of groups and individuals by the ruling sovereign; hence their focus tended to be on what today we would conceptualize as the equal protection of the law—the insistence that, to use Locke's formulation, there should be "promulgated established laws, not to be varied in particular cases, but to have one rule for rich and poor, for the favorite at Court, and the countryman at plough."[1] In eighteenth-century France, the paradigmatic arbitrary inequality surrounded the institution of the several estates, together with the invidious distinctions of political representation, taxation, and the like that came with it. Equality, in this context, tended to center about the establishment of equal political status for all citizens *qua* citizens. Descriptively speaking, then, it would seem accurate to describe the ideal of equality as an expression of what Edmond Cahn calls "the sense of injustice." As he writes, "inequalities resulting from the law must make sense. . . . The sense of injustice revolts against whatever is unequal by caprice. The arbitrary, though indispensable to many of law's daily operations, is always suspect; it becomes unjust when it discriminates between indistinguishables."[2]

As a result, appeals to the ideal of equality are most effective and meaningful in the context of denouncing specific forms of political discrimination that seem nonsensical or obsolescent. When adherents try to turn the ideal of equality into an abstract blueprint for utopia, the outcome is less than satisfactory. Giovanni Sartori summarizes the pattern this way:

> Writers on the subject of equality are eloquent and persuasive as long as they give us a *cahier de doléances* denouncing the evils of inequality. But their arguments become thin and far less convincing as soon as they have to deal with the question of how the ideal of equality is to be realized. In this matter their outstanding characteristic seems to be ingenuousness. As an ideal expressing a protest, equality is intelligible and appealing; as an ideal expressing proposals—I mean as a constructive ideal—it is not.[3]

Indeed, whenever we try to envision what perfect or complete equality might actually look like, the speculative model seems to be patently chimerical or positively repellent. There are simply too many spontaneous and (at least partly) benign differences among human beings to imagine in any compelling way how they—and the functional inequalities that attend them—could ever be done away with short of imposing severe and destructive restrictions on almost everyone. It becomes hard, in fact, to understand why—in light of these differences among us—we would even *want* to do away with them and, by implication, to do away with their unavoidable consequences. As a limit condition, perfect equality is a dream world, radically at odds with the particularities that create our very identities. Perhaps this is a moral tragedy. At any rate, it is a serious difficulty indeed, and one that becomes patently evident once the kind of constructive thought experiments alluded to by Sartori are candidly entertained. This is why, in Michael Walzer's words, "equality literally understood is an ideal ripe for betrayal." Its appeal "is not explained by its literal meaning," he continues. "Nor would many of us who are committed to equality be happy with the regime necessary to sustain its literal meaning: the state as Procrustean bed."[4]

As a final problem, the ideal of equality seems in some obvious respects to be prima facie counterintuitive. No one seriously believes that human beings match up equally on any of the various metrics associated with the skills and attributes people value. In light of that fact, any serious and candid insistence upon the norm of equality has to sound paradoxical at best. Walter Lippmann put that insistence this way, explicitly to acknowledge its paradoxical status: "There you are, sir, and there is your neighbor. You are better born than he, you are richer, you are stronger, you are handsomer, nay, you are better, wiser, kinder, more likable; you have given more to your fellowman and taken less than he. By any and every test of intelligence, of virtue, of usefulness, you are demonstrably a better man than he, and yet—absurd as it sounds—these differences do not matter."[5] For many who have considered the matter, in fact, this "absurdity" is too much to accept. It produces a cognitive dissonance they find unbearable, and hence they are driven to resolve it. The resolution can go in opposite ways, of course: the ideal may be relaxed or abandoned in face of the obdurate realities in tension with it or the realities may be obfuscated on principle. The former path is taken by elitists and technocrats of various stripe. And the inanities of linguistic political correctness, with their euphemistic dissemblings about differential human capacities, exemplify the opposite way of reducing the tensions between perception and aspiration in this context.

The ideal of equality, in sum, is ambiguous, problematic, and in some respects counterintuitive when taken as a constructive norm for political organization and policy. It makes sense and has great resonance as a protest ideal when directed against specific instances of hierarchical differentiation which are experienced as arbitrary and oppressive. It is harder both to specify and to defend as a general rule or final good. Yet it still remains, and should remain, as one of the defining ideals of democratic liberalism. The point of observing the ambiguities and vicissitudes of the ideal of equality is not to debunk it or to discard it. Rather the point is that it is necessary to clarify and specify and justify this ideal—that it is not sufficient simply to adopt it as a dogmatic moral intuition, particularly when doing so involves endorsing equality as a final or maximizing social good. In a democratic age, with its ruling passion for equality, one may be allowed to get away with such unreflective and unsubstantiated stipulations. Indeed, to call for reflection about and justification of the ideal of equality may seem faintly sinister and subversive. But the invocation of equality as an imperative absent such specification and substantiation is likely to be either self-defeating or pernicious. The failure to situate equality within an integument of human purposes and other moral imperatives may leave the ideal weightless, unpersuasive, utopian in the pejorative sense. Or it may push us willy-nilly toward the Procrustean bed Walzer properly derides.

In what follows, then, I want to clarify and defend what I characterize as the civic liberal interpretation of the ideal of equality. And to do so it is first necessary to attend to questions about the grounds and the point of political equality. Why is it good? Why is it proper? With respect to what attributes or what metric can we reasonably construe human beings as equals? Only after giving some answer to these questions can we try to make reasonable judgments about the proper extent and venues of equality in the good society.

To anticipate the central conclusions to come, the burden of my argument will be that equality should be construed as a different kind of ideal than liberty/ autonomy. Autonomy, I have argued, should be seen as a constitutive good. Equality, in contrast, functions as a moral postulate and as an instrumental good. In its function as a moral postulate, the ideal of equality embodies two fundamental ontological and ethical claims. The first of these is that, to invoke Edmond Cahn's words once again, "as human integers, [individual human being] are indistinguishables." This fundamental belief, he argues, serves as "one of the fixed stars of an anthropocentric jurisprudence: nature has made man a prime which positive law cannot justly differentiate."[6] Whatever its force in law, this moral commitment is one of the fixed stars of liberal theory. The other fundamental claim is that these human integers possess great—possibly ultimate—worth.[7] A commitment to the moral postulate of human equality, then, embodies the belief that human lives are valuable and that what makes them valuable in the last reckoning is something they have in common.

In its role as an instrumental good, equality serves to sustain and promote a whole range of the other liberal goods and values, beginning with liberty and fraternity. Where citizens are greatly unequal, the autonomy of those on the downside of the hierarchy is compromised or debilitated. Where citizens are deeply unequal, civic friendship is undermined and the bonds of democratic community weakened or destroyed. Wherever inequality is extreme, or unjustified, or present in inappropriate venues, the civic virtues proper to liberal democracy are made more difficult to cultivate. Democratic procedures and legitimacy are damaged. And political stability—valuable to all regimes, including liberal democracies—suffers.

Equality as Moral Postulate: The Grounds for Equality

The ideal of equality functions within liberalism, in the first instance, as a moral postulate. That postulate is based on the deep belief that human beings are in certain fundamental respects "indistinguishables" and that these human qualities entitle us to attribute positive value to human existence. For some analytical or normative purposes, the class of human beings may be divided into subgroupings in accordance with differences in their physiognomy or capacities or behavioral inclinations or whatever seems relevant. But these are always subcategories. The basic category is a constant, and it points toward certain features displayed by human beings *qua* human beings, even if in some cases these features may be deemed to exist more potentially then actually. To put it in Aristotelian terms, these features are those that establish membership within a species rather than the ontologically less fundamental qualities or "accidental" properties that distinguish individuals or subgroupings from each other. But what are these defining features, and why are they valuable? In trying to answer these questions, a good place to look for clues is the historical record of answers that have previously been given by those concerned with issues of human equality (or inequality) and their political implications.

Classical Greek political philosophy, specifically the Platonic and Aristotelian accounts of *dike* (justice or right order), provides an important negative reference point for thinking about political equality. Neither Plato nor Aristotle would have denied that all human beings shared certain defining attributes, but when it came to those attributes bearing upon political roles and status they both found the differences among subgroups more determinative than the similarities. In Aristotle's view, now infamous to contemporary democratic sensibilities, these politically determinative differences included not only gender differences—which he considered a sufficient basis for assigning men and women to different social roles and political status. They also included the claim that some were fitted by nature with the capacity to rule and others—"slaves by nature"—with capacities and inclinations that fitted them to be political subjects only. Similarly, Plato promulgated his "noble lie," the "myth of the metals," that conveyed his belief that human beings came in different types, each of which corresponded in the myth to a different alloy in the soul. Each of these types he depicted as governed by a different ruling passion, by a different part of the soul. And, because these parts of the soul fell into a natural and normative hierarchy of proper control and submission, the different human types were properly destined to play different—and unequal—roles in the polis.[8]

This emphasis upon the politically determinative differentiation of fundamentally distinctive human types was soon challenged by Christian and Stoic universalisms. For both the Christian theologians and the Stoic philosophers, all people—at least, all competent adults—were deemed to possess in common attributes which made them moral creatures and equals. Christian theology held that all human beings—male and female, rich and poor, Jew and Gentile—were created in the image of God. And the Stoics maintained that all competent human adults possessed what they called "right reason," the moral and intellectual capacity to intuit the basic moral order of the world and thereby to distinguish right from wrong. This meant that for the Stoics, everyone was at least theoretically capable of being a "philosopher" in Plato's sense: they could all see and know and embody the human good. The notion of the *imago Dei* was more complex and multifaceted, but overlapping. To be made in God's image meant *inter alia* to know good and evil, to have a free will, to have the capability to be a faithful will—i.e., to remain true to personal and moral commitments through time—and to be able to participate in the saving dance of grace. These crucial moral capacities, again, were not limited to particular classes or castes or cultures or ethnicities. They were constitutive of being human, available universally and on an equal basis to all.

On a moral level, then, to recall Hegel's phrase, the Christians and Stoics knew already that "all were free." That insight did not await, as Hegel alleged, "the Germanic peoples." But Hegel was right to observe that "this realization first arose in religion" and that "to introduce it in the secular world was a further task which could only be solved and fulfilled by a long and severe effort of civilization."[9] The spiritual radicalism and democratic implications of Stoicism and Christianity were buffered from spilling over into the political domain—into the secular world, as Hegel put it—for centuries. The principal causes of this persistent gap between the presumed ultimate moral equality of all human beings and the perennial entrenchment of political hierarchy is probably better explained by Marxist sociology than by the history of ideas. Ideas may have consequences, but material conditions often are more determinative of political arrangements. Roman feudal corporatism and Catholic patriarchal authoritarianism together created strong barriers against secular and political egalitarianism. Classical cosmology and Christian anthropology and soteriology also included elements that functioned ideologically in support of traditional hierarchical institutions. The idea of the "great chain of being" lent itself readily to the justification of social hierarchy.[10] Augustinian insistence upon the distinction between the City of God and the City of Man, together with the emphasis upon the fallenness and corruption endemic to the latter, made it easy to write off social domination as wages of sin that should be endured in this world for the sake of final salvation in God's eternal and redeemed polity to come. Instead of insisting that slavery was a profound violation of the moral equality of mankind, then, Augustine could counsel Christian slaves to accept their lot as part of God's will for a sinful world and to be obedient to their masters.

It was the combined effects of the Reformation, the Enlightenment, and the bourgeois revolution that broke apart the dikes that had contained moral egalitarianism and kept it from having a democratizing impact on political institutions.

The Reformation was predicated upon a challenge to hierarchy and authoritarianism in matters of scriptural interpretation. Ideas such as the "priesthood of all believers" and the "inner light" obviated the need for submission to a clerical hierarchy in matters of doctrine. This democratization quickly carried over into the area of church governance. John Wise, a New England Congregationalist minister, exemplified the logic of this development in his 1717 treatise on church government. Quoting both from scripture and from sources such as Plutarch and Ulpian, Wise wrote that Nature has "set all men upon a level and made them equals." We are equals first of all because we share the same conditions of natality and mortality: "The noblest mortal in his entrance on to the stage of life, is not distinguished by any pomp or passage from the lowest of mankind; and our life hastens to the same general mark. Death observes no ceremony, but knocks as loud at the barriers of the Court as at the door of the cottage." We are all equal, moreover, in possessing "right reason," which is "founded in the soul of man" and is "part of God's image." This divinely ordained natural and moral equality among human beings, Wise then argued, vindicated ecclesiastical democracy. Ecclesiastical monarchism was "a poison poured into the church." And "aristocracy is a dangerous constitution in the Church of Christ." So that "if there be any of the regular government settled in the Church of God it must needs be a democracy."[11]

This democratic lesson was clearly pertinent to secular politics as well. The English Levelers were particularly direct and eloquent in making this connection. As John Lilburne wrote, since human beings are "by nature all equal and alike in power, dignity, authority, and majesty" none of them have "any authority, dominion, or magisterial power one over or above another" except by "mutual agreement or consent."[12] And in the wonderfully pithy words of Colonel Thomas Rainborough in the Putney debates, the lesson was equally clearly set forth: "For really I think that the poorest he that is in England hath a life to live, as the greatest he; and therefore truly, sir, I think it's clear, that every man that is to live under a government ought first by his own consent to put himself under that government." Hence, he concluded, "I do hear nothing at all that can convince me, why any man that is born in England ought not to have his voice in election of burgesses."[13]

It is perhaps worth noting in this secular age that the more worldly Enlightenment theorists were initially less insistent upon the politically democratic implications of moral equality than were the theologically oriented children of the Reformation. Like Plato, they had serious doubts about the common man and they sought to insinuate knowledge into politics from the top down. Thus Voltaire was prone to display a Menckenesque condescension toward the masses and to seek the ear of modernizing princes. But the Cartesian epistemology that underlay the Enlightenment was freighted with egalitarian implications. It undermined authority with its program of critical doubt, and it foresaw a not-too-distant future in which peasants could—by apprehending the pellucid truths of a simplifying science— become the cognitive peers of today's philosophical few. As the eighteenth century wore on, and the bourgeois social revolution undermined the traditional ruling hierarchies of clerisy and court, later Enlightenment figures such as Condorcet, Paine, and Jefferson could paint a more egalitarian scenario of progress. In Condorcet's account, for example, the path of enlightenment went not from princes to people but rather the other way around. Once again, the key sustaining ideas behind Enlightenment egalitarianism were, first, that all competent adults had the capability to intuit fundamental moral truths: in Condorcet's words, "every class of society whose education went beyond the catechism and the alphabet" were capable of "an understanding of the natural rights of man." And second, all human beings shared the same basic moral constitution and attendant moral passions: "nature has implanted in the hearts of all," Condorcet averred, "habits of an active and enlightened benevolence, of a fine and generous sensibility . . . whose flowering waits only upon the favorable influences of Enlightenment and freedom."[14]

Kant traversed within his own intellectual journey the path from early Enlightenment elitism to later Enlightenment recognition of the fundamental moral equality of all people. As he wrote of himself, he at first "despised the common man who knows nothing," but Rousseau "set me right" and taught him "to respect human nature."[15] What Kant learned from Rousseau was that all human beings are worthy of respect because of the "spirituality of [their] souls," and the essence of this spirituality, what distinguishes human beings from beasts, is their capacity for "free agency" and the "consciousness of this liberty."[16] And in Kant's interpretation, picking up on Rousseau's account of conscience and on his insistence that this free agency expressed itself though law-giving (and that all true law must take a general object), the corollary was a belief that all human beings had the capacity to perceive and act upon "the moral law within." It is this participation in the noumenal world of free rational self-determination that gives human life its dignity, its transcendent worth. It "raises my value infinitely, as an intelligence, through my personality; for in this personality the moral law reveals a life independent of animality and even of the entire world of sense. This [purposeful determination of my existence according to this law] . . . radiates into the infinite."[17]

Thus, when Rawls addresses the question of "the basis of equality" in *A Theory of Justice*, the answer that he gives is generally in keeping with the Western tradition of moral philosophy. People are properly to be treated in accordance with the principles of justice—i.e., they are properly treated as moral equals—because they possess the attributes of moral personhood: the "two moral powers" as Rawls now terms them. "Moral persons are distinguished by two features: first they are capable of having (and are assumed to have) a conception of their good (as expressed by a rational plan of life); and second they are capable of having (and are assumed to acquire) a sense of justice, at least to a certain minimum degree." Moreover, "the minimal requirements defining moral personality refer to a capacity and not to the realization of it." And it is assumed that "the overwhelming majority of mankind" possess this capacity.[18]

What this very cryptic review of the traditional warrants offered on behalf of a belief in human equality reveals is a pattern of considerable continuity and overlap. Across a variety of historical eras, cultural perspectives, and religious and philosophical beliefs, the core basis of the doctrine of human equality is the universal and common capacity of all competent human beings to fashion for themselves a plan of life and to distinguish right from wrong. Human beings are moral equals because they are (at least potentially) all free, morally rational, and responsible agents. There are eddies and subcurrents which compromise this consistent pattern somewhat, to be sure. Hobbes, for example, bases his claim of equality in "the natural condition of mankind" more on grounds of parity in natural capacities than on common possession of the moral powers. People are equal enough in strength for all political and practical purposes, he tells us, in that "the weakest has strength enough to kill the strongest, either by secret machination, or by confederacy with others." And they are basically intellectual peers as well: "And as to the facilities of the mind . . . I find yet a greater equality among men, than that of strength."[19] Another important view, moreover, focuses more upon the presumed equality of human beings with respect to their passive sentience rather than to their active moral capacities. Bentham exemplifies this approach, for example, with his argument that the crucial desideratum about human beings is not whether they are free agents but whether they suffer. The French socialist Mably wrote similarly that nature "has given us all the same needs to make us continually aware of our equality."[20] And more recently, Ronald Dworkin combines the free agent/moral powers criterion with the sentience/suffering criterion by placing them in tandem as his justification for what he construes as "the liberal conception of equality."[21] But despite these subcurrents, the dominant criterion of and justification for the demand that human beings be treated as equals is their common possession of what Rawls designates as the two moral powers: the capacity to formulate a plan of life and the capacity to act upon a sense of right and wrong—together with a freedom of will and responsibility for one's actions that Rawls, as we saw earlier, departs from tradition by circumscribing in notable ways.

Against this background, the civic liberal claims regarding the moral postulate of equality can be stated rather summarily. They consist of two propositions about the content of human moral equality, one proposition about its foundations, one proposition about its status, and one practical implication drawn from these propositions and stated in the form of an imperative. None of these claims is novel. Indeed, in this context civic liberalism is perhaps more (morally) traditionalist than most of its competitors.

Proposition One: All people are moral equals, regardless of the particular defining features which differentiate them—features such as gender, race, and ethnicity.

Proposition Two: This is an equality of infinite worth, not a merely relative condition of indeterminate value. It is an equal standing beside which particular differences in skill, intellect, strength, beauty, and other valued attributes are of relatively minor moment.

Proposition Three: The principal ground for insisting that all people are of equal and infinite worth is that they are all actually or potentially rational self-governing agents who have a "conscience"—i.e., the capacity to acknowledge valid moral restraints upon their desires and impulses.

Proposition Four: These three claims are not attached to any single metaphysic or comprehensive religious or philosophical doctrine; but the insistence upon human equality is a moral conception that transcends the particular mores of any contingent democratic culture.

Imperative: No policy or institution is morally acceptable if it is incompatible with either the postulate of human moral equality or its basis.

These precepts, given their continuity with long-standing traditional beliefs rooted in a variety of religious and philosophical doctrines, may understandably seem rather banal. They are, no doubt, less controversial than some of the other claims about the value and proper political incarnation of human equality to be found in the rest of this chapter. These precepts are, nonetheless, highly consequential. And they are not by any means universally accepted, even within what passes for the liberal democratic tradition. A couple of polemical claims may be pertinent here to sharpen and sustain these contentions.

The first polemical implication of this relatively traditional set of precepts concerning human equality is that there are limits to the propriety of what is sometimes called the pragmatic or hermeneutic turn in contemporary normative political theory generally and in democratic theory in particular. One significant instance of this shift in perspective is that found in Rawls's more recent formulations of his views, in which he seeks to move away from what was previously (mis-?)understood by many of his readers to be a neo-Kantian "foundationalist" theory of justice to what is now presented as a merely "political" hermeneutic account of widely accepted democratic conventions and values. This shift is reflected to some extent in the somewhat different rationales for democratic equality he provides in *A Theory of Justice*, on the one hand, and twenty years later in *Political Liberalism*, on the other. In the earlier work, Rawls embraced the idea of a "natural basis of equality," an idea that—whatever else it might mean—would seem clearly to suggest that the belief in human equality was more than a purely contingent product of a specific political culture. In his more recent accounts of the rationale for his entrenchment of the norm of equality among the intuitions behind his principles of justice, however, he seems to argue that the notion of the person and its moral powers—from which the precept of equality is derived—is itself an artifact of "our" particular political culture and nothing more. "Since we start within the tradition of democratic thought," he writes, "we also think of citizens as free and equal persons."[22]

The civic liberal view here accords with that of the early rather than the later Rawls. If the precepts set out above are valid, then it follows that the moral commitment to human equality undergirds the democratic tradition rather than vice versa. This is a logical and normative claim rather than an empirical and historical one, but I believe that it could stand up as a historical point as well. If the fashions and prevailing intuitions of contemporary democratic societies were to change in ways adverse to the acceptance of the postulate of equality, say by a more ardent and unqualified embrace of a technocratic view of governance as scientific management, the civic liberal response would not be to say that the prevailing and hence proper standards had changed but rather to say that the tradition had lost its moorings and become morally illegitimate. This point also means, *inter alia*, that civic liberals would have agreed with Lincoln's position on slavery in his debates with Stephen Douglas, that civic liberals do not share Richard Rorty's ironic detachment *vis-a-vis* democratic ideals, and that civic liberals would be reticent in making and acting upon a condemnation of a caste society only because of prudential considerations and not because of doubts about the moral impropriety of caste systems. "Light-minded aestheticism" and "shared understandings" have their limits.

A second polemical point issuing from the argument on behalf of equality as a moral postulate is that civic liberalism is hostile to what could be called the Benthamite account of equality. The Benthamite approach to equality is insufficiently differentiated from the more traditionalist argument offered here. And its influence is potentially pernicious. Benthamism, recall, is generally egalitarian in its moral consequences for the central reason that everyone counts as one in the utilitarian calculus: all pleasures and pains, and all individual sites of pleasure/pain, are valued equally. Within the parameters of its own metaphysic and its own moral anthropology, then, Benthamism endorses the first precept of the moral postulate—the one according equal moral status and hence equal consideration to all people. The difficulty arises, however, from the metaphysic and the moral anthropology and from the resulting status accorded to the equal persons. These tenets in turn serve potentially to legitimate forms of political control and types of political institutions which should profoundly disturb all democratic liberals.

The heart of the problem is that the Benthamite argument grounds human equality not upon the common and universal capacity for exercising the moral powers of rational self-governance and a sense of justice, but rather upon the common capacity to suffer. Resting equality on these alternative grounds has significant and not always benign consequences. It means that people are treated with equal concern but not with equal respect. Indeed, in a profound sense they are not treated with respect—the appropriate stance toward free and morally responsible agents—at all. They are treated instead with compassion as suffering animals. Bentham, recall, was willing to style himself as "the most benevolent man who ever lived," but he was at the same time utterly dismissive of the idea that the objects of his benevolence had any rights. The notion of rights he saw as nonsense because, among other things, it presupposed what he saw as a prescientific conception of human beings as something other or more than pleasure/pain mechanisms. The objects of his beneficent reformism thus were to be treated the way an animal-lover treats his or her pets. Hence democracy for him was all results and no process, government for but not necessarily of and by the people. It was then not at all accidental that Bentham's most cherished institutional proposal, one he pursued with constancy and diligence for forty-five years, was his plan for a model prison, the Panopticon. The genius of the Panopticon, in which the inmates were subject to constant surveillance, was that it institutionalized an almost perfect system of control and domination. That, he averred, was "the fundamental advantage" of his proposal.[23]

The lesson drawn by civic liberalism from this paradigmatic case can be succinctly stated. It is crucial that the postulate of human equality be grounded upon a recognition of the moral powers uniquely exhibited by human beings and not merely upon a nondiscriminatory form of benevolence. Equal concern without equal respect is not only insufficient; it is positively dangerous. What is lost is human dignity, the moral standing that makes all human beings the proper object of deference and not merely of pity. When that dignity is lost, the content and point of equal treatment changes decisively and disastrously. That change may be masked for a time by the genuinely good intentions of those beneficent guardians who seek to treat their charges kindly. But benevolence is not enough. Unless the moral respect proper to beings who possess the moral powers is also there, the outcome may well become the imposition if the kind of philanthropic despotism exemplified by the Panopticon and relentlessly unmasked by Foucault.

Equality as Instrumental Good

In recent years, arguments on behalf of political, social, and economic equality have generally been arguments predicated upon claims about distributive justice. No doubt Rawls, the critical reaction to his theory of justice, and the attempt by some to improve upon his arguments have been extraordinarily important in this respect. From the civic liberal perspective, however, this tight linkage between considerations of distributive justice and conceptions of social equality—however productive and illuminating some of the discussions have been—has been unfortunate in several respects. In the first place, the arguments for egalitarian distributive policies on the grounds of social justice have not proved entirely compelling.[24] More important still, this focus of discussion has diverted attention from the highly valuable instrumental consequences of political, social, and economic equality (or at least significantly constrained inequality), especially with respect to several other salient liberal purposes. Thus I have found, for example, that students in my classes in democratic theory often seem to think that once they have discovered the weaknesses—as they see them—of egalitarian claims about social justice, the matter has been settled: they no longer need to take equality—beyond basic legal and formal political equality—that seriously as a social ideal. The civic liberal, however, would insist that the argument has then only just begun—and that we need to pay very careful attention to the important ways that relative equality of condition conduces to other social goods and virtues. Simply because rigorously egalitarian conceptions of social justice are not entirely convincing does not mean that other more inegalitarian conceptions win the day: they fall equally short of being fully compelling. We inhabit a morally tragic world in which no rules of distribution can be entirely fair. Since no definitive answer can be given to issues of social, political, and economic equality solely on grounds of justice, a lot remains to be decided on prudential grounds—on the way that degrees and modes of equality and inequality bear upon other important social goods.

When the focus turns from the justice of equality to its prudential consequences, it turns out that quite a bit can be said on its behalf. A good argument can be made that relative equality has multiple beneficial effects *vis-a-vis* other liberal values in particular and other social goods in general. Indeed, it can be argued that the prudential consequences of equality are sufficiently profound to establish—in concert with the moral postulate discussed earlier—a very strong presumption on its behalf. A liberal society, we can say, should favor equality wherever that option presents itself in the absence of compelling overriding considerations. There are times and places in which such overriding considerations arise, or at least so I argue shortly. But the presumption always has to be strongly in favor of a relative equality of condition among citizens in a liberal democratic regime. The relevant prudential reason underlying that presumption is that deep inequalities subvert other important liberal values and aspirations.

Consider first the bearing of equality upon personal autonomy. Libertarians like to argue that we should simply maximize individual freedom and then let the chips fall where they may in terms of equality. But this argument presumes that the resulting inequalities have no reciprocal bearing upon the conditions of autonomy, and that is a presumption hard to sustain. There are reciprocal causal relationships here that must be taken into account. The causal reciprocity between equality and autonomy is perhaps most easily recognized by observing that the negative limit case for each of these values is the same: namely, the master/slave relationship. To be the slave of someone else is to be, at one and the same time, in the most unequal political relationship possible and also to have the least possible autonomy. That coincidence of deprivation should prompt even the most ardent advocates of individual freedom to reconsider their initial assumption that considerations of liberty and equality can be kept entirely independent. If autonomy is a great good at all points in time and not only at the initiating moment of a society, even libertarians would seem to need to be concerned about the possibility of a self-undermining dialectic of political and economic laissez-faire—the possibility that an initial and unrestrained liberty can lead down the road to the destruction of the conditions of liberty for all. Those who care about autonomy have to be vigilant that it not become cannibalized by the long-term dynamics of its own unleashing. Without some restraints on inequality, autonomy may produce relations of servitude and hence the end of autonomy for some.

This potential for the self-undermining of autonomy need not be limited, moreover, to the unlikely development of legalized slavery. Extreme socioeconomic inequality can produce a kind of de facto servitude of unacceptable dimensions. Hence Rousseau's fundamental limit on the permissible extent of economic inequality. Among the reasons for valuing equality, he tells us, is that "liberty cannot exist without it." This should not be taken to mean, he continues, "that the degrees of power and riches are to be absolutely identical for everybody, but that power shall never be great enough for violence, and shall always be exercised by virtue of rank and law; and that, in respect of riches, no citizen shall ever be wealthy enough to buy another, and none poor enough to be forced to sell himself." And, he concludes, "it is precisely because the force of circumstances tends continually to destroy equality that the force of legislation should always tend to its maintenance."[25]

The civic liberal endorses Rousseau's conclusion here, a conclusion that arguably is especially pertinent to a competitive capitalist economy and to any society where family ties and loyalties have significant distributive consequences, especially when compounded over generations. Both free markets and strong families have claims to moral legitimacy and practical value. But, especially in tandem, they do function to "destroy equality," as Rousseau puts it. And the force of law and public policy should thus be a countervailing force in this context. From the civic liberal perspective, moreover, the stipulation that none should "be poor enough to be forced to sell himself" should be read as meaning that no one should be poor enough to be precluded from participation in the common life or the political process of the society. As Michael Walzer has aptly reminded us in this context, there is a "sense in which every political community is in principle a 'welfare state.'" That is, "there has never been a political community that did not provide, or try to provide, or claim to provide, for the needs of its members as its members understood those needs."[26] What exactly these "memberships needs" are must be, so long as resources are scarce, a matter of social deliberation and political choice. But it would seem that, in addition to basic security and welfare, they must include in a democratic society those resources necessary to be a citizen and not merely a subject. Any society that takes seriously its claims to be a democratic community must, like ancient Athens, be prepared to underwrite and invest in the maintenance of its civic life. The Athenians were not particularly committed to economic redistribution for its own sake or in obedience to putative claims of social justice. But they were "as a body . . . prepared to lay out large sums . . . to make it possible for each and every citizen to participate in public life," and these outlays had there and would have in any society the effect of countering to some significant extent privately generated inequalities.[27]

A significant degree of political, social, and economic equality is also conducive to—arguably a necessary condition of—democratic community and civic friendship. Friends must be, in fundamental respects, equals. That does not mean, of course, that perfect equality of every attribute, capacity, or status is necessary; otherwise, no one would ever be friends. But it does mean that the attitudes and behavior patterns inescapably produced by permanent and pervasive gaps of wealth, power, and status are incommensurate with the mutuality of genuine friendship. People who interact across the divide of ingrained inequality may be cordial with each other, but they relate more as patron and client, creditor and debtor, champion and minion. There are, we might say, thresholds of deference, supplication, and hierarchy, the crossing of which violates the demands and requisites of friendship. That structural incompatibility of hierarchy and the mutuality, reciprocity, and spontaneity of friendship is why sergeants and privates, managers and employees, doctors and patients, teachers and students are—even where respect and affection are present—never exactly "friends." And that is also one of the (several) reasons that amorous relationships across these lines are generally suspect.

There is, moreover, a strong element of causal reciprocity at work in the relationship between equality and friendship. If fundamental equality is a necessary condition of friendship, friendship likewise creates incentives and inclinations that work on behalf of equality. Friends (and lovers)—if they really be such—always take care to eliminate where possible and soften where impossible elements of superiority and inferiority which they tacitly understand tend to contaminate their relationship. Consider in this context the unlikely source of Herbert Spencer, who wrote that "every one must have observed the carefulness with which those who are on terms of affectionate intimacy shun anything in the form of supremacy on either side, or endeavour to banish from remembrance, by their behaviour to each other, whatever of supremacy there may exist."[28] In short, wherever a fundamental equality of status obtains between people, there is at least the possibility of establishing a friendship, and wherever there is friendship, care is taken to maintain the enabling condition of relative equality.

A significant degree of political equality is also a precondition for genuine democratic deliberation. Since civic liberalism attaches great importance to democratic discourse and deliberative approaches to political decision-making, this connection creates yet another reason for civic liberals to value equality.[29] A healthy democratic forum requires the closest approximation to equal access a society can manage. (Habermas calls this "symmetry of access" and thematizes it as part of his "ideal speech situation.") And the participants in the democratic conversation must have equal standing so that their arguments are accorded respect during the proceedings. Practical discourse among those who are vastly unequal in wealth and power may have some real utility in regulating and mitigating the domination that otherwise attends or could attend the relationship between the unequal parties. This happens because the terms of discourse embody what Kurt Baier calls "the moral point of view" and hence provide some countervailing force against the temptations of unalloyed self-interest, either because of promptings of conscience or because of the force of public opinion. But conversation between those embedded in hierarchical patterns of differential power and control is always distorted because of the background knowledge that the whole process is in a sense contingent upon the tolerance of the dominant parties, who might if sufficiently provoked terminate the forum and dictate the outcome through their power advantage. Civic liberals, therefore, will always seek—other things being equal—to encourage equality of power, access, and standing if for no other reason than to sustain the health and legitimacy of the deliberative procedures they consider so central to the logic and moral purposes of democratic governance.

A society complacent about deep and persistent inequalities in its midst is also a society that fails to acknowledge and to compensate for the profound contingency of human life and fortune. Such a society lacks the morally essential recognition that "there, but for the grace of God, go I." The sense of contingency is morally essential because it is the fount of both humility and charity. These latter virtues follow logically from the understanding that differences in social standing are in large part the result of dumb luck or the fruit of others' efforts and generosity. Conversely, a false sense that all differences in wealth and social standing are somehow exclusive products of cosmic *dharma* or personal moral meritoriousness leads to stupid condescension and cold-heartedness. Proper recognition of the force of contingency in human life, therefore—an awareness of the power of "morally arbitrary" factors over our individual fate—represents a crucial component of moral enlightenment, one that any good society must take to heart.

Equality does not produce social or individual virtue. Hell could quite conceivably be a society of equals. But a concern for social equality is so closely linked with certain virtues that a lack of egalitarian concern is a sure sign of moral failings in a society. Civility, respect, friendliness, humility, and *caritas* are all inducements to minimize social inequality—to constrain and counteract the social divides and hierarchical subordinations that estrange people from each other and blight the prospects of the less favored. As Matthew Arnold put it: "A community having humane manners is a community of equals, and in such a community great social inequalities . . . are . . . a menace and an embarrassment. . . . A community with the spirit of society is eminently, therefore, a community with the spirit of equality."[30]

Equality is an instrumental good to a political society in one last way: it conduces to political stability. Ever since Aristotle sought to explain the causes of revolution and to delineate the features of what he called the "most generally practicable" regime, it has been a staple of political science in general and of the civic republican tradition in particular that multiple advantages accrue to societies with a large middle class. Conversely, societies polarized between rich and poor are likely to be highly contentious and unstable for some of the reasons canvassed earlier. "It is," writes Aristotle, "the greatest of blessings for a state that its members should possess a moderate and adequate property. . . . Where the middle class is large, there is least likelihood of faction and dissension among the citizens."[31] Those who fall toward the middle of the economic spectrum have enough to feel that they have a stake in the society, and they are likely to be relatively self-reliant. They therefore are likely to be productive and loyal citizens. The wealthy, on the other hand, may be exploitative and prideful, and they make a fat

target. The very poor have little reason to support the regime and may easily become larcenous and seditious out of necessity and resentment. Rousseau accordingly lays out the hypothetical imperative that seems to follow: "If the object is to
give the state consistency, bring the two extremes as near to each other as possible;
allow neither rich men nor beggars. These two estates, which are naturally insep-
arable, are equally fatal to the common good; from the one come the friends of
tyranny, and from the other tyrants. It is always between them that public liberty
is put up to auction; the one buys and the other sells."[32] Marx's belief in the inevitable demise of capitalist politics traded directly upon Rousseau's maxim. It
was the fate of capitalism to dig its own grave by polarizing itself between the im-
miserated and alienated poor and the exploitative and concupiscent rich. All
societies, and democratic societies in particular, have very good practical reasons—wholly apart from considerations of fairness and charity—to avoid entering upon this fateful path.

The Venues of Equality

The ideal of equality thus comes vested with strong moral and practical warrants.
But where exactly is it appropriate? There are numerous venues in a society within
which people might be equal or unequal. Given the moral postulate of equality
and given the instrumental value of equality with respect to several other important liberal purposes, should equality be maximized across the board? Or are different kinds and degrees of equality appropriate within different contexts?
Specifically, people may be equal or not before the law, they may be equal or not
in political status, they may be equal or not in terms of the economic resources
they have at their disposal, and they may be equal or not in their social standing.
Additionally, we might demand that people be politically equal in the sense that
they exercise equal influence over policy formation and political decisions or we
might demand only that they have the same formal rights and powers, leaving the
actual distribution of influence to be determined by individual choice and multifarious social forces.

   Although in its inception liberalism had to fight battles on behalf of legal and
formal political equality, these venues of equality are not really controversial today. No significant liberal viewpoint or liberal theorist would contest, for example, the norm of equal protection of the law, and none would contest the norm of
universal suffrage. But this unanimity disappears when it comes to whether and
how the ideal of equality should bear upon the other venues. Libertarians generally insist, for example, that equality is a valid norm *only* in the context of legal
and formal political standing. Beyond that, choice reigns. In their view, no moral
affront or social scandal whatever arises when even very great inequalities of actual political influence, social status, or economic power come from the free
choices and activities of legally equal citizens. Egalitarians, in contrast, tend to
suppose that equality is a valid norm in all of these contexts indiscriminately. For
Rawls, for example, the principle of redress—and hence the domain of the differ-

ence principle—applies to all "primary goods," and primary goods are taken to include not simply formal rights and liberties but actual opportunities and powers, income and wealth, and the sense of one's own worth that comes from the social affirmation of a person's ends and endeavors.[33] Civic liberalism is situated in abstract terms somewhere between these contending viewpoints. Unlike libertarianism, it subscribes to equality as an ideal on a par with that of autonomy; but unlike egalitaranism it conceives and justifies equality as a moral postulate and an instrumental good rather than as a maximizing good or as an omnibus principle of distributive justice. What if anything distinctive, then, does civic liberalism have to say on this issue of the proper venues of equality?

Three things, principally. First, civic liberals side with egalitarians on the question of whether social practices and institutions should be devoted to promoting an actual as opposed to a merely formal equality of influence over political decision-making. Second, civic liberalism considers the issue of economic equality to be a highly complex one upon which valid moral and prudential considerations can legitimately be invoked that push in different directions. Hence it would see the best distributive norms to consist of some mixture of these countervailing standards, and it would insist that the balance among these is something properly left to democratic deliberation and bargaining rather than something to be determined by market forces acting in a political vacuum, by philosophers, or by bureaucrats. Third, civic liberalism would seek to put renewed emphasis upon that subset of social equality that we can designate as civic equality. Recognizing that social standing and esteem is properly and unavoidably largely a matter of private judgments that lie outside the realm of public determination, civic liberalism would nonethless insist that judiciously contrived public institutions and enterprises both can and should promote and concretely embody a real sense of civic equality among citizens.

First, the issue of actual versus merely formal equality in the sphere of political decision-making. On the civic liberal view, a democratic community is first of all a community of moral equals, possessed of infinite worth and human dignity. This fundamental equality of moral worth implies not only that everybody should count for one in any decision-making calculus, but also that everybody should, prima facie, have an equal say in the making of these decisions. That is what self-governance in a community of equals means—government for the people and by the people. As a normative limit condition, therefore, formal and legal equality does not suffice. Given all the sometimes profound inequalities that develop from differential capacities and the dynamics of free choice and autonomous activity, mere formal equality inevitably permits great discrepancies between the "equal say" standard and the actual distribution of political power. To the civic liberal, this discrepancy not only allows but mandates legal constraints upon sources of unequal political influence in order to protect the integrity and legitimacy of democratic decision-making.

This does not mean that a democratic society should undertake a futile quest to prevent spontaneous and consensual political differentiations stemming from uneven interest levels, rhetorical skill, and charisma quotients. Nor does it mean

that all-out warfare must be declared upon the functional requisites of organization. As Michael Walzer says, "we may dream of a society where power is shared,
and everyone has exactly the same share. But we know that equality of that sort
won't survive the first meeting of the new members. Someone will be elected
chairman; someone will make a strong speech and persuade us all to follow his
lead. By the end of the day we will have begun to sort one another out—that's
what meetings are for."[34] Some, moreover, may feel they have better things to do
than to attend the meetings, preferring to immerse themselves in other more felicitous (to them) enterprises and accepting the consequences of their absence on
the results of the meeting as a reasonable price to pay for relief from the burdens
of a participation they find onerous. In a free society, they have a right to make
that trade-off.

The norms of democratic legitimacy and the ideal of political equality do allow
and even call for, however, measures to insulate the decision-making process from
the distortions that unequal power, social standing, and wealth will create absent
some defenses against their colonization of the political domain. The freedom to
speak, to organize, and to petition have both moral standing and constitutional
protection in our democratic system. But these rights need not and should not be
construed in such a way as to sacrifice the basic integrity of the democratic process.
The structural issue here is the need to protect the autonomy of, and the relevant
distributive norms within, the different spheres of society. A democratic society
cannot stand idly by and allow political access and influence to be commodified.
Money has its privileges, but among them is not the right to buy office or to dominate the flow of political information and ideas. To allow that is to countenance in
secular politics what simony represents in ecclesiastical politics. Just as the right to
free speech does not entail having the right to drive a sound truck through the
streets at night with the decibel level cranked up high, so free political speech does
not entail having the right to monopolize the political media.

The civic liberal, therefore, believes it perfectly proper—indeed mandatory—
for a democratic society to take care to defend the integrity of its political process,
and that includes defending the capacity of all citizens to have their say and influence over the outcomes. Doing so will, in a free society, always involve an element
of swimming upstream against the economic, sociological, and psychological
forces that create inequalities of power and control. Perfect equality of influence
may be an illusory goal, but it nonetheless remains a valid standard of democratic
moral legitimacy. That is why measures to regulate financial contributions to can-
didates for political office or to give all groups and perspectives a chance to be
heard in the democratic forum are consonant with the civic liberal understanding
of the imperatives of equality. Purely formal political equality, in the absence of
such affirmative steps to translate it into actual practice, is likely not to be enough.

What then about the second of these highly contested issues concerning the
proper venues of equality, the question of economic equality? Do liberal democratic ideals require that economic resources be distributed as equally as possible,
subject only to the prudential limitation that everyone not be made worse off in
absolute terms, as Rawls would contend? Or are economic fortunes instead prop-

erly left to the freely contracted exchanges of the marketplace, with equality not a relevant norm in this context apart from having the law protect and enforce in a nondiscriminatory way the results of market transactions? Should the civic liberal side with the libertarians or the egalitarians here? The answer, I think, is that the civic liberal sides with both, hence with neither. Civic liberalism recognizes multiple moral imperatives and prudential considerations that in some respects work in opposition to each other when it comes to establishing the criteria for allocating economic resources in a society. None of these conflicting norms can be set aside without moral impropriety. Hence the final outcome must involve reaching some compromise among valid but contrary standards. And in a democracy the ultimate arbiter in such cases must be the deliberations and judgments of the cit-||
izenry. The civic liberal position on the question of economic equality, then, is complex, indeterminate, and procedurally democratic.

The civic liberal begins as a prima facie egalitarian. Absent overriding considerations to the contrary, the civic liberal would endorse equality as the proper rule in the economic domain as well as in the domains of law and politics. Three reasons drive this initial predisposition on behalf of economic equality. The first is what we have called the moral postulate that stipulates the equal status and value of all human beings. In a sense, Locke gave expression in theological terms to this postulate as it bears upon economic distribution when he said simply that God gave the earth to mankind in common. No one can claim a disproportionate share of the world's resources on the grounds of being better than anybody else. In a more contemporary and secular voice, Bruce Ackerman institutionalizes the same prima facie egalitarian standard when he stipulates that control over resources in a liberal society is to be determined by an authoritative conversation in which any claim will be invalidated if it can be shown to depend upon a claim to be intrinsically better than others.[35]

The second reason for extending the ideal of equality into the economic realm is that, as Rawls properly insists, differences in economic fortune are to a very substantial degree the result of morally arbitrary causes. People do better or worse economically in large measure because of differential capacities they have inherited or been accorded by circumstance. Hence the inequalities are undeserved to that same extent; and undeserved inequalities are unjust. This is, then, a second potent moral foundation for economic equality. And to these two moral reasons, finally, we can add the powerful prudential considerations adduced earlier regarding the instrumental benefits of equality of condition among citizens. Equality of condition conduces, it may be recalled, to autonomy, to civic friendship, to democratic deliberation, to civic virtue, and to political stability.

So it would seem prima facie that equality should be the standard for the distribution of economic resources in a democratic society. But further reflection turns up countervailing considerations, both prudential and moral, that have to be taken into account. The principal prudential consideration on behalf of relaxing the demand for complete economic equality is the one qualifying factor recognized by Rawls. And that is the fact that some incentive in the form of a more-than-equal share of the proceeds of the economy may be practically necessary to induce the more talented members of society to develop and deploy their productive abilities. For that reason, as Rawls recognizes, a rule of absolute equality may leave everyone worse off, including those who would be on the lower end of a distributive scheme involving some inequality.

This is a very important and compelling consideration that argues for the practical necessity of some deviations from economic equality simply to make a nonslave economy function. Marx, of course, tried to argue that such a concession represented a reification of capitalist psychology and a failure to recognize that "socialist man" would be motivated by the more altruistic incentives of a genuine "species-being." And along similar lines, Joseph Carens has argued that a free market economy could still be productive if people were socialized to feel bound by a social duty to maximize their pre-tax income even if their post-tax income would reduce them (or raise them) to an equal share.[36] Apart from other possible objections to these optimistic hopes for socialization into economic altruism, the extraordinary rigor—hence unlikelihood of success—of such socialization schemes is made apparent by the realization that these unselfishly toiling citizens would have to be not only altruistic but irrational.[37] That is, they could not only not govern their actions by self-interest: they could not even be allowed to be disinterested utilitarian welfare maximizers. The problem here is one of collective rationality. Assume that I can control only my own work habits and no one else's. In that case, even adhering disinterestedly (i.e., unselfishly) to the utilitarian maxim would tell me to be a shirker rather than a worker. The reason is that shirking my chores would produce a clearly discernible gain in pleasure/loss of pain for me, while the effect on everyone else would be—spread out over 250,000,000 others—literally unnoticeable. Hence it would be rational and proper by the utilitarian standard of greatest good for the greatest number for each to be a slacker. The problem arises in the aggregate and not in the individual case. In short, to work utterly without regard to incentives, people must go beyond public spiritedness to being irrationally (i.e., for no noticeable benefit to anyone) self-sacrificing.

Beyond this powerful prudential inducement to permit unequal returns for differential productivity, there are also three legitimate moral arguments on behalf of unequal outcomes. The first of these is an argument from desert. The straightforward intuition here is that people deserve different returns for different inputs of effort. If I offer ten dollars to my two sons for mowing the yard and one of them chooses to go swimming while the other does the job, it would be not only imprudent but positively unjust to give each of them five dollars at the end of the day. Rawls's argument that effort is the product of character and character in turn the product of circumstance is, in this context, something of a red herring. The point of remunerating work as a dictate of justice is simply to recompense the sweat and sacrifice of time and energy involved. It is not based on some imputation of generically superior moral character. Economic desert is simply and only that; it is not a function of some omnibus moral deservingness. This point needs emphasis, perhaps, because the Protestant ethic has often blurred this distinction, attributing economic productivity and success to such (presumed) general virtues as industriousness, diligence, thrift, and self-denial. In fact, someone's superior economic output may be the product of avarice, cupidity, vanity, and obsessive-compulsive neurosis. The successful entreprenuer may neglect his family and be a miserly philistine. But he still deserves to receive a larger share than I who works less because I am more devoted to my family and have a better sense of values. I have made my choices and receive different rewards. Mr. Rich-guy may not deserve my equanimity or the affection I receive from my family, but I also don't deserve his greater wealth. Justice may require redress of some inequalities, but it must validate some other inequalities as morally warranted.

Accepting some economic inequality as morally legitimate is also a correlate of respect for the integrity of persons. Rawls wants to argue that all individual talents are properly to be treated as common assets because we didn't do anything to deserve them. Hence I am as entitled as Michael Jordan to the returns on his athletic ability and as entitled as Pavarotti to the royalties on his compact discs. But their lack of (complete) desert is not by itself sufficient to sustain that alleged entitlement on my part. For Jordan's legs and Pavarotti's voice are, however undeserved, a part of them. These attributes are not merely "assets" external to them; they are constitutive components of who they are. It does not require buying into a strong doctrine of "self-ownership," then, one that says they are entitled without qualification or remainder to every penny generated by their talents, in order to reject as presumptuous a claim by me or anyone else to be, in effect, their part owner. At the least, people are related to their talents in a different and more intimate way than anyone else, and, regardless of desert, respect for their integrity as persons constituted in part by these economically valuable talents would seem to require that they be accorded privileged standing *vis-a-vis* the fruits of their talents and labor.

A final moral consideration that works at cross purposes to the prima facie commitment to economic equality is what we might call the moral legitimacy of the gift-relationship. The problem here is that justice is not the only morally valid form—and arguably not even the highest form—of moral relationship that binds people together. Justice is measured and impartial. Love and friendship are highly partial and are at least somewhat unmeasured and uncalculating on principle. Friends and lovers, that is, do not interact through a calculus of justice. Fairness may be necessary, but it clearly is not sufficient as a transaction norm for those linked by *amicitia, caritas,* or *eros.* Indeed, if someone you consider a friend or lover keeps a constant and assiduous ledger sheet of the costs and benefits of your dealings with each other, you may reasonably begin to suspect that you misunderstood—and overestimated—the nature of your relationship. Justice demands a close accounting. Love and friendship, based on mutuality of purpose and free giving and taking, demands transcendence of such narrow economizing.

The problem that love and friendship present to justice, then, is that these also are morally legitimate and valuable relationships. Indeed, they are arguably "higher" and more valuable forms of relationship than those more distant relationships properly governed by what Hume called the "remedial virtue" of justice. But the distributive consequences of love and friendship disrupt the principles of justice because they involve prejudicial giving. As a loving parent, I give care, affection, nurturance, and resources to my children—unfairly so, both in the sense that what is given is not determined by desert or equity and also because I do not bestow similar benefits upon the other children in the world, all of whom may be equally deserving and many of whom are more needy. The moral conundrum facing a society dedicated to justice and the ideal of equality then is this. If the spontaneous distributive consequences of love and friendship are permitted to occur, these will bring with them unfairness and inequity. But if the society seeks to preempt these inequities by interdicting the gifts occasioned by love and friendship, it seems both to delegitimate these higher forms of human association and also to discourage them. Christianity, along with other serious moral traditions, has always contended that grace trumps fairness. (Consider here not only the parable of the Prodigal Son but also the depiction of God as a vineyard owner who will reward those who come late to labor in his vineyard on a par with those who came earlier.) Does a commitment to the democratic ideal of equality demand that we stand that moral intuition on its head?

By raising these questions I don't mean to imply that society should not attempt to constrain the inequalities created and exacerbated by the beneficences of love and friendship. We properly do constrain them, for example, by laws governing inheritance, gift taxes, and the like. My own view, indeed, is that American public opinion and policy is more permissive than it should be in allowing intergenerational bequests to skew the distribution of wealth and power in our society. Even that archcapitalist Andrew Carnegie was of the opinion that "the growing disposition to tax more and more heavily large estates left at death is a cheering indication of the growth of a salutary change in public opinion. . . . It is desirable that nations should go much further in this direction."[38] The point is simply that recognizing and accommodating the moral value of love and friendship (and the enormous prudential value of the support and nurturance so generated, as well) necessarily involves some compromises with egalitarian norms and aspirations. That is why, for example, the institution of the family has always been a stumbling block for adherents of the most ambitious schemes for promoting social and economic equality.[39]

It turns out, then, that applying the ideal of equality to the economic domain is a somewhat messy business. On the one hand, valid moral imperatives and important prudential considerations justify the imposition of significant limitations on the permissible extent of economic inequality in a democratic society. Economic inequality tends to corrupt the integrity of the democratic decision-making process, to undermine the conditions of civic friendship, to compromise the autonomy of less advantaged members of society, and to ratify and reenforce the basic unfairness of life—of the genetic lottery and the historical contingencies that consign people to undeservedly divergent fortunes. It also can polarize and destabilize a democratic polity, rendering everyone's life less commodious and secure. On the other hand, a society cannot create incentives for economic productivity without allowing for potentially unequal economic outcomes. And not only the toleration of but the moral legitimation of some degree of inequality seems a necessary consequence of giving due compensation for effort and self-sacrifice, of respecting the personal integrity of individuals, and of validating the particularized commitments of kinship, affection, and cultural affiliation.

The practical inferences that seem to follow are these: first, a well-ordered liberal democratic society should give credence and weight to all of the sometimes-conflicting moral claims and prudential concerns canvassed here. A good society is obligated to accredit and factor into its allocative criteria recognition of contingency, respect for desert, regard for personal integrity and autonomy, concern for friendship and stability, and the need to protect political equality. As a consequence of the need to acknowledge the validity of these different moral considerations and social goals, the quest for some simple and determinate allocative algorithm seems not only chimerical but almost inescapably perverse. Any such simple and determinate rule must deliberately ignore some relevant ethical considerations and/or compelling social purposes.

It follows from these claims about the intrinsic and unavoidable messiness and complexity of considerations relevant to the norms of distributive justice that the moral endorsement and the political enforcement of unmitigated and unqualified market allocations is indefensible. It also follows that the attainment and implementation of some form of "moral geometry" *vis-a-vis* social justice is not a legitimate possibility. The civic liberal, therefore, must be what Rawls calls an "intuitionist." That is, the civic liberal believes that "the complexity of the moral facts defies our efforts to [establish definitive priority rules] and necessitates a plurality of competing principles . . . [with regard] to which we can only say that it seems to us more correct to balance them this way rather than that."[40]

In the absence of simple and definitive standards to determine the legitimate extent of permissible economic equality in a democratic society, how then should the requisite determinations be made? Who should do the unavoidable balancing among the plural, valid, and competing moral and prudential considerations that factor into establishing the rules of economic distribution? In a democracy, the only answer must be that this is the proper task and the unavoidable burden of the democratic citizenry as a whole. The relevant answers cannot be provided—and should not be dictated—by philosophical decree or by judicial fiat. That means that these decisions are necessarily and properly made through the normal processes and institutions of democratic politics: deliberation, bargaining, voting, and compromise. The rules for allocating the benefits and burdens subject to collective control will be decided as the democratic populace determines and prioritizes its purposes, effectuates its moral judgments, and pursues its interests. Conservatives have worried since the inception of democracy that the unpropertied or less-propertied majority would use its power to expropriate the justly acquired earnings and assets of the wealthier members of society. Marxists and democratic leftists have complained to the contrary that the failure of this expropriation to occur indicates the presence of false consciousness within and the power of economic control over the democratic public. But neither of these sets of worries, forecasts, and explanatory claims are terribly convincing. Many of the more economically successful members of contemporary democratic societies doubtlessly believe that their assets have been justly acquired and are taxed at morally improper confiscatory rates. And equally unquestionably the power of money skews the policy outcomes of legislative politics. But both the empirical record of allocative policies in modern democracies and what we know of public opinion suggests that the reliance on market allocations heavily modified by welfare redistributions reflects a compromise among the competing moral intuitions and prudential concerns that pull not only groups but even individual citizens in different directions. We should, I think, expect this messy and contentious process of moral contestation, pragmatic calculation, and interest contention to be a permanent feature of democratic politics. In a corrupt society this political contest may degenerate into a morally unconstrained clash of economic self-interest. But in a well-ordered society, the moral intuitions and acknowledged obligations of citizens—their sense of justice—will be prominent both in the public deliberation over these issues and in the determination of individual behavior.

The moral judgments and political priorities I endorse lead me to believe that the dynamics of a "winner take all" society generate excessive inequalities at the upper end of the income scale, and the labor market, in tandem with the necessary security net at the lower end of the income scale, generates a disproportionately small premium for relatively unskilled workers *vis-a-vis* both the more highly skilled and the nonworking segments of the population.[41] As a result, I would favor the implementation of a higher marginal tax rate at high income levels, significant constraints on the intergenerational transfer of wealth, an expanded earned income tax credit, and the universal provision of basic health care. But these are claims that must be pressed upon my fellow citizens in the political forum by appealing to their own judgments and priorities. The norms and aspirations of civic liberalism provide touchstones for the greater degree of economic equality I would champion, but they give me no warrant for bypassing the legitimately determinative processes of democratic dialogue and negotiation.

One final and important point about the civic liberal account of the proper venues of equality in a democratic society. Although the civic liberal endorses substantive and not merely formal political equality and although the civic liberal likewise endorses placing significant constraints upon the extent of economic inequality created by a capitalist economy, an equally important concern is with a kind of equality that overlaps with but exists alongside of and can be differentiated from political and economic equality *per se*. This kind of equality is sometimes called "social equality," but I prefer and use here the term "civic equality."[42]

Civic equality can be defined as a social condition wherein there are numerous situations and experiences in which people function on a par as valuable and valued participants solely and sufficiently by virtue of their (equal) role and status as citizens of the democratic body politic. These may include but are not limited to specifically political experiences. And although these situations and experiences may be very difficult to create in a setting of significant economic inequality, they by no means require a parity of income among the citizens in question. Civic equality is embodied and experienced in various settings and occasions in our public life. We experience it when standing in line at the voting booth: that scene graphically expresses the fact that we are all equal members of the sovereign *demos*. It makes no difference whether we are relatively young or old; black, white, or brown; able or handicapped; rich or poor; secular or religious; we all stand in the same line at the same place and cast an equally weighted vote. We experience civic equality as students in public schools, where the same resources and opportunities are available to all indiscriminately and where the teachers care mostly about your performance and deportment and where your classmates care mostly about your personality and athleticism. We experience civic equality in the military—a paradigmatically hierarchical institution to be sure, but one in which the ranks are not a function of outside political, social, or economic status. We experience it when we use public libraries, when we enjoy public parks, and when we visit the metropolitan zoo or museum. We experience it when we participate in programs of local arts councils and when we attend local civic festivals. We experience it to some degree when we rub shoulders with people from all walks of life on the streets, in shopping malls, and in the neighborhood tavern. In each of these settings, we are entitled to be there by virtue of our status as a citizen; we function on a par with others by virtue of our equal status as citizens, and we experience ourselves as (equally) valuable persons because of this entitlement and this function.

To a civic liberal, one of the most dispiriting trends in the past several decades is the considerable deterioration that has occurred in many of these venues of civic equality. So many of our public schools have become unsafe and ineffectual. Public libraries and public parks suffer from underfunding and are inadequately defended against abuse. Replacement of the draft by a volunteer army fairly effectively eliminates the children of the prosperous from this venue of civic equality. And the segmentation of residential areas into class and ethnic enclaves seems to proceed apace. This deterioration of our public sphere has not only been encouraged by ideologues and activists on the libertarian right of our political spectrum. It has also been exacerbated by the preoccupations and priorities of the egalitarian left. The derogation of the public sphere by the libertarian right is, of course, not terribly surprising. Libertarians have always held that the public sphere could be beneficially dissolved into a multiplicity of private domains. They do so in part on the grounds of efficiency, contending that public enterprises are always subject to the destructive dynamics exemplified in the "tragedy of the commons."[43] They do so also because they place no intrinsic value on civic equality. Thus they would be quite happy to privatize schools, parks, libraries, and, if possible, even the public highways. These claims, however, are subject to two simple rejoinders which could be elaborated in considerable detail but which I here state summarily: civic equality and social solidarity are important aspects of a good society, and the tragedy of the commons can largely be alleviated by judicious policing and diligent maintenance if a society considers that worth doing.

What is more remarkable and more depressing is that political egalitarians in this country have in recent years done relatively little to promote a healthy public sphere. Indeed, some very prominent left organizations have actively—if possibly inadvertently—accelerated its decline. The paradigm case here is the American Civil Liberties Union, which has championed a kind of expansive and unnuanced version of individual rights that in many instances destructively undermines the integrity of public spaces and public institutions. I have no quarrel with the proposition that society needs to make provision for treating the mentally deranged, for assisting the homeless and addicted, and for according educational opportunity even to poorly socialized children. But these social obligations and individual entitlements need not and should not entail allowing these individuals to inflict serious damage on public spaces and institutions whose functioning they thwart by converting them to other purposes or by obstructing them. If schools are forced to allow obstreperous students to disrupt their classrooms, they cannot educate. If libraries must allow alcoholics to use them as drying-out stations, those who want to use them for their intended purposes will go elsewhere. If public parks must become havens for drug users, mothers will neither take nor send their children to play there. If disturbed individuals are given leave to defecate and intimidate on the public streets, others will avoid and abandon them.

When the consequences of the decline of the public sphere on the lives of the working poor are contemplated, it should be apparent that a strong effort needs to be made to reverse this decline in the name not only of community but also in the name of civic equality and social justice. Where those of modest means can enjoy safe streets, inviting parks, accessible libraries, and successful schools, their lives can be pleasant and dignified. Where, in contrast, the streets are dangerous, the schools unsafe and ineffectual, the parks and libraries seamy or chaotic, then those without the financial resources to escape into suburban enclaves will lead much more difficult, anxious, and impoverished lives. They will have every right and reason to believe that their society's invocations of the ideal of equality are hypocritical at best.

A good case can be made that a dedication to fostering civic equality is the real test of a society's commitment to what I have termed the moral postulate of equality. It is the presence or absence of this commitment that indicates whether or not all people are truly held to be moral equals not only in the eyes of God—a claim that easily can degenerate into a cheap and empty nostrum—but also in the eyes of the society. But civic equality and its sustaining arrangements are fostered only by a society willing to promote and protect the strength and integrity of its public sphere. By that standard, American democracy has failed the test in recent decades, and few on either side of our current political spectrum seem all that interested in facing up to the challenge.

Notes

1. Locke, *Second Treatise*, XI, 142.
2. Edmond Cahn, *The Sense of Injustice* (Bloomington: Indiana University Press, 1949), 14–15.
3. Giovanni Sartori, *Democratic Theory* (New York: Praeger, 1965), 328.
4. Walzer, *Spheres of Justice*, xi.
5. Walter Lippmann, "Why Should the Majority Rule?" in *The Essential Lippmann*, ed. Clinton Rossiter and James Lare (New York: Random House, 1965), 8.

6. Cahn, *Sense of Injustice*, 15.

7. Compare William Galston's account of what he calls the "triadic theory of the good" that he argues informs all the most credible defenses of liberalism. The first of the triad is a belief in "the worth of human existence." Liberals, he writes, "cannot be satisfied to say that all human lives are equally worthy. They must also say that each life has positive worth, greater than zero." See "Defending Liberalism," *American Political Science Review* 76, no. 3 (September 1982): 625.

8. See Aristotle, *Politics*, book I, chapter 5; and Plato, *The Republic*, III, 414–15.

9. G. W. F. Hegel, *Reason In History*, trans. Robert Hartman (Indianapolis: Bobbs–Merrill, 1953), 24.

10. See Arthur O. Lovejoy, *The Great Chain of Being* (Cambridge: Harvard University Press, 1936).

11. John Wise, "A Vindication of the Government of New England Churches," in *Political Thought in America*, ed. Levy, 38–44.

12. John Lilburne, *The Free-Man's Freedom Vindicated*, cited in Sanford Lakoff, *Equality in Political Philosophy* (Cambridge: Harvard University Press, 1964), 63.

13. Cited by Lakoff, *Equality in Political Philosophy*, 67 and 64.

14. Condorcet, *Progress of the Human Mind*, 144, 192.

15. Immanuel Kant, "Fragmente," in *The Philosophy of Kant*, ed. Carl J. Friedrich (New York: Random House, 1949), xxiii.

16. Rousseau, "Discourse on the Origin of Inequality," in *The Social Contract and Discourses*, trans. G. D. H. Cole (New York: Dutton, 1950), 207–8.

17. Kant, "Critique of Pure Practical Reason," in *The Philosophy of Kant*, ed. Friedrich, 262.

18. Rawls, *Theory of Justice*, 505, 509, and 506.

19. Hobbes, *Leviathan*, part one, chapter 13.

20. Quoted by Lakoff, *Equality in Political Philosophy*, 117.

21. "I presume that we all accept the following postulates of political morality. Government must treat those whom it governs with concern, that is, as human beings who are capable of suffering and frustration, and with respect, that is, as human beings who are capable of forming and acting on intelligent conceptions of how their lives should be lived." Ronald Dworkin, *Taking Rights Seriously* (Cambridge: Harvard University Press, 1977), 272–73.

22. Rawls, *Political Liberalism*, 18–19. Rawls may not be wholly of one mind on the issue, however, as he seems to equivocate a good bit regarding the status of the relevant conception of the person. See, for example, *Political Liberalism*, 18, 20n.

23. See the account in my *The Irony of Liberal Reason*, 109–21.

24. Some of my remarks in the chapter on Rawls and later on in this chapter are pertinent to the reasons for this failure. See also my "The Antinomies of Social Justice," *The Review of Politics* 55, no. 2 (Spring 1993): 193–216.

25. Rousseau, "The Social Contract," in *The Social Contract and Discourses*, 50.

26. Walzer, *Spheres of Justice*, 68.

27. Walzer, *Spheres of Justice*, 71. See also in this context the argument of Charles Beitz in *Political Equality* (Princeton: Princeton University Press, 1989), which bases its egalitarian claims on the importance of establishing conditions sufficient for all the members of a democratic society to be able to participate effectively in democratic citizenship.

28. Herbert Spencer, cited by Lakoff, *Equality in Political Philosophy*, 153.

29. See my *Reason and Democracy*, 126–44 and Benjamin Barber, *Strong Democracy*, 173–98.

30. Matthew Arnold, "Equality," in *Essays Religious and Mixed*, ed. R. H. Super (Ann Arbor: University of Michigan Press, 1972), 289.

31. Aristotle, *Politics*, IV, II.

32. Rousseau, "Social Contract," 50.

33. Rawls, *Theory of Justice*, 92 and 441–42.

34. Walzer, *Spheres of Justice*, xi.

35. Bruce Ackerman, *Social Justice in the Liberal State*, 11.

36. Joseph Carens, *Equality, Moral Incentives, and the Market* (Chicago: University of Chicago Press, 1981).

37. See, for example, James Fishkin, *Justice, Equal Opportunity, and the Family* (New Haven: Yale University Press, 1983), 137–43.

38. Andrew Carnegie, "Wealth," *Political Thought in America*, ed. Levy, 332.

39. One of the best recent analyses of some of these moral dilemmas is provided by James Fishkin in his *Justice, Equal Opportunity, and the Family*. As he argues in this context, "the basic liberal approach to equal opportunity does not amount to a coherent ideal once complications involving the family are systematically taken into account," 6.

40. Rawls, *Theory of Justice*, 39. I have here substituted the phrase "establish definitive priority rules" for Rawls's "give a full account of our judgments" because that seems closer to the crucial difference here. The "intuitionist" can give as full an accounting of his or her judgments as Rawls can. What is disclaimed is not the capacity to account for the judgments but the ability to adjudicate any tensions among them by recourse to determinative and explicit criteria. It should also be noted in this context that it is not only "intuitionists" in this particular sense of the term who must rely upon their moral intuitions. As Rawls himself acknowledges, "any ethical view," including his own, "is bound to rely on intuition to some degree at many points," 40.

41. Robert H. Frank and Philip J. Cook, *The Winner-Take-All Society* (New York: Free Press, 1995).

42. Mickey Kaus uses the term social equality in his endorsement of that goal. My account overlaps considerably with his argument. But social equality can misleadingly connote venues and criteria of social differentiation that take place in private arenas which are inevitably and properly beyond the direct control of public policy. The term civic equality invites instead our attention to more public venues. See Mickey Kaus, *The End of Equality*, esp. chapters 3, 4, 6, and 10.

43. Common properties, that is, are always subject to being destructively overexploited and undercared for by those who use them, precisely because the individual users don't bear the entire cost of the properties' overexploitation or reap the entire benefit of their nurturance.

7

Civic Friendship in Liberal Society

Liberty and equality should not be seen as the only goals or ideals guiding the liberal democratic project. In this chapter and the next, I want to examine the most important additional goals, goods not so specifically and distinctively liberal, that need to be included within any compelling account of liberal purposes. These goals are civic friendship and civic virtue.

Many liberal theorists, especially twentieth-century ones, have deemed friendship and virtue as purely private matters beyond the proper concern of liberal regimes. And other theorists who, conversely, have considered friendship and/or virtue central to a well-ordered society have allowed these concerns to take them beyond or outside the liberal project altogether, whether to illiberal conceptions of solidarity and liberation or to illiberal versions of moral perfectionism. My argument that these goods are properly to be included among the animating purposes of liberalism, therefore, necessitates taking issue with both of these theoretical orientations in the process of making two central claims. The first claim is that liberalism properly understood encompasses a concern for friendship and virtue and has a place for them in the public domain. The second claim is that the nature and political role of friendship and virtue must be understood in a way consistent with the constitutive good of autonomy, the moral postulate of equality, and the recognition of the limits and fallibility of our moral knowledge.

Objections to incorporating virtue and friendship among the purposes of liberal regimes are partly moral and partly empirical. Liberals of various orientation have deemed the inclusion of these goods to be improper or infeasible or both. Why they consider them improper on liberal grounds varies, of course, with their own axial moral concerns. When it comes to virtue, for example, most liberal realists consider a commitment to the virtuous life to lie beyond the reach of liberal regimes, given their generally Hobbesian account of human motives and interests.[1] Libertarians, deontological egalitarians, and difference liberals, on the other hand, are more concerned that a pursuit of virtue must compromise their own most treasured goals. The libertarian worries, for example, that the individual would lose the freedom to define and pursue his or her own conception of virtue. The egalitarian worries that the embrace by the state of a particular account of virtue would violate the crucial insistence upon treating citizens as equals. And difference liberals worry that any official doctrine of virtue involves the hegemonic imposition of one identity and hence the construction of difference as otherness.

When it comes to friendship, the objections are grounded more in practical doubts than in moral worries. The latter are still at issue to the extent that friendship is understood as encompassing what Aristotle considered to be the fullest and highest form of friendship—to wit, friendship based upon a common commitment to the good; for that kind of friendship would seem to entail the specification of what is in fact good and hence would be subject to the concerns just canvassed regarding an official conception of virtue. Beyond that, the doubts about maintaining "fraternity" on the liberal masthead are mostly practical. The realists reprise Hobbes's objections to the classical view that humans are naturally sociable, citing all the conflicts over gain and glory endemic to political life. And liberal theorists of various persuasion express serious and legitimate doubts about whether friendship can remain a viable political goal in very large and diverse societies. When we extend the sphere of the body politic, there may well be some beneficial consequences, as Madison argued, regarding the dynamics and consequences of factionalism; but political friendship would seem to be discouraged at the same time and for the same reasons that the formation of a tyrannical majority faction is made less likely. Similarly, the "fact of pluralism"—the profound moral and religious differences encompassed by most contemporary liberal polities—would seem to militate against any robust form of civic friendship. Rawls wants to maintain his hope that liberal citizens will be motivated to "share the fate" of their fellows, of course. And Connolly hopes that care will survive and even be inspired by agonistic contention. But, given the terrain they sketch, these hopes seem somewhat wistful. Hence most liberal theorists conclude that as a practical matter, liberal societies should base their hopes for civic comity upon self-interest rightly understood as expressed most crucially in the willingness to fulfill contractual obligations, to respect the rights of others, to keep one's promises, and to live and let live.

It is not, then, that these liberal theorists dispute the value of friendship or the importance of virtue. It is simply that they think these goods cannot be properly embodied within the public domain of a liberal regime committed to individual liberty and to the equal treatment of all citizens; nor can the content of these goods be adequately specified for political purposes by any philosophy that recognizes and respects the limits of our epistemic competency in matters moral. Thus virtue and friendship need not be denigrated, but they should be consigned to the private realm. Let each pursue virtue and friendship in his or her own way in accordance with his or her own conceptions. As for the liberal regime, however, it should pursue neutrality rather than promote virtue; and it should seek to constrain and enlighten self-interest rather than try to engender friendship among liberal citizens.

Against the many liberals who doubt that friendship and virtue have any significant place among the animating purposes of liberal regimes, I want to argue that these traditional political goods have an important and valid role to play in the liberal democratic ideal of a well-ordered society. I would even hazard the conjecture that the inappropriate neglect or unnecessary banishment of friendship and virtue from liberal democratic aspirations may have much to do with the widespread view that liberalism is morally tepid and even perverse. Liberals, of course, cannot simply embrace the classical ideals of political friendship and of politics as a partnership in human virtue *in toto* or uncritically. The specific form these ideals took in classical political theory and in premodern polities was a function of philosophical assumptions we no longer accept and of sociological contingencies we no longer inhabit. Any persuasive account of friendship and virtue as viable and valid liberal purposes, then, must differ from the classical account in ways necessary to conceive these goods as consistent with liberal goals and assumptions that premodern (or illiberal) societies did (or do) not endorse. My claim is that this is not an impossibility. Properly understood, friendship and virtue can be endorsed as political goods fully compatible with liberalism's commitment to liberty and equality and with liberalism's acceptance of moral pluralism and fallibilism. The case can be stated even more boldly, in fact. I believe that properly liberal conceptions of civic friendship and civic virtue are complementary with and help to sustain the definitive liberal commitment to liberty and equality. Indeed, I would argue that a political society devoid of civic friendship will be unable to sustain any profound and practically consequential commitment to the ideal of equality. And it may also be unwise to expect a political society to maintain a serious commitment to civil liberty and social tolerance absent the understanding that autonomy is both a civic virtue and a constitutive feature of a good human life.

Before turning to consider the nature of civic friendship and its role in a well-ordered liberal society, let me make three further preliminary points that are necessary to contextualize the claims about civic friendship and civic virtue that follow. First, the adjective "civic" here attached both to the politically relevant conceptions of friendship and virtue signalizes the fundamental importance in this context of the distinction between the public and private realms and what is pertinent and proper to each. Rawls's distinction between "comprehensive" and "political" goods and virtues is very much on target here. No liberal theory can officially endorse and no liberal society can legitimately seek to create comprehensive forms of friendship and virtue. Such an attempt would violate the moral humility and epistemic fallibilism that are central and legitimate aspects of the liberal tradition. And such an attempt would result in oppressive policies that would violate the liberal commitment to human dignity and autonomy. But the endorsement and pursuit of more delimited and partial (i.e., "political" in Rawls's sense) forms of civic friendship and civic virtue may be not only permissible by liberal standards but even intrinsic to the liberal project considered as a whole. Rawls's endorsement of what he calls the "political virtues" serves, in fact, to demonstrate how this distinction between comprehensive and partial goods may be crucial in this regard.[2] It is, then, important to be very clear from the outset that the ideals of civic friendship and civic virtue I endorse as important parts of the liberal project are partial and constrained subsets of friendship and virtue. Were civic friendship not a limited form of friendship, it would not be a possibility—especially in a pluralistic society. And were civic virtue not limited to one specific domain of the humanly good life, it would not be legitimate for a liberal regime to affirm and promote it.

Second, the inclusion of civic friendship and civic virtue among liberal purposes is not inconsistent with a steadfast devotion to the defining liberal norms of liberty and equality. At least there is much more synergy than tension among these several liberal ideals so long as liberty and equality are understood as the preceding chapters argue they should be understood. The recognition of the propriety and significance of civic friendship and civic virtue within liberal politics, however, may well be rendered exceedingly difficult within the framework of some alternative conceptions of liberty and equality. Civic friendship and civic virtue become anomalous, for example, in the context of a purely decisionist account of liberty or in the context of a conviction that democratic equality is what Allan Bloom has characterized as "genial nihilism." Where the ideal of liberty is understood, on the other hand, as a devotion to human autonomy and where the ideal of equality is understood as grounded in universal respect for the dignity of all people, the same problems of reconciling these various liberal purposes do not arise or at least do not present themselves so starkly. That is not to say that—as in any case of multiple valid goals—questions about which end to prioritize in specific cases never arise. It is to say that there is no problem of fundamental irreconcilability to be dealt with—one that would, as a consequence, mandate banishing one or more of these purposes from the liberal project. In my view, this is but one more good reason for the superiority of the civic liberal understandings of liberty and equality set out earlier.

Finally, the civic liberal endorsement of civic friendship and civic virtue should not be seen as some kind of radical innovation within or heretical departure from the liberal tradition. Rather, as even a rather cursory revisiting of many canonical liberal texts from John Locke to John Dewey would suggest, this concern with political friendship and civic virtue represents a recovery of a dimension of liberal aspirations that was suppressed or subordinated for the most part very recently. Because they were not morally pyrrhonic and because they incorporated within their own assumptions some strands of the classical philosophical tradition, earlier liberals found no great problem with accepting "fraternity" as one of the liberal goods. And they likewise found no great difficulty in assuming that liberal politics had, like all other regimes, the right and the need to be concerned with the formation of "good character" among its citizens. Had they been acquainted with the insistence found in much contemporary liberal theory upon a rigorous form of principled neutrality about the human good, one could reasonably surmise that they would have considered it a self-defeating moral asceticism produced by a failure of will and/or conviction. And had they been confronted with the claim that liberal societies could not properly and realistically seek to engender a sense of community or civic friendship among its members, they would almost surely have considered this renunciation to be a potentially dangerous impoverishment of liberal aspirations. I don't want to make too much of this reading of the liberal tradition in the context of my constructive argument on behalf of civic liberalism. Arguments from (previous) authority should not count for a great deal. The earlier liberals may well have embraced aspirations that can no longer be sustained in the setting of contemporary postindustrial pluralist societies. Or they may have simply been wrong—philosophically inconsistent, morally perverse, or politically unrealistic. It is, nonetheless, worth recognizing that the arguments and the moral frame of reference of this chapter and the next do not represent some radical departure from previous liberal concerns. Instead, they represent an attempt to resuscitate ideals and aspirations that—whatever their fate in the hands of recent deontological or conventionalist forms of liberalism—are by no means foreign to the liberal tradition as a whole.

The Good of Friendship

Our concern in this chapter is with civic friendship. But before discussing a species, one needs to know something about the genus. It would be difficult to reach an understanding of the nature and possibilities of civic friendship without having a sense of what friendship is, where it comes from, and why it is a human good—something that most people seek and value as part of a satisfying human life.

Friendship is a complex phenomenon. Moreover, it is analogous to and overlaps with other forms of affective association. As a result, one finds conflicting accounts and definitions offered by those who have reflected upon friendship. One can also argue that the English language is somewhat conceptually crude and impoverished when it comes to identifying and discriminating among variant forms of human affective ties. The word "love," for example, is applied in English usage indiscriminately to the partly overlapping but also importantly distinctive forms of affection the Greeks distinguished as *philia, eros, caritas,* and *agape.*

For our purposes, it is not necessary to canvass or adjudicate the various disagreements about the proper conceptual boundaries of friendship, but it is important to provide a working definition of friendship.[3] And, although no such definition can fully satisfy all adherents of the different accounts of friendship, our working definition should incorporate as much as possible of these accounts and of the conventional understandings they have engendered. With these concerns in mind, the working definition of friendship that will be used here is this. Friendship here is understood to mean a condition of mutual enjoyment, affection, and good will among people who have some degree of mutual understanding. The hallmark consequences of this relationship include a propensity to seek each others' company, to communicate with each other, to engage in joint endeavors, to trust each other, and to provide some degree of mutual assistance when requested or deemed necessary. This is a definition, it may be noted, that incorporates most of the elements of friendship that Aristotle identified in his classic account in the *Nicomachean Ethics*. In Book Eight of that work, for example, one finds reference to the core features of "mutual goodwill," "fondness for each others' society," "trust," "aid," "knowledge," and "communication." Our definition does not, however, commit us to all of the distinctive particulars in Aristotle's account regarding the moral and psychological bases of friendship, its subtleties, or its consequences. Deploying this definition of friendship, in other words, is highly consonant with Aristotle's insightful analysis, but doing so does not require us to embrace all the features of his moral philosophy, his political sociology, or his philosophical anthropology.

Friendship, so understood, is generally—and, I think, properly—recognized as an important human good. In the process of exploring with my students the value of friendship as an irreducible part of a good human life, I have on occasion proposed a bargain to them. Suppose that I offer you a life in which you have complete freedom, unlimited wealth, and vast powers over other people, I begin by saying. Their eyes light up eagerly at the prospect. There is, however, one catch, I continue. You can have no friends at all—none, ever. That's the price of your limitless freedom, wealth, and power. Their eyes fall. It was a trick proposal, a Faustian bargain: gain the whole world, as it were, but sacrifice your soul, a basic element of your humanity. They all, by their reactions, recognize and affirm that a life devoid of friendship is really not in their eyes a life worth living. In short, they confirm Aristotle's claim that "friendship is necessary to the good life [and] is in itself a good and beautiful thing." They agree that "no one would choose a friendless existence on condition of having all the other good things in the world."[4]

Aristotle goes on to distinguish among different types of friendship, types that correlate with what he regards as the three different bases or sources of friendship. There are, he argues, three answers to the question, "what is it that awakens friendship?" These are the good, the pleasant, and the useful. When the last two of these—the pleasant or the useful—are what awakens friendship, he continues, "what the friends are thinking of is their own good." In these cases, then, it can be said that the friendships "are grounded in an inessential factor" and the friends are only friends *per accidens*. These lesser forms of friendship are, as a consequence, often transient. When friends *per accidens* are no longer agreeable or useful to one another, their friendship "dies a natural death." This death is natural because "with the disappearance of the motive, the friendship itself disappears, for it had no other *raison d'être*."[5] Aristotle thus views those friendships grounded upon a common attachment to and embodiment of goodness as the highest form of friendship. Indeed, one could say that this is the only genuine kind of friendship and that those based upon utility or pleasure are mere simulacra and counterfeits of the real thing. It also follows that for Aristotle only those who are good can really be friends in the fullest sense.[6]

Now in making these analytical distinctions and associated judgments regarding different types and grounds of friendship, Aristotle is onto something important. But I would want to argue that he doesn't get it quite right. And the way in which he doesn't get it quite right will prove to have some bearing upon our understanding of the possibilities and limitations of effectuating civic friendship within pluralistic societies. In distinguishing among the kinds of friendship, I would argue, the crucial distinction does not lie where he claims it does. It does not lie, that is, between the useful and/or the pleasurable on the one hand and the good on the other, with the only real friendship being based on the latter. Instead, I would argue, the crucial distinction actually is between what Alasdair MacIntyre calls "internal goods" and "external goods."[7] This is a distinction not between pleasure and the good—with the former being largely assimilated to utility—as Aristotle's argument would have it. Rather it is a distinction between importantly different forms of taking pleasure and enjoyment in a good thing or activity. Moreover, to the extent that MacIntyre is correct in saying this distinction proceeds from "an Aristotelian view of pleasure and enjoyment," then this is a distinction that Aristotle had available to him and arguably should have invoked in his account of the nature and pleasures of friendship.[8] "Internal goods" are things or activities enjoyed and found satisfying in and of themselves. Having them or doing them is intrinsically rewarding, wholly apart from any incidental benefits or valuable consequences that may attend or follow from them. "External goods," on the other hand, are things or activities we value only on account of the incidental or consequential benefits attached to them. Thus a Mozart symphony is an internal good for the music lover, and money is almost the paradigmatic external good—valuable only for what it can buy—unless one happens to suffer from some Midas-like form of fetishism. The same thing or activity may also be valued or experienced differently by different people, such that one values it internally and the other externally. MacIntyre offers the apt example of the contrast between Benjamin Franklin's "external" account of sex and D. H. Lawrence's "internal" riposte: "When Franklin asserts, 'Rarely use venery but for health or offspring . . . ,' Lawrence replies, 'Never use venery.'"[9] A fairly straightforward definition of an internal good, then, is that it is something valued and enjoyed "without regard to consequences."[10]

True friendship occurs, then, when people find pleasure and satisfaction in each other's company in an intrinsic, noninstrumental way. Friends enjoy and seek each other's company "without regard to consequences." The correlates and beneficial consequences of having friends need not be disdained, of course. But in genuine friendship, these external benefits are not themselves the main reason for the association. If you are my friend, I may appreciate receiving your aid and succor; but our friendship will survive its absence. It will survive, at least, if you are unable to offer needed assistance. If, on the other hand, you are able but prove consistently unwilling to help me, the friendship may come to an end. But this happens because I conclude from your actions that you must never have really been a friend in the first place, since mutual aid is such a natural product of friendship that its complete absence may reasonably be taken as a sign of friendship's failure. If one person valued another solely for the collateral benefits of associating with that person, then the relationship was never one of genuine friendship but only a kind of contractual relationship that each party maintained on a *quid pro quo* basis. True friendship, in contrast, always has a "convenantal" dimension to it.

Aristotle is therefore justified in his claim that some shared good plays a crucial role in the formation of friendships, for people will only take continued delight in each other's company when they share some common love, passion, or purpose. Friendship arises only when people are *simpatico*—only when they have a *pathos* together. And this common feeling must have an object. As C. S. Lewis writes, "friendship must be *about* something." That is why "we picture lovers face to face but friends side by side." And it is also "why those pathetic people who simply want friends can never make any. The very condition of having friends is that we should want something else besides friends."[11]

Human goods thus factor crucially into friendship because they are the common objects friendship is about. They are the objects of the shared passion, feeling, enthusiasm that makes us value the company of a friend in and of itself without regard to any other external and incidental benefits our association may confer. Without some good in common, a genuine friendship—as contrasted with its external-good oriented utilitarian counterfeit—will never arise. Once engendered, the friendship may survive the disappearance or demise of the shared good, because the pleasure of the association itself may become self-sustaining. The shared good has become a shared past or a shared set of experiences. One example of this phenomenon is the persistence of friendship among war veterans who once fought side by side. They are soldiers no longer, but the sense of attachment and affection remains.

Aristotle sometimes speaks as if it is only a mutual pursuit of The Good in some comprehensive, specifically moral, essentialist sense that constitutes genuine friendship. But that claim is misleading. Clearly, a common devotion to a deeply held set of moral goals and ideals provides the basis for a profound kind of mutual identification and affiliation. But the goods in question can in fact be very particular and more practical than moral. It doesn't require a common apprehension of and erotic attraction to the Agathon to constitute a genuine friendship. Instead, C. S. Lewis is more on target here when he amends his insistence that "friendship must be about something" with the phrase "even if it were only an enthusiasm for dominoes or white mice."[12] Friendships so created may not be "perfect," as Aristotle puts it.[13] They may, however, be quite genuine and may become quite deep and lasting. This is a point that bears some emphasis because it has significant consequences for assessing the possibilities for friendship in pluralistic societies—an issue considered specifically and in some detail later in this chapter.

Although relationships with other people entered into purely for utilitarian reasons are not genuine friendships but only quasi-contractual *quid pro quo* exchanges, friendships bring with them important incidental benefits. Even as he disparages pseudo-friendships founded solely "on the expectation of some advantage to be received," Aristotle immediately invokes the instrumental advantages of friendship in his account of why a friendless existence is so dismal.[14] There are arguably a host of these benefits incidental to friendship, but three of them seem most significant in their potential political implications.

The first of these advantages of friendship is the aid and assistance friends bring to one another. Friends spontaneously help each other through their trials and tribulations out of their spontaneous concern for each other's welfare. Friends are allies and resources. As the ads suggest, "friends don't let friends drive drunk." Moreover, friends don't let friends fight their battles alone or sink into destitution when circumstances make them unable to provide for themselves. Thus, as Aristotle puts it, "in poverty and all the other misfortunes of life the thoughts of men turn to their friends as their one refuge. Truly friends are an aid."[15]

Second, friends provide us with communicative or deliberative partners. As Hannah Arendt points out, one of the things well understood by the Greeks was that the world "remains inhuman in a very literal sense unless it is constantly talked about by human beings." And thus "the essence of friendship consisted in discourse."[16] Human language is not some incidental or sporadic phenomenon. Rather it embodies and serves as the primary vehicle of the communicativeness which is part of the essence of a genuinely human existence. And although one can talk with those who are not one's friends, it is really only among friends that discourse and deliberation are most effectively carried on. The mutual understanding and common purposes that characterize friendship provide the starting points and frame of reference necessary for a fruitful exchange of ideas. And the mutual caring for each other's welfare is a potent motivation that fosters and animates the discussion. Enemies may threaten each other and occasionally negotiate. Strangers and instrumental allies may bargain and communicate in ways needful for their strategic interaction. But only those who are in some sense and in some measure friends will enter fully and seriously into the sharing of thoughts and feelings that characterizes human deliberation in its highest form.

Finally, friendship is one of the most potent sources—perhaps an essential one—of affection and self-esteem. Friendship occasions and is marked by the spontaneous expression of affection. And although the conduct of friendship may consist more in the giving than the receiving of affection, the mutuality of friendship means that the state of being friends with another inevitably brings with it the receipt of some measure of affection.[17] Not only is receiving this affection pleasurable in itself. It also brings with it a validation of one's sense of worth: it enhances one's self-esteem. When affection comes our way from someone we consider an estimable person—and a genuine friend would have to qualify—we are thereby given objective grounds for thinking that we are ourselves estimable. We become more confident and justified in considering ourselves to be good and valuable people.

Friendship in sum, is a good and precious thing, as Aristotle insists. It is good and pleasurable in itself. And it is valuable for the additional benefits it confers.

One last issue deserves comment before moving to consider the role that friendship plays in politics and the role that it should play in contemporary liberal democratic theory and practice. This issue is one of those hoary old "perennial questions" of political theory, but it needs at least some answer to be given to it here—however cryptically—because this answer has some bearing upon the normative claims that follow. The issue in question is whether human beings are "friends by nature" or whether, to the contrary, they are naturally at war with one another. The juxaposition of Hobbes with Aristotle famously poses this issue.

Aristotle insisted that human beings are naturally social—that a human being "is by nature an animal intended to live in a polis." Moreover, he added comparatively, "man is a being meant for political association in a higher degree than bees or other gregarious animals." He supports his claim by offering as evidence the widespread agreement that friendship is "necessary to the good life," the fact that solitary human beings are not self-sufficient, the faculty of language, and the "perception of good and evil" this faculty makes possible.[18] Hobbes seems directly to challenge Aristotle's account of natural human sociability. Bees and ants, he says, may be naturally sociable, but not human beings. The Greek belief that man is a creature "born fit for society," he says, is "certainly false, and an error proceeding from our too slight contemplation of human nature." Human beings do seek association with each other, but not for friendly or cooperative purposes. Human beings come together to achieve physical security, economic gain, and personal esteem or glory. But each of these ends would actually be more fully obtained by achieving dominion over others than by cooperative endeavor. The result is that "men have no pleasure, but on the contrary a great deal of grief, in keeping company, where there is no power able to overawe them all."[19]

In *Liberalism and Community*, this Hobbesian moral psychology is said by Steven Kautz to be the classical liberal view. "Classical liberalism," he writes, "is a doctrine of acquisitive individualism, and teaches that man is by nature solitary and selfish, not political or even social. . . . Human beings are not friends by nature."[20] But this identification of Hobbesianism and liberalism on the issue of the naturalness of human friendship seems excessively one sided. Locke's views, after all, were much more widely embraced than Hobbes's by his contemporaries. And Locke argued that God had "made man such a creature" that he was "under strong obligations of necessity, convenience, and inclination" to join society. Locke, in fact, was happy in this regard to cite with approval "the authority of the judicious Hooker" to the effect that "we are naturally induced to seek communion and fellowship with others."[21] And Richard Hooker was an Anglican divine who drew his inspiration on this matter from Thomas Aquinas, who in turn was drawing heavily upon Aristotle. The fact is that, appearances to the contrary, it is not really necessary for us to choose between the Hobbesian and the Aristotelian accounts of the natural human propensities toward friendship or competition. The two accounts are not so contradictory as Hobbes's language would suggest. A somewhat misleading impression to that effect is created by the faulty supposition, embodied in abstractions about the natural and the artificial, that the circumstances of human existence are the product of some unified agency—"nature"—animated by a coherent pattern of purposiveness. When that supposition—commonly and tacitly embraced by both Hobbes and Aristotle—is suspended, we should be able to see that both the Hobbesian and the Aristotelian accounts are grounded in real features of the social world and that we therefore need to synthesize their insights rather than choose between them.

The claim of Aristotle (and Locke, following Hooker) that human beings naturally and spontaneously seek the company of others out of both convenience and inclination has a strong evidentiary basis. In *The Moral Sense*, James Q. Wilson canvasses some of the studies that seem most convincingly to demonstrate what he characterizes as the human "predisposition to attachment."[22] Despite the great variability and malleability of human cultures and behaviors, human infants appear to arrive in the world programmed for and profoundly interested in social interaction. These predispositions of the neonate, absent some very strong over-riding circumstantial forces to the contrary, develop into more mature forms of social desire and behavior that produce the general belief alluded to by Aristotle that friendship "is one of the things which life can least afford to be without."[23] Hence, there are ample warrants for the proposition that we are a species predisposed by our very nature to be sociable and to value friendship. This conclusion, however, need not entail the corollary that these predispositions toward friendship will unproblematically reach fruition or that they may not encounter resistance and difficulties stemming either from countervailing propensities and desires or from other circumstances of human existence. And, in fact, these contrary propensities and circumstances are also part of the human condition. Specifically, human beings naturally seek security, need and want material possessions, and desire esteem and recognition. Unfortunately, as Hobbes insisted, the pursuit of these valued ends brings us into competition with each other. Thus it seems reasonable to conclude that "nature"—i.e., the combination of internal human passions and the external circumstances of social existence—inclines us to be sociable but also set us at odds. We want to be friends but we are driven to be enemies in some respects, nonetheless.

To the extent that this synthetic appropriation of Aristotle's and Hobbes's apparently contrary views is persuasive—to the extent that it is accurate to see human beings as predisposed by nature both to cooperate and to conflict—an important practical lesson emerges for those who value civic friendship. That lesson is that a society cannot adopt a *laissez-faire* posture toward civic friendship in the confidence that it will be attained spontaneously and unproblematically. The dynamics of natural enmity inescapably present in all human societies make that confidence naive and delusionary. On the other hand, a society seeking to enjoy the benefits of *fraternité* among its citizens need not write off that hope as a futile attempt to be "at war with nature," to borrow a piece of Burkean rhetoric. The appropriate attitude, instead, is a wary optimism that can inform and sustain thoughtful and diligent efforts on behalf of civic friendship. If—as I argue in more detail shortly—the presence of civic friendship is a great social good, then we need to fashion our institutions and policies to nurture and promote it. Our propensity to be sociable makes that possible; our propensity to war with each other makes that necessary.

Friendship in Politics

Friendships are not always confined to relationships between two individuals or even among a very few people. They spill over, in a somewhat attenuated fashion no doubt, into larger collectivities. The political consequences of friendship patterns and affiliations, moreover, can be quite significant. As a result, the dynamics of group friendliness and/or enmity are a proper concern of social theory and social practice, even in a liberal society that respects the integrity of the private realm. The appropriate analogy here, perhaps, is with marriage and family relationships. These cannot be—or should not be—created or mandated by social fiat. And there are important aspects of the relationships into which the larger society should not intrude. On the other hand, all societies wind up having to account for, accommodate, and in some respects shape and regulate these relationships. It is not always an easy matter to decide exactly where the society may and should involve itself in marital and family relationships. And the boundaries of their involvement shift over time with changes in prevailing mores and practices. Consider in this respect, for example, recent legal changes regarding contraceptive usage and marital rape. Laws concerning child custody, adoption, community property, alimony, and spousal benefits offer further examples of the inevitability and the mutability of social involvement in and regulation of relationships that are in their essence and origin quite private and voluntary. Because they do not produce new and dependent members of society in the form of children, friendships neither require nor merit the kind of legal regulation that attaches to marriage. But the patterns and modes of friendship and enmity —affiliation and estrangement—among the citizens of a society have important consequences for the overall health and success of the social enterprise. And various social policies and practices, in turn, have considerable influence upon the shape of these patterns and modes of affiliation. Hence the patterns and the practices that shape them are a proper object of concern for both normative theorists and political leaders.

The dynamics of friendship spill over into collectivities because both the subjective and the objective bases of friendship are extendable. It is true, of course, that friendship can never be as perfect or complete or as intense among the members of a large association as it can be between intimates. That is because the depth of friendship varies with the depth of the friends' understanding of each other and with the extent and closeness of their mutual endeavors. In a somewhat attenuated fashion, however, friendship can transcend the boundaries of intimacy and occur on a larger scale. The subjective grounds of friendship are "good will" and the desire for pleasing companionship. Both of these are capable of being generalized. Regarding good will, Aristotle points out that *philia* functions as a virtue—i.e., as a state of character. Among good people, friendliness is a "confirmed disposition."[24] The good human being is positively disposed toward others, including mere acquaintances and even strangers. Generalized *philia* inclines one to be neighborly. And people can, of course, take pleasure in the companionship of others with whom they are not intimate. The objective bases of friendly association also can be found on a scale that exceeds the dimensions of personal intimacy. It is not only close friends who may share the common interests, common attachments, common purposes, and common values that generate the behavioral cohesion of amicable and cooperative association. Quite large groups of people may share these goods in common, and on the basis of pursuing them together they may form the quasi-erotic bonds of social concord Aristotle referred to as *homonoia*: "friendship between the citizens of a state, its province being the interests and concerns of life."[25]

The political consequences of friendly associations are by no means unequivocally benign. Indeed, when the bonds of the associative relationship are powerful and their extent limited to distinct subsets of the populace, friendship dynamics can be a threat to social comity and political stability. Friendship "is both a possible benefactor and a possible danger to the community," as C. S. Lewis observes.[26] Its potential for benefaction will be canvassed in some detail momentarily. But it is necessary to recognize as well the very real dangers it can present to society. The reason for the danger is that "every real friendship" among specific subsets of the population "is a sort of secession, even a rebellion."[27] The interest or enthusiasm or purpose that fuels the union of friendship tends at the same time to distinguish and hence potentially to separate those included in the friendship from the rest of society. These others may be perceived merely as the uninitiated or they may be more negatively construed as the "other" in a stronger sense. Benjamin Constant captured the structural dilemma presented to the larger society by powerful subset friendships when he remarked that profound loves and friendships amount to an "egoism a deux." Or, on a larger scale, they can create the collective egoism of partial associations. Friendship groupings can function as cabals or cliques that are exclusionary and that seek to profit at the expense of the excluded. This is why Rousseau was so hostile to such partial associations. They are, he said, "formed at the expense of the great association" and "the will of each of these associations becomes general in relation to its members, while it remains particular in relation to the state." Thus he thought that ideally "there should be no partial society within the state" or, failing their complete elimination, "it is best to have as many as possible and to prevent them from being unequal."[28] Rousseau's favored solution was extreme and, if enacted, would function to the real detriment of a society. But his animus was based upon his recognition of a social dynamic quite pertinent to friendship groups: they can function as factions in the Madisonian sense, with all the dangers and pitfalls attendant to factious behavior.[29]

On the other hand, even in their "partiality," friendship groupings can be beneficial to the larger society. Not only do they provide the satisfactions of conviviality to their members and not only do they at times perform very useful functions that help their members become successful contributors to the society economically and politically; they also can function as seedbeds of civic virtue. Just as families function as small partial associations that socialize children, so particular friendships arouse and nurture capacities for trust in, cooperation with, and affection for other members of society. Through habituation and generalization, dispositions toward *eunoia* and *caritas* learned within small-scale friendship associations can be crucial instrumentalities for countervailing our natural narcissism and turning us toward being good neighbors and good citizens.

Civic friendship in the full and complete sense may be said to obtain when the range of *eunoia* ("good will") and *homonoia* ("like-mindedness" or "concord") is coterminous with the boundaries of the society as a whole—when these positive dispositions and the behavioral patterns induced by them characterize "the citizens of a state" and not merely some specific subset thereof.[30] This definition does not require the inclusion of each and every person resident within the boundaries of the state in question. That constitutes a limit condition that never, realistically speaking, could ever occur. Every society encompasses criminals, hermits, aliens, and incompetents. Civic friendship thus admits of degrees and can never be perfect. It can, however, exist to an extent sufficient to have significant political consequences if and when the vast majority of the citizenry regard their fellow citizens—on the basis of their common membership—as in some sense their friends: as people in the same boat, as it were, who share important interests, concerns, purposes, and values and who therefore are *prima facie* predisposed to communicate, trust, cooperate with, and assist one another. Real-world civic friendship relates to the unattainable perfection of its ideal type as polyarchy relates to democracy.[31] It is an approximation only, but a meaningful and consequential approximation. It meets the ideal defining criteria only partially and imperfectly, but it does so to an extent sufficient to distinguish it and its results from instances where the criteria are met more sporadically or not at all.

The Good of Civic Friendship

A society that succeeds in generating a sense of civic friendship among its citizens benefits in numerous ways. The lives of its members are richer, more pleasant, more secure. The society's capabilities of performing its principal functions are significantly enhanced. It is more stable, its economic performance is facilitated, and its capacity to mobilize the community to deal effectively with social problems is improved. As Jacques Maritain put it: "While the structure of society depends primarily on justice, the . . . internal creative force of society depends on civic friendship."[32] Moreover, as I argue shortly, it is precisely those societies that are pluralistic, liberal, and democratic that benefit the most from and stand most in need of civic friendship. This latter claim may seem surprising, since it is commonly supposed that civic friendship is an attribute only generated by and only functionally adapted to premodern, compact societies—to the Greek polis, perhaps. But the truth of the matter is that civic friendship conduces not only to universally valuable political goods such as stability and prosperity, it also conduces to the attainment of specifically liberal and democratic goods such as equality, toleration, civil liberty, deliberation, and compromise.

Like friendship itself, civic friendship is good both intrinsically and instrumentally. It is pleasing and satisfying to human beings in and of itself, insofar as they are to a certain extent "naturally sociable" (Aristotle) "species-beings" (Marx). In addition, it serves instrumentally to help produce other very important benefits.

Most people find friendly interaction with their fellow citizens satisfying and desirable in itself, wholly apart from any other social and personal benefits that might come with it. The pleasures of life are more enjoyable and the sorrows and burdens of life more bearable when they are shared with others. Thomas Jefferson invoked the intrinsic value of civic friendship—even as he implicity acknowledged, at the end of an intensely contested electoral campaign, its elusiveness—when he spoke in his First Inaugural of the need to "restore to social intercourse that harmony and affection without which liberty and even life are dreary things." Conversely, when Hobbes enumerated the ills of civil warfare, the first of the dismal adjectives he invoked was "solitary." Where social comity is wholly absent, we are miserably isolated and not really human. Harmony with and affection for our fellows are important components of the good life. Where these are present in our daily association with others, we experience ourselves as validated and confirmed as moral creatures, and we experience the comfort and psychic gratification of human solidarity. We enjoy the mirror of recognition and the warmth of helping hands. Where there is civic friendship, we feel better about ourselves and about life in general.

One way to get a concrete sense of the intrinsic value of civic friendship and the misery of its absence—the contrast between what Jefferson hoped for and what Hobbes feared—is to reflect upon the social distance between two vignettes that found their way into the newspapers in recent years. Both involved young women named Catherine. The first and more famous event happened on March 13, 1964; the other occurred on July 15, 1995. The first involved twenty-eight-year-old Kitty Genovese:

> As she returned from work around 3 A.M. to her apartment in Queens, a stranger stepped from the shadows. For over half an hour, at least thirty-eight of her neighbors listened as the young woman's desperate screams shattered the morning stillness: "Oh, my God, he stabbed me! Please help me!" Yet not one of her neighbors came to her aid or telephoned police as the assailant stalked, stabbed and then raped her in three separate attacks over a thirty-five minute period. The rapist/murderer sauntered away, leaving Kitty Genovese dead and mutilated, three doors from her home.[33]

The second vignette involved seventeen-year-old Katie Fisher, who took a lamb she had raised to auction during a summer in which she was engaged in a painful and arduous battle with a form of cancer known as Burkitt's lymphoma.

> " We sort of let folks know that Katie had a situation that wasn't too pleasant," said Roger Wilson, auctioneer for the Madison County (Ohio) Fair's Junior Livestock Sale. He began the sale, hoping his short introduction might push the price per pound for Katie's lamb above the average two dollars. It did, and then some. "It first went for $11.50 per pound, and then that person gave it back," Wilson said. "That started a chain reaction. Families bought it and gave it back; businesses bought it and gave it back. We sold that lamb thirty-six times." The effort raised $16,620. . . . The last buyer gave back the lamb for good.[34]

Forget for the moment the costs and benefits suffered and enjoyed by the two young women in these two cases. And set aside the question—however interesting and pertinent this may be—of the causes of the radically different forms of social behavior the cases manifest. The point here is simply to reflect upon the different sense of self and of life occasioned by participation in these radically disparate social dramas. In the first story, the words "neighbors" and "home" leap off the page with savage tacit irony. This is a world without neighbors—people who know, care, and help—and without a home—a place of security and belonging. The second story invokes neither of those terms but exemplifies both. This is a world where people sympathize and give aid to their fellow citizens and where one can feel at home—both in the sense of feeling secure and feeling oneself a member of the human community. The distance between these two worlds can be seen as a measure of the intrinsic value of civic friendship.[35]

Pleasant and gratifying to enjoy in and of itself, civic friendship is also of great instrumental value—both to individual citizens and to the community as a whole. It is a good that brings many other goods in its wake. Some of these collateral benefits would be of value to any political regime. Others are of particular benefit to liberal democratic regimes because they promote specifically liberal and democratic goals. It would be hard, in fact, to overstate the importance of these collateral advantages of civic friendship, for they encompass some of the essential attributes of successful polities generally and some of the core goals of liberal democracies in particular.

The first collateral benefit accruing to societies that enjoy a significant degree of civic friendship is actually a cluster of intimately related political advantages: stability, cohesion, and legitimacy. All societies require some emotional and motivational forces that work to create the social bonding necessary for collaborative endeavor. Absent these sources of cohesion, a society devolves into a disorganized agglomeration of individuals who regard each other with some mixture of estrangement, hostility, and mutual indifference. This is the specter of social atomism or, to borrow Emile Durkheim's term, *anomie*. To function at all well, other than by hegemonic command, societies require filaments of cohesion and spontaneous interaction. And the most powerful and durable sources of these bonds of social affiliation are not calculative but—in the very broadest and most generic sense of this term—"erotic." It is true that, as Adam Smith famously insisted, people perform economic services for each other most reliably from their own self-interest and not from benevolence. But people create their social institutions, and also are able to create certain economic institutions such as corporations and cooperatives, only because they are impelled to cooperate with each other through a recognition that they share common affections, aspirations, and values. Market transactions may be the result of self-interest. But the larger social order that sustains the markets—as Adam Smith also well understood—is generally not the creature of mere self-interest or for that matter of an abstract sense of justice. It is the product of sympathy, sociability, and friendship.

In their different ways, both Freud and John Stuart Mill recognized this essential role of quasi-erotic bonding in forming and sustaining organized society. Freud wrote that "civilization is a process in the service of Eros, whose purpose is to combine single human individuals, and after that families, then races, peoples and nations, into one great unity, the unity of mankind." This instinctive libidinal bonding, he added, however, was opposed by the similarly instinctual human impulsion toward death and destruction.[36] And Mill, clearly influenced here by Comte, believed that the psychic sustenance for the triumph of utilitarian morality would be "the desire to be in unity with our fellow creatures, which is already a powerful principle in human nature, and happily one of those which tend to become stronger, even without express inculcation, from the influences of advancing civilization."[37] Neither of these accounts is particularly clear or convincing in its invocation of some rather amorphous, mystical or instinctual, universal causal force out there governing human behavior. The dynamics of social bonding are, for the most part at least, more mundane, more rational, and more specifiable than these accounts suggest. Where Freud and Mill are correct, however, is in their recognition of the fundamental importance of emotional affiliation among human beings to the creation and maintenance of social institutions. As did Edmund Burke, who protested against a society conceived and conducted as "nothing better than a partnership agreement in a trade of pepper and coffee, calico, or tobacco . . . to be taken up for a little temporary interest and to be dissolved at the pleasure of the parties," they understood that polities held together only by calculative self-interest—and devoid of bonds of civic friendship inspired by mutual dedication to and pursuit of common goods—were ultimately not viable.[38] Without the contribution to social cohesion provided by lineaments of friendship, it not only becomes exceedingly difficult to inspire the individual sacrifices that all societies must sometimes ask of their citizens, whether to defend the country, provide for future generations, or to accommodate the general good. It may even become difficult to achieve those basic habits of self-restraint and the willingness to abide the law that are necessary for any society to function in an orderly and effective manner.

Along with its capacity to motivate the centripetal forces of willing cooperation necessary to counterbalance the centrifugal force of competing interests that challenge every society, the presence of civic friendship is a primary source of political legitimacy. Regimes enjoy legitimacy—in the Weberian sense of that term—when their citizens believe that its purposes and practices are morally proper. Citizens may be supportive of their political regime out of self-interest, of course. But that kind of support is inherently precarious and volatile. It is subject to rapid erosion when circumstances become difficult. And it is also inclined to get steadily chipped away by the human propensity to exaggerate the benefits others have and simultaneously to exaggerate the costs and burdens they must bear. As Hobbes noted wryly, we all come equipped with passions and self-love that make "every little payment appeareth a great grievance."[39] Relying upon inevitably distorted perceptions of personal advantage, therefore, is not a safe recourse for any political regime wanting a form of popular loyalty warmer, deeper, and more consistent than the more shallow and evanescent support occasioned by the fickle felicific calculi of individuals. That kind of deeper and more consistent support can come only from a widespread belief among the citizenry that adherence to the regime is warranted by moral and not merely prudential considerations—that its purposes and procedures are in a real and significant sense morally right and proper.

Political legitimacy is therefore linked with and sustained by civic friendship in two respects. In the first place, they both are generated in part by the same cause, namely the belief that the members of the society have certain goods in common to which the efforts of the social union are devoted. In this sense, it could be said that political legitimacy and civic friendship are largely twin-born. Once established, however, civic friendship reinforces political legitimacy in another way as well. For those who are considered under the rubric of friendship must be understood as morally worthy and valuable people. As a consequence, governmental or societal efforts to promote the general welfare or the welfare of other citizens can be seen as morally worthy endeavors in their own right and not simply as a burden or as an illegitimate disbursement of common resources.

By promoting cohesion and sustaining legitimacy, civic friendship conduces to stability and civil peace. It also, however, is an important enabling condition—possibly even a necessary condition—of a society's economic health and productivity. The evidence for this proposition has recently been laid out in illuminating fashion by Francis Fukuyama in his book *Trust: The Social Virtues and the Creation of Prosperity*. As Fukuyama argues there, it is a serious mistake "to regard the economy as a facet of life with its own laws, separate from the rest of society." The fact of the matter is that "there is scarcely any form of economic activity, from running a dry-cleaning business to fabricating large-scale integrated circuits, that does not require the social collaboration of human beings."[40] It follows, then, that the economic success of a society is predicated in part upon its "social capital," its capacity for voluntary cooperative endeavor, grounded in "a community based on mutual trust."[41,42] These communities of mutual trust are in turn a function of "the degree to which communities share norms and values and are able to subordinate individual interests to those of larger groups."[43] And this subordination of narrow individual interest to a more general good must be accomplished voluntarily rather than by the imposition of external force. All of which is to say that it is the existence of civic friendship—a situation of trust, mutual goodwill, and willingness to cooperate, grounded in shared values—that conduces to economic attainment and prosperity.

Civic friendship conduces to economic success for several reasons. In the first place, civic friendship sustains and facilitates what Fukuyama terms "spontaneous sociability": "the capacity to form new associations and to cooperate within the terms of reference they establish."[44] Civic friendship and its corollary, trust, also minimize economic "transaction costs": every economic exchange does not need to be carefully hedged, regulated, enforced, and possibly litigated. Moreover, the organizational capabilities of societies rich in social capital and civic friendship are enormously enhanced. It is much easier in these societies to create large and complex organizations, such as the modern corporation.[45] These organizations can be more innovative and adaptive. And workplaces can be more flexible and efficient, capable of spreading authority and responsibility widely among their employees.

The organizational capabilities engendered by the phenomenon of spontaneous sociability—and hence by the civic friendship and trust that fuels it—are not, moreover, limited to the economic domain. Instead, they are available to a society in all its efforts to cope with social problems and to pursue its social goals. Where citizens are basically "friendly" in their interactions with each other, they are generally able to create informal cooperative associations to act together on behalf of their common interests: neighborhood associations, PTA's, charitable associations of all kinds, churches, service organizations like Kiwanis and Rotary, arts councils, local youth athletic associations, choral societies, support groups, cause-oriented groups like the Sierra Club and Mothers Against Drunk Driving, and so on. We often take this remarkable array of self-organized cooperative associations for granted, but an astute observer like Tocqueville was quick to note upon his visit to American shores how important this pattern of behavior is for the functioning of a democratic society. When civil society withers, the result must be an overextended state, a hypertrophied marketplace, an impoverished communal life, or some combination of these three unhappy results. And where no lineaments of civic friendship are present to sustain the habits, ambitions, and expectations necessary for it to function, civil society will in fact wither. People will not associate spontaneously, productively, and effectively with others whom they regard with wariness and suspicion as nothing more than strangers and hostile competitors.

Finally, it is also worth noting along with Alan Wolfe and Robert Putnam, that whereas overextended governments and markets may eat away at the health and strength of civil society, a strong civil society does not weaken states and markets so much as it makes them more effective. A healthy civil society works on behalf of governmental and market effectiveness principally by allowing them to concentrate on functions they can perform well rather than becoming saddled with functions they perform more poorly and with great difficulty. Moreover, the civic habits, attitudes, and capacities nurtured by civic friendship permit the satisfactory functioning of political linkage institutions and the more participatory and decentralized institutions of governance such as town councils, citizen commissions, and juries. Thus Wolfe concludes, after surveying the recent careers of the American and Scandinavian welfare states, that "when civil society exists as a sphere alongside the market and the state, it contributes to the more effective working of both of them; when the market and the state exist without civil society, neither can work as promised."[46] Similarly, Putnam concludes, after reviewing the contrasting performance of regional government institutions in different areas of Italy, that "social capital, as embodied in horizontal networks of civic engagement bolsters the performance of the polity and the economy, rather than the reverse: Strong society, strong economy; strong society, strong state."[47]

Civic friendship, together with its correlates of social trust and strong civic associations, can reasonably be seen, therefore, as a significant contributing factor to a host of important social goods desired by all societies: stability, cohesion, legitimacy, and organizational capability. But civic friendship is also highly conducive to the attainment of additional social goods specific to the needs and aspirations of liberal and democratic societies. If all societies should value civic friendship, therefore, liberal democratic societies should value it all the more. This claim deserves some emphasis because the conventional view tends to be that civic friendship may have been central to the functioning and the self-understanding of morally and culturally more homogeneous premodern polities but that it is not particularly relevant to the needs and purposes of contemporary liberal democracies. In contrast with that view, I want to insist that civic friendship—even if it is more problematic to create and sustain in large-scale pluralist democracies—deserves recognition as an especially desirable goal for precisely those societies to pursue.

Consider first the facilitative role played by civic friendship *vis-a-vis* key liberal ideals. Two of the most fundamental liberal goals are toleration and limited government. Liberals believe that a good society is one in which individuals enjoy sufficient social space, sufficient latitude from the impositions of both the government and their fellow citizens, to live free and independent lives—to be true to their own values and identity and to be autonomous and self-governing. When we inquire into the social conditions conducive to these core liberal goals, however, it seems clear that civic friendship is one of the most crucial of these enabling factors. It might be supposed prima facie that the way to limit government power is simply to maximize individual liberty. Individual liberty and government hegemony are direct opposites, so increasing the one would seem to translate directly into decreasing the other. But appearances here can be misleading. Governments exert power and control where they have tasks to perform. Some variable portion of state dominance is, no doubt, pathological in normative terms: ruling elites exercise what Marcuse calls "surplus repression"—unnecessary control—because they are arrogant, exploitative, or paranoid. But the state exists and exercises power largely because it has work to do. Some instrumentality must enforce the laws, protect the society from predators, socialize and educate the next generation, promote and regulate industry and commerce, and so on. Where the society is unorganized, incompetent, and anarchic, therefore, state power will almost inevitably flow into the vacuum. The real opposite of state power, then, turns out to be not individual liberty, negatively defined, but self-governance. Strong and competent civil societies provide the setting and the resources for government that is both effective and limited. Weak and anomic societies, if they are not to lapse into total disarray, will invite and even necessitate overextended and intrusive states. And, as we have seen, the activities and attitudes associated with civic friendship are primary factors in a society's ability to organize and govern itself.

Liberalism's dependence upon a strong civil society and the elements of civic friendship that sustain it is well captured by Fukuyama when he writes that

> a liberal state is ultimately a limited state, with government activity strictly bounded by a sphere of individual liberty. If such a society is not to become anarchic or otherwise ungovernable, then it must be capable of self-government at levels of social organization below the state. Such a system depends ultimately not just on law but on the self-restraint of individuals. If they are

not tolerant and respectful of each other or do not abide by the laws they set for themselves, they will require a strong and coercive state to keep each other in line. If they cannot cohere for common purposes, then they will need an intrusive state to provide the organization they cannot provide themselves.[48]

Once again, Putnam's comparative study of the different regions of Italy provides empirical confirmation of this logic and leads Putnam to make the following observation:

> Lacking the confident self-discipline of the civic regions, people in less civic regions are forced to rely on what Italians call "the forces of order" that is, the police. . . . Citizens in the less civic regions have no other resort to solve the fundamental Hobbesian dilemma of public order, for they lack the horizontal bonds of collective reciprocity that work more efficiently in the civic regions. In the absence of solidarity and self-discipline, hierarchy and force provide the only alternative to anarchy. In the recent philosophical debate between communitarians and liberals, community and liberty are often said to be inimical. No doubt this is sometimes true, as it was once in Salem, Massachusetts. The Italian case suggests, however, that because citizens in civic regions enjoy the benefits of community, they are able to be more liberal.[49]

Societies marked by civic friendship can "be more liberal" in another significant respect, as well. Besides being enabled to limit state power and thus protect space for individual autonomy, these societies find it easier to promote toleration. The causal logic here is relatively straightforward, and most of us can confirm it by our own experience. A certain amount of "tolerance" can, of course, simply be legislated. Laws can be hedges—Robert Frost's "good fences" that restrain our desire to dictate to others and give them space to live in ways they see fit in accordance with norms and beliefs they accept. Some of these mandates in our own society are directed at the governing majority: "Congress shall make no law respecting an establishment of religion, or prohibiting the free exercise thereof; or abridging the freedom of speech, or of the press." Others are directed at individuals or corporations acting within the public domain: for example, civil rights laws prohibiting discrimination on the basis of race or gender or sexual orientation. These mandates, however, don't come down like manna from heaven. They are positive laws that must arise from and be sustained by cultural norms or moral precepts accepted by the society that creates them. The real question, then, concerns these norms and precepts together with the motivations and experiences that produce them. What is it that inclines an individual or a society to be forbearing and tolerant?

A disposition to be tolerant is the fruit either of necessity, of respect, or of affection. It seems fairly evident that the modern practice of liberal toleration emerged in the first instance substantially as an expedient of necessity. After trying for more than a century to convert, extirpate, or subdue each other, European adherents of competing religious faiths eventually came to realize that the only alternative to a policy of religious tolerance was a terrible cycle of enmity, oppression, and recurrent bloodshed. They reluctantly came to recognize the futility and the dangers of their respective quests for social hegemony and resigned themselves to accepting the presence of the "heterodox" in their midst. In the *politique* spirit of a Henry of Navarre, who allowed that "Paris was worth a mass," they decided that achieving social peace was worth tolerating religious dissent. Insofar as tolerance became touted as a virtue, it was a classic instance of making a virtue of necessity.

So long as everyone, or at least most people, continue to affirm the practical necessity of religious, moral, and cultural forbearance for the sake of social comity, this kind of modus vivendi toleration can be perpetuated. But tolerance so motivated is always grudging, hence guarded, hence fragile and subject to revocation. Toleration becomes more durable and reliable only when it is informed and motivated by some degree of respect or friendship. (This is the reason that John Rawls is leery of modus vivendi conceptions of democratic consensus more generally conceived. "An overlapping consensus," he insists, "is not a mere modus vivendi . . . [because] the object of consensus . . . is itself a moral conception, and it is affirmed on moral grounds." This status of the democratic consensus is practically as well as theoretically important, he then adds, because of its implications for political stability. It "means that those who affirm the various views supporting the political conception will not withdraw their support of it should the relative strength of their view in society increase and eventually become dominant. . . . This feature of stability highlights a basic contrast between an overlapping consensus and a modus vivendi, the stability of which does depend on happenstance and a balance of relative forces."[50]) If toleration is not to be grudging, unstable, and subject to quick revocation whenever circumstances so permit, then, the crucial issue becomes: What gives a stance of toleration moral weight? What sustains the belief—essential for toleration to be seen as morally imperative and not merely circumstantially expedient—that other people are worthy of our tolerance? The answer, I would argue, is a combination of respect and friendship, each of which depends to some extent upon the other. Simply and somewhat dogmatically stated, then, my claim is that the acceptance of the liberal norm of toleration as a moral conception depends upon certain *minima* of respect and friendship, which in turn depend in part upon each other.

Anyone who looks down upon members of another ethnic group, or despises a particular religion, or finds an alternative sexual orientation distasteful or reprehensible has a motive and a prima facie rationale for bullying and suppressing these "others." The motivation stems from the natural animus toward those who believe or act in ways that contradict our own cherished views and favored way of life. And the rationale is that these others are, after all, some form of miscreant: animals, devils, heretics, or perverts. But as all sorts of anecdotal evidence—and possibly introspection—strongly suggests, these hostile sentiments and aggressive inclinations are almost unfailingly mitigated to a great extent when one forms a friendship with someone from the heretofore problematic groups or when it is discovered that an already valued friend is of the problematic persuasion. Those of us among the cognoscenti are taught to deride protestations of nonprejudice that take the form: "but some of my best friends are _____." But as both common sense and the theory of cognitive dissonance tell us, it is very hard to have a good friend across racial lines and be deeply racist or to have a prized gay friend and be a rabid homophobe. When we know someone else to be a morally worthy human being— and all friends must qualify as such—any particular attribute of theirs we would otherwise be inclined to attack is reduced to an accident of their existence we can tolerate. And, by extension, all those others who share that attribute can no longer on that basis alone be considered fair game for tyrannizing.[51]

In addition to its conduciveness to the core liberal goals of limited government and toleration, civic friendship also promotes and sustains a number of important democratic purposes and procedures. It is probably too much to claim that elements of civic friendship are necessary conditions without which these democratic purposes are unattainable and these democratic procedures inoperable. But bonds of civic friendship and their behavioral and attitudinal correlates go a long way toward enabling democratic societies to deliberate meaningfully and productively, to fashion necessary compromises, to promote political and social equality, and to motivate communal support for the disadvantaged.

Consider first the relationship between friendship and equality. These two conditions are clearly related and interact with each other in important ways. Commentators have differed on how tight the connection is, but all who have thought carefully about friendship recognize that some degree of equality is requisite for friendship to exist and that the presence of friendship exerts strong pressures toward creating and maintaining equalities of status and condition among the relevant parties. Friendship consists of free and uncoerced interaction. It consists in reciprocity and requires some degree of openness and self-disclosure to the other. All of these elements of friendship, in turn, are possible only when the parties are roughly equal and are not enormously divergent in status, power, or wealth. Aristotle cites in this respect the maxim "caritas est paritas." That does not mean that friendships require absolute equality in all respects. There are ways to adjust and compensate for some measure of unequal status, power, or wealth and to maintain sufficient parity to sustain the consensuality, reciprocity, and openness essential for friendship. But it does mean that there are real limits to the extent of inequality friendship can survive. "We cannot," Aristotle notes, "fix the exact point (i.e., of inequality) up to which and no farther men can go on being friends . . . but when a great gulf is fixed, as between God and man, there can be no friendship." As a consequence, the natural home of civic friendship is democracy, for in a democracy the citizens are political equals and they rule and are ruled in turn: "We cannot maintain that there is much room for friendship and justice between rulers and ruled under a tyranny. They are most adequately realized in democracies, the citizens of a democracy being equal and having many things in common."[52] It follows then that those who value democratic equality should value civic friendship as well, even if for that reason alone.

A sense of civic friendship is also, as an extension and corollary of these dynamics, a very important resource for those who believe that some form of economic redistribution to sustain the life chances of the disadvantaged is necessary in a good and decent society. In recent years, the dominant tendency of defenders of the welfare state and those arguing on behalf of communal obligations toward the less fortunate has been to argue their case in the language of social justice and fairness. Rawls's theory of justice, in this context, is but a paradigmatic and philosophically profound exemplar of a general moral orientation and rhetorical strategy. Despite its salience, this line of argument has, I would insist, very real limitations and dangers. One basic difficulty here stems from what I have elsewhere called "the antinomies of social justice."[53] Simply put, the gratuitous causes of human suffering render any allocation of its burdens arguably unfair. Moreover, what Aristotle called proportional conceptions of social justice still have a very widespread appeal. Persuading a democratic majority that fairness alone dictates that they support other people's children as well as their own or that justice alone demands that the state take their hard-earned dollars to allocate to others who are (or are believed to be) less industrious can be a very hard sell. Here is where a sense of civic friendship can be crucial in motivating people to be concerned about and responsive to the needs of less fortunate fellow citizens. It is part of friendship to see the other as involved in a common enterprise, to see the other as someone of genuine worth, and hence to desire to see the other prosper. With that sense of community and *eunoia* ("good will") comes a disposition to assist the other that takes on a sense of obligatoriness. "With an intensification of friendship there naturally goes an increase in the sense of obligation between the friends."[54] Friendship "implies the obligation on Self of taking care of and being concerned about the impact of his actions on Other . . . [and] friendship implies mutual and shared responsibility."[55] Hence, as Empedocles observed long ago, one empirical consequence of friendship is that it leads to the sharing of goods and property. Proponents of the communal provision of core "primary goods" needful for a good life, therefore, should be the first to give credence to and work on behalf of civic friendship in a democratic regime.

Civic friendship also provides enormously important sustenance to democratic deliberation. It does so in two ways. In the first place, it provides a motivating passion to stimulate discursive interaction with our fellow citizens. As Hannah Arendt has said, "the essence of friendship consists in discourse."[56] Friends seek a "sympathetic consciousness" of each other's existence, and a primary means of attaining this awareness is "conversing and exchanging ideas" with each other.[57] Friends are impelled toward mutual understanding. They want to know each other's thoughts, feelings, perceptions, and desires. This impulsion fuels many if not most of the conversational behavior of human beings—from schoolyard banter to gossip between neighbors over the back fence on up to the more formal, public, and explicitly political dialogue found in journals of opinion, legislative debates, and judicial opinions. Without the curiosity and affection attendant to friendship and "natural sociability," we would not be struck entirely dumb, but a vast proportion of our conversation would wither and die.

Some element of friendship or the generalized disposition thereto is also highly instrumental if not essential in making the conversation of democracy genuinely deliberative in the fullest and truest sense. Each party to a process of what Habermas calls "discursive will formation" has to accredit the other participants in the dialogue as moral equals and to recognize the validity of their wants and needs. If the telos of the dialogue is to be the ascertainment of what is in the best interests of the society as a whole, this accreditation and recognition is essential. Some degree of friendship, then, is highly conducive to empowering the norms of communicative competence. We abide by the terms of what Habermas calls "universal validity claims" (intelligibility, sincerity, orientation toward the truth, and the acceptance of legitimate norms) only as a consequence of the kind of faithfulness and trust that characterize relationships among friends. Were our interlocutors aliens or enemies, the moral logic of the discourse would change altogether. In warfare, we don't strive for intelligibility but send our messages in codes we hope cannot be broken. Our communications are not "sincere" but calculated. We seek not to reach consensus or truth, but to prevail. To put it in the context of domestic politics, then, we can say that the conversation of democracy will have realistic hopes of approximating the conditions and aspirations of communal practical reason only when citizens are to some degree civic friends. Absent *eunoia*, democratic talk degenerates into little more than verbal gaming—the tactical deployment of words for the sake of factional advantage. When it comes to what Ben Barber has called "strong talk," reason may set the rules; but it is the warmth of civic friendship that supplies the spirit of the law and the impulsion to act in accord with its mandate.[58] The partisans of deliberative democracy, therefore, need to be at the same time cultivators of the sociological sources of civic friendship if they do not want to see their democratic ideals dissolve into abstract utopianism.

Last, civic friendship sustains democracy by its capacity to sustain a spirit of compromise. It goes too far to claim that compromise is the central mechanism or overriding ethical norm of democratic politics. But it is nonetheless patently obvious that democratic policies and practices are always fashioned in significant measure by finding a way to resolve the conflict among competing interests by giving partial satisfaction to the different parties while pleasing no one altogether. That is what the honest brokerage of democratic politicians and deal-makers is all about. Without creative compromise, the democratic policy process would grind to a halt. The bargains reached have the practical virtue of bringing closure and some measure of reconciliation to a political problem or dispute. And they have the moral virtue of according some satisfaction to the legitimate desires of all or at least most of the relevant parties rather than licensing the hegemony of one party over the others. But compromises are rarely liked, just as compromisers are rarely honored. If the conflict is one of interests, half a loaf seems always inadequate; if the conflict is one of principle, any concession seems morally disreputable.

The brokered compromises that make up a large part of everyday democratic politics, then, are absolutely essential to its functioning, but they are also generally experienced as unpalatable. In this context the function of civic friendship is to make it easier for the perpetually somewhat disappointed citizenry who never get exactly what they want to swallow the bitter pill of partial concession with some measure of grace and equanimity. What is crucial here is the sense that the re-

sources denied me are nonetheless being put to good use or that my favored principles have been thwarted in part in order to accommodate other principles that
possess prima facie legitimacy. And it is much easier to have this perception if I
recognize the competing needs and principles as emanating from those I experience as being civic friends: morally worthy human beings who bear me no ill will
and who are involved with me in common endeavor. If, on the other hand, I perceive all my competitors as enemies and as "other," I will be inclined to instruct my
political representatives to draw lines in the sand, concede nothing, and take no
prisoners. Not only the partisans of deliberative democracy, then, but also liberal
realists and democratic pluralists such as Robert Dahl and David Truman should
place a high value on civic friendship as an instrumental good.

We can summarize the argument of this section, then, in the following way:
civic friendship should be prized in the first instance as an intrinsic good because
most human beings find a sense of community, the good will of fellow citizens,
and participation in common enterprise gratifying in and of itself. It is, moreover,
an important instrumental good for all forms of political society because it conduces to stability, prosperity, and the capacity to deal effectively with all manner
of social problems. And it is an instrumental good of particular value to liberal
democracies because of its favorable impact upon other cherished liberal and
democratic goals including limited government, toleration, political and social
equality, deliberation, compromise, and communal support for the less well-off.

The Stumbling Block of Pluralism

Even were all these contentions about the value of civic friendship conceded to be
true, some would argue that the consequence is merely to find ourselves ensnared
within a demoralizing catch-22. Perhaps liberal democracies, even more than
most societies, would prosper and benefit greatly by achieving some significant
measure of civic friendship. But these same liberal democracies, at least within
their real-world contemporary settings, are precluded from attaining and even
from legitimately attempting to attain the constituent elements of civic friendship. This impasse is the product of the confluence of three things: (1) the necessary grounds and conditions of civic friendship; (2) the social and moral
heterogeneity of present-day liberal societies, what Rawls capsulizes in the phrase
"the fact of pluralism;" and (3) the moral constraints on public action implicit in
the norms of liberty and equality, or essentially what Rawls has labeled—not entirely felicitously—as "the fact of oppression."[59] The heart of this undermining argument *vis-a-vis* according civic friendship acceptance among the goals of liberal
democracy, then, is twofold. The first claim is that the "fact of pluralism" renders
the conditions of civic friendship unattainable. The second claim is that the "fact
of oppression" renders attempts to effectuate these conditions illegitimate. We can
call the first of these claims, with apologies to Kenneth Arrow, the "impossibility
theorem" and the second claim the "impropriety theorem." I postpone a full consideration of the "impropriety theorem" until the next chapter, since the same is-

sue surfaces *vis- a-vis* the notion of liberal civic virtue. Here I want to focus on the "impossibility theorem." My contention is that it represents a seriously misleading half-truth about the nature and prospects of civic friendship in a pluralistic liberal society. The element of truth captured by the impossibility theorem is that civic friendship in a free and pluralistic society is subject to limitations and constraints not present in a morally and socially more homogeneous society. Liberal civic friendship cannot be as complete, as easy, or as uncomplicated as civic friendship might be in a society united upon a single comprehensive conception of the human good (if indeed any such political society has ever really existed outside of utopian theory or romantic retrospective interpretations of, say, Greek city-states). But this half-truth is seriously misleading when it is taken as implying that pluralistic societies are precluded entirely from enjoying the presence and benefactions of civic friendship. For the fact is that civic friendship need not be built solely on common allegiance to some single, all-embracing moral creed. Instead, it can take—and to some extent will take even within morally more homogeneous societies—the form of a complex web of overlapping and multiple bonds of affection and common endeavor generated by a wide variety of quite particular enterprises and enthusiasms. And there is no reason that pluralistic societies are prevented from achieving this constrained but nevertheless quite real and consequential form of civic friendship. As Robert Putnam argues and to some extent demonstrates empirically, neither modernization nor social and moral pluralism needs to "signal the demise of the civic community."[60]

Political theorizing cannot, of course, produce civic friendship. That is a task—Aristotle thought it to be the "special business"—for political leaders (and for ordinary citizens) to accomplish. But political theorizing can function therapeutically in this context by clearing up conceptual confusions or misconceptions that misdirect our political practices. In Wittgenstein's apt metaphor, philosophy's task is to help the fly get out of the fly bottle—to escape those invisible linguistic traps that hamper its free movement. In politics as well, we are often constrained unnecessarily and in damaging ways by conceptual inhibitions that convert into behavioral prohibitions. My claim here is that the belief that meaningful civic friendship is inaccessible to pluralist democracies is an example of precisely this kind of self-induced entrapment. The "impossibility theorem" is a damaging "do not enter" sign that perhaps can be removed by careful reflection.

The idea that nurturing a civic community is not a realistic possibility for a pluralist society is based on a number of assumptions about the nature and causes of civic friendship that don't withstand close examination. Two of these assumptions are related to each other and are taken over from Aristotle's influential account. The other assumption is of more recent origin and relates to our understanding of the nature and dynamics of a conceptual system.

Although Aristotle distinguishes friendship from love, *philia* from *eros*, in some respects he does not draw the contrast with sufficient clarity and sharpness. In places, his account seems to suggest that love and friendship are structurally identical and that the difference is essentially one of degree or intensity. For example, he tells us that "what we mean by love is affection for a friend carried beyond a certain point."[61] He also assimilates his account of friendship to the Platonic understanding of *eros* in the sense that he sees the affectivity of "perfect friendship" as essentially aroused by the "goodness" embodied in the character of the friend. Only the truly good, therefore, can in his view really be friends in the full sense of the word.

Besides blurring the different bases and dynamics of love and friendship, this way of conceiving friendship has the unfortunate corollary of setting the bar excessively high when it comes to the possibility of having civic friends. Only the truly good need apply, and their friendship must replicate the face-to-face character of love and border on its emotional intensity. But as we saw earlier and need to insist upon here, an important difference between love and friendship is obscured by this account. Lovers, as C. S. Lewis has said, we picture as facing each other but friends we see as standing side by side. The good thing desired by lovers—the object of their amour—is each other: it is the good or the attributes of the human good embodied in the other that stirs love to life. Hence lovers embrace the desired qualities or goods by embracing each other. But the affectivity of friendship arises from a common enthusiasm for a good that exists outside of the participants themselves. Their bond is formed from their common affection for an object that they do not embody but rather appreciate. Friendship must be about something, and this something cannot be simply the friend or the quality of friendship itself. It may be about art or music or sport or a special place or whatever, but it must be about something out there in the world.

The political importance of insisting upon this structural difference between love and friendship is that it vastly enhances the possibilities for and hence the potential political role of friendships among citizens. To be friends, people need not almost love each other. And they need not be "truly good" people in any strong sense. They need only to be people of some good will who have an enthusiasm for some good thing in the world that others also appreciate. Instead of being a condition so demanding and elevated as to be attainable only rarely and with great difficulty, friendship has many occasions and it can be enjoyed by the common range of humankind and not only by the truly and fully virtuous.

Another conceptual barrier to our understanding and pursuit of civic friendship stems from the locution: "the human good." The related verbal formulations of "the good," "the good life," and "the human good" also appear in classical Greek philosophy, and we are rolling along in the conceptual ruts they established when we employ them. This univocal and noun-oriented linguistic mode of apprehending the object of human desire and fruition arguably might have made sense in the context of Greek philosophical essentialism and its allied notion of the forms: hence, the Agathon as the form of the Good. But it is a highly problematic and misleading linguistic formulation apart from that philosophical context, and it was arguably even within that context a very awkward way of conceiving the nature and function of things that arouse and fulfill human desires and aspirations. Because of the role that the good or a good plays in creating friendship, moreover, any awkwardness and distortion created in this way also affects our understanding of friendship and its possibilities.

Instead of jettisoning what we can call the "singular noun" mode of conceiving the ends of human desire, however, recent liberal political philosophical formulations have arguably not only adopted this conception uncritically but have deepened and compounded its distortions and its woodenness. In post-Kantian philosophy, of course, the assumption that there is a univocal, objective, and universal human good is rejected as an artifact of a time before we ingested the "distasteful . . . fruit of the tree of knowledge" and recognized that consciously guided human actions are governed by "irreconcilably antagonistic values" that are in turn produced by a "series of ultimate decisions."[62] On this account, there is thus no single human good but rather plural "conceptions of the good." These conceptions are then implicitly understood as having the structure and function of Kuhnian paradigms. That is, a conception of the good is taken to be an overarching and all-encompassing conceptual framework (or language game) in which the meaning of each part is determined by the framework's core models and conceptual premises. Different conceptions thus confront each other as impermeable, inadjudicable, and even mutually incomprehensible moral perspectives.

This (neo-Kantian, neo-Weberian, Kuhnian) manner of conceiving how people have and are affected by their ideas of the good is clearly visible and important in Rawls's construction of the possibilities and limitations of a pluralistic democracy, for example. Perhaps the single most important empirical premise informing his whole enterprise centers about what he terms, borrowing from Hume, "the circumstances of justice." These circumstances, in turn, comprise both "objective" and "subjective" circumstances. The objective circumstances of justice are those Hume cited: the conditions of moderate scarcity. But equally important for Rawls's enterprise is his stipulation of what he styles as the subjective circumstances, "namely, that persons and associations have contrary conceptions of the good . . . and these differences set them at odds and lead them to make conflicting claims on their institutions. They hold opposing religious and philosophical beliefs, and affirm not only diverse moral and political doctrines, but also conflicting ways of evaluating arguments and evidence when they try to reconcile these oppositions."[63] These putative "subjective circumstances of justice" are what turn the "fact of pluralism" into such a quandary for a society that seeks to be based on consent and also seeks to be a cooperative enterprise with a moral basis. Accepting this premise leads to the conclusion that a pluralist democracy cannot be a community or even an association and that its animating moral consensus must center around what is right and not what is good in human life.

But this supposition, steeped as it is in the belief that "conceptions of the good" function like all-embracing and mutually exclusive philosophical paradigms, is once again a profoundly misleading partial truth. It comes closest to capturing real patterns of belief and behavior in cases where Shi'ite theocrats collide with democratic liberals, where secular feminists encounter Christian fundamentalists, where homosexual activists denounce the Catholic Church, or where the Nation of Islam confronts white America. Important and highly contentious, hence highly visible, political conflicts such as those over abortion, Salman Rushdie, and sex education or prayer in the schools do have their roots in the clash between broad, deep, and divergent moral and religious belief systems.

Despite its applicability in instances like these, the whole "subjective circumstances of justice/competing conceptions of the good/fact of pluralism/impossibility of civic friendship based on goods in common" line of argument is highly inaccurate in other—arguably in most—instances. It is inaccurate and misleading for the central reason that the linkage between fundamental moral and religious precepts or beliefs on the one hand and concrete political judgments and specific attachments to human goods on the other is by no means so tight or univocal or determinate as the model suggests.

In the first place, people for the most part—and this includes theologians and political philosophers—do not and cannot derive their judgments on concrete political questions in some simple deductive manner from their basic moral or religious world view. It is not really plausible in most instances to say that I believe in the contents of the Apostles' Creed and therefore I support political policy X or that I am a utilitarian or a Kantian and hence I support policy Y. These moral and religious doctrines provide only very general moral norms which have to be mediated by a host of more particularized ethical and practical judgments and by a vast array of particular empirical beliefs as well. Thus, not all Moslems are theocrats. Adherents of the Kantian maxim, like John Rawls and Robert Nozick, can and do diverge widely in applying it to concrete questions such as property rights. And Christians can and do reach opposing positions on issues of social justice, on church-and-state separation, and on abortion. Just as the adherents of the same broad moral or religious persuasion may wind up on opposing sides of a policy question, moreover, they may wind up as allies of others who have what Rawls refers to as "opposing religious and philosophical beliefs." This is part of the reality behind the old bromide about politics making strange bedfellows.

Second, not only can we not deduce our specific political allegiances directly from our basic moral and religious beliefs, our apprehension of and attachment to particular human goods usually occurs by direct experience unmediated in any significant way by our doctrinal affiliations. What do my fundamental moral doctrines have to do, for example, with the way I have acquired a passion for specific human goods such as classical music, jazz, and rock; the artistry of Matisse, Picasso, Michael Jordan, and Steffi Graf; the beauty of Glacier National Park; laughing children, good schools, and safe streets; our civil liberties and democratic self-governance; Pilobolus and Dostoyevsky; deep-dish pizza and Hunan chicken; sailing and hiking; scientific genius and poetic imagination? These appreciations and affections were not somehow generated by and from within some distinctive and hermetically sealed religious or philosophical "conception of the good." How could they be? Instead, we acquire our enthusiasms for such particular human goods by direct encounter. We came, we saw, they conquered.

These observations about the multiplicity and the specificity of human goods, about their apprehension via direct experience, and about their detatchability for the most part from allegedly "comprehensive" "conceptions of the good" may seem banal. But they carry profound implications regarding the potentialities for civic friendship and civic community in a pluralistic society. They effectively undermine what I earlier termed the impossibility theorem. If civic friendships are created by mutual attachment to goods apprehended and appreciated and pursued in common, and if human goods are multiple and highly particular, and if people acquire their affectivity toward them in a direct fashion rather than by derivation from some "comprehensive conception of the good," then there is no reason to suppose that pluralistic societies are bereft of the constitutive conditions of civic friendship. Civic friendship in a pluralist society for the most part will not take the form of bonds of association generated by mutual acceptance of some single all-embracing moral creed—although some elements of this form of *homonoia* may in fact occur by widespread attachment to some basic political moral norms such as liberty, fairness, or the work ethic. But by virtue of its very breadth and generality this form of civic friendship tends to be somewhat tepid and abstract in any case. Instead, the topography of civic friendship in a pluralist society will be a highly complex web of overlapping and diverse associations that take their life from the many and varied vocations and enthusiasms of the citizenry.

One way to visualize this topography is to imagine every household in a community hosting a holiday open house to which all of its friends are invited. Each gathering would encompass a wide array of clusters of friends: work friends, neighborhood friends, PTA friends, tennis or golf buddies, school chums or fellow alumni, church friends, fellow members of civic clubs or professional associations, friends from gardening groups or bridge clubs or choral societies, and so on. Throughout the holiday season people would wind up under many roofs socializing with some people with whom they had many common interests and with others with whom they had but one thing in common. Each would see some other guests several times; others they might encounter only once. Some partygoers would share a specific moral or religious belief system; others would share only an enthusiasm for a particular good. In our own society and probably in most others, distinct groupings and boundaries along lines of class and ethnicity would be clearly visible. In some towns and cities, these groupings would be sharply etched; in others—including those communities with the healthiest and most vibrant civic cultures—these boundaries would be less distinct and more permeable. Only in very polarized and hence politically troubled societies would we find this web of civic association divided into circumscribed and mutually isolated sectors marked by identifiable and opposing comprehensive moral orientations. The topography of the web of civic friendships would look different in different societies, and from these differences perceptive social scientists could no doubt distinguish various levels of the societies' social capital and the strength of what Putnam calls their civic community. But, given the nature and bases of civic friendship, there is no reason to assume that pluralist democracies are precluded from coming in on the higher end of the scale.

Conclusion

The burden of our argument in this chapter, then, has been this. The cluster of social attributes referred to by terms such as civic friendship, a sense of community, trust, *homonoia*, and *eunoia* are important and valuable to any society. They are intrinsically gratifying. And they bring with them a host of associated political goods. Some of these additional goods are desired by all societies: stability, prosperity, and enhanced capacity to address social needs and to cope with social problems. Other goods to which civic friendship is so conducive are of particular concern to liberal democracies: limited government, toleration, civic equality, a capacity to engage issues deliberatively, the ability to reach compromises where legitimate interests come into conflict, and a willingness to accord communal assistance to the less fortunate. Despite confronting complications and limitations in their pursuit of civic friendship, pluralistic societies have the wherewithal to seek and attain a considerable measure of that social good and its concomitant blessings—unless circumstances and/or its own negligence convert pluralization into polarization.

A civic liberal would therefore insist that what used to be called "fraternity" needs to be put back onto the masthead of liberalism along with liberty and equality. The term "fraternity" today seems antiquated and sounds sexist, and the term "civic friendship" comes across as rather academic. Perhaps "community" would be the most apt candidate for rhetorical purposes. Whatever the term of choice, the important thing is to recognize that those earlier liberals who embraced "liberty, equality, fraternity" were correct to affirm that each of these goods is important, that each helps support the others, and that none was reducible to the others. For a variety of reasons, it is fraternity that has slipped into the shadows of the liberal mind. But it lingers there to haunt the liberal project, the rhetorical ghost of a dimly perceived but largely unacknowledged need and longing.

If there is anything to the argument set out here, its practical moral is that the political leadership of contemporary pluralist liberal democracies—maybe more than the leaders of any other form of political regime—should heed Aristotle's admonition that it is "the special business of the political art to produce friendship."[64] So far from this admonition being the accoutrement of defunct sociological contingencies and an obsolete philosophy, it is especially pertinent to the needs and aspirations of today's democratic polities. It is we who need to prize and to nurture those lineaments of civic friendship we can create, unless we want to preside over a slide into an atomized and balkanized society, increasingly less able to function effectively as an economy, as a civil society, and as a polity.

These lineaments of civic friendship, moreover, are a proper concern of the political art because—even though they may to some extent emerge from the spontaneous social interactions within civil society—they will not survive and flourish without a certain amount of explicit recognition and careful nurturance. Civic friendship in a pluralist society is a possibility because its citizens have the impulsions of natural sociablility and because they share many goals, values, and interests. But its attainment is by no means a sure thing because pluralism compounds the fissiparous impact of the universal sources of social conflict that Hobbes so sharply limned for us —greed, vanity, and fear—with the additional hurdles created by the impact of differing moral, religious, and cultural orientations and identities. As Bernard Crick once wrote: "Fraternity does mean creating by public policy, as well as by individual example, common purposes and cooperation both in working life and in leisure."[65]

From the civic liberal perspective, one of the most striking and dismaying aspects of the prevailing theories of liberalism is the way that they ignore, distort, and subvert the understanding and pursuit of civic friendship. Liberal realists ignore it because they consider it beyond the capabilities of a selfish and diffident humanity. Libertarians either consider it irrelevant to the public domain or imply that it occurs as spontaneously and unproblematically as do self-interested responses to market imperatives. Liberal egalitarians seem to think that it consists in state-mandated transfers of resources. And difference liberals seem to think that it either is hegemony in sheep's clothing or that it can emerge from the combat of self-assertive identity groups. None of these accounts, I have argued, is theoretically convincing. And each of them in various ways discourages or deflects us from achieving whatever measure of civic friendship is available to us in today's pluralistic democracies.

The irony here is that, by discouraging or misleading us in this way, these influential theoretical accounts not only weaken the prospects for the health and success of liberal democratic regimes, but they damage the chances of attaining their own most cherished goals. The realists prize security and toleration. Libertarians prioritize limited government and prosperity. Egalitarians seek to end social discrimination and to guarantee that all citizens have access to the resources necessary for a good life. But, as I have tried to demonstrate here, every one of these social goals is made much easier to reach by the trust and willingness to cooperate that are part of the good that Enlightenment liberals called fraternity.

These days, those who tout the virtues of community, of public spirit, of civic friendship are often derided by self-styled more worldly wise colleagues for indulging in nostalgia or romanticism. I recall a very able political theorist remarking at a conference that talk about community made him want to throw up. He had spent much of his life in New York City, where the conflicts between ethnic groups and interest groups are particularly bruising, so his cynicism was understandable. But it still should be resisted. The charge that advocacy of civic friendship is an exercise in nostalgia offers an empty epithet in place of argument. Simply because some social good was more appreciated in the past than it is today tells us nothing about whether it is either desirable or attainable in present circumstances. As Christopher Lasch once wrote, to call a social theory nostalgic "substitutes sloganeering for the objective social criticism with which this attitude tries to associate itself. The fashionable sneer that now automatically greets every loving recollection of the past attempts to exploit the prejudices of a pseudoprogressive society on behalf of the status quo."[66] Charges of nostalgia have real content only if it can be assumed that the recommended attribute—in this case, civic friendship—has as its necessary conditions certain nonreplicable circumstances found only in the past. But that contention is not in this instance persuasive. It is of course obvious that the particular form and the specific institutional vehicles of civic friendship in today's pluralist democracies cannot be the same as in earlier and different forms of society. But that does not mean that civic friendship cannot be generated or sustained in different patterns and by different means.

The charge of romanticism is similarly misguided and can even be turned against the accusers. The element of truth in this charge is that civic liberalism—by virtue of its insistence upon the importance and the possibilities of civic friendship—must indeed maintain some degree of faith in the better angels of our nature. That is a faith sometimes difficult to sustain in the face of the daily catalog of hostilities and animosities we read about in the morning paper. But the real romantics are those who think that a free, pluralistic, and democratic society can be stable, successful, prosperous, tolerant, deliberative, and dedicated to citizen equality when it does not enjoy and continually nurture the civic friendships that bring people together and motivate their common endeavors. With its tendency to fixate upon its historically more novel and distinctive commitments to liberty and equality, liberalism has tended over its career to lose sight of its own earlier, less novel dedication to fraternity. Civic liberalism counsels an end to that neglect. Forgetfulness about important things can be dangerous.

Notes

1. See, for example, Steven Kautz, *Liberalism and Community* (Ithaca: Cornell University Press, 1995); and Patrick Neal, "Vulgar Liberalism," *Political Theory* 21, no. 4 (November 1993): 665–90.

2. See Rawls, *Theory of Justice*, 106, and *Political Liberalism*, 194.

3. For a useful review of some of these disagreements among Greek and Roman philosophers, see Horst Hutter, *Politics as Friendship* (Waterloo, Ontario, Canada: Wilfrid Laurier University Press, 1978).

4. Aristotle, *The Nicomachean Ethics*, trans. J. A. K. Thomson (Baltimore: Penguin Books, 1955), book eight, chapter 1.

5. Aristotle, *The Nicomachean Ethics*, book eight, chapters 2 and 3.

6. "But it is only between those who are good, and resemble one another in their goodness, that friendship is perfect." Aristotle, *The Nicomachean Ethics*, book eight, chapter 3.

7. MacIntyre, *After Virtue*, 184–85.

8. MacIntyre, *After Virtue*, 184.

9. MacIntyre, *After Virtue*, 185. One might fairly comment that Franklin's own behavior actually gave the lie to his own stated account and instead justified Lawrence's view of the matter—unless, that is, one grants him a very broad interpretation of "health."

10. MacIntyre, *After Virtue*, 185.

11. C. S. Lewis, *The Four Loves* (London: Fontana Books, 1963), 63.

12. Lewis, *Four Loves*, 63.

13. Aristotle, *Nicomachean Ethics*, book eight, chapter 3.

14. Aristotle, *Nicomachean Ethics*, book eight, chapter 3.

15. Aristotle, *Nicomachean Ethics,* book eight, chapter 1.

16. Hannah Arendt, *Men in Dark Times* (Harmondsworth, England: Penguin Books, 1968), 31–32.

17. "Now friendship surely consists in giving rather than accepting affection." Aristotle, *Nichomachean Ethics,* book eight, chapter 8.

18. The quoted phrases are from his *Politics,* book one, chapter 2 and *Nicomachean Ethics,* book eight, chapter 1.

19. The last of these quotations is from *Leviathan,* part one, chapter 13. The other is from Hobbes's *English Works,* ed. William Molesworth (London: John Bohn, 1839), II, 3.

20. Kautz, *Liberalism and Community,* 28.

21. Locke, *Second Treatise,* chapters 7 and 2.

22. James Q. Wilson, *The Moral Sense* (New York: Free Press, 1993), esp. chapter 6.

23. Aristotle, *Nicomachean Ethics,* book eight, chapter 1.

24. Aristotle, *Nicomachean Ethics,* book eight, chapter 5. See also Hutter, *Politics as Friendship,* 115–16.

25. Aristotle, *Nicomachean Ethics,* book nine, chapter 6.

26. Lewis, *Four Loves,* 65.

27. Lewis, *Four Loves,* 75.

28. Rousseau, *The Social Contract,* book two, chapter 3.

29. Even though they saw the bonds of friendship as crucial to the health of the *polis,* Greek political analysts could have had no illusions on this score. The Greek *hetaery,* the "union of friends" that was quite salient in Greek society throughout the history of classical Greece, in numerous instances functioned as an institutional basis of conspiracy, collusion, corruption, and manipulation in Athens and other Greek cities.

30. Aristotle, *Nicomachean Ethics,* book nine, chapter 6.

31. For the notion of polyarchy and its relationship to the ideal type of democracy, see Robert Dahl, *A Preface to Democratic Theory* (Chicago: University of Chicago Press, 1956), esp. chapter 3.

32. Jacques Maritain, *The Rights of Man and Natural Law,* trans. Doric C. Anson (New York: Scribner, 1943), 22–23.

33. Harold Takooshian and Peter J. O'Connor, "When Apathy Leads to Tragedy," *Social Action and the Law* 10, no. 1. (1984): 26.

34. "Bidders Show Their Heart," *Columbus (Ohio) Dispatch,* 23 July 1995, 1A.

35. It might be objected that these cases do not necessarily speak directly and without remainder to the phenomenon of civic friendship, for we do not have dispositive evidence of the motivations of those offering assistance in the positive example. We cannot know for sure, in other words, that the assistance offered was not an example of generalized compassion for someone who was suffering—that it had nothing to do with some of the hallmarks of civic friendship, such as shared values or common identity. That is a possibility, and one that no interview data or other relevant evidence is available to disprove. It seems to me not an unreasonable conjecture, however, that the Ohio "bidders" acted as they did at least in large measure because the young woman in question was seen by them to be "one of us" in a way that embodies the criteria of civic membership. She was, in other words, related to them not so intimately as by kinship and not so generically as by mere common humanity, but rather as a member of the community—as a fellow American, Ohioan, and citizen of the town of Big Plain.

36. Sigmund Freud, *Civilization and Its Discontents,* trans. James Strachey (New York: Norton, 1961), 69.

37. John Stuart Mill, *Utilitarianism* (Indianapolis: Bobbs–Merrill Co., 1957), 40.

38. Edmund Burke, *Reflections on the Revolution in France* (New York: Liberal Arts Press, 1955), 110.

39. Hobbes, *Leviathan*, II, 18.

40. Francis Fukuyama, *Trust: The Social Virtues and the Creation of Prosperity* (New York: Free Press, 1995), 6.

41. See James S. Coleman, *Foundations of Social Theory* (Cambridge: Harvard University Press, 1990), 300–321.

42. Fukuyama, *Trust*, 8.

43. Fukuyama, *Trust*, 10.

44. Fukuyama, *Trust*, 27.

45. Fukuyama presents considerable evidence to support his contention that "there is a relationship between high-trust societies with plentiful social capital . . . and the ability to create large, private business organizations." *Trust*, 30.

46. Wolfe, *Whose Keeper?* 258.

47. Robert D. Putnam, *Making Democracy Work: Civic Traditions in Modern Italy* (Princeton: Princeton University Press, 1993), 176. I am not sure however, that Putnam's evidence or logic functions to contradict the claims of theorists such as Rousseau, Madison, or Mancur Olson to the effect that highly institutionalized informal political associations may function to weaken the larger society and to hamper collectively rational government policy-making. (See Putnam's remarks about Rousseau's and Olson's worries on pp. 90 and 176 respectively.) Instead, I would insist that we need to differentiate subcategories of the genus "civic association." Most of those associations canvassed by Putnam and enumerated by me as exemplary of the domain of civil society function to enrich the lives and accomplish the purposes of their participants without doing harm to—and often in fact contributing to—the welfare of nonparticipants. Associations formed primarily to press particularist demands or interests upon the larger society in ways that are, to borrow from Madison's definition of a faction, "adverse to the public interest or to the rights of others" are a different story. The local PTA, Kiwanis Club, and Habitat for Humanity generally do not do anything to damage my life as a nonmember of their groups and indeed benefit me by their contributions to the community. The AARP, the NRA, and the American Dairy Association, together with the plethora of other particular interest lobbies, may have as a central goal obtaining private benefit at general expense. The enthusiasts of civil society from Tocqueville to Putnam are essentially right about the importance of vibrant civic associations for democratic life. But the critics of factions should not have their very reasonable concerns neglected. There is no necessary contradiction between them.

48. Fukuyama, *Trust*, 357–58.

49. Putnam, *Making Democracy Work*, 112 (emphasis added).

50. Rawls, *Political Liberalism*, 147–48.

51. For one captivating account of this phenomenon, see Osha Gray Davidson, *The Best of Enemies* (New York: Scribner, 1996). This book tells the story of a friendship that developed from the initially antagonistic public encounters of a white, male Klan sympathizer and a black, female political activist. It should be noted that it was precisely this form of friendship/alliance that Southern progressives historically hoped and worked for and that Southern economic elites consciously worked to undermine through racist scaremongering when their political hegemony seemed threatened. One of the most depressing aspects of the contemporary political scene is watching self-styled political progressives in effect serving reactionary purposes through their insistence that such understanding, cooperation, and even amity across the lines of "difference" are unattainable and suspect. It is

time to recognize that this kind of pseudosophisticated principled cynicism is, to put it bluntly, both stupid and perverse. It is empirically falsifiable and politically destructive.

52. Aristotle, *Nicomachean Ethics*, book eight, chapter 11. The other quotations in this paragraph also come from book eight of that work, chapter 7 and 8.

53. See the article of that title in *The Review of Politics*, 55, no. 2 (Spring 1999): 193–216.

54. Aristotle, *Nicomachean Ethics*, book eight, chapter 9.

55. Hutter, *Politics as Friendship*, 11.

56. Hannah Arendt, *Men in Dark Times*, 31.

57. Aristotle, *Nicomachean Ethics*, book nine, chapter 9.

58. Benjamin Barber, *Strong Democracy* (Berkeley, California: University of California Press, 1984), 173–98.

59. Rawls, *Political Liberalism*, 37.

60. Putnam, *Making Democracy Work*, 115. As Putnam notes, his argument and his findings "contradict most classical accounts" of the social causes and correlates of a vibrant civic community. "Many theorists," he notes, "have associated the civic community with small, close-knit, pre-modern societies . . . Quite the contrary, our studies suggest. The least civic areas of Italy are precisely the traditional southern villages. The civic ethos of traditional communities must not be idealized." 114. Nor, conversely , should the civic potentialities of modern pluralistic societies be underestimated.

It is important in this context not to lose sight of the distinction between pluralistic and polarized societies or to think that they are structurally and functionally pretty much identical. A pluralistic society is one that encompasses a multiplicity of moral, religious, and possibly ethnic orientations or ways of life. Polarized societies are societies divided between or among highly self-conscious, intense, and competitive moral, religious, or ethnic groupings. It is no doubt exceptionally difficult for such polarized societies to enjoy civic friendship that transcends these divisions. But then these societies suffer, partly as a corollary of this incapacity, from all sorts of significant dangers and debilities. Pluralistic societies may become polarized, of course, but they need not suffer this fate.

61. Aristotle, *Nicomachean Ethics*, book nine, chapter 10.

62. Max Weber, "The Meaning of 'Ethical Neutrality,' in Sociology and Economics," in *The Methodology of the Social Sciences*, ed. and trans. Edward Shils and Henry Finch (New York: Free Press, 1949), 18.

63. John Rawls, "Kantian Constructivism in Moral Theory," *The Journal of Philosophy* LXXVII, no. 9 (September 1980): 536.

64. Aristotle, *Eudemian Ethics*, 1234b.

65. Bernard Crick, *In Defense of Politics*, 2nd ed. (Harmondsworth, England: Penguin Books, 1982), 234.

66. Christopher Lasch, *The Culture of Narcissism* (New York: Norton, 1979), 24.

8

Civic Virtues in Liberal Regimes

Human virtues, encompassing both valuable capacities and moral excellences, may be important to political theory and practice in two ways. First, a political society may find it necessary or at least highly advantageous to foster certain of these virtues as instrumental to its survival and success. These virtues we can call the specifically civic virtues, excellences that promote the well-being of a particular society. These excellences are, as Aristotle observes, "relative to the constitution" of the society in question.[1] The civic virtues are, to put it in Rawlsian terms, specifically "political" virtues and not necessarily the lineaments of a "comprehensive" conception of the good life. Second, it is possible but by no means necessary that a political society may embrace as one of its purposes the fashioning of its citizens into "comprehensively" good human beings, in accordance with its understanding of what that entails. A society may understand its statecraft to be "soulcraft." It may endorse a conception of the humanly good life taken to be universally valid, a conception not confined to those virtues instrumentally conducive to its own success, and seek to make its members into good people in this transcendent sense.

In this chapter, I want to consider the relationship between a well-ordered liberal democratic society and each of these forms of human virtue: those civic or "political" virtues specific to particular regimes and those virtues that might be deemed constitutive of some "comprehensively" good life. Regarding the question of civic virtue in liberal regimes, my argument is that liberal regimes depend upon certain citizen excellences for their flourishing—excellences that can be specified by their relationship to the basic ideals of liberty, equality, and civic friendship canvassed in the preceding chapters. Regarding the question of the (comprehensive) human good in liberal regimes, the argument will be that—for several reasons relating to these same basic ideals—it is neither proper nor necessary for a liberal society to endorse and seek to fashion its citizens in accordance with such a putatively universal norm of human excellence. I also argue that a liberal society is entitled to promote those civic virtues it requires, that doing so will necessitate that it will *de facto* not be wholly neutral *vis-a-vis* competing comprehensive conceptions of the human good, and that it need not apologize for this unavoidable departure from total neutrality regarding the human good so long as it promotes the liberal civic virtues in a procedurally liberal manner.

Liberal Civic Virtue

Civic virtues can be defined as the moral and intellectual abilities and habits necessary or highly valuable to the preservation and success of a particular political regime. These are virtues that serve as important resources for the society as it meets its needs, pursues its goals, and conducts its business. Liberal civic virtues, then, are virtues that conduce to the success of liberal regimes.

John Stuart Mill provided an admirable statement of the logic of civic virtue in the first chapter of his *Considerations on Representative Government.* "Political machinery," he wrote, "does not act of itself." It is not only made by human beings, it also "has to be worked by men and women, and even by ordinary men and women. It needs not their simple acquiescence, but their active participation; and must be adjusted to the capacities and qualities of such people as are available." This necessity implies three conditions, Mill continued:

> The people for whom the form of government is intended must be willing to accept it; or at least not so unwilling, as to oppose an insurmountable obstacle to its establishment. They must be willing and able to do what is necessary to keep it standing. And they must be willing and able to do what it requires of them to enable it to fulfill its purposes. The word "do" must be understood as including forbearances as well as acts. They must be capable of fulfilling the conditions of action, and the conditions of self-restraint, which are necessary either for keeping the established polity in existence, or for enabling it to achieve [its] ends.[2]

The criteria of civic virtue specify what it means to be a good citizen of a particular regime. They are not definitive of what it means to be a good human being in any absolute, universal, or comprehensive sense. The norms of good citizenship and of civic virtue are more limited and less complete than are the standards of human virtue *tout court*, especially in the context of liberal societies with their bounded public sphere. Criteria of civic virtue are also by their very nature and logic relative to the particularities of specific societies. Hence they may well differ from place to place, from one regime to another. Some human virtues are probably useful to practically any society, but some traits prized by one kind of society might be otiose or even counterproductive in another.

Conceptions of civic virtue are justified and defended, then, largely on instrumental grounds. One need not try to make the case that the particular capacities that go into a conception of civic virtue are intrinsically good or virtuous. Instead, it is necessary only to provide a reasonable showing that these capacities help the society in question achieve its objectives. Nevertheless, it probably would be false and misleading to suggest that a people's understanding of what it means to be a good human being is irrelevant to or has no bearing upon their willingness to embrace a particular conception of civic virtue, whatever the needs of their regime. For just as adherents of a particular regime—in order to consider it legitimate—have to believe that it is morally acceptable, they must *pari passu* consider the character traits of a "good citizen" to be at least compatible with and probably even partly constitutive of the features of a good human being *simpliciter.*

Owing to its more limited scope and reference points, a conception of civic virtue will generally be somewhat open ended *vis-à-vis* comprehensive conceptions of the human good and therefore compatible with multiple conceptions thereof. At the same time, however, no account of civic virtue can be wholly open-ended without becoming trivial or empty. Therefore, adopting any nontrivial account of civic virtue will unavoidably involve the rejection of—or at least the exaction of certain costs upon—some possible comprehensive conceptions of the good life. (Because of their principled proclivity toward geniality, antinomianism, and consensualism liberal theorists sometimes lose sight of or positively try to suppress the hard truth that all moral conceptions are not always reconcilable with each other. This theoretical blindness can translate practically into a self-defeating lack of resolve, a problem we return to later on.) Liberal conceptions of civic virtue, for example, are generally compatible with such diverse human ideals and ideal types as the Christian saint, the strong poet, the good-old-boy, the capitalistic go-getter, the yuppie aesthete, and many others we could identify. But any liberal conception of civic virtue clashes with conceptions of the human good that are profoundly antirationalist, inegalitarian, or intolerant.

Some versions of liberalism have virtually denied that civic virtues in the populace are necessary for the success of liberal regimes. In their different ways, for example, both Bernard de Mandeville and Immanuel Kant took issue with the traditional civic republican claim that a republican regime could survive and prosper only so long as its members remained virtuous—only so long as they were willing to subordinate selfish inclination to the public interest. Mandeville and others insisted that public good could be produced out of private vice, that society as a whole would function at its best when its citizens were not moralistically badgered to be altruistic but were instead given free rein to pursue their own self-interests. And Kant wrote that

> many contend that a republic must be a nation of angels, for men's self-seeking inclinations make them incapable of adhering to so sublime a form of government. But now nature comes to the aid of that revered but practically impotent general will, which is grounded in reason. Indeed, this aid comes directly from those self-seeking inclinations, and it is merely by organizing the nation well (which is certainly within man's capacities) that they are able to direct their power against one another, and one inclination is able to check or cancel the destructive tendencies of the others. The result for reason is the same as if neither sets of opposing inclinations existed, and so man, even though he is not morally good, is forced to be a good citizen. As hard as it may

sound, the problem of organizing a nation is solvable even for a people composed of devils (if only they possess understanding.)[3]

The half-truth embodied in these contentions is that liberal citizens need not
be republican saints, thanks to the socially useful effects of key liberal institutions.
"Self-interest rightly understood" can be generally benign in its consequences
when it is deployed within the disciplinary constraints of the marketplace and the
separation of powers. It is in fact a genuine advantage of a market economy that,
as Adam Smith put it, we don't have to rely upon the altruism of farmers and gro-
cers in order to eat. And although their practical effects are not always optimal,
constitutional systems of checks and balances have generally been successful in
blunting majoritarian hegemony. That much conceded, it is nonetheless now recognized with increasing unanimity that even the sparest (in terms of the goals and
functions it assigns to the political system) and the most optimistic models of liberal governance cannot escape the need for some form of civic virtue in their constituencies. No liberal polity can make a convincing case that it will function well
in the absence of certain capacities and behavior patterns its citizens need in order to perform the roles and carry the burdens assigned to them.

The least demanding forms of liberalism when it comes to the civic virtues required of their members would logically seem to be the libertarian and realist
variants—market liberalism and the liberalism of fear. But even they have to demand something of their citizens. Libertarians characteristically boast of the ability of their system to produce a free and prosperous society out of selfish and
greedy people. Upon reflection, however, it becomes apparent that a market system depends upon elements of mutual respect and forbearance on the part of the
participants for the system to work properly. Libertarian citizens may be profoundly concupiscent, but they must be willing to play by the rules, to respect the
property rights of others, and to be self-reliant. If all or most are sluggards,
thieves, and free riders, even the invisible hand loses a lot of its magic. Adam
Smith certainly understood that the market-based system he espoused depended
upon moral virtues and habits derived from other venues in the encompassing
civil society, primary among them being the church and the family. It also turns
out, as readers of Milton Friedman's *Capitalism and Freedom* are made well aware,
that it would be enormously helpful to the market system's ability to produce optimal outcomes if people would refrain from engaging in special pleading and
paternalism. That is, the system doesn't work if people constantly use political
channels to evade market discipline when it comes to the allocation of social resources to them and their causes. And people also need to refrain from using political power to curtail other people's freedom to allocate their resources as they
see fit. Friedman may not be moralistic in the same way or to the same degree as
the "evangelical" bees derided by Mandeville in his fable, but even he winds up
having to do some preaching to his fellow democratic citizens.

Similarly, liberal realists might seem able to avoid counsels of civic virtue,
given their relatively constrained political aspirations and their candid recognition of human limitations and antisocial propensities. But as even that prototyp-

ically realistic exponent of checks and balances, James Madison, understood, even the best system of countervailing power imaginable cannot obviate the need for some elements of moral probity among the public. People may not be angels, but they had better not be a race of devils either: "Were the pictures which have been drawn by the political jealousy of some among us faithful likenesses of the human character," he wrote, "the inference would be that there is not sufficient virtue among men for self-government; and that nothing less than the chains of despotism can restrain them from destroying and devouring one another."[4] A recent commentator has also pointed out that even that archrealist exponent of a liberal *modus vivendi*, Thomas Hobbes, must be understood as being in some respects a virtue theorist.[5] Hobbes demands of his citizens—however acquisitive, vain, and power hungry they may be—that they be willing to seek peace, that they keep their promises, that they respect the rule of reciprocity when it comes to rights and liberties, that they be forgiving of those who are genuinely repentant, and that they not be guilty of contumely. And contemporary exponents of a liberalism of "fearful accommodation" have also recognized that such a political order demands certain virtuous character traits in liberal citizens. As Steven Kautz writes, even such a modest liberalism requires "uncommon self-restraint or moderation." And Judith Shklar identifies "a self-restraining tolerance" as fundamental to the practice of her liberalism of fear. "Far from being an amoral free-for-all," she writes, "liberalism is, in fact extremely difficult and constraining . . . and a liberal character can readily be imagined."[6]

More ambitious versions of liberalism place additional demands upon the capacities and attitudes of their citizens. As John Rawls has acknowledged with increasing explicitness and specificity over time, his "political" liberal regime entails a conception of what he calls "the political virtues." He presumably adopts this term to emphasize terminologically that these virtues are not (at least directly) derived from a comprehensive conception of the good and that their scope is governed by the limits of the public sphere. But the logic of their derivation and justification is perfectly consonant with that of traditional conceptions of civic virtue.[7] Political liberalism, he writes, despite its purported desire to be "neutral in aim . . . may still affirm the superiority of certain forms of moral character and encourage certain moral virtues. Thus, justice as fairness includes an account of certain political virtues—the virtues of fair social cooperation such as the virtues of civility and tolerance, of reasonableness and the sense of fairness."[8] It might also be noted that his ideal of the well-ordered society requires in addition a sufficient measure of *caritas*, compassion, *eunoia*, and/or sympathetic imagination to enable his citizens to be able to recognize the terms of the original position as a legitimate "device of representation" and to be willing to "share one another's fate."

Difference liberalism also clearly would demand certain virtues of its citizens in order to be workable. The members of William Connolly's "agonistic" democracy, for example, would need to have the character traits necessary to sustain an ethos of "respect for difference" and "care for life," absent which the agonistic tensions built into his system would deteriorate into anarchic hostility. And the citizens in Iris Young's "egalitarian politics of difference" would have to possess the charity or self-restraint needed for them to be able and willing to "affirm" those who are "other." These are, one might add, demanding and not altogether common virtues that would seem to need some promotion.

Two of the most thoughtful arguments about the liberal civic virtues, finally, have been provided by Stephen Macedo and William Galston.[9] Macedo espouses a version of political liberalism that accords specific endorsement to certain traits of character he recognizes as being essential to the successful functioning of liberal regimes. Central among these traits are such virtues as autonomy, the willingness to offer reasons in justification of one's policy choices, and respect for diversity. Galston, pursuant to his insistence that liberalism is not neutrality incarnate but rather a way of life informed by a specific and contestable morality that should be affirmed and defended, generates from his account an extensive set of human capacities and dispositions important to the flourishing of liberal societies. As he writes: "the operation of liberal institutions is affected in important ways by the character of citizens (and leaders), and at some point, the attenuation of individual virtue will create pathologies with which liberal political contrivances, however technically perfect their design, simply cannot cope. To an extent difficult to measure but impossible to ignore, the viability of liberal society depends upon its ability to engender a virtuous citizenry."[10] Among these needful or useful virtues Galston includes: (1) "general" virtues, such as courage, law-abidingness, and loyalty; (2) "social" virtues, such as independence, fidelity, and tolerance; (3) "economic" virtues, such as the work ethic, punctuality, reliability, entrepreneurship, and adaptability; (4) "virtues of citizenship," such as respect for others, good judgment, moderation, and self-discipline; and (5) "leadership" virtues, such as the capacity to forge common purposes among disparate individuals, energy, impartiality, and resistance to the temptations of demagoguery.

The conception of civic virtue consonant with the political ideals of civic liberalism overlaps considerably with these accounts. This overlap is unsurprising, since all of the theories in question are variants of liberalism and therefore have more commonalties than differences, however important some of those differences may be. We have, in this work, focused for the most part on the differences between civic liberalism and the alternative conceptions of liberalism—for obvious practical and polemical reasons. But it is worth remembering from time to time that this is in fact an intrafamilial controversy. The principal differences here are two. First, the civic liberal conception of civic virtue tends to be somewhat more demanding and complex than the other versions because it is a function of a more complex set of goals. Second, many recent liberal theories tend to downplay their involvement with claims about civic virtue: when it comes to recognizing and affirming the civic virtues conducive to the goals they espouse and the procedures they endorse, they often tend to follow what Rawls terms, approvingly, the "method of avoidance." Primarily, I think, this reticence is a function of two things: first, a fear that espousing an explicit notion of civic virtue is rhetorically imprudent, damaging their chances of cultivating potential adherents and allies; and, second, a fear that endorsing a conception of civic virtue clashes with the norms of liberty and/or equality. Both libertarian and egalitarian liberalism tend to be highly decisionistic in their understanding of morality: individuals are free to designate what they conceive to be good. Hence affirming a specific conception of the civic virtues seems to clash with a mandate to accord individuals the right to make their own choices and a mandate to accord equal respect to these individuals and hence to the competing conceptions of the good which they espouse. This reticence, in short, is the function of a deep and unresolved tension within these theories, a tension that produces some discomfiture when it breaks surface. The paradigmatic instances of this discomfiture appear, for example, whenever libertarians have to instruct others to prioritize negative liberty over all other goods and when Rawls laments that "at this point we may have no alternative but to deny [a competing prioritizing of goods] and hence to maintain the kind of thing we had hoped to avoid."[11] In contrast to this reticence, civic liberalism can be candid about its acceptance of certain standards of civic virtue and can be forthright in endorsing their promotion because—in contrast with the dominant strands of libertarian and egalitarian theory—civic liberalism understands liberty and equality as themselves being contestable substantive moral goods requiring endorsement and defense on that basis instead of construing them as instances of refraining from imposing moral judgments on others in ways inconsistent with a decisionist and subjectivist understanding of morality.[12]

Our substantive account of liberal civic virtue begins with the central ideals surveyed in the three preceding chapters: liberty, understood not as negative freedom or positive fulfillment but as autonomy; equality, understood as a moral postulate with political corollaries; and civic friendship, understood in ways consonant with legitimate pluralism. It also begins with the definitive political tasks and processes of a civic liberal regime: self-governance, deliberation, rule of law, and respect for the rights of others. Taking these fundamental purposes and procedures as their reference point, the liberal civic virtues can be clustered under seven general headings. Analytically, these headings are not entirely neat; some cover a family of constituent virtues and some overlap with others. But this logical sloppiness is not only inevitable but justifiable when the task at hand amounts to translating a coherent ethos or way of life into an itemized list.

The first cluster of liberal civic virtues are those capacities and habits necessary to a politics of autonomy: independence, self-reliance, and responsibility. Autonomy is a preeminent, constitutive good for liberal politics. But it is not possible to operate a political system premised upon the value and the reality of personal autonomy unless the populace is in fact capable of behaving in the manner that characterizes those who are genuinely self-governing. You could not, for example, run a kindergarten in an entirely democratic way because its constituents are not yet capable of full autonomy. Liberal freedom has its flip side: the obligations, duties, and abilities necessary to sustain an autonomous mode of existence.

The good liberal citizen, therefore, is someone who is independent; independence here means nondependent; it does not and could not mean subject to no external restrictions whatever. An independent person will submit to rational and legitimate authority but will not accept a position or role of subordination out of habit or subservience. An element of assertiveness is part of being autonomous.

"Don't tread on me" is a legitimate liberal motto. But if autonomy warrants assertiveness, it likewise precludes attempts to leech off the efforts of others. Free riders are not good citizens. Autonomy implies and demands self-reliance. Both politically and economically the good liberal citizen does not depend on others to provide for him or her. When the toddler insists "I do it myself," he or she is taking the first steps away from the encompassing narcissism and dependency of infancy and toward the requisites of democratic citizenship. These are only the first steps, to be sure. But the "terrible twos," however trying on parents, deserve a measure of applause from the standpoint of democratic citizenship. If we never went through that stage, we would be on our way to being the proverbial nation of sheep. One price of this legitimate autonomy and assertiveness, however, is some degree of acceptance of the work ethic. By that phrase I mean in this context not all the particulars of Weber's "Protestant ethic," nor do I refer to an ethic of ascetic self-denial. I mean simply that the virtue of self-reliance entails more than the pleasures and rights of self-assertion. It also entails the correlative responsibility to cover the costs of one's own upkeep and the upkeep of those one has willfully brought into the world who are in a state of (temporary) dependency themselves—i.e., one's children—insofar as it lies within one's abilities to do so. This obligation to be self-supporting to the extent commensurate with one's abilities, it should be emphasized, does not mean that some economic goods are not properly objects of communal provision. Nor does it mean that the more able are not subject to moral and prudential considerations requiring them to provide assistance to the less able in their midst. It means simply that no one can coherently claim those fundamental liberal rights proper to the status of autonomous personhood while demanding at the same time to be supported by others. Legitimate excuses are available from this moral obligation, but they are exactly that: pleas on the basis of defensible warrants to be exempted from normal expectations and demands.

The capstone virtue under this heading, then, may be said to be that of responsibility. As an autonomous being, the good citizen of a liberal polity is willing to stand answerable for his or her actions. Responsible individuals accept the status and burdens of agency. They acknowledge that they are doers of deeds and not merely loci of reactions. They are not wholly independent variables, for that would be to style themselves as creators *ex nihilo*, i.e., as gods. But they are also not merely dependent variables, for that would be to sink into the realm of unmediated heteronomy, i.e., back into the status of animals who dumbly and unreflectively follow the impulses of nature. Good liberal citizens know that their actions have consequences, they try to foresee those consequences to the extent possible, and they stand ready to put those consequences on their own tab.

As Samuel Scheffler has astutely and pointedly argued in a recent article, and as I suggested in earlier chapters of this book, this issue of the nature and political implications of personal responsibility is one of the touchiest spots within the philosophical and political universe of contemporary liberalism.[13] Most contemporary liberal theorists, I believe, including those Scheffler examines, intuitively realize that venturing very deeply into an examination of the idea of responsibility would lead them into philosophical *aporiae,* reveal some of their own moral confusions and contradictions, and present them with unwelcome political dilemmas. Specifically, they recognize the deep intractability of the problems of free will and natural causality, they have difficulty fully reconciling their various moral intuitions (as reflected, for example, in the glaring gap between the premises of Rawls's theory of distributive justice and his dicta regarding retributive justice), and they fear that the accreditation of standards of individual responsibility would give aid and comfort to what they see as a morally unenlightened right-wing tendency to heap blame on those victimized by social oppression and unfortunate circumstances. Thus there is within liberalism a very strong reflex toward suppressing discussion of this issue.

However understandable it may be, my sense is that this intellectually repressive defense mechanism *vis-a-vis* the norm of responsibility is exceedingly unfortunate. It weakens liberal theory, damages liberalism's political prospects, and at times leads liberalism to embrace policies that are at once morally dubious, practically destructive, and ultimately profoundly inconsistent with what historically has been and properly should be the moral heart of a truly vital and humane liberal politics. It is inconsistent to build one's embrace of liberty and equality around ascribing great moral weight to individual choices and decisions, for example, and then unqualifiedly to endorse Foucault's denunciation of Sartre's account of bad faith as a form of moral terrorism. It is damaging to liberalism's persuasiveness to base its distributive principles upon a wholesale rejection of notions of merit and desert. And deliberately expunging all questions about the impact of social policies on the nurturance of responsible behavior clearly has perverse consequences.

It is, of course, incontrovertibly the case that, as Rawls insists, no one can be held responsible for choosing his or her genes or family circumstances. But just because we all are born into a world we did not make and did not choose does not mean that a liberal democratic society—or any other society for that matter—should consign its citizens to total moral passivity, relieve them of any obligation to or deny their capacity to make the best of their circumstances, and distribute blanket exculpations for any derelictions or depredations they may commit. It is also no doubt the case, as Connolly insists, that "we are not predesigned to be responsible agents."[14] Indeed, we are, it has been said, born with an insatiable appetite at one end and no sense of responsibility at the other. But we cannot remain in that condition, not only because that would require others to provide for and clean up after us, but also because we would then never attain the status of a moral being. As Connolly acknowledges, "we cannot dispense with practices of responsibility."[15] Therefore, even if it should—in recognition of the frailties of its human material—proceed with charity rather than with malice or resentment, a liberal society can forthrightly and unapologetically insist upon and seek to nurture within its citizenry a strong sense of personal responsibility.

A second liberal civic virtue is respect for human dignity. As Galston points out, even the most minimalist versions of liberalism assume "the worth of human existence, the worth of human purposiveness and of the fulfillment of human purposes."[16] A liberal citizen, then, should acknowledge the positive worth of each of his or her fellow citizens and should likewise acknowledge their moral status as purposive and responsible human agents. Some important nuances and distinctions are pertinent here. In the stylized libertarian polity, citizens regard each other with what might be best characterized as benign indifference. Each citizen claims an expansive private space and freedom of action to do his or her thing and grants that same space and freedom to others. The dominant egalitarian ethos tends to center around compassion, a kind of latter-day offspring of Rousseau's "natural pity": citizens should feel each other's pain, and the state should respond to this pain with benevolent solicitude. Respect, in contrast, is more than indifference and different from (both more and less than) benevolence. Respect requires intervention and assistance where the conditions of human dignity are not met. But it requires a restrained form of intervention that takes due regard of the (sometimes only potential) autonomy of all parties. Liberal citizens should be seen neither as strangers nor as each other's keepers. The former account neglects their partnership in a common social enterprise. The latter account both demands and permits too much: think of the connotations packed into words and phrases like "zookeeper" and "kept woman." Liberal citizens should, out of respect and mutual good will, be each other's helpers. And that should be the dominant motif of the liberal state as well. The liberal state, pursuant to respect for the dignity of its citizens, should not be merely a neutral umpire who leaves people entirely to their own devices, sink or swim. But it also should not turn into what both Tocqueville and Foucault feared in their different ways as the possible fruit of democratic liberalism: a benevolent, intrusive, and condescending nanny state that diminishes its clients as it "takes care of" them.

The behavioral hallmarks of the civic virtue of respect, or course, are tolerance and the honoring of civil rights and liberties. These demands are common to all specifications of liberal civic virtue. The only thing that distinguishes the civic liberal account here is that the point and purposes of rights and tolerance are construed in light of the differences just canvassed. This can be important at the margins. When it comes to specifying what rights people should have, for example, the civic liberal will address that issue not by asking about what liberties are appropriate for equal consumers/producers in the marketplace nor what entitlements are appropriate for equal clients of the welfare state—but rather by asking what are the rights and liberties that necessarily pertain to democratic citizens. Similarly, the civic liberal mode of toleration incorporates a positive concern and affirmation for one's fellow citizens that is absent from the minimalist construction of toleration as benign indifference. But it does not rise to the kind of "recognition and affirmation" demanded by Iris Young. Toleration does not necessarily mean approval. Liberal citizens may well disapprove—on moral, practical, or aesthetic grounds—of some uses their fellow citizens make of their freedoms. In such cases, the requirements of good liberal citizenship do not preclude them from voicing their disapproval. Liberal respect for the dignity and autonomy of others instead requires that each must refrain from forcible intrusions and prohibitions based on that disapproval. As Mill wrote in *On Liberty*, we may well at times view some actions of other citizens as "immoral and fit subjects of disapprobation." In such instances, liberal virtue does not require that we swallow our tongue or feign admiration. Instead, "we may express our distaste, and we may stand aloof from a person as well as from a thing that displeases us; but we shall not therefore feel called on to make his life uncomfortable."[17] (Several other civic virtues, to be canvassed shortly, do however suggest the need for serious constraints upon such expressions of distaste or disapproval. I refer here to the virtues of friendliness, humility, and magnanimity. Taken together, these virtues would seem to require that no citizen should go out of his or her way to be another's moral censor, that critique should not be condemnation, that disapproval generally not be voiced unless it is somehow pertinent to behavior or policy in the public domain, and that the corrigibility of one's own moral standards be recognized even as they are given voice.)

A third cluster of liberal civic virtues emerges from the characterological requisites of the rule of law. Although the full spirit behind the rule of law has taken something of a battering in recent decades, as both in theory and practice the normativity of rules taking a "general object" (Rousseau's term) has been submerged beneath the particularities of interest-group bargaining, nothing is more fundamental to legitimate and effective democratic self-governance. Democratic policies should be expressed in the form of general and explicit rules that apply to all evenhandedly. And conflicts are to be resolved as much as possible by courts of law rather than by private vengeance, acting with an impartiality symbolized by the blindfold worn and the balanced scales held by the goddess of justice. These norms and the procedures that embody them can be effectual, as Mill pointedly noted, only under certain conditions. The most important of these conditions relates to the character and moral habits of the citizenry. Specifically, a system of law requires the very important liberal virtues of self-restraint and a capacity for "objectivity." It is essential that most citizens have the ability to refrain from acting directly upon the immediate impulses produced by their passions and self-interest. They must allow these passions and interests to be pursued through and regulated by the applicable rules and procedures. And they must be able to be somewhat "objective" in their approach to policy choices and conflicts in the sense that they can stand back, abstract from their personal biases, and approach what Kurt Baier calls "the moral point of view." They must have some ability, as Hume put it, to "form some general unalterable standard" to inform their moral judgments. It is natural and even proper, Hume wrote, "that private connections should commonly prevail over universal views and considerations." Otherwise our attachments and affections for friends and family "would be dissipated and lost." But still, he continued, "we know here . . . to correct these inequalities by reflection, and retain a general standard of vice and virtue founded chiefly on general usefulness."[18]

Without the ability to rely upon these virtues of self-restraint and moral objectivity, the rule of law founders. Private violence, vigilante justice, and mob rule shoulder aside the courts of criminal law. And that displacement of law by force will be hastened as jurors abandon impartiality in favor of their personal biases or group loyalties. The enforcement of rules becomes an occasion for private enrichment *via* the extortion of bribes by both bureaucrats and supposed "officers of the law." Legislative politics becomes an exercise in beggar-thy-neighbor. The sense of justice that Rawls properly includes among his designated political virtues likewise disappears as the capacity for objectivity which sustains it is lost. Not only the policy process, then, but the judicial system and the conduct of everyday life descends into a largely unmediated free-for-all governed by private advantage and the exertion of force. The virtues of self-discipline and self-transcendence, then, have to rank very high on the list of the liberal virtues.

The capacity for attaining moral objectivity and with it some sense of justice and fairness points toward another entry in the civic liberal catalog of significant virtues. Call this one "democratic humility." Humility here should not be construed as a form of moral masochism or obsequiousness. It does not connote the unfortunate tendency of some liberals to issue wide-ranging *mea culpas* for all sorts of social ills—a tendency that has subterranean linkages with vanity and the will to power. And it does not imply the demeanor of a Uriah Heep. The core conviction animating democratic humility, instead, is captured in the tag line of "The Farmer and the Cowman" from *Oklahoma*: "I may not be better than anybody else; but I'll be damned if I ain't just as good." Democratic humility, in short, is the flip side of a proud assertion of one's moral stature and equality. No masochism here. Instead, it embodies the recognition and cheerful acceptance that each of us is one among equals.

Democratic humility manifests itself in the absence of three things: vanity, *pleonexia* (the insistence upon getting more than one's fair share), and dogmatism. It has both distributive and epistemic dimensions. In its largest sense, perhaps, *pleonexia* actually subsumes vanity. For vanity is one particular form of insistence upon receiving more than one's share of something: it demands an excess measure of honor and esteem. The same general vice extends also to the other two of the three objects of natural passion Hobbes identified as problematic in human affairs: namely, wealth and power. In its distributive dimension, then, democratic humility refers to the absence of making arrogant demands for more than one's share of honor, of wealth, or of power—all in the context of the fundamental postulate of the ultimate equal moral worth of every human being. The epistemic dimension of democratic humility is manifested by the absence of dogmatism. Good liberal citizens refrain from making unwarranted and unwarrantable claims about the status of their beliefs—not only their moral beliefs, but also their empirical beliefs where these outrun a definitive evidentiary basis and are pertinent to political choices. Just as democratic humility generally requires neither moral masochism nor obsequiousness, so in the area of politically pertinent knowledge claims about goodness, rightness, or truth it does not demand the abandonment of one's convictions. And it certainly does not mandate pyrrhonism or moral skepticism. It demands only the willing recognition that even one's deepest and most cherished convictions have—to borrow an apt term invoked by Michael Polanyi in this context—a fiduciary basis.[19] That is to say, the good liberal citizen recognizes and affirms that ultimately his or her beliefs about both moral truths and matters of empirical fact are just that: beliefs. However confident we may be of their truth, we cannot demonstrate their correctness in any incontrovertible and definitive way. When contested issues are put to a vote, we are entitled to vote our convictions. Moreover, *contra* Rousseau, we are not obligated to conclude when we wind up on the losing side that we were mistaken. But we are not entitled, ever, to be sure that we are right. We therefore cannot legitimately try to force our own views upon others. Above all, we cannot try to consolidate the triumph of our views by closing off the democratic forum. We should, in affirming the contingency of the perspective of the majority, never confuse dissent with sedition. And we should try, wherever compatible with the needs of public order, to allow some space for conscientious objection and principled civil disobedience.

Democratic humility—especially in its epistemic dimension—also provides the inspiration for and part of the logic behind the next set of liberal civic virtues: the deliberative virtues. Where people differ in their goals and where these differences arise in significant part from contestable beliefs, we owe our fellow citizens an accounting for our actions. We stand under a moral obligation—particularly since we concede that those with whom we disagree are our moral equals and even our civic friends—to explain ourselves. It is an obligation of good liberal citizenship to provide a candid presentation of the reasons or justifications for our actions that impinge upon others. As Jefferson acknowledged in the preamble to the Declaration of Independence, "a decent respect to the opinion of mankind requires that [we] should declare the causes which impel [us]" to our political stances and political actions.

The deliberative virtues include both dispositions of the will and capacities of the mind, both moral and intellectual virtues. The first of these is "reasonableness" in the sense of a willingness to give reasons. As Stephen Macedo writes: "being a self-critical reason-giver is the best way of being a liberal." Because the antithesis of legitimate government according to liberalism is, as Locke made clear, arbitrary government, "liberal citizens expect to be answered with reasons rather than mere force or silence."[20] The paradigmatic manifestation of this moral obligation of liberal citizenship to offer justifications for one's political decisions and actions may be the practice of writing judicial opinions. But, as Macedo properly insists, it is not only judges who need to give reasons to their fellow citizens. "In a liberal political community no one is above needing publicly to justify the exercise of political power. . . . Principled adjudication merely solemnizes and makes official a process of argument and reflection that could, and should, go on in politics all the time."[21] Legislators, after all, give speeches. Political journalists and commentators write editorials and op-ed pieces. And citizens, in their turn, write letters both to their legislators and to the editor. These also, properly done, are exercises in the declaration of causes.

The phrase "properly done" here introduces the other deliberative virtues. Reason-giving is done properly when the speaker is, to borrow Habermas's term, "truth oriented." The liberal citizen's disposition of will must be to ascertain and act upon the "truth" of the matter, both in the practical and theoretical senses of that term. Liberal discourse seeks to discern what Madison called "the permanent and aggregate interests of the community." And it also seeks to identify those features of the empirical world that have a bearing upon how these goods in common should most effectively be pursued. Contributions to democratic discourse should exemplify respect for what Habermas calls the "pragmatic rules that form the infrastructure of speech situations in general."[22] That is, the speaker should intend his or her remarks to be comprehensible, truthful, and appropriate. These justificatory declarations must embody what Michael Polanyi calls "universal intent." They must embody a striving, against the background of acknowledging the partiality of one's perspective, toward a more comprehensive vision of reality, a "submission to the compelling claims of what in good conscience I conceive to be true."[23] Put into the simplest terms, then, the moral deliberative virtues are forthrightness, candor, sincerity, and dedication to the truth.

The intellectual deliberative virtues are encompassed by the phrase "capacity for exercising good judgment." There are intrinsic limits upon the extent to which the particulars of good judgment—whether in science, law, or politics—can be rendered fully explicit. The very notion of judgment incorporates recognition of the uncertainties and the tacit dimension involved in such cognitive feats.[24] In general terms, however, we can nonetheless identify some of the components of good judgment. One of these is the capacity for achieving critical distance from both oneself and the subject matter. James Fishkin thematizes this capacity, for example, in his ideal of a "self-reflective society." And Amy Gutmann captures the point of such critical and reflective self-awareness when she writes that people "without a developed capacity for reasoning are ruled only by habit and authority and are incapable of constituting a society of sovereign citizens."[25] A second element of good judgment is a sense of what constitutes relevant considerations, the capacity to recognize what is and is not pertinent to the issue at hand. And third, the most formal element of good judgment is the ability to abide by canons of logic and consistency in argument and appraisal: the determination and capacity to avoid embracing contradictory warrants for one's assertions and to recognize and respect the need for a coherent linkage between these warrants and the prescriptive conclusions they purport to justify.

Three final points under the heading of the deliberative virtues of a liberal politics. First, the principal vices in this domain are moral cynicism, sophistry, and demagoguery. The moral cynic believes practical discourse to be delusive and/or fraudulent. Moral argument is but a cover for self-interest and the will to power. Hence the cynic either boycotts democratic discourse or participates in it subversively and manipulatively, as does his cousin, the sophist. If practical discourse is a fraud, then one can only seem to participate in it. The norms of sincerity, honesty, and universal intent can be ignored and argumentation can be consciously deceptive manipulation. "Just gaming," the cynic and sophist undermine the faith in and the legitimacy of democratic debate and push a liberal society down the slope toward the war of each against all, laughing all the way. And the demagogue, for personal or partisan advantage, deliberately appeals not to the better judgment of the people but to their darker passions, tempting opponents to respond in like fashion and unleashing a deliberative version of Gresham's law in which bad discourse drives out the good.

Second, it merits remarking that the practice of the deliberative virtues links up with and reinforces the previously cited virtues of self-restraint. Serious democratic deliberation has this effect because it forces upon the participants the virtue of "objectivity." It drives people toward the "moral point of view" by reference to which their own partisan and particular goals can be judged and constrained.[26] Here, as elsewhere, the liberal civic virtues cohere, overlap, and reinforce one another.

Finally, I think it important in speaking of the deliberative virtues clearly to understand the norm of "reasonableness" as a procedural rather than a substantive norm. The deliberative virtues of liberalism should be conceived adverbially and not adjectivally. To be reasonable, then, means that one: (1) acknowledges the moral imperative to justify one's views and actions to one's fellow citizens, (2) engages in practical discourse with sincerity and universal intent, thereby adopting the moral point of view and enforcing what Rawls terms the formal constraints of the principles of right, and (3) offers relevant reasons in support of one's favored policies and outcomes. These procedural requirements are not, of course, entirely neutral in substantive terms. They render egoism mute, for example. They tend strongly to enforce, *de facto*, the postulate of moral equality. And they privilege the common good against particular interests. Moreover, in a liberal democracy, "good reasons" include appeals to the core social goals of liberty, equality, and civic friendship. But beyond these important but relatively general and open-ended substantive considerations the norm of reasonableness must not go. What needs to be resisted here is what might be called the Platonic temptation—inconsistent with epistemic fallibilism and respect for the competence and sincerity of those with whom we differ—to construe reasonableness as a description of those who basically share my own good sense and hence see things my way. My impression, although it is not too easy to say for sure, is that Rawls—in embracing reasonableness as one of the political virtues—does not altogether avoid this temptation. It is not easy to say for sure, because—although in his recent work Rawls invokes the norm of reasonableness ubiquitously—he does not offer a fully satisfactory definition of that term.[27] As he concedes, " I grant that the idea of the reasonable needs a more thorough examination than *Political Liberalism* offers."[28] On behalf of my worries here, I offer two pieces of evidence, admittedly not dispositive. First, Rawls tends to use reasonable as an adjective, as when he talks about "reasonable comprehensive doctrines" and "reasonable pluralism." These formulations seem to suggest that "reasonableness" demarcates a constrained subset of substantive beliefs rather than a set of procedures for arriving at the beliefs. Second, he argues that "any comprehensive doctrine that leads to a balance of political values excluding that duly qualified right [to abortion] in the first trimester is to that extent unreasonable."[29] Since the fact is that at least some opponents of abortion are perfectly reasonable people in the sense of meeting all the criteria of rational argumentation I set out above, the suspicion grows that "reasonable" for Rawls means those people who think like me. It means those who defend abortion rights and share the moral beliefs that sustain the difference principle.[30]

Whatever Rawls's understanding of the parameters of "reasonableness" may be, I want to be clear that my account of the deliberative virtues of liberalism is not so substantively particular and exclusionary. The deliberative virtues refer to how one reaches and defends his or her political views together with the substantive constraints imposed by the logic of moral discourse and by what in a liberal culture can count as relevant moral considerations. But we should reject any imputations that universal adherence to the deliberative virtues would somehow resolve our moral disagreements about such vexing issues as abortion and distributive justice. It wouldn't. And any claim to the contrary is either delusionary or an exercise in tendentious self-congratulation. Here, as in the case of many important disputed questions of politics and morality, fully reasonable people both can and do differ. In this context Isaiah Berlin's recognition of moral pluralism and tragedy is more fitting than Rawls's aspirations for a moral geometry.

We can deal more quickly with the next two sets of liberal civic virtues, which are close kin, not because they are less important but because they are less complicated. The first set encompasses the dispositions of heart and will conducive to civic friendship. Call these the virtues of neighborliness. The basic disposition of will is what Aristotle described as friendliness or good will—the generalized readiness to relate to others in a positive and helpful way. The good liberal citizen is no saint. He or she cannot be obligated to embody all the dimensions of *caritas* euologized by Saint Paul in his letter to the Corinthians. And the obligation to be friendly is binding only, as Hobbes put it *vis-a-vis* the obligation to obey the laws of nature, in foro interno: "that is to say, they bind to a desire they should take place: but in foro externo; that is, to the putting them in act, not always." For, Hobbes continues, those who are modest and tractable and keep all their promises "where no man else should do so, should but make himself a prey to others, and procure his own certain ruin."[31] Good liberal citizens are asked to be friendly, but they are not required to be chumps. The virtue of liberal *eunoia* is grounded in the postulate of moral equality and the assumption that, as Galston insists, this is an equality of positive worth. And it encompasses the recognition that any functional society is, to borrow Rawls's phrase, "a scheme of social cooperation." It furthermore is based on the realization that this requisite cooperation must either be spontaneous or it will be compelled: people must associate and cooperate willingly and voluntarily on behalf of public goods or else they will be dragooned into doing so by state power. The willingness to be cooperative generated by the disposition to be a good neighbor, then, is in this context part of the price of freedom.

Hence the logic behind the closely associated participatory virtues lauded in their different ways by the Athenians, by John Stuart Mill, and by the Students for a Democratic Society in their Port Huron Statement days. The good liberal citizen is "public spirited," as Mill put it. He or she is not merely compelled to appreciate the concerns and adopt the standpoint of the general good by the discipline of democratic discourse and the checks and balances of democratic constitutionalism. That may be what pushes him or her in that direction, but ultimately the good citizen of liberal democracy comes to identify with the interests of the whole. The reason Mill put so much emphasis on the extension of democratic suffrage was his somewhat overly optimistic belief that the process of voting—along with the performance of other public duties such as serving on juries—was a "school of public spirit" in the sense that it forced people to identify with the general good. The citizen so occupied is pushed to transcend his privatism and partiality. "He is called upon, while so engaged, to weigh interests not his own; to be guided, in case of conflicting claims, by another rule than his private partialities; to apply, at every turn, principles and maxims which have for their reason of existence the general good. . . . He is made to feel himself one of the public, and whatever is their interest is his interest."[32]

However inflated was Mill's estimation of the beneficent consequences of exercising the franchise and performing public duties, he was not entirely off the mark about the impact such responsibility has upon many. And he was correct to eulogize the willingness to identify with and to contribute to the general good as an important liberal virtue, absent which democracy might not survive and certainly wouldn't prosper. Liberalism, including the civic liberal variant here endorsed, does not expect its citizens to subordinate or sacrifice themselves to the larger society in the manner that the enthusiasts of republican virtue at times have done. We are rightly as appalled as we are impressed by tales of Spartan youths who allow their entrails to be devoured rather than disrupt their cohort by crying out and by stories of Spartan mothers who affect not to regret the loss of their soldier sons so long as their side prevailed. This is public spiritedness carried to excess and turned into a vice. It neglects morally legitimate self-concern and the morally worthy particular affections and care due to family and personal friends. Civic liberalism does not ask too much. It asks only that liberal citizens be willing to do their part, that they affirm the priority of public good over particular advantage, and that they understand that if they and their fellows are not willing to make some sacrifices and bend some efforts on behalf of the common good then it will not be achieved. Good liberal citizens need not sacrifice their entrails or their children on the altar of the state. But they should, even if childless, be willing to institute taxes to support public education; if among the financially sound elderly, they should not demand that their routine medical services be paid for by the working poor; if affluent they should not insist that the children of the less well-off bear all the dangers of mutual defense. They should, when it comes their turn, serve on juries, help out at soup kitchens, lead the PTA, coach in the youth league, and so on. If the public good is to be served, someone must serve it.

These then are the most significant liberal civic virtues: responsible self-reliance, respect for the human dignity of all fellow citizens, law-abiding self-restraint, democratic humility, reasonableness and good judgment, neighborly *eunoia,* and the public-spirited willingness to participate in civic service. This demanding and capacious array of liberal virtues stands over against an equivalent array of contrasting vices which have surfaced in the course of our account: irresponsibility, dependency, snobbery, dogmatism, *pleonexia,* sophistry, demagoguery, the lust to dominate others, and privatistic self-absorption. We noted on several occasions in our survey, moreover, the overlap, interplay, and mutual reinforcement among the various liberal virtues. These are not so much a catalog of discrete and disparate traits of character as they are the most salient features of a complex and coherent mode of civic life. Were we to seek a single term to encompass this whole mode of civic existence, to comprise the various virtues, we could do worse than adopt and adapt one recently put forward by Amy Gutmann and Dennis Thompson: civic magnanimity.³³ On their definition, civic magnanimity stands for three things: acknowledging the moral standing of one's opponent, keeping an open mind *vis-a-vis* opposing positions, and seeking to minimize the rejection of these alternative moral positions. I would like to appropriate their very apt term along with the spirit behind it and broaden it to encompass and to capture the unity of the liberal civic virtues I have identified in this chapter.

The term magnanimity in the context of characterological typologies builds upon the metaphor of largeness. The magnanimous are those who are "great souled," those whose lives manifest and express a largeness of spirit in some sense or other. The hallmark of the great soul in whatever version is some form of generosity of spirit. My suggestion here is that, taken together, the particular traits associated with the liberal civic virtues add up to and produce exactly that. People who respect the deep human worth and dignity of all their fellow citizens, who are tolerant of those who differ from or with them, who exhibit democratic humility, who communicate candidly and seek to achieve moral objectivity, who are warm and friendly, and who contribute freely toward the achievement of common goals live their lives in a mode of generosity. This specifically democratic mode of greatness or generosity or grandeur of soul, however, is very different from the kind of greatness of soul praised by Aristotle and Nietzsche. For them, magnanimity is a species of aristocratic hauteur, an expression of perceived moral superiority. The Aristotelian aristocrat behaves in a grand and "generous" way toward his inferiors, those who are "mechanics and laborers" and who therefore "cannot pursue the things which belong to excellence."³⁴ And the "generosity" of the Nietzschean "overman" is the expression of his consummate disdain for the little people he despises. In both cases, the magnanimity in question is in part a largeness of ego, and the generosity is akin to that of the grand signeur or grande dame who signalizes his or her superior status and virtue by occasionally sweeping the crumbs from his or her table to the rabble. Nothing could be further from the democratic magnanimity generated by the liberal virtues. For the generosity of the democratically magnanimous is grounded in dedication to the proposition that, in Benjamin Barber's wonderful phrase, we are "an aristocracy of everyone." It expresses the *caritas* of civic friendship for prized equals vested with the dignity of reason and autonomy.

It is no doubt hazardous to attempt to put specific faces on a moral archetype of the sort embodied in the idea of democratic magnanimity. And it is in the very nature of this particular archetype that anyone designated as exemplifying the virtues encompassed by it would demur. But the month during which I was trying to chisel out this archetype happened to see the deaths of two notable public figures: Jimmy Stewart and Charles Kuralt. Occupied as I was in meditating upon the lineaments of liberal civic virtue, I was struck by the reactions to their passing.

Both deaths prompted a widespread outpouring of expressions of respect, affection, and appreciation. The traits of character cited in each case as the reason for the aforementioned respect and affection largely coincided. And these traits largely coincided in turn with many of the particulars I was touting as the constituents of liberal virtue. Both were praised for their genuine humility, for being unaffected and "down to earth," for their warmth and good will, for their capacity to discern and celebrate the extraordinariness of ordinary human beings, for their self-discipline and attendant good craftsmanship, and for their willingness to shoulder common burdens whether by volunteering to fly in combat or by raising funds for a school of social work. The lives of these two men were celebrated and their losses mourned, the people who knew them said in effect, because they were examples of democratic magnanimity.

We are, with good reason, reluctant and reticent when it comes to speaking of civic virtue and good citizenship. The very terms tend to reek of sanctimony, of Boy Scout jingoism and Sunday school moralism, of priggishness and prudishness and self-righteousness and ostentation. A democratic era, moreover, is loathe to discriminate in any way—even between vice and virtue. Under the aegis of what Allan Bloom famously lampooned as our "genial nihilism" we often behave as though tolerance were the only virtue, discrimination the only vice. Hence to speak of virtue is itself a vice. As I observed the reaction to the losses of the good actor and the good journalist, Stewart and Kuralt, however, it occurred to me that a democratic people understands civic virtue in the same way that another Stewart, Justice Potter Stewart, once reported that he understood obscenity: they may not be able to define it but they know it when they see it.

Soulcraft in Liberal Regimes

It should not be surprising that the norms of civic virtue are more extensive and demanding in liberal democracies than in other political regimes. Because they are democracies, their citizens are collectively sovereign. Therefore these citizens must possess at least some of the moral and intellectual virtues requisite of those who rule. Because these democracies are liberal, they leave as a matter of principle significant areas of social space free from governmental supervision and control. Therefore their citizens must be capable of exercising self-restraint and creating forms of social order on their own recognizance. It is an intrinsic part of the logic of both democracy and liberalism that its adherents be capable of governing well and of governing themselves. Liberal democratic societies are highly permissive toward their citizens, but at the same time and for some of the same reasons they are very demanding of them as well. To be successful, liberal democracies depend upon a wide dissemination of traits and capacities often thought to be the province of the few rather than the many.

Should fostering the liberal civic virtues also be considered one of the final ends or purposes of these regimes? Should the nurturance of these virtues be deemed not only an instrumental but a teleological good? And/or should some additional "supra-" or "extra-" civic virtues be so enshrined and pursued as one of the defining goals of liberal democratic practice? In his justificatory rationale for the superiority of representative (i.e., democratic) regimes, John Stuart Mill insisted, for example, that the "principal element" of "good government" was "the improvement of the people themselves." Hence, "the first question in respect to any political institutions is, how far they tend to foster in the members of the community the various desirable qualities, moral or intellectual."[35] Should it be a fundamental goal of liberal democratic societies, then, to produce human selves shaped in accordance with a conception of human perfection?

The basic answer here has to be a qualified "no." It cannot properly and legitimately be a purpose of a liberal regime to produce "good people" in a specific and comprehensive sense. That does not mean that a liberal regime is nihilistic, relativistic, or hostile to its citizens' efforts to live a good life and pursue human perfection as they understand it. Indeed, a liberal polity provides its citizens with both some of the infrastructure and the necessary social space for their pursuit of the human good. But it is beyond the competence and hence outside the proper scope of a liberal regime to endorse and promote one particular conception of human perfection in preference to and at the expense of all alternative conceptions. This is the important truth encapsulated in the otherwise rather misleading stipulations about the moral "neutrality" of the liberal state.

This circumscription of the moral aspirations and commitments of a liberal regime is generated by the confluence of three of its core principles. The first of these is the epistemic humility consequent upon the recognition of the fallibility and limits of human reason, especially with regard to moral and religious matters. Locke made this point memorably and pertinently in his *Letter Concerning Toleration* with specific reference to "speculative" religious doctrines. And subsequent experience and reflection have amply confirmed his point with regard to all comprehensive moral doctrines. It is simply a fact of life that even reasonable people differ on such issues, and there exists no process or device to adjudicate these disagreements in any certain and reliable way. The second core principle is the liberal respect for individual autonomy. And the third principle is the liberal insistence on the equal moral worth and political standing of all liberal citizens. Taken together, these three core commitments lead to the conclusion that it is impermissible for a liberal regime to endorse and privilege a single comprehensive moral doctrine—something that would be necessary in order to sustain any effort to make the creation of comprehensively "good people" a legitimate liberal purpose. This is what Rawls terms "the fact of oppression" and what I have called "the impropriety theorem."

The conclusion that it is improper, as a consequence of its own core principles, for a liberal regime to make the creation of comprehensively "good people" one of its purposes is subject to the following qualifications, however. The first of these is that the civic virtues a liberal regime is entitled to promote are *de facto* "partially comprehensive." The liberal civic virtues, that is, are not indiscriminately compatible with all comprehensive ethics. Even a cursory review of their content, for example, makes it clear that they cannot really be made to cohabit in any coherent or consistent fashion with moral codes which are racist or irrationalist, which distinguish "supermen" from the *hoi polloi,* or which demand unquestioning deference of one caste to another. This kind of "partial comprehensiveness" is inevitable and common to all civic ethics: to the extent that these ethics have any substance, they cannot be so protean as to be entirely nondiscriminatory *vis-a-vis* comprehensive moral doctrines. Whether one chooses to lament this fact of life and logic, it should be forthrightly acknowledged and need not be occasion for apology. A civic ethic cannot escape this kind of *de facto* bias with respect to comprehensive moralities by some form of strategy of prescinding or method of avoidance of the kinds counseled by Charles Larmore or John Rawls.[36] To escape such bias, to be genuinely and entirely neutral with respect to divergent comprehensive conceptions of the good, a civic ethic would have to be not merely constrained but empty.

The second qualification to the negative conclusion concerning the propriety of a liberal regime taking the creation of virtuous people *tout court* as one of its animating purposes is this: it is perfectly licit to offer as a supplementary or secondary warrant for the liberal civic virtues the observation that they are congruent with and play a role within several more comprehensive ethical systems which have illustrious pedigrees and which garner wide respect—both within and beyond modern liberal cultures. It would, in fact, occasion significant doubts about the general meritoriousness of liberalism and its civic virtues were this not the case. It would be a source of proper concern if the liberal virtues were widely conceived as vices by most serious moral traditions. In point of fact, however, champions of the liberal civic virtues may justifiably be encouraged by the appearance of these virtues within other and more comprehensive moral systems. By itself, this fact would not be sufficient to override the impropriety theorem and justify the endorsement and promotion of these virtues—given that some liberal citizens might reject them. The primary justification of all civic virtues—especially so within liberal regimes—must be instrumental, prudential, and "political." But that does not make it irrelevant or inappropriate for civic liberals to invoke as auxiliary grounds for their civic virtues their accreditation by Judeo-Christian, Greek, or Enlightenment moral traditions. Specifically, they may take comfort in noting the Judeo-Christian endorsement of humility and *caritas,* the Socratic endorsement of *eunoia* and the deliberative virtues, Mill's and Kant's endorsement of autonomy and mutual respect, and so on. In this sense and in this context, then, one could say without embarrassment or apology that the liberal civic virtues may be defended as "partially comprehensive" virtues in a positive way and not merely in a *de facto* negative way. Or, as Roberto Alejandro has expressed it, even a resolutely "political" liberalism—a liberalism that properly confines its soulcraft to the specifically civic or political virtues—may be seen as a form of "minimalist perfectionism."[37]

Rawl's attempt to draw a sharp distinction between his putatively political liberalism and John Stuart Mill's allegedly comprehensive liberalism, therefore, turns out to be more misleading than helpful. The difference here is one of degree and not of kind. When push come to shove, even reticent political liberals such as

Rawls will not inappropriately find themselves making (minimally) perfectionist arguments on behalf of their "political" virtues. Thus Rawls concedes that "in affirming a political conception of justice we may eventually have to assert at least certain aspects of our own comprehensive (by no means necessarily fully comprehensive) religious or philosophical doctrine." And he later in the same essay finds himself, in confirmation of this concession, insisting that "the virtues of political cooperation that make a constitutional regime possible are, then, *very great* virtues" (emphasis in original).[38] Even a self-styled political liberal cannot escape the invocation of at least partially comprehensive ethical claims, then, when facing challenges from illiberal or antiliberal quarters. In these instances it is not useful to offer the purely "political" and instrumental argument that the liberal civic virtues should be endorsed because they conduce to the success of liberal regimes. It is precisely the merits of liberal regimes that are at issue.

Promoting and Defending the Liberal Civic Virtues

The conclusions of the argument in the preceding section are that liberal regimes (as distinct from more private associations within them, such as families and churches) should confine their promotion of character and the virtues to the domain of the specifically civic virtues, that these socially useful capacities and character traits should be forthrightly acknowledged and championed even though they are inevitably *de facto* (or as Rawls would say, "in effect") "partially comprehensive," and that liberal regimes may also take encouragement from the appearance of many of their civic virtues within other more comprehensive accounts of human perfection. But how, one might fairly ask, should these virtues be promoted? And how can their active cultivation be defended against recent specific complaints from both postmodernist and traditionalist perspectives that such a policy is improper and hegemonic? In the remainder of this chapter I want to indicate in somewhat summary form what I believe to be the proper response to these queries.

First, how should the liberal civic virtues be promoted? By what agencies should they be promoted and by what means? Judith Shklar is for the most part correct to admonish us, I believe, that the acquisition of a liberal character "is not to be forced or even promoted by the use of political authority."[39] The state is not the best or the most appropriate agent for promoting the liberal civic virtues because of the confluence of several considerations: first the state has a monopoly of legitimate force in the society; second, liberal societies are fallibilist in moral epistemology and respect what Godwin called the "right of private judgment," and third, character development occurs through education and habituation rather than through coercion or indoctrination. Hence, a liberal society is properly very leery of putting the task of moral education and habituation into the hands that hold the sword, as it were. For the use of force is neither effective nor proper in moral socialization. A liberal state is not really in the business of telling its citizens how to be good, even when the virtues in question are political or civic and not comprehensive in their scope and rationale. We don't look to the state as a proper moral tutor, and the powers of the state could not be effectively put to work in this regard even were it proper for them to be so deployed. How, after all, could anyone effectively be commanded to respect others, to be autonomous, to be neighborly, to deliberate candidly and sincerely, to exhibit democratic magnanimity? For reasons both of propriety and of practicality, then, the liberal virtues must be inculcated more by the institutions of civil society than by the state.

Shklar's admonition against the deployment of political authority to promote the liberal civic virtues should not, however, be interpreted or applied in a rigid and absolute way. There are times and ways in which public figures and public institutions may properly and effectively play a role. The prohibition against using force should be firmly adhered to, the maxim that liberal virtues be encouraged only in a liberal manner firmly respected. But these canons of liberal propriety need not, for example, prevent public figures, including officeholders, from using their bully pulpits to praise and encourage displays of civic virtue. There is nothing the matter with the President according recognition and praise to someone of modest means who gives her life savings for a scholarship, for example. And there is nothing wrong with the Speaker of the House wearing a Habitat for Humanity pin and praising the work of members of the organization. If we don't like their judgments about what should be honored as good citizenship, we can criticize them or elect someone else.

It is also acceptable for public institutions involved in the socialization of the young to thematize and seek to foster the liberal civic virtues under the rubric of good citizenship. These institutions, preeminent among them the public schools, should in these endeavors clearly abide by the constraints of both scope and mode entailed by the norms and limits of liberal regimes. Specifically, the virtues or character traits in question must carefully be limited to the civic virtues and not extend to particular comprehensive ethical norms. And any such character education should proceed by example and discussion rather than by some form of heavy-handed indoctrination (which would likely be as ineffective as it would be inappropriate). "Character education" in public schools in a liberal society should not consist in catechizing students in the norms of good citizenship, much less in the norms of being good Christians, good Muslims, or whatever. Instead, it should consist primarily in the school, its teachers, and its staff demonstrating to students by their own actions and procedures how democratic citizens should treat each other: e.g., with respect, with tolerance, with friendship, with candor and honesty, and so on. It also may consist in inviting students to reflect upon these procedural and behavioral norms and the reasons for them.

For some interpreters and critics of liberalism, however, even this kind of social promotion of a particular and contestable conception of civic virtue is deemed improper. It is seen as an immoral, possibly by some standards illiberal, form of social hegemony in which some ways of life are privileged over others. Such practices are therefore condemned as repressive impositions that should be avoided rather than encouraged. How, then, can the endorsement of a specific account of the liberal civic virtues and the admonition to promote them be defended against these charges? Specifically, how can advocacy of the liberal civic virtues be defended first against Foucauldian arguments that such advocacy must be seen as a form of presumptively illicit disciplining and normalization? And second, how can such advocacy be defended against claims from moral traditionalists that it represents the *de facto* imposition of secular humanist norms upon all liberal citizens, including adherents of religious persuasions who consider such norms anathema?

Bonnie Honig's critique of Rawls provides a good example of the first of these lines of argument. I am not here concerned to defend all the particulars of Rawls's argument that come under Honig's indictment. But the generic version of her argument against Rawls's normative conception of democratic personhood and against his account of the political virtues would seem equally pertinent to my civic liberal accounts of civic virtue and good citizenship. Her objections are equally pertinent here not only because the civic liberal does openly what Rawls does only reluctantly and reticently (endorse a civic ethic), but also because some of the elements of Rawls's account of political virtue and good citizenship to which she objects appear in the civic liberal ethic as well: for example, the endorsement of self-restraint and reasonableness. The burden of Honig's complaint is that the promotion of liberal civic virtue results in the exertion of "normalizing pressures" on the members of a liberal society. These pressures are, as in Foucault, construed as intrinsically oppressive *vis-a-vis* human material, which is neither naturally constructed nor spontaneously inclined to conform to the dictates of "normality." And they are, moreover, unequal and discriminatory in their impact: they bear more heavily against some people—against some character types—than they do against others.

Honig worries in particular about the treatment within a liberal regime of those she styles as "irresponsible rogues and idiosyncratic misfits." These become, in her view, "silenced others" in Rawls's well-ordered society. "What is it like," she ponders, for those who are "odd" or "underachievers" to "live among these [Rawlsian] citizens, with their . . . rational capacities and their confidence in their own ways of life?"[40] "What about promiscuity, spontaneity, experimentation, the will to live in the present? The promiscuous or spontaneous subject is not as supported by the regime as are Rawls's rational deliberators. Deliberative rationality is a voluntary activity but one held in high—and public—esteem. Although rational deliberation is an option, not a requirement, there is nonetheless some moral pressure to conform with its requirements."[41] And what about that curious figure Rawls conjures up in *A Theory of Justice,* the fellow whose life occupation, whose personal understanding of the good life, is to sit in the park and count blades of grass? Isn't he consigned to the fate of a Rodney Dangerfield? He just doesn't get any respect: "those (like Rawls's grass counter) who deviate from [the society's] norms find that their rights are protected but that they themselves are (at best) disrespected."[42]

The basic answer to these complaints is simply to say that the stance Honig attributes to Rawls *vis-a-vis* the rogues and misfits is entirely the proper one: their rights are protected but they themselves are not honored for or encouraged in their promiscuity, irresponsibility, or mindlessly neurotic compulsions. There is an important ambiguity or bivalence in the term "respect" that needs unpacking here. These odd or rebellious characters are indeed "respected" by the society precisely in having their rights protected: they are recognized as moral equals, as beings who possess human dignity and integrity, as autonomous moral agents. What they do not receive is "respect" in the sense of "honor." Their behavior and their character traits are not in fact those most conducive to the flourishing of the liberal public order, and there is accordingly no legitimate basis for the rogues and misfits to demand that their fellow citizens confer honor upon them.

The demand or the moral expectation upon which Honig's complaint—and, for that matter, a great deal of Foucauldian social criticism—is predicated turns out upon reflection to be not only wildly unrealistic but substantively incoherent. First, misled by their pan-political effacement of the distinction between the personal and the political, those who levy this demand fail to recognize that, in the words of Richard Rorty, "the sort of autonomy which self-creating ironists like Nietzsche, Derrida, or Foucault seek is not the sort of thing that could ever be embodied in social institutions." At least some of the conduct of a Nietzschean quest, of creating oneself in the mode of a "strong poet," has to "be reserved for private life."[43] By respecting their rights, a liberal society gives strong poets—and rogues and misfits—the necessary social space to fashion their life projects; but a liberal regime cannot leave its public sphere and its own norms to be a function of these plural and changeable life projects. It is not realistic to expect or proper to ask any regime, liberal or otherwise, to undermine itself by according honor and support indiscriminately both to practices and forms of character that sustain it and to those that either do not do so or that positively weaken it.

Honig's complaint is, moreover, incoherent in the sense that it fails to understand that by its very nature honor is not something that can be conferred universally or indiscriminately. This is a misconception Rawls invites, to be sure, as a consequence of his inclusion of self-respect as a primary good—hence something "at the disposition of society." But it is a misconception nonetheless. The fact is that honor is intrinsically relative and this in two respects. It is relative, first, in the sense of being contingent upon the value of the human purposes the promotion of which occasion it. And it is relative, second, in the sense that some people and some actions will inevitably contribute more than others to the attainment of these purposes. If a society accords equal honor to all actions, it has no purposes. If it honors everything, it honors nothing. Hence, any "respect" of the sort demanded by Honig that it might confer would eventually lose all value. This process of the self-deconstructing of honor *via* its indiscriminate universalization is something, indeed, that all of us have witnessed at one time or another. Words of praise from someone who, it turns out, is utterly undiscriminating and who has only good words for any and all lose their currency altogether. When a child perceives that the nice lady down the street who had good words about him or her would compliment the little pyromaniac next door for creating a pretty glow when he torched his house, then that child will henceforth exhibit not only a lack of appreciation but active disdain for any future praise from that source. Honig's criticism of the discriminatory impact and putatively "normalizing pressure" of a liberal regime's affirmation and promotion of the civic virtues that sustain it, then, may be an understandable lament: it is indeed a pity that whoever we are and whatever we desire to do are not necessarily of great value to our peers and to our society. But her criticism is not a valid indictment because it asks the impossible and the incoherent. Any attempt to hand out some kind of awards for "best blade counter" or "most promiscuous" would occasion hilarity rather than respect—and rightly so.

Honig may well be right to charge Rawls with aspiring to what she calls "a politics without remainders."[44] He clearly wishes to consign a large part of what ordinarily is thought to be the subject matter of political contestation to pre- or postpolitical determination—to a consensus about fundamental distributive rules that attains quasi-constitutional status and to judicial and bureaucratic decisions. But her complaints about the impropriety and oppressiveness of promoting the liberal civic virtues should be rejected. A liberal society is perfectly justified in saying to its "irresponsible rogues and idiosyncratic misfits" something like the following: "You have all the very considerable rights and privileges of citizenship in our democratic society. Pursuant to our respect for personal autonomy, our recognition of the fallibility of practical reason, and our belief in the sanctity of the private sphere, we are happy to accord you the space to do your thing. But we have no reason and are under no obligation to accord you honor, and we have no incentive to encourage others to behave as you do. We are trying to build and sustain what we consider to be a well-ordered society; and in pursuit of that goal we are prudentially required and morally entitled to promote those traits of character and those excellences among our citizens that will conduce to our success in this venture."

The response may be even a bit more pointed than that. Honig's complaint, it could be argued, trades upon a systematically misleading tendency to abstract character traits and identities from their social contexts. Social critics influenced by Foucault and Derrida seem at times not only to romanticize social deviants but also to avert their gaze entirely from the likely social consequences of the character types whose marginalization concerns them. Promoting the liberal civic virtues, whether in Rawls's account of the political virtues or in an account like the one in this chapter, accordingly becomes depicted as a kind of irrational and inappropriate privileging of the dull and stodgy above the gay and spirited. "There is little room here," Honig complains, "for the Nietzschean 'spirit who plays naively'—that is, not deliberately but from overflowing power and abundance."[45] But this is a delusion occasioned by decontextualization. Whether Rawls prefers stodgy folk to free spirits I do not know. I don't. The reason the liberal virtues may sound like the stigmata of the dull and repressed has nothing to do with personal style of life and everything to do with the fact that it is the impact of one's actions on others—on the society as whole—that drives the content of conceptions of civic virtue. Hence the emphasis on such apparently stodgy traits as responsibility, self-restraint, humility, toleration, and the like.

Conversely, the civic liberal regime's proper response to what Honig calls "the promiscuous or spontaneous subject" depends upon the social contextualization not provided in her complaint. The proper response does not turn around the subject's attitude; it turns around the actions engendered by that lifestyle—and in particular by the consequences these actions have for the lives of other citizens. If "promiscuity, spontaneity, experimentation, and the will to live in the present" mean simply that one lives with artistic flair and is a great party animal, then there is no problem pertinent to good social policy or to a desirable social ethos. No civic liberal commisar—and I presume no Rawlsian apparatchik either—will appear to try to browbeat "the promiscuous and spontaneous subject" into being less poetic and fun-loving. If, however, promiscuity entails the production of progeny for whom the spontaneous subject takes no responsibility or entails the heedless transmission of the AIDS virus, if spontaneity means driving while intoxicated down the wrong side of the highway, if the will to live in the present means leaving others to provide for your old age, then the tolerance, neutrality, and generosity of the civic liberal regime has reached its limit. Any liberal society, perhaps any decent society—must incorporate into its behavioral norms some version of Mill's harm principle and some fair terms of social cooperation. Just as actions that violate these principles are properly sanctionable, so the character traits that produce the violations may not only legitimately not be celebrated or honored, but they may be positively disdained and discouraged.

From the quarter of moral traditionalism comes a formally parallel but substantively very different version of what I have called the "impropriety theorem." Like Honig, the traditionalists argue that promoting liberal civic virtue is morally improper and politically hegemonic. Rather than worrying about the discouragement and disrespect putatively directed by a liberal ethos toward rogues and misfits, however, their complaint is that promoting a liberal conception of civic virtues oppresses and discriminates against adherents of objective morality. The liberal ethic, in this view, directly contradicts the convictions and self-understanding of moral traditionalists and absolutists by presupposing a decisionist, secularist, relativist, and hedonistic account of the human good. In one sense, this is the direct opposite of the post-Nietzechean critique: the latter deems defenders of liberal virtue to be insufficiently and inconsistently decisionist—and hence to be inadequately generous and tolerant. The traditionalists, in contrast, see defenders of liberal virtue as dogmatically decisionist—and hence as genial nihilists who behave oppressively toward those who believe in an objective human good. Both camps, however, find the content of the liberal virtues objectionable and see their promulgation as an oppressive imposition upon them and their cohorts.

The proper response to these traditionalist concerns, I believe, is as follows. First, it is emphatically not the case that the civic liberal conception of the civic virtues constitutes a secularist or a relativist ethic, much less that it forces secularism or relativism upon liberal citizens. It is a secular ethic, in the sense that it applies to this world and not to a world to come, to the City of Man and not to the City of God, to the public sphere and not to our private pursuits or convictions. It is a political and not a comprehensive ethic in Rawls's sense of those adjectives. It consists of norms intended to regulate and facilitate peaceful accommodation and

social cooperation among people who have different convictions about the meaning of life but who must cohabit politically. No tenet of the liberal civic virtues
forces a particular account of the meaning of life upon anyone. That forbearance
does not imply that there is no such meaning or that there is no objective truth
about the human good. It simply recognizes that the liberal regime is not competent to make that determination and that it therefore has no warrant to impose
such a determination upon any of its citizens.

Similarly, liberal civic virtue is "relative" to the specific, substantive, and contestable purposes and values of the liberal polity. It does not understand itself and
should not present itself as moral truth incarnate, as a definitive account of what
is good for human beings universally and absolutely. But that is not at all the same
thing as embracing or implying the truth of moral relativism, which is, in fact one
version of precisely the kind of universalist ethical stance that the liberal civic
virtues do not pretend to embody. And the civic liberal account of the civic virtues
is certainly not consistent with, much less an incarnation of, a hedonist ethic. The
traditionalist complaint has an object, but it is not liberalism, at least not a liberalism properly understood and properly practiced. One can indeed argue that
mature capitalism tends to generate a consumerist ethos of self-gratification. And,
of course, this development may in a sense be laid at liberalism's door, since liberal regimes—for both moral and prudential reasons—rely at least to some extent
on market mechanisms and incentives in the economic sphere. But a consumerist
ethos and a liberal ethic are decidedly not the same thing. Instead, as Daniel Bell
has convincingly observed, capitalist consumerism is in important respects profoundly at odds with core norms and patterns of moral habituation historically
associated with and important to the continued health of liberal societies.[46] It is
not only moral traditionalists who worry about the moral failures and the disin-
tegrative consequences of consumerist hedonism: defenders of the liberal virtues
properly and logically worry about them, as well. Stephen Macedo therefore must
be seen, from the perspective of civic liberalism, to have overreached himself and
given an unfortunate and distorted depiction of the liberal character and the liberal virtues when he writes that "liberalism holds out the promise, or the threat, of
making all the world like California," including the favoring of character traits
such as inconstancy ("Liberalism creates a community in which it is possible to
decide that next week I might quit my career in banking, leave my wife and children, and join a Buddhist cult"), "superficiality, self-absorption, or even narcissism."[47] This account confuses character traits properly privileged by liberalism as
civic virtues with traits that may result from a capitalist economic system with its
pressures toward commodification or from a decisionist metaphysical or moral
doctrine.

The charges of enforced secularism, relativism, and/or hedonism are not, then,
sustainable complaints *vis-a-vis* the civic liberal account of the civic virtues. That
does not mean, however, that Catholic, Protestant, and natural-law-affirming
critics of liberal society such as Francis Canavan, Stephen Carter, and the editors
of the journal *First Things* do not have some legitimate complaints to make about
a secularist assault against religious communities and people of faith that gets car-

ried on through liberal institutions and under the guise of liberal values.[48] Their complaints may not be properly directed at the kind of liberal regime depicted and defended in this book. But they are neither delusionary nor paranoid: they have real enemies out there. One influential subset of the liberal elites in our society does in effect function as a crusading secularist party (Stephen Macedo calls them "evangelical atheists") who seeks to marginalize religious faith and institutions and to proselytize against them in the public schools and elsewhere.[49] These evangelical atheists or crusading secularists believe, *inter alia*, that conceptions of the good are social or personal constructs, that sexual persuasions are morally indifferent, that science disproves the idea of a Creator God, and so on. Resistance to these beliefs is construed as benighted, "bigoted," and "undemocratic." Public educators, these evangelical atheists therefore believe, are perfectly justified in instructing their captive audiences accordingly and in denigrating any contrary beliefs held by their students' parents and churches.

Nothing in civic liberalism, including its account of the civic virtues, provides any legitimacy or justification for such a secularist project and such proselytizing endeavors. On the contrary, conducting such a crusade directly violates the civic liberal insistence upon democratic humility, democratic magnanimity, and respect for the dignity and autonomy of fellow citizens. As Macedo pointedly and properly observes, "children from religious families are not the only ones who need lessons in tolerance."[50] Permitting public institutions to function as coercive (via school attendance laws and tax policies) and authoritative venues for promoting such comprehensively secularist moral views, moreover, represents a clear violation of the spirit and logic of the establishment clause. It is no more proper for someone standing in front of the public school classroom, vested with state authority, to make pronouncements about contested matters of sexual morality, say, than it is for that person to lead prayers or to make pronouncements that Jesus is the "one true way." Either way, the state lends its authority to the imposition of contestable and comprehensive moral views upon unwilling subjects who have every right to be protected against such coercive proselytizing.

(In this context, I would even say that civic liberals, without necessarily endorsing their demands, should nevertheless accord respect to some of the complaints voiced by the fundamentalist plaintiffs in the widely discussed case of *Mozert v. Hawkins County Board of Education*, 827 F.2d 1058 (6th Cir., 1987). The plaintiffs in this case were unhappy that their elementary school children were required to participate in a reading program in which the text included some 47 stories referring to or growing out of religions. Of the religions involved in these 47 stories, as one of the judges observed," only three were Christian, and none Protestant." In the context of a country that historically has been dominantly Christian and Protestant these statistics are quite remarkable. The superintendent of the Hawkins County schools was either ingenuous or deliberately deceptive in claiming that the program in question simply taught "reading, not values." The federal court and Stephen Macedo (in "Liberal Civic Education," cited above), in contrast, defended the text as a reasonable way of teaching the students tolerance by "exposing [them] to diversity." Civic liberalism encourages the promotion of liberal civic virtues, and tolerance—properly conceived—is one of those. But there is a serious question here, I would argue, regarding the wisdom and the moral propriety of using such a text for such young children under the guise of teaching reading skills. Democratic humility and magnanimity require respect for and forbearance toward the considered moral and religious convictions of our fellow citizens. And it seems very hard to square such respect and forbearance with using this kind of text, with its clear implicit challenge to particular religious convictions, for such young students. Later on, when students are more mature and have time both to assimilate and reflect upon the beliefs in which they were raised, using such a text would be much more pedagogically appropriate. I would endorse in this context the sensitivity to the complexities and nuances of legitimate liberal authority in the socialization and education of children exhibited in the chapter on "Liberal Education" in Bruce Ackerman's *Social Justice in the Liberal State.* I would commend to uncritical defenders of the Hawkins County reading program and other similar efforts the dialogue on pages 142–143 of that work. Ackerman's conclusion is that "during the early years of secondary education, the curriculum must be especially respectful of the strong parental interest in continuing control over the child. Hence, the early stages of a liberal curriculum will content themselves with the elaboration of life options relatively close to those with which the child is already familiar." Only later on, Ackerman writes, "as the child ages and parental interest in control declines, a firm foundation will have been laid for confrontations with cultural forms that provide more challenging interpretations of the youths' evolving pattern of resistances and affirmations."[51])

One last objection sometimes raised from the ranks of moral objectivists or communities of faith deserves a bit more attention. People of faith and moral absolutists do not understand their moral commitments in a voluntarist way. They do not see themselves as "choosing," much less as "constructing," their moral obligations. Rather, they experience these obligations as due submission to claims and demands placed upon them from the outside—from the natural moral order or from God. In Michael Sandel's words, they "regard themselves as claimed by religious commitments they have not chosen."[52] Is, then, the civic liberal insistence upon the promotion of autonomy and the deliberative virtues violative of this self-understanding? And does this insistence impinge illegitimately and destructively upon—i.e., is it oppressive toward—religious communities within the liberal state? I believe the answer is no.

In addressing these questions, it is crucial to keep in mind two important differences between a "decisionist" conception of autonomy and the kind of autonomy defended by civic liberalism. First, decisionism is grounded in a specific metaphysic—one that is incompatible with religious conceptions of the world; the civic liberal conception is not. Decisionism presupposes a neo-Kantian metaphysic that depicts the objective would as itself devoid of moral content. Life has, apart from human choice, no moral meaning. It "runs on as an event in nature," to use the words of Max Weber. Moral meanings, then, do not derive from a purportedly purely heteronomous natural order but from "a series of ultimate decisions through which the soul chooses its own fate, i.e., the meaning of its activity and existence."[53] It is understandable that believers in God and in natural law cannot accept such a metaphysic, which would have to appear as both false and blasphemous to them. But the civic liberal account of autonomy is not dependent on such a doctrine. Second, civic liberalism understands autonomy as a constitutive good, not as a teleological good. It does not claim, then, that unconstrained choice provides the content of the good human life. It is not tied to the claim that the moral hero is someone who—like Weber's Atlas, Sartre's Orestes, or postmodernism's strong poet—produces the meaning of his or her life through an act of radically free self-determination. Civic liberal autonomy has none of these cosmic dimensions. It does not mandate moral constructivism in lieu of gods; it only mandates political self-governance in defiance of domination by other people. Decisionist autonomy seeks to make good a presumed absence of moral meaning in the cosmos. Civic liberal autonomy seeks only to prevent the exercise of absolute and arbitrary power in the polis.

The autonomy insisted upon and promoted by civic liberalism then—together with the capacity for deliberative reflection that accompanies and sustains it—is not inconsistent with or oppressive toward religious convictions or legitimate religious practices. It is not incompatible with "regarding oneself as claimed by religious commitments that one has not chosen," to recall Sandel's characterization. Instead, it merely insists upon creating and defending the conditions in which and the capacities by virtue of which anyone could coherently be said to "regard oneself" as anything. "Choosing" in the decisionistic sense is not presumed by civic liberalism to be the substance of the good life. What civic liberalism presumes, instead, is that having some capacity for self-determination—a capacity which may perfectly legitimately be exercised in knowing and willing submission to moral demands by which one sees oneself as "claimed"—is a necessary part of having a life at all: having a human life, that is, rather than existing as an artifact or responding uncomprehendingly and unquestioningly to impulse or outside determination.

The only religious practices that would run afoul of civic liberal commitments and demands, then, would be practices which are effectively cultic. The civic liberal insistence upon society's obligation to assist in cultivating their citizens' capacities for self-governance poses no threat to communities of faith or to religious people. It only poses a threat to those religious people who seek—whether from sincere religious motives or not—to exercise absolute and permanent dominion over their fellow citizens, including their parishioners or their children. Liberalism was born in and remains today animated by its fundamental opposition to the exercise of absolute and arbitrary power by one human being over another. The authority of God is another matter entirely. Liberalism sets itself not against God's dominion over those of its citizens who recognize and accept it. It sets itself instead against anyone—including those inspired by or under the cover of religion—who seek to play God with the lives of others.[54]

There is much about the culture of contemporary liberal societies to cause legitimate dismay to people of faith. The tendency of modernity and mature capitalism to foster concupiscence, hedonism, egoism, narcissism, sexual antinomianism,

and impiety can understandably lead adherents of the traditional religions to conclude that what might be called, in a pardonable if somewhat misleading ellipsis,
"liberal culture" is slouching toward Gomorrah—that it is a civilization moving
"towards chaos, not order; towards breakdown, not stability; towards death, destruction, and darkness, not life, creativity, and light."[55] And religious communities
have legitimate grounds for complaint against some forms of liberalism: not only
against comprehensively secularist liberalism but also against versions of political
liberalism that use overly stringent and/or tendentious definitions of reasonableness to silence or confute them. But there are, I have argued here, no legitimate
grounds for people of faith to complain about civic liberalism or about the civic
virtues it espouses. In the context of a pluralist society, a civic liberal regime would
give to religious communities the most they could legitimately ask for and the best
they could reasonably hope for. The ethical commitments of civic liberalism do not
contradict their religious values, and a civic liberal regime would both defend them
against Macedo's "evangelical atheists" and give them the social space to live in accordance with their beliefs.

The civic liberal virtues do not add up to human virtue *tout court*. And the
civic liberal regime is not the City of God. People of faith must always seek to govern their lives in accord with moral norms more expansive and specific to their
beliefs than any political ethic could properly be. What the civic liberal regime
provides is room for them to form their religious communities and to work out
their salvation in compliance with their understanding of God's mandate—just as
it provides a setting for "strong poets" to pursue their Nietzschean quests and for
all other citizens to seek happiness in their own ways. What the civic liberal virtues
do is sustain a political order that accords these pursuits integrity and allows them
to flourish.

Notes

1. Aristotle, *Politics*, 1276b.
2. John Stuart Mill, *Considerations on Representative Government* (Chicago: Henry Regnery, 1962), 5.
3. Immanuel Kant, "Perpetual Peace," in *Perpetual Peace and Other Essays*, trans. Ted Humphrey (Indianapolis: Hackett, 1983), 124.
4. James Madison, *Federalist*, #55.
5. See David Boonin-Vail, *Thomas Hobbes and the Science of Moral Virtue* (Cambridge: Cambridge University Press, 1994).
6. Kautz, *Liberalism and Community*, x; Shklar, *Ordinary Vices*, 5.
7. "Keep in mind here," writes Rawls, "that the political virtues are identified and justified by the need for certain qualities of character in the citizens of a just and stable constitutional regime. . . . They characterize the ideal of the good citizen of a democratic state."
Political Liberalism, 194–95.
8. Rawls, *Political Liberalism*, 194.
9. Macedo, *Liberal Virtues;* Galston, *Liberal Purposes,* esp. chapter 10.
10. Galston, *Liberal Purposes*, 217.
11. Rawls, *Political Liberalism*, 152.

12. See Sandel's account of this linkage in *Liberalism and the Limits of Justice,* 175–77. The notable exceptions to this general pattern of reticence are Galston and Macedo. See Galston, "Defending Liberalism," *American Political Science Review* 76, no. 3 (September 1982): 621–29; and Macedo, *Liberal Virtue,* 254–63.

13. Samuel Scheffler, "Responsibility, Reactive Attitudes, and Liberalism in Philosophy and Politics," *Philosophy and Public Affairs* 21, no. 4 (Fall 1992): 300–314.

14. Connolly, *Identity\Difference,* 116.

15. Connolly, *Identity\Difference,* 116.

16. Galston, "Defending Liberalism," 625.

17. John Stuart Mill, *On Liberty* (Indianapolis: Bobbs–Merrill, 1956), 95–96.

18. David Hume, "An Enquiry Concerning the Principles of Morals," in *Moral and Political Philosophy,* ed. Henry D. Aiken (New York: MacMillan, 1948), 220.

19. See Michael Polanyi, *Personal Knowledge* (Chicago: University of Chicago Press, 1958), esp. chapter 8.

20. Macedo, *Liberal Virtues,* 59, 41.

21. Macedo, *Liberal Virtues,* 115.

22. Jurgen Habermas, "What Is Universal Pragmatics?" in *Communication and the Evolution of Society,* trans. Thomas McCarthy (Boston: Beacon, 1979), 27.

23. Polanyi, *Personal Knowledge,* 65.

24. Again, Michael Polanyi is a valuable resource here. See *The Tacit Dimension* (Garden City, N.Y.: Doubleday, 1967).

25. Fishkin's account is found in his *The Dialogue of Justice: Toward a Self-Reflective Society* (New Haven: Yale University Press, 1992). Gutmann's words are found in her *Democratic Education* (Princeton: Princeton University Press, 1987), 51.

26. For an elaboration of these dynamics, see my *Reason and Democracy,* 134–39.

27. See for example his "Reply to Habermas," *The Journal of Philosophy* 92, no. 3 (March 1995): 132–80. At one point in this essay, Rawls uses the word "reasonable" or some variant twenty-seven times in two pages.

28. Rawls, "Reply to Habermas," 150.

29. Rawls, *Political Liberalism,* 243.

30. Perhaps this suspicion is unfair to Rawls. The problem is that he makes it so desperately difficult to know exactly where the parameters of "reasonableness" are when it comes to these issues of political morality and public policy.

On behalf of the inference that Rawls seeks to use the rubric of reasonableness to privilege his views on abortion and distributive justice, one can cite his characterization of opposition to a first trimester abortion right as "unreasonable." And one can note the various characterizations in *Political Liberalism* and elsewhere that led Michael Sandel to conclude that regarding disagreements about distributive justice, "Rawls's reply must be that, although there is a fact of pluralism about distributive justice, there is no fact of *reasonable* pluralism. Unlike disagreements about morality and religion, disagreements about the validity of the difference principle are not reasonable." Sandel, "Political Liberalism," *Harvard Law Review* 107 (1994): 1784.

Since Sandel wrote these words and since I first drafted this chapter, Rawls has written a second introduction to *Political Liberalism* that seems to back off from these characterizations, but only partially and still without fully clarifying the parameters of the term "reasonable." Indeed, he there introduces new categories, such as "for the moment reasonable," whose parameters and criteria are themselves left inadequately defined. The difference principle is now styled as the "most reasonable" conception of distributive justice, but not the only reasonable conception. Any reasonable conception, however, must at least "guar-

antee for everyone a sufficient level of adequate all-purpose means;" so libertarian conceptions, as Sandel suggested, indeed do seem to stand disqualified as unreasonable—as perhaps do current welfare policies in this country, depending upon what "sufficient level" and
"adequate" are taken to mean.

His dicta on abortion rights Rawls now says constituted an "opinion" but not an argument. But he asserts the belief that "a more detailed interpretation" of certain political values he supports in *Political Liberalism* "may, when properly developed at public reason,
yield a reasonable argument. I don't say the most reasonable or decisive argument; I don't
know what that would be, or even if it exists." He then cites an article in favor of abortion
rights by Judith Jarvis Thompson but says he would "want to add several addenda to it,"
which he does not specify. ("Introduction" to paperback edition of *Political Liberalism,*
xlviii–xlix, lv–lvi.) This kind of formulation is not very helpful. It says, in effect: Don't ac-
cuse me of calling your position unreasonable, even though I said it was, because I never
gave you an argument to that effect. But I will assert a belief that I could make such an argument if I really wanted to, although I will neither do so here nor provide clear criteria of
what counts as reasonable and what doesn't.

31. Hobbes, *Leviathan,* part one, chapter 15.

32. Mill, *Considerations,* 72–73.

33. Amy Gutmann and Dennis Thompson, *Democracy and Disagreement* (Cambridge:
Harvard University Press, 1996), 82–85.

34. Aristotle, *Politics,* 1277b.

35. Mill, *Considerations,* 55, 32.

36. See Charles Larmore, *Moral Complexity* (Cambridge: Cambridge University Press,
1987).

37. Roberto Alejandro, "What Is Political about Rawls's Political Liberalism?" *Journal of
Politics* 58, no. 1 (February 1996): 17. Rawls essentially concedes this point when he acknowledges that political liberalism is not and cannot be neutral in its effects vis-a-vis
competing comprehensive moral doctrines even if it "hopes to satisfy neutrality of aim"
(*Political Liberalism,* 194).

38. Rawls, "The Idea of an Overlapping Consensus," (ms version), 18, 22. See also *Political Liberalism,* 152.

39. Shklar, *Ordinary Vices,* 5.

40. Bonnie Honig, *Political Theory and the Politics of Displacement* (Ithaca: Cornell University Press, 1993), 149.

41. Honig, *Politics of Displacement,* 151.

42. Honig, *Politics of Displacement,* 130.

43. Richard Rorty, *Contingency, Irony, and Solidarity* (Cambridge: Cambridge University Press, 1989), 65.

44. Honig, *Politics of Displacement,* 127.

45. Honig, *Politics of Displacement,* 154.

46. Daniel Bell, *The Cultural Contradictions of Capitalism* (New York: Basic Books,
1976).

47. Macedo, *Liberal Virtues,* 278.

48. See, for example, Francis Canavan, *The Pluralist Game* (Lanham, Md.: Rowman &
Littlefield, 1995); and Stephen Carter, *The Culture of Disbelief: How American Law and Politics Trivialize Religious Devotion* (New York: Basic Books, 1993).

49. Stephen Macedo, "Liberal Civic Education and Religious Fundamentalism: The
Case of God v. John Rawls," *Ethics* 105, no. 3 (April 1995): 487.

50. Macedo, "Liberal Civic Education," 487.

51. Ackerman, *Social Justice in the Liberal State,* 157.

52. Sandel, *Democracy's Discontent,* 65.

53. Max Weber, "The Meaning of 'Ethical Neutrality,'" 18.

54. Demands by devout parents or by communities of faith to be allowed to "protect" their charges by preventing them from developing or exercising a will of their own, it can be argued, are as indefensible theologically as they are indefensible politically by liberal and democratic standards. Consider in this context the pertinent query of John Locke: even assuming that there is "but one truth," he wrote, "what hope is there that more men would be led into it if they . . . were put under the necessity to quit the light of their own consciences, and blindly to resign themselves to the will of their governors and to the religion which either ignorance, ambition, or superstition had chanced to establish in the countries where they were born?" It would "ill suit the notion of a Deity," he continued, that "men would owe their eternal happiness or misery to the places of their nativity." Locke's remarks were directed at state mandated religious observances, but they apply equally to overreaching religious authorities. John Locke, *A Letter Concerning Toleration* (Indianapolis: Bobbs–Merrrill, 1950), 19–20 and 35.

55. Malcolm Muggeridge, "The Great Liberal Death Wish," in *The Portable Conservative Reader,* ed. Russell Kirk (New York: Penguin Books, 1982), 611.

Conclusion: A Civic Liberal Agenda

Hazards attend any attempt to generate concrete recommendations about policies and institutions from the necessarily more general and abstract specification of broad social goals. The complexities, uncertainties, and obduracies of the real world intervene and disrupt any neat and unequivocal practical inferences. We can move from aspirations to tactics only by wading into murky and contestable issues of social fact and causal relationships. Philosophers can talk about moral principles and human goods on their own, but they can become political counselors only with the aid of political scientists, sociologists, economists, and psychologists. And since these students of social dynamics are often in deep disagreement, no exercise in political casuistry can be anything but precarious.

These dangers conceded, it nonetheless seems imperative—upon pain of suspicions of irrelevancy—to say something about the practical differences it might make to adopt the conception of democratic purposes I have championed in the preceding chapters. Moreover, I would argue that these differences are real and in some cases quite significant. It is not merely an academic question whether we should be guided by the precepts of civic liberalism or by one of the currently more prevalent variants of democratic ideals. These differences manifest themselves in the area of specific social policies, and they also have an important bearing on the way we should understand the powers and duties of the liberal state and the rights and responsibilities of liberal citizenship. In many important cases, the normative structure of civic liberalism leads us toward policies that diverge from the usual left/right alternatives. Moreover, taken as a whole the civic liberal responses do not fall into some set position on the conventional ideological spectrum. What is important to insist here is that this pattern is indicative not of confusion or incoherence within the civic liberal perspective but rather of the poverty and inadequacy of the conventional notion of a unidimensional ideological spectrum defined by laissez-faire at one end and statist egalitarianism at the other. That notion of unidimensional ideological space is, in fact, itself a factor in reinforcing the poverty of much public policy analysis in contemporary liberal society: it tends to force us into choices between oversimplified and stylized strategies that fit into established ideological pigeonholes rather than to open the field to more complex strategies which take multiple social goals seriously.

When it comes to welfare policy for example, the impulse of egalitarian liberals is to advocate greater generosity toward recipients. These recipients seem to fall naturally into the category of "the disadvantaged," and the egalitarian imperative—whether it be simply to maximize equality of results or to apply the difference principle—is to enhance the economic standing of the less well-off. Libertarians, in contrast, emphasize the entitlement of everyone to their earned or freely given economic assets and the moral and tactical advantage of letting the market discipline behavior and allocate resources. Egalitarians seek to maximize welfare allocations, possibly in the form of a guaranteed minimum income. Libertarians seek to minimize such reallocations and would accomplish those that remain through mechanisms, such as a negative income tax, that leave market forces in play as much as possible.

The civic liberal norms of autonomy, civic equality, and civic friendship lead in a different direction. From the civic liberal perspective, the greatest evils of the welfare system—apart from the way that it blights the life prospects of the children caught within it—are captured by the terms "dependency" and "underclass." Dependency denotes the absence of the capacity—whether circumstantial or internalized—for genuine self-governance on the part of the recipient population. And the concept of an underclass signifies the deep rupture of basic civic equality between the recipient population and the larger populace. The damage to civic equality in turn seriously erodes the prospects of civic friendship, since mutual respect and a basic equality of status are prerequisites of the latter good.

Dedicated to citizen autonomy and to civic equality and impelled by civic friendship—which obliges us to "wish for the good of the other" (Aristotle, *Ethics*, VIII, 3) and to come to each other's assistance—civic liberals would seek neither to expand nor to contract our system of welfare provision so much as to transform it. The truly incompetent and disabled we shall always have with us, and they will require direct support sufficient to accord them dignity and freedom from genuine want. For everyone else, the goal should be inclusion within the institutions of economic production, together with the human dignity, social status, economic self-sufficiency, political purchase, and personal responsibility that inclusion entails. To pursue these ends, it would be necessary to allocate significant resources to job creation and/or provision, to child care subsidies, to job counseling, and to job training programs. It is likely that, in the short run at least, making provision for these services will be more costly than simply doling out cash subsidies at the current level. Down the road, these policies would probably lead to social savings for a whole host of reasons. But even if that were not the case, even if such a transformation of the welfare system were an economic loser, that approach would be worthwhile nonetheless. For the goods aspired to are not merely economic benefits but the larger social benefits of autonomy, civic equality, and civic friendship. Even if there were to be a permanent economic price to be paid rather than a temporary one for orienting welfare policy this way, it would be—by the civic liberal calculus—a price well worth paying.

The same general principles bear upon the question of social security reform, an issue that becomes increasingly more imperative to face. The current system with its financing methods, its eligibility criteria, and its payment levels was a product of demographic assumptions that no longer apply. Accordingly, corrections and adjustments are no longer avoidable. Once again, however, the leading reform strategies generated by libertarian and egalitarian norms are, by civic liberal standards, inappropriate and counterproductive. Libertarians predictably counsel a policy of privatization. They would abandon a system of common provision in favor of private and individualized pensions. Many of those with egalitarian sympathies, on the other hand, would seek to preserve and amplify the current system's redistributive effects while making it actuarily more viable by turning social security into a means-tested program.

From the civic liberal perspective, neither of these reform strategies is desirable and each would send messages that would reverberate destructively throughout the society. The privatization strategy would inevitably intensify rather than mitigate the effects of economic inequality on the disparate retirement lives of rich and poor. And it clearly conveys the message that even where it comes to providing for the needs of our aged population the basic rule is everyone for himself or herself. The sense of civic equality and the bonds of civic friendship would clearly be damaged by such a policy. And that damage in turn would impact negatively upon attitudes, behavior, and institutions that sustain a strong civil society.

Converting social security into another means-based program would be equally damaging in other ways. The system would no longer be one of common provision for a universal need, a system in which all contribute during their productive years and all benefit during their retirement years. It would no longer be a sign and symbol of common interest and mutual responsibility. Instead it would be transformed and degraded into another "welfare" program that takes from Peter and gives to Paul, a system that, rather than embodying our unity and commonality, instead establishes and reifies the division of the citizenry into a class of productive donors and one of insufficiently competent charity cases. Sending social security checks to financially comfortable retirees may not seem sensible when measured by a short-term utilitarian calculus, by criteria of straightforward need, or by egalitarian conceptions of distributive justice. But the symbolic value of fulfilling the established social obligation to contribute to the retirements of all those who have done the same for others during their work lives is enormous: it enhances the perceived legitimacy of the system, it forestalls any stigma that might otherwise attach to recipient status, it testifies to and reinforces social solidarity, and it sustains support for a system of old-age provision that carries justifiable redistributive consequences. The dollars saved by means-testing would be fool's gold.

The civic liberal imperative, then, would be to preserve the basic commitment to a scheme of common provision for all citizens in their postproductive years.

This commitment is what should be nonnegotiable. Exactly how that commitment can best be carried out, however, is a matter for prudential calculation to decide—with the best economic advice available. It might be possible, for example, to maintain the main features of the current pay-as-you-go system, making the necessary adjustments by some combination of raising the eligibility age for benefits, raising or eliminating the ceiling on income subject to the social security tax, treating all social security receipts as taxable income, and somewhat flattening the differences in benefit levels. Alternatively, it may make more economic sense, as Martin Feldstein has argued, to convert to a prefunded system.[1] And some portion of that system could even be composed of individualized accounts. Besides the putative economic advantages, such a partial quasi-privatizing of the system could have the collateral benefits of bolstering personal responsibility and enhancing citizens' sense of being stakeholders in the national economy. What must strenuously be avoided, however, would be either the abandonment of common responsibility for the aged and infirm or the conversion of that enterprise of mutual support among civic equals into a means-tested charitable benefaction from one class to another. For either of those strategies—the one sometimes championed by the right and the other by the left—would seriously damage our aspirations to maintain and strengthen the civic equality and the civic friendship fundamental to a truly well-ordered liberal democratic regime.

In the areas of health care and immigration policy, the civic liberal perspective points toward positions remarkably similar to those articulated by Michael Walzer in his *Spheres of Justice.* Or perhaps the similarity here is not so remarkable after all. For although Walzer styles his general logic of justification as a conventionalist appeal to "shared understandings," a close look at the more specific arguments he makes and the more specific and substantive criteria he invokes in these cases reveals his reliance upon the same norms of civic friendship and strong citizenship that distinguish civic liberalism from its rivals. The deployment of these norms as relevant policy criteria, moreover, in civic liberalism as in Walzer's argument, yields prescriptive guidelines that do not array themselves consistently on the usual ideological spectrum.

The "conservative" side of civic liberalism emerges in the assessment of immigration policy. In some respects, the distinctive norms of civic liberalism are neither distinctive nor determinate *vis-a-vis* immigration. We cannot, for example, infer from these norms exactly what the appropriate levels of immigration are or how immigration quotas should be allocated among the various groups of applicants at the door. These determinations have to be made through the normal channels of democratic decision-making, and they will presumably be decided by some mixture of prudence, humanitarianism, and interest-group bargaining. What is distinctive to civic liberalism is the insistence that decisions about immigration are ultimately decisions about membership in a political community of civic equals and that the criteria for and dynamics of attaining such membership are serious matters.

From the civic liberal perspective, the criteria for admission to membership in a (liberal democratic) society turn properly on the responsibilities inherent in (liberal democratic) citizenship and the capacities necessary for the fulfillment of these responsibilities. They also turn on the reciprocal obligations of the society to its potential members, specifically to the society's capacity to incorporate these newcomers into its communal life and its obligation to treat them as full civic equals. It follows from these considerations, then, that when setting its immigration policies a liberal democratic society operates within a set of certain permissions and constraints.

A democratic society is permitted, as a part of its self-determination as a political community, to set immigration standards consistent with its constitutive values, purposes, and identity as a community. Membership is not merely geographic residence but incorporation into a political way of life. It is, therefore, morally permissible as well as prudent for the society to grant admission only or at least primarily to prospective members who may reasonably be deemed to have the relevant capacities and inclinations to become full and contributing citizens of a liberal democratic regime. What it means to be a "full and contributing citizen" in the ideal sense can best be defined by the criteria of liberal civic virtue discussed in the previous chapter. In a more minimal sense it means to have the capability to become literate, to be economically productive, to respect the rights of others, to accept the rule of law, and to be tolerant of different creeds and ethnicities. In establishing its immigration criteria and quotas, then, it is perfectly appropriate for a democratic society to discriminate in favor of the competent, the tolerant, and the law-abiding. Not to discriminate in this fashion is not morally praiseworthy even-handedness but sheer folly. What Justice Jackson once said of the Constitution can also be said of immigration policy: it need not be construed in an act of misconceived high-mindedness as a suicide pact.

If a liberal democracy is permitted to be self-regarding (apart from the humanitarian considerations proper to granting political asylum and reuniting families) in setting its criteria for admission into its ranks, however, in another respect it faces an important constraint—a constraint attendant upon the same considerations regarding the meaning of membership in a democratic community. Specifically, a well-ordered liberal democracy is not free to admit outsiders into its domain on a permanent or long-term basis with the intention of denying them full civic equality, instead relegating them to perpetual second-class status. Societies are most tempted to do this in the case of "guest workers" of some sort or other—people who are admitted to perform economic tasks or services unattractive to native workers. But to do so violates the standards of fundamental political justice inherent in the norms of civic equality and civic friendship. Michael Walzer states the relevant constraint here succinctly and pointedly:

> Democratic citizens, then, have a choice: if they want to bring in new workers, they must be prepared to enlarge their own membership; if they are unwilling to accept new members, they must find ways within the limits of the domestic labor market to get socially necessary work done. And those are the only choices. Their right to choose derives from the existence in this particular territory of a community of citizens; and it is not compatible with the destruction of the community or its transformation into yet another local tyranny.[2]

The same values—community and civic equality—that give a partially "conservative" cast to the civic liberal approach to immigration point in a more "liberal" direction when it comes to health care policy. In each instance, the central consideration is the same: namely, that membership in the political community of civic equals is a very serious matter, replete with both important privileges and significant obligations. Conversely, the larger political community operates under a powerful set of obligations and constraints *vis-a-vis* its members but is entitled to expect in return certain contributions and self-restraints on their part.

What a political community owes its members is always legitimately contestable, and it is also unavoidably and properly particular and parochial. Those obligations are a function of the constitutive purposes of the political association and of what is reasonably deemed necessary to full membership in the community and to the capacity to participate in its communal life as civic equals. An important part of democratic deliberation always will and should concern the evolving purposes and identity of the communal enterprise and what, accordingly, should be communally provided to its members as a necessary condition of their status and function as civic equals. No final and definitive answers to these questions are ever available. Although it can persuasively be insisted that all morally acceptable political societies are subject to the obligation to respect a core of fundamental human rights—to personal and physical integrity, to human dignity, and to autonomous agency—there are, to borrow a phrase from Benjamin Barber, no "independent grounds" to adjudicate issues concerning the proper scope of communal provision. The answers here are a function of the answers to the questions "Who are we?" and "What are we about?" And the answers to these latter questions are pervasively social constructs, matters for collective self-determination. Thus, as Michael Walzer notes, the ancient Athenians provided public baths and gymnasiums for its citizens but not anything like unemployment insurance or social security. This choice was, he observes, produced "by their understanding of what the common life required," and "it would be hard to argue that they made a mistake."[3] Alongside the question of the purposes of a particular association is another relevant consideration, also particular to specific societies. And that is the level and the nature of the resources available to the society. What may be unavailable to anyone in a subsistence economy may be deemed a subject of private provision in a somewhat more prosperous society and may be more properly a subject of communal provision in an affluent society.

Against this backdrop, the case for universal health care can be very succinctly stated. Even the most minimal versions of the liberal state have assumed that among the advantages and entitlements of membership—indeed the rationale offered for voluntarily leaving a state of nature and joining the society—are the protection of one's life, liberty, and estate. In the context of a relatively affluent liberal democratic society possessing well-developed medical technology, it would seem difficult to deny that the society's obligation to protect the lives of its members must extend to protection against the threat of predations from nature and not merely from other human beings—protection against hostile bacteria and not only against criminally inclined fellow members and outside enemies. Where that protection is a technological and economic possibility, the failure of the society to provide it evinces a clear abdication from the constitutive purposes of a legitimate liberal regime. And the exclusion of some rather than all from this protection speaks volumes about the absence of civic equality and civic friendship. The logic of liberalism thus suggests that, in the context of a relatively affluent society, some level of basic medical care and protection against catastrophic illness and preventable infirmity should be made available. And the logic of civic liberalism requires that this provision be made available to all citizens, as moral equals and civic partners.

The defining norms of civic liberalism would therefore make imperative, in advanced industrialized societies at least, the provision to all citizens equally of some form of basic health care: basic "wellness" care and coverage for catastrophic illness. How exactly this medical protection should be provided is a matter for economists, physicians, and political authorities to determine, and the many vexing and complex issues surrounding these "how to" decisions cannot begin to be pronounced upon here. It is also important to add, however, that the logic of civic liberalism—specifically the logic of citizen obligations discussed under the heading of civic virtue—make it morally proper (and not simply prudentially advisable) for such a system of provision to incorporate strong incentives for taking personal responsibility for maintaining one's own good health and strong disincentives or prohibitions against wasteful use of scarce health care resources and against shifting the foreseeable costs of willful risk-taking to others. It also must be recognized and accepted that painful decisions have to be made *via* democratic deliberation regarding the limits of communal obligations in this area. Even in a relatively affluent society, resources are scarce and some medical interventions are extraordinarily costly. It is not morally mandatory, for example, for a society to provide heart transplants to ninety-year-old patients or unlimited fertility treatment to couples desirous of large families when that society is struggling to provide a good education and decent housing for all its children.

It may well turn out that making these kinds of difficult choices is not a political possibility. And that incapacity in turn will doom the attempt to enact the kind of universal health care system that civic liberal ideals would commend to us. The recent unhappy fate of the state of Oregon's effort to implement a system along these lines testifies to the many difficulties and obstacles such a program will encounter. But our current system, with its mix of commodification, entitlement, and neglect seems clearly indefensible. For what we have is a system where the rich can purchase excellent health care, the most dependent segments of the populace are given health care as an entitlement *via* Medicaid and charitable donation by providers, and self-supporting citizens of modest means are often left without. This situation can be seen as the largely predictable outcome of a polity whose policies result from a tug-of-war between libertarian and egalitarian ideologies. But it is a situation that should help us appreciate why these ideological perspectives are inadequate and their domination of our politics undesirable.

In the original version of this chapter, I said nothing about two of the most controversial policy issues of recent years: abortion and affirmative action. When one reader asked why that was so, my response was that these issues turn largely around competing conceptions of justice, divergent prudential calculations, and—in the case of abortion—metaphysical disputes about when human life begins. Judgments on these matters are rationally indeterminate and legitimately contestable. Civic liberalism, as a conception of democratic ideals, claims no capacity to adjudicate disputes of this sort in any definitive way. Indeed, part of civic liberalism is the insistence that no moral geometry is available to canonize one particular account of social justice and that it is precisely one of the legitimate purposes of democratic politics to deal with such disagreements. And civic liberals have no corner on prudential calculation.

These considerations notwithstanding, the ideals and aspirations championed by civic liberalism do at least have some bearing on these issues even though they cannot pretend to resolve them. The real but limited bearing of civic liberal ideals on these vexing questions results from the civic liberal insistence that however a democratic society deals with such issues it must do so in a way that seeks to promote civic equality and respects the human dignity at the heart of that ideal, respects and seeks to promote the autonomy of its citizens, seeks to engender civic friendship, and respects the imperatives of democratic magnanimity.

Applied to abortion, these imperatives and aspirations might lead to the following admonitions to the opposing sides in the debate. To those who would criminalize abortion, a civic liberal would say: it is incumbent upon you as a democratic citizen to respect the autonomy of your fellow citizens with regard both to their ability to control their own lives and their right to make their own moral judgments on issues that divide serious people of good will. You must also recognize the strong considerations of both justice and prudence that make it problematic to empower the state to force a woman to bear a child she does not want and cannot, for whatever reason, nurture and support. To abortion's defenders, on the other hand, a civic liberal would say: you must recognize that many of your fellow citizens consider abortion to be a moral wrong and that many more consider it not always wrong but nonetheless a matter of serious moral moment. You must also recognize that these citizens' doubts about the morality of abortion are grounded in the same respect for human dignity and the sanctity of human life that inform a democratic society's respect for human rights and concern for civic equality.

In policy terms, these considerations would seem to suggest that abortion should be legal, preferably by legislative enactment reflecting the community's collective judgment rather than judicial decree. But this legal permission should be attended by hedges and procedural requirements manifesting the community's serious concern about decisions to abort and their insistence that such decisions not be made lightly. What exactly these hedges and requirements should be are, once again, subject to the normal course of democratic decision-making. My own view, for example, is that public funding of abortion is inappropriate because democratic magnanimity requires avoidance whenever possible of forcing fellow citizens not merely to tolerate but to support financially (or in other ways) and thereby to promote actions they find abhorrent.[4] But these issues are for the democratic collectivity to decide through the normal political channels.

Regarding affirmative action, a civic liberal would say to its opponents: our democratic ideals require us to provide all our citizens and not merely more fortunate elites with the circumstances and, as far as reasonably possible, with the social resources needed to enable them to achieve autonomy, participate as equal citizens in the life of the society, and to pursue happiness. That imperative is relevant to all citizens of whatever race, creed, color, or gender who find themselves on the lower end of the socioeconomic hierarchies that are at some level inevitably present in any society. But it applies with particular force and urgency to those whose disadvantage was produced historically by the society's violation of its own democratic norms and ideals. Not only social justice but civic friendship and a devotion to civic equality thus require special concern for those who were improperly discriminated against in the past. And if those so discriminated against were racially identified, then this mandatory special concern may legitimately take the form of racially conscious preferences.

To supporters of affirmative action, a civil liberal would say: as time goes on, race-conscious preferential allocations increasingly take on the guise of benevolent but nonetheless invidious double standards that not only are understandably resented by those discriminated against but also serve as a badge of inferiority to and a derogation of the genuine achievements of the preferred groups. To avoid these inevitable intimations of inferiority, and to justify the perpetuation of the double standards, moreover, the governmentally favored groups are driven to fixate upon, sometimes to exaggerate, and perhaps even to fabricate instances of social discrimination against them—thus deepening suspicions and resentments all around.[5] Race-conscious policies not only compromise the legitimacy of democratic governance, then, by undermining the perception that everyone is treated equally by the government, they also undermine racial comity and cooperation.

Moreover, a civic liberal must insist, it is improper and unacceptable to substitute for the goal of civic equality an attempt simply to replicate within all racial groups the current patterns of social and economic hierarchy that prevail within historically dominant racial groups. That is the best that affirmative action standards and policies have to offer, and although such an outcome would be an improvement upon racially specific hierarchy, it essentially amounts to a game of musical chairs that does nothing to ameliorate the larger inequalities of class stratification. However important racial and ethnic inclusiveness is for the creation of a good society, a preoccupation with that project should not be allowed to substitute for or deflect attention from the quest for enhanced civic equality across the board.

The policy consequence of these considerations arguably would be: first, a forthright and unapologetic recognition that many, though not necessarily all, of the affirmative action programs employed to date have been morally proper and practically necessary means of dismantling the systemic biases and institutionalized discriminations of an inherited and democratically illegitimate caste order and, second, the continued attenuation and eventual abandonment of race-specific policies, which inescapably become corrupt, demeaning, and divisive if they are allowed to calcify into permanency. But with the attenuation and eventual abandonment of race-specific policies must come another crucial addition to the policy mix: a significantly enhanced commitment to guaranteeing that *all* disadvantaged children have access to the social resources needed to allow them to develop their talents and succeed in life. And that in turn means, in my view, not only some form of universal health care but vastly improved security in lower income areas and a near-fanatical determination to transform weak and failing schools into safe and productive learning environments—by any means necessary and without obeisance to the stale pieties or entrenched interests of either right or left. Concretely, this latter determination would involve not only a willingness to increase public funding of schools in some instances but also a willingness to experiment with voucher plans where parents believe their children are trapped by incompetent and unresponsive public school authorities.[6] The core goal, in any case, should be to lessen entrenched patterns of hierarchy and dominance within as well as across racial/ethnic groupings and to do so by improving the life chances of those on the lower end of extant hierarchies.

Finally, the logic of civic liberalism indicates why it is so important for a well-ordered democratic society to have a strong and vital public realm: effective public schools, accommodating public spaces, inviting public parks, accessible public libraries, and fiscally viable public hospitals. Much of our lives in a liberal democratic society can be conducted in the private domains of market enterprises, families, and spontaneous associations. But a healthy public sector is indispensable as a symbol and progenitor of civic equality and civic friendship. A democratic society cannot be merely an aggregation of unequal coteries devoted to private purposes. Somewhere we must meet and experience ourselves as democratic citizens: full equals in a cooperative social endeavor. And such encounters and experiences can hardly occur absent the effective presence and functioning of important public institutions. Democratic deliberation and democratic will formation, moreover, require visible and effective public forums in which they can occur.

The libertarian and individualist right does not accept the legitimacy of a strong and viable public sphere, and the contemporary egalitarian left often seems not to understand or appreciate the need for it. Libertarians have always championed the privatization of virtually every social endeavor. They would reduce public agency to the tasks of policing and adjudicating. They would convert democratic armies into mercenary forces, sell off the public parks to private entrepreneurs, abandon the regulation of radio and television on behalf of public interests, and even privatize long-distance turnpikes.[7] They consistently disparage the public domain as a residual space for losers. Hence they advocate dismantling whatever public programs they can and starving the rest by denying them adequate funding.

What is more surprising and alarming than this expectable opposition of the libertarian right to a strong public sphere is its neglect or abandonment by the egalitarian left. One way to appreciate this neglect is to reread Rawls's *A Theory of Justice* with a view to asking "what is the role of the public sphere in his well-ordered society?" The clear answer would seem to be "not much at all." The democratic goals of equality and fraternity are championed. But both are conceived in an economizing fashion and pursued through strategies of allocation: social equality is construed largely as a function of patterns of possession of primary goods, and fraternity is dissolved into the mutual ownership of each others' assets. The public domain is that of governmental functions, and all of the latter seem to turn about the management of distributions to competing claimants. Thus the government is composed of four branches: the allocation and stabilization branches, which "together are to maintain the efficiency of the market economy generally," and the transfer and distribution branches, which reallocate goods in accordance with the principles of justice.[8] What seems missing from this account is any understanding of or concern about the concrete phenomenology of civic equality and civic friendship and any sense of the way that institutionalized public spaces, public activities, and public endeavors—as contrasted with merely governmental regulation of goods production and distribution—are essential to these social purposes.

In contrast to the libertarian disparagement and the recent egalitarian neglect of the public sphere, civic liberalism distinguishes itself by its forthright insistence on the importance of robust public enterprises in a well-ordered democratic society. Civic liberalism winds up in this posture as champion of public spaces and endeavors because of its inclusion of civic equality and civic friendship as central democratic goods—and because it understands that neither of these goods can be achieved merely by governmental manipulations of the allocation of economic resources and opportunities. From the perspective of the right, then, civic liberalism seems to be noxiously "liberal." It endorses public financing and public management of some important social activities, and it is happy with the egalitarian redistributive consequences of such policies. From the standpoint of many on the conventional left, however, the civic liberal posture incorporates a very significant "conservative" component. For if the public sphere is to perform effectively both its explicit (educating, recreating, etc.) and its latent (promoting civic equality and civic friendship) functions, it must be vested with sufficient power and authority to protect the integrity of its institutions and their capacity to achieve their purposes. And that power and authority must be exercisable against those who would undermine these public institutions by compromising their integrity and/or by diverting their resources to other purposes. The venues and enterprises of the public sphere are not merely commonly held empty spaces available for people to appropriate for whatever ends they may choose. Hence, public schools must have the authority to deal decisively with students who disrupt the educational process, public avenues need not be ceded to panhandlers or drunk drivers, public parks are not required to serve as homeless shelters or as drug dens, public libraries should not have to function as drying-out tanks for displaced alcoholics, and public housing projects can and should be kept safe from depredation by gangs and drug merchants. Civil liberties are indeed a precious good and an essential entitlement of liberal democracy. But the point, the justification, and the scope of individual liberty is misunderstood if it be deemed to incorporate the right to, in effect, steal from the public purse by interfering with the intended uses of public places and institutions and/or by usurping them for different uses altogether.

State, Society, and Individual

The review of selected policy issues in the preceding section is very cryptic and certainly incomplete. It should, however, serve to substantiate and illustrate the central contentions that animated it: first, that the civic liberal argument concerning democratic purposes is not purely theoretical and academic but instead carries with it implications for practice and policy; and, second, that the policy directives generated by the civic liberal perspective are in significant respects distinctive and different from those characteristically generated by other versions of liberalism. Civic liberal policies are different from those advocated by libertarians and egalitarians because civic liberalism embraces *both* liberty and equality as important democratic purposes but construes neither of them as maximizing goals. Moreover, civic liberalism understands the essence of liberty to be the absence of dependency rather than the absence of impediment, and it understands the essence of equality as more a matter of moral and civic standing than of private economic resources. And finally, civic liberalism accords to civic friendship an important place in the complex of social goods and makes civic virtue a legitimate concern of liberal regimes.

This same distinctive conception of democratic purposes is linked with conceptions of state, society, and citizenship that also can be usefully contrasted with the parallel conceptions associated with more conventional viewpoints. These contrasts are capsulized in figure 1.

In the civic liberal model of the well-ordered democratic society, the individual members are conceived as what Ben Barber has called "strong citizens." They are also understood to be, in some respects at least, "socially constituted" selves— to borrow a phrase recently championed by Michael Sandel. They are separate individuals whose integrity and particularity must be respected. But they are people whose lives and identities and aspirations and activities are all generated *via* their association with others in their families, neighborhoods, churches, schools, clubs, traditions. It is insisted that they are capable of functioning as responsible and self-governing agents, but it is recognized that this is an achievement rather than a natural fact: they are not born autonomous but become so through a complex and sometimes arduous process of socialization, acculturation, and education. They are understood as people who seek to flourish in multiple concrete and specific ways which they learn and pursue in a pragmatic and particularistic manner. They are encouraged to embody the liberal civic virtues and to relate to each other as civic equals.

This means that a civic liberal society does not understand its members as purely private individuals. It does not treat them simply as preference maximizers, economizing "rational" choosers who pursue preconceived selfish desires. It does not assume that they are governed by entirely divergent comprehensive conceptions of the good or that they should be dealt with as representative types of identities. This is why citizenship and immigration are more serious matters for civic liberals than for either libertarians or egalitarians: clients and consumers can be relatively unproblematically accommodated by states and markets, but citi-

Figure 1

	Individuals	Society	State
Libertarian	Consumers/producers, legally equal preference maximizers	Voluntary associations of individuals; market contracts from self-interest	Nightwatchman state, umpire
Realist	Potentially aggressive private actors, defenders of hearth and home	Factions with inclinations toward tyranny, cruelty	Nightwatchman state, countervailing power source
Egalitarian	Equally deserving rational actors, possessing a sense of justice and divergent conceptions of the good	Advantaged and disadvantaged groups who (1) cooperate economically and (2) compete over allocation of social benefits, burdens	Welfare state; protector of persons, enforcer of distributive justice, grantor of goods, services
Difference liberalism	Bearers of different identities arising from social groups	Agonistic identity groups	Welfare state, plus arbiter, equalizer, and recognizer of groups
Civic liberalism	Socially constituted strong citizens, who (1) pursue happiness, (2) are civic equals and friends, and (3) embody liberal virtues	Multiple spheres of voluntary associations born of common purposes and mutual interests, that compete and cooperate with each other	Enabling state: develops capacities of strong citizens and their associations

zens—full and flourishing and equal members of a good society—have to be nurtured and incorporated.

When it comes to the realm of civil society, most forms of liberalism conceive this domain under the rubrics of factious behavior or economizing behavior, or some combination thereof. That is, civil society is seen as occupied by some form of interest groups, whether these interests be preference groupings or identity groupings. These groups are seen as essentially in conflict for power and resources. Where cooperation occurs, this is seen as tactical collaboration in pursuit of goods in short supply, a network of *de facto* contracts among self-seeking individuals. Civic liberalism recognizes these important constituent elements of civil society. But it also insists that civil society is composed of many spheres and several modes of behavior. Not all the purposes around which civic associations develop are factions, and not all common ventures are the product of economizing modes of behavior. Social cooperation is not merely a matter of economic necessity. In large part, this voluntary cooperation occurs because many dimensions of a flourishing human life are intrinsically "political": they either require or are best carried out through common endeavor. To make good music, we may need a band or a chorus. To educate our children, we need schools and PTA's. To play games, we need teams. To help less fortunate neighbors, we need charitable organizations. In short, in civil society we both compete and cooperate. And in a well-ordered society, the nonfactious cooperative associations need to be both various and vigorous. If they do not exist, our lives have big holes in them. If they are colonized by or subsumed under either the state or the market or both, they are weakened and/or distorted.

The classic models of the liberal state, which often contend with each other for acceptance, have been those of the "nightwatchman" state and the welfare state. The former of these has traditionally been championed by libertarians, the latter by egalitarians. In the nightwatchman state, government roles are essentially and exhaustively those of police and umpire. The function of the state is to enforce the conditions of a healthy and lawful marketplace: to protect people and property, to enforce contracts, and to adjudicate conflict and enforce settlements and terms of agreement. The welfare state also does these things, but adds other significant functions to its repertoire. Besides undertaking to regulate economic institutions and to promote prosperity, the welfare state also undertakes significant redistributive functions on behalf of politically endorsed principles of social justice or utility.

The normative conceptions of the state generated by liberal realism and the liberalism of difference seem for the most part to be variants of these two models. The realists' state must above all prevent cruelty and tyranny. It is, therefore, akin to the nightwatchman state in its focus upon erecting an effective police power to protect individuals against depredations of their persons, properties, and basic human rights. Beyond its policing functions, the realist state pursues its largely defensive and protective purposes by creating decision-making procedures based on countervailing power, hence encouraging compromise and moderation. Difference liberalism does not, for the most part, focus upon state functions. Moreover, the images of the state that emerge from the writings of William Connolly and Iris Young—to cite the two theorists I discussed as leading examples of this orientation—are far from identical. But both of these theorists seem to endorse or assume the propriety of a welfare state that engages in economic regulation and redistribution; they would add to these functions the task of providing social space and legitimacy to various identities. In Iris Young's account, the state role would be particularly noteworthy in this context: it would not only bear responsibility for the "recognition and affirmation" of nondominant identity groups but would deploy its power very pervasively on these groups' behalf.

The normative conception of the state most consistent with civic liberal ideals and most coherent with the civic liberal understanding of citizenship and civil society is what has recently been called "the enabling state."[9] If the members of a democratic society are construed fundamentally under the rubric of *homo economicus*—as consumers and producers who rationally pursue preference-maximizing strategies—the state may logically be seen as properly no more than an umpire or nightwatchman. If the members of society are seen, on the other hand, as rights-bearing clients of a collective scheme of social cooperation, the state appears under the guise of manager and provider of services. Where the members of the society, however, are seen as "strong citizens" who bear both rights and responsibilities and who are socially constituted selves, capable of and flourishing through self-governance, the state logically becomes an "enabler": it must provide the background resources and institutional framework through which citizens can become "prime agents of their own development."[10]

Since people are not born autonomous, government properly serves as the creator and sustainer of the conditions of autonomy. It need not stand passively by, watching citizens fail to develop the capacities necessary for the "pursuit of happiness" in accord with their plans for life. Especially in the case of children, who are by necessity dependent upon others for resources they need to grow and prosper, government may need to serve as an agent of collective provision. But because persons who deserve respect and possess human dignity, who are likely to flourish in the long run, and who can function as contributing citizens need to be self-determining and responsible agents, the state should not assume the role of patron—reducing its citizens to the status of votaries, petitioners of largesse from the public till, and obedient (or recalcitrant) objects of bureaucratic "management." Fundamentally, the role of government in a civic liberal regime should be to provide the institutional framework and the resources necessary and proper to help people help themselves—both individually and as members of their voluntary civic associations.

This normative conception of the liberal state arguably has a wider appeal and a broader following than either the libertarian or the egalitarian alternatives. In a 1997 public opinion survey of 1000 American voters, to cite one warrant for this claim, pollster Mark Penn posed the following question: "Which of the following is closest to your own thinking about the proper role of the federal government? Government should solve problems and protect people from adversity; government should help people equip themselves to solve their own problems; government should stay out of people's lives so they can solve their problems without interference or regulation." Only 12 percent of the respondents endorsed the first, arguably paternalistic, conception of the state. Thirty-four percent opted for the libertarian "stay out of people's lives" model. And 52 percent endorsed the "help people equip themselves" option that corresponds most closely to the conception of the enabling state outlined above.[11]

If these results are in fact reasonably representative of the views of the American citizenry, they indicate that civic liberals begin with a very strong base of intuitive support but that they still have polemical and political work to do. The data also seem to indicate that civic liberalism has more adversaries within the current American electorate to its libertarian right than to its egalitarian left. But it is also clear from Penn's data and from other data about elite attitudes that a disproportionate number of Democratic Party activists subscribe to the welfare paternalist persuasion. What is most remarkable, perhaps, is that the most widely endorsed position is the one that arguably is most bereft of a clearly defined and articulated theoretical model to inform and support it. Part of the burden of my argument in this book is that this theoretical vacuum can be filled by the civic liberal understanding of democratic ideals. For if libertarian market models, modus vivendi theories, and the liberalism of fear push us toward a relatively passive and neutral nightwatchman state, and if welfare utilitarianism, Rawlsian deontological liberalism, and some leading versions of "difference liberalism" push us toward a benevolent but sometimes overbearing collectivism, the interpretation of democratic ideals offered here leads us in a different direction. It encourages us to seek a democratic society where citizens are viewed and treated as full civic equals, where they are enabled to become autonomous and responsible participants in social life, where they enjoy the pleasures and benefits of nonhegemonic forms of civic friendship, and where the liberal civic virtues are prized and nurtured. These are multiple aspirations, complex in conception and certainly difficult to achieve. But to seek anything less is to aim too low and to fail to keep faith with what is best in the liberal tradition.

Notes

1. Martin Feldstein, "A New Era of Social Security," *The Public Interest*, no. 130 (Winter 1998): 102–25.

2. Michael Walzer, *Spheres of Justice*, 61. This stipulation, it should be noted, would not prohibit some form of intermediate arrangement for those who wish to retain their citizenship in their home country but to work elsewhere on a periodic basis. (See Walzer, *Spheres of Justice*, 60.) What is unacceptable as a matter of principle is the consignment of some subset of the population to the status of permanent resident alien, forever precluded from becoming full citizens.

3. Walzer, *Spheres of Justice*, 67.

4. Abortion activists often argue in opposition to this view that poor women should not be left without the financial means to seek an abortion if they want one. But private institutions could provide the loans or grants necessary for this purpose. The latent reason for insistence on public financing, at least as important as the concern for social justice, is a desire to gain official sanction for the view that abortion is morally indifferent—and hence to help prevent any sense of guilt for having an abortion. It is neither proper nor prudent for any government, however, to attempt to play moral arbiter or to serve as grantor of absolution in cases so deeply contested.

5. Ben Gore, "Hate Crime Hoaxes Unsettle Campuses," *Chronicle of Higher Education*, 8 January 1999, 55–56.

6. Most of the reasonable objections to voucher programs, such as legitimate worries that private schools could utilize them to "cream" the best and easiest to educate students out of the public system, would lose much of their force if any school where vouchers were applicable were required to accept its students (or at least its voucher-using students) randomly from their pool of applicants.

7. These examples are culled from Friedman, *Capitalism and Freedom*.

8. Rawls, *Theory of Justice*, 276.

9. See Neil Gilbert, *Welfare Justice: Restoring Social Equity* (New Haven: Yale University Press, 1995).

10. This phrase comes from Will Marshall and Martin Schram, quoted by Gilbert, *Welfare Justice,* 152.

11. Mark J. Penn, "The New Democratic Electorate," *The New Democrat* 10, no. 1 (Jan./Feb. 1998): 6–9.

Index

abortion policy, 256
Ackerman, Bruce, 165, 242
affirmative action, 86, 257–58
Agassi, Andre, 99
agonistic democracy, 96–102
Alejandro, Roberto, 89, 233
Alger, Horatio, 20
American Civil Liberties Union, 171–72
Anderson, Charles, xi, 141
Aquinas, Thomas, 184
Archer, William, 22
Arendt, Hannah, 198
Aristotle, 31, 50, 56, 73, 116, 188, 228,
    230; on civic friendship, 72, 176,
    179–85, 197; on civic virtue, 213; on
    equality, 150–51, 161; on friendship,
    72, 176, 179–85, 197
Armey, Richard, 22
Arnold, Benedict, 125
Arnold, Matthew, 161
Arrow, Kenneth, 200
Augustine, Saint, 97, 152
autonomy: as constitutive good,
    124–26, 136; as threshold good,
    126–28, 136

Baier, Kurt, 160, 223
Barber, Benjamin, 129, 260
Beiner, Ronald, xvi
Bell, Daniel, 44, 46–47, 240
Bentham, Jeremy, 29, 43, 46, 65–66, 101,
    117, 154, 156–57
Bentley, Arthur, 3
Berkeley, George, 140
Berlin, Isaiah, 111, 115–17, 119, 123–24,
    133, 228
Bernstein, Richard, 7

Berra, Yogi, 47
Bloom, Allan, 17, 178, 231
Boaz, David, 32, 42, 44
Bowers v. Hardwick 478 U.S. 186 (1986),
    136
Buddha, 47
Burke, Edmund, 11, 13, 30, 117, 185
Bush, George, 16

Cahn, Edmond, 147–49
Calvinism, 28
campaign finance, 164
Canavan, Francis, 240
Carens, Joseph, 166
Carnegie, Andrew, 20, 168
Carter, Stephen, 240
categorical imperative. *See* Kantian
    maxim
Chausiriporn, Jenny, 45
Churchill, Winston, 3
civic republicanism, 45–46
communitarianism, xvi, 113, 136
community, 201; Connolly on, 102;
    Rawls on, 70–71
comprehensive liberalism, 70, 128–32,
    177, 205, 232–34; Rawls on, 53–56
compromise, 13, 199–200
Comte, Auguste, 191
Condorcet, Marquis de, xvi–xvii, 41,
    100, 120–21, 139, 153
Connolly, William, xi, xv, 80, 82, 83,
    176, 221, 262; on agonistic
    democracy, 96–102; on civic virtues,
    217
Constant, Benjamin, 115–16, 139, 187
Crick, Bernard, 17, 111, 207
Croly, Herbert, 20

About the Author

THOMAS A. SPRAGENS, JR. is professor of political science at Duke University. He has written extensively on political theory, with particular attention to democratic theory and the liberal tradition. Among his books in this area are Reason and Democracy (Duke University Press, 1990), The Irony of Liberal Reason (University of Chicago Press, 1981), and The Politics of Motion: The World of Thomas Hobbes (University Press of Kentucky and Croom-Helm Publishers, 1973). He has served on the editorial boards of The Journal of Politics and The Responsive Community.

60 - 9
74
110
127
136
158 - 72
198
207
220
235-9